Connect the Dots

THE COLLECTIVE POWER OF RELATIONSHIPS, MEMORY AND MINDSET IN THE CLASSROOM

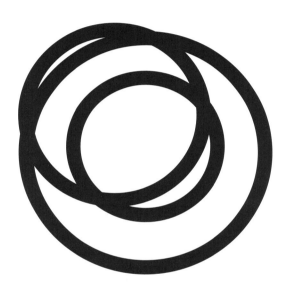

Tricia Taylor
with Nina Dibner

Illustrated by Oliver Caviglioli

First Published 2019

by John Catt Educational Ltd,
15 Riduna Park, Station Road,
Melton, Woodbridge IP12 1QT

Tel: +44 (0) 1394 389850
Email: enquiries@johncatt.com
Website: www.johncatt.com

Opinions expressed in this publication are those of the contributors and are not necessarily those of the publishers or the editors. We cannot accept responsibility for any errors or omissions.

ISBN: 978 1 912906 36 9

Set and designed by John Catt Educational Limited

Acknowledgements

Thank you, teachers, for the investment and expertise you extend every day to young people everywhere. Your work is exponential. Without you, where would we be? A special appreciation to all of the teachers whose ideas and experience are scattered throughout this book. We owe you. Thank you to Shirley Edwards for your passion for social justice, your courage to organise – and your decision to hire both Nina and me many years ago. Thank you to the young people who inspire us to keep coming back for more. We learn from you too.

To all of the researchers who have spent decades examining what works best in schools and helping us, educators, to improve how we teach, we are indebted. You feature heavily in this book. Every single person I asked to be interviewed for the book said yes. Thank you for your insights. And for the insights of those who generously read early drafts for Nina and me. We know it wasn't easy.

When I was given the green light to write this book a long time ago, I had no idea how incredible our publisher John Catt would be. Without fail, the team have been supportive each step of the way. A big warm thank you to my new friend Oliver Caviglioli, who illustrated this book. I have seen so much with you. Thank you for challenging me, teaching me and bringing this book alive.

Nina and I would like to thank our families and friends for their encouragement, advice and putting up with late nights and long phone calls. A special thanks to Nina's daughter, Naomi, for her understanding and youthful perspective. And lastly, thank you, Nina, without whom this book would not have been written. We talked about it for so many years and here it is. You are smart, principled and patient. You are my thought partner and confidant – the kind of friend everybody wishes they had.

CONTENTS

Introduction

This educator-to-educator book, grounded in evidence, is shaped by our journeys teaching young people in two countries. This intro shares the story of how we learned to connect the dots.

MOVING TO BROOKLYN

At age 26, I was unemployed and unsure I had what it would take to be a teacher – even though I had just finished a master's degree and two years of additional teacher training. Still undecided and decidedly unconvinced of my career choice, I moved to New York City to look for work. Within a few weeks, I found myself in my first job interview, sitting in a small storage area which had been converted into an office, in an overcrowded school in one of the most impoverished neighbourhoods in NYC. The actual building was part of another school that had some spare space. A temporary home, it was overcrowded and bleak. For the first time in a long time, a decision felt right.

Nina and Tricia in front of mural of Shirley Edwards, former Principal of EBC High School for Public Service – Bushwick

Seated across from me was Shirley Edwards, principal of EBC Bushwick High School for Public Service, a woman I would come to know as a visionary and activist. I was eager to talk about my experience volunteering in Washington, DC and training in Georgia; I wanted to show off my illustrated teaching portfolio and letters of reference. As I spoke, however, Shirley kept a laser focus on getting to know me as a person – why I wanted to teach and why I had chosen a school in Bushwick, Brooklyn. Her approach seemed informal and too personal for a job interview; yet, once hired, I learned that this one-on-one conversation was a core practice for both the school and its sister organisation, East Brooklyn Congregations (EBC), an interfaith not-for-profit organisation that helped found the school. The intent of the one-on-one: to get to the bottom of someone's story. Building relationships, they espoused, drives learning, social change and teaching.

> Personal stories can fuel a movement

BUILDING RELATIONSHIPS STARTS WITH A STORY

My second interview took place the next day in a car. I was picked up by Sister Kathy, a stern-faced and straight-talking Catholic nun, who was also an ardent and skilful EBC activist. Sister Kathy took me on an insider's tour of the area as a way for me to get to know the community and its story. We started in East New York, where 55% of adults were unemployed or not in the labour force, only 27.5% were high school graduates, and the incidence of AIDS was doubling each year. (Thabit, 2005, p. 229–230) Sister Kathy and I then made our way to Bushwick, an adjacent neighbourhood

Long before it was a school, this building was a popular Vaudeville theatre.

Illustration credit: Brooklyn Public Library, Brooklyn collection. DeKalb Theatre (1911).

with similar statistics yet remnants of a more affluent past. We drove past vacated brownstones, a grand Baroque church and then stopped in front of an abandoned vaudeville theatre to speak. The shooting of two teenagers at point-blank range at a nearby high school spurred the idea to start a new school in this neighbourhood, poor in resources yet high in expectations and care. The Board of Education had promised to convert this vaudeville theatre in order to house an EBC school in this neighbourhood, but on this day the building still looked empty and neglected.

TEACHING IN BROOKLYN: BREAKING BIG PROBLEMS INTO WINNABLE ISSUES

Although hired to teach English, I was asked to take on the role of Community Action teacher to start. I was given minimal direction or space to teach. I created my own classroom in a section of our library. Devoid of books, I used cardboard boxes to create temporary walls in this empty space. Shirley gave me flexibility regarding my curriculum, allowing for student-driven skill-building projects based on their interests. I designed a course based on the EBC philosophy of social change through collective power whereby students could find a salient issue in their community and work on changing it. It was based on the idea that students would be motivated by having choice and empowered by a structure within which to work.

PAULO FREIRE

LISA DELPIT

Our student-run school newspaper documents the perseverance of these young activists.

I was also deeply influenced by progressive educationalists like Paulo Freire and critical pedagogy – the belief that disenfranchised people can become empowered through the knowledge and skills to challenge the status quo – and Lisa Delpit's call to educators to explicitly teach the codes of the 'culture of power' within our society in order to open access to all. As a school, our mission was to instil a belief that one can effect change and learn tools to do so. My students took on the status quo with issues ranging from changing the school uniform to starting an all-girls basketball team. One initiative stood out and would impact us all for years to come. What started as a small group project – 'Miss, we want to get the building we were promised' – turned into a school-wide, whole-community campaign involving teachers, students, parents and local church members that spanned several years.

As the class project to get a new building developed, the students organised a petition, a relentless calling campaign to the chancellor's office and finally a sit-in at the board of education that brought out so many parents, staff, and students that we could hardly fit in the room. As planned, one by one, starting with the students, we faced the chancellor and then turned, leaving the room silently as a sign of solidarity and strength. The event was ostensibly led by me and my students, but orchestrated behind the scenes by Sister Kathy, my mentor with considerably more experience. The students came in early and stayed late to make phone calls and write letters. This continued until several months later when the board of education finally gave us a move-in date. As we entered the front doors in the autumn of 1998, the feeling of accomplishment and love was palpable from students to parents to staff. Our building was a symbol of success born of the perseverance and grit of a community that was often disenfranchised. The students were my heroes.

RELATIONSHIPS AT THE CENTRE: STRUCTURING THE DAY TO MAKE IT WORK

EBC Bushwick 'walked the talk' by prioritising social-emotional wellbeing and relationships in the school community through its Advisory programme, which has aspects of England's PSHCE (Personal, Social, Health and Citizenship Education) and form time. An advisor (a teacher similar to a form tutor in England) meets with a small group of about 15 students on a ritualised basis (e.g. three times a week) to build a supportive peer group, develop a positive relationship with an adult and gain social-emotional skills that foster wellbeing. As an advisor at EBC, I facilitated discussions and activities in our 25-minute, single-gender sessions about topics that ranged from grades to goals, to peer pressure, to power, to puberty. My girls and I were a family.

The programme's success was due to Advisory's ability to foster a sense of camaraderie and belonging. While there was no curriculum for our school's Advisory programme (yet), advisors created community and social-emotional skills through team-building activities, discussions and service learning projects. High levels of trust and respect permeated the larger school culture. Most teachers knew the names of every student and my mobile number was written on the chalkboard the first day of class for all students to use if needed. I wrote letters to all of my students at the start of year introducing myself; and they wrote back, introducing me to bits of their personality, culture and life.

A year after I started at EBC, Nina Dibner joined the school as a global studies teacher. She also held a deep-seated drive for social justice, having originally come into teaching through anti-racist organising. Nina found her passion in Advisory and hers was alive with activities and excited students. There, students made pop-up books to teach primary students conflict-resolution skills and offered peers advice (such as how to tell your parents that you ran up a £400 phone bill). Down the hall, I was blindfolding my Advisory girls for an activity about trust and getting them to work as a team to solve challenges like making peanut butter and jelly sandwiches as a pair with only one arm each. We went to great lengths to teach collaboration! When we found the time, Nina and I informally shared ideas to integrate social-emotional learning skills into our Advisory classes. These short exchanges would someday lead, decades later, to this book.

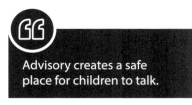

Advisory creates a safe place for children to talk.

BROADENING OUR PRACTICE, YET LITTLE SCOPE AND SEQUENCE

Our principal was on a mission: although community building took centre stage, she also wanted our students to be thinkers. In Shirley's wisdom, all teachers at EBC were trained in how to teach what I now call 'metacognitive skills' in our content classes through such strategies as 'think alouds' whereby students talk through how to tackle a difficult task. We were teaching discussion protocols that provided clear, explicit guidelines for students to listen to each other, and we explored content using the 'jigsaw method', a well-researched

Pedagogy focused on getting students to think about learning and communicate ideas.

and highly effective cooperative learning activity detailed more in the Research and Classroom sections We had a strategy toolkit that I still use when I train and teach.

As the school grew up, it was clear that the real obstacle wasn't lack of opportunity to implement new pedagogy, but the school's lack of systems or a broader scope and sequence for what's taught when. At the beginning of each year, it was like starting from scratch. I'd pull books out of the cupboard and ask students in my English classes which ones they hadn't read yet because there was no overall plan for curriculum delivery. Periodically, teachers would meet as an English department, but there were no department leaders and no whole-school priority from which to ground the work. Our focus was more on individual kids or teaching tools, not the continuum of curriculum or collaboration for delivery.

It was not a completely smooth transition.

After five years at the Brooklyn school, I was itching to see a bit more of the world. I had recently travelled to England and bought a directory of secondary schools in London just to see what was out there. When I got back, I – without contemplation – borrowed a fax machine and sent my CV to a long list of London schools. I got one call back – but that was all I needed. I was hired at Pimlico School and moved to London in August 2001, intending to stay for a year. That was almost two decades ago.

CULTURE SHOCK: FINDING MY WAY AS A TEACHER IN LONDON

It was not a completely smooth transition – moving to another country to teach in a comprehensive state school, not an international school like some of my friends had done. I didn't know my SATs from my GCSEs and I called full stops 'periods'. When I received my teaching timetable on the first day, I was absolutely shocked, prompting me to contact the head of English immediately about what must be a mistake: 'Is this right? I'm teaching years 7, 8, 9, 10 *and* 11? And what is PSHCE?' Then, several days later, also during the first week of school, I was told that a school inspector from some organisation called the Office for Standards in Education (Ofsted) would be observing me teach my challenging Year 9 English class. Despite the culture shock, I was able to hold it together until the next afternoon when I received a call from my sister telling me that the World Trade Center and Pentagon had just been hit by aeroplanes. The following day at school, on September 12th, the headteacher at Pimlico came up to me to ask if I was OK. I wasn't. It was my first week teaching in London and there I was crying in front of the boss.

I soon realised that I had miscalculated the scale of what I had entered. I had just left a small school of about 500 students whom I knew mostly by name to come to a high school almost three times the size. A sea of 1200 adolescents all dressed exactly the same. At EBC Bushwick, I taught only 9th and 12th grade English, so I had only two different lessons to prepare per day. In England, I could have six different preps on some days. Stunned, I still managed to adapt. Looking back now, I smile to think of how naive I was and how quickly my English timetable became so accepted as the norm. To question it appeared odd: 'But this is how we have always done it,' colleagues would say. I recently recounted my timetable culture shock story while interviewing Lucy Crehan, international education

IT TAKES TIME TO LEARN
The deeper culture and language of your school and students.

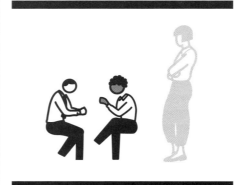

consultant and former UK teacher, for this book. Crehan (2018a) summed it up well: 'Teachers in England have just come to accept this [timetable] despite its inefficiency for teaching and demand on workload.'

Although American teachers teach an average of 26.8 hours a week compared to 19.6 hours for English teachers, English teachers in Britain spend on average more time planning, marking and doing administrative tasks. (OECD, 2018) I quickly discovered that there was little time to form relationships or connect emotionally with the 30 kids in my form and the 150 or so kids in my English classes, let alone memorise names and small details that are so important for building positive relationships with young people. Time to explore was limited. In the first week of teaching Year 11 (10th grade), I tried to get students to facilitate 'popcorn' (a discussion strategy that was a hit with my Brooklyn kids). As students were calling out their feelings and thoughts as we read a Maya Angelou poem, a Year 11 student interjected: 'Is this on the exam? Otherwise, it's a waste of time.'

> Mindset and character development can change over time

LOOKING FOR BALANCE AND THE BEST OF BOTH WORLDS

My years of teaching were accompanied by a constant companion: the desire to integrate the academic framework of England with strategies to build positive relationships and thinking skills that I learned in the US. I welcomed the structure of the English system I knew what I had to teach at each year level and I could follow a very specific criteria for marking. The national curriculum and exam boards dictated which texts I could teach, which was surprisingly reassuring. And finding resources was easy. I was given pre-prepared schemes of work, which outlined what I could do with students each lesson and proved to be a survival kit for teaching so many different year groups in a given day. What English teacher doesn't have a box file of resources for *Of Mice and Men*, partially created by someone else? But there was still little collaboration time and I greatly missed the freedom I had had in New York to teach what I wanted and customise content to integrate the seeds of social change and youth voice. And I missed Advisory.

This led to a late-night text: 'I think I'm having a mid-life career crisis.'

Meanwhile, Nina, the recipient of this text, had taken a significant professional journey of her own. Following my departure from EBC, she became the school's Advisory coach, mentoring advisors creating curriculum, and systematising the programme so that it would be more sustainable and engaging. In 2006, she left EBC and founded a consulting firm with a focus on Advisory and social-emotional learning. Under Dibner Consulting Services, Nina and Donna Mehle (also a former EBC Bushwick teacher) consulted for a range of schools in NYC, supporting them to design or redesign their Advisory programmes. In 2014, Nina rebranded her company as PowerTools and expanded her team and focus to include school culture and climate. Nina and I had been in contact from time to time; we shared a similar approach to pedagogy and vision for the purpose of education.

Unsure whether I was needing a soundboard to think through my discomfort (I was) or actually having a breakdown (I wasn't), she quickly responded with, 'Come to New York.'

A few months later, I found myself in Brooklyn, shadowing Nina as she conducted Advisory programme training and then in the Bronx, joining in as we co-facilitated a Young Women's Day retreat for students. I was catapulted into the world of educational research when Nina introduced me to the work of Carol Dweck, Stanford professor and author of *Mindset: The New Psychology of Success*. In *Mindset*, Dweck (2016a) documents her three decades of research in the fields of business, sport and education, showing how a growth mindset – the belief that our most basic abilities can be developed through dedication and hard work – has an impact on success, and the understanding that our brain strengthens with effort and

CAROL DWECK

practice. I was captivated by the prospect of helping children develop perseverance and an attitude to embrace challenge. This reminded me of my kids in Brooklyn.

LEADING A CULTURE SHIFT WITH ALLIES ON THE INSIDE

Back in London, I stayed in contact with Nina via weekly FaceTime calls to bounce around ideas and tackle research. I shared my excitement about mindsets with others and the buzz grew. By this time, I had moved on to a different school and moved up the hierarchy to Head of Faculty for the Creative Arts. New ideas about education were surfacing and now possibilities for my role in the field of education started to percolate. At the time, I was fortunate enough to be working at Dunraven School, a school in London for students aged 5 to 18. David Boyle, the principal, did something few heads of school do. He gave me the autonomy to develop strategies to embed growth mindset throughout the school.

We started with small shifts in how teachers offer feedback to students about their successes and how we spoke about mistakes and challenges. We saw our fastest results at the primary level, where Assistant Principal Lowri Millar became my co-conspirator, teaching each and every child that we can all get smarter. Students as young as five learned about neural pathways and how our brains get stronger at a particular skill with practice and effort. 'Students now come up to us and ask for a challenge,' reported one teacher. Every single member of the school counted. Lowri, whose enthusiasm was infectious, grabbed parents and carers at drop-off and pick-up to convince them to attend our workshops. Supervisors who monitored the playground and receptionists at the main office were making small talk with students about working hard and persisting. Conversations in the lunchroom, where children explored new foods or battled with cutlery, were opportunities to practise perseverance and resilience. Teachers and parents – both from the primary and from our adjoining secondary school where I also worked – would recount stories about how a particular child became more willing to have a go, leading to a significant improvement of his handwriting, or how another student developed the courage to speak more in French class.

RESEARCH INTO PRACTICE: A SIMPLE CONCEPT, COMPLEX TO IMPLEMENT

DANIEL WILLINGHAM

At the same time, a surge of interest in the 'science of learning' and how it informs and shapes pedagogy started to change the tide. The push for more traditional teaching methods (such as explicit instruction and a knowledge-rich curriculum) surfaced. The UK seemed to be taking the lead on educational research in schools, apparent in a March 2018 article in *The Economist*: 'England has become one of the world's biggest education laboratories.' My understanding of learning sciences expanded at ResearchED conferences, by reading blogs by the Learning Scientists in the US and fantastic writers like Daniel Willingham, author of *Why Don't Students Like School?* (Willingham, 2010). At a Learning and the Brain conference (San Fran and NY) where Nina and I were presenting, John Dunlosky's research stood out the most: there is a big gap between what the research says are the most effective ways to learn (which actually feel intuitively wrong) and what students think are the most effective ways to learn (and

N

what they do, because that's what feels right). Helping young people learn how to learn was an obvious no-brainer for us.

Anyone who has sat through a student assembly about study and memory techniques will know the disappointment of finding out later that only your best students actually listened and took on board the suggestions. Knowing how to do something – even under the best instruction – doesn't guarantee they will do it. Unsurprisingly, we also saw that our growth mindset initiative was not a silver bullet. In our work with schools to infuse a growth mindset, we found that teachers' messaging, our collective pep talks, and even strategies were not enough to sustain motivation. A part of the formula was missing. I reflect back on my students from EBC Bushwick HS. It wasn't enough to tell them they could get their own school building; we had to teach them the skills to do so and they needed to have the mindset that they could be powerful and successful.

EDUCATORS NEED AN INTEGRATED APPROACH – RELATIONSHIPS, MINDSET AND MEMORY

By now, I had left Dunraven and founded TailoredPractice, an education consultancy partnering with schools to synthesise the research and tailor evidence-based strategies for both teachers and students. Following Nina's lead (but in England), I spent my days delivering trainings, meeting new students and visiting classrooms. I spent hours reading the research, combing blogs and investigating tweets by teachers, scientists and educationalists putting research into practice – a luxury I didn't have as a teacher. Nina and I started to incorporate more about cognitive science into our work – and our phone catch-ups. As I expanded my work across three themes – relationships, memory and mindset – I was struck by how interconnected they were. I would do a session on memory but feel compelled to discuss mindset. (For the memory strategies to work, students have to value effort.) Or we'd look at mindset, but I couldn't help but give strategies on memory. (To make sure their effort pays off, we must teach them the most efficient strategies.) And no matter what the topic, I started with the power of positive relationships as the bedrock of them all. Each on its own has merit, but together there was a collective power.

Good practice is often tucked away in individual classrooms. Teachers need to collaborate.

I knew that in this moment it was time to put my thoughts to paper and get these ideas out there. With the invaluable help of Nina each step of the way, this book is written out of the deep respect we have for educators, their passion and their time. It is a culmination of experiences in Brooklyn and London and a result of hundreds of hours of weekly FaceTime and phone calls between these two places, pulling apart the research and figuring out how to make the information practical. As explained at the start, it is an educator-to-educator book. It is grounded in evidence and shaped by experience. This book argues that to do this right, we need to integrate three approaches – build positive relationships, develop a learning mindset and utilise our understanding of memory. In other words, we must connect the dots.

How this Book Works

Use this guide to navigate the book.

Connect the Dots has three chapters, each containing three sections.

Chapters:

- **Relationships:** creating a sense of belonging, establishing norms and high expectations; and understanding barriers, like unconscious bias and misconceptions, in order to break them down
- **Memory:** managing cognitive load, using effective learning strategies, planning for long-term retention and application of knowledge
- **Mindsets:** building self-efficacy, developing metacognitive skills, and using feedback, goal setting and talk effectively

Sections in each chapter:

- **Research** worth knowing: key findings from experts in the field
- In the **Classroom**: strategies aligned with the research
- **Leadership** and professional learning: guidelines for whole-school application

We refer to these throughout as Research, Classroom and Leadership.

Use the guide at the top of page to know where you are:

1
CHAPTER

RELATIONSHIPS | MEMORY | MINDSET

RESEARCH | CLASSROOM | LEADERSHIP

A
SECTION

There is a detailed table of contents at the start of each chapter to find what you are looking for.

Things to know:

Dig in. Although we recommend starting with Relationships (relationships are the bedrock for all effective teaching and learning, after all), this book was designed so that you can start wherever you like.

Sit back. When reading the Research section, you may be eager to see how these ideas can be used in the classroom. We've got you covered. Each concept and finding from Research is aligned with strategies in the Classroom section.

Mind the spelling gap. This book is written with British spellings. For example, we spell 'practise' with an 's' if it's a verb and with a 'c' when it's a noun.

In the margins there are side notes. These are interjections – things we really want to let you know. It's also great for taking notes of your own. Side notes include:

- Recommended reading. Most of these are also listed at the end in Recommend Readings and Resources, but if we really wanted to tell you now then it's here.
- Classroom (when we want to point you to a classroom strategy)
- Connect to Research (when we want to remind you of some research)
- Connect to other chapters
- Teacher Tips
- Definitions quotes and captions.

Ages: We've kept our age ranges wide with the understanding that you will adapt strategies to the appropriate level for your students.

- Very young students (EYFS/Pre-K)
- Younger students (Reception to Year 4/K–3rd grade)
- Older students (Year 5 to Year 13/4th grade to 12th grade)
- GCSE/A level (specifically high school)

Repetition of graphics: You'll find that some of the same graphics appear in two sections (e.g. in Research and Classroom). This is done when a graphic used in Research is perfect for making a point in Classroom.

Pronouns: They? We've chosen to use the pronoun 'they' when referring to a person to keep it simple and gender neutral.

RELATIONSHIPS

RELATIONSHIPS: RESEARCH

Relationships: Research
worth knowing

Relationships influence every aspect of our teaching – in ways we might not have thought. Research reveals the power of positive relationships.

INTENTIONAL, EVERYDAY AND EXPECTED

At the end of each school day, every child at Clapham Manor Primary School in South London shakes the hand of an adult. 'Good afternoon,' says a Year 1 (kindergarten) student as he extends his hand to David Pittard, his Year 1 teacher. 'Good afternoon, Max,' David responds. 'You had a great day today. I noticed you worked really hard on your letters.' The teacher and student shake hands. Zlata Camdzic, the teaching assistant, is there too. 'I always rush back at the end of the day for this moment,' Zlata tells me when I visit the classroom. David and Zlata stand by the door every afternoon, connecting with each child in the class as their parents or caregivers come to the door to pick them up.

This is the golden handshake rule, which goes back at least 15 years at Clapham Manor. It's just what they do and it's for everyone – from the nursery (Pre-K) child who gets handed over to parents to the Year 6 (5th grade) students who leave school on their own. The children with whom I chat in the playground tell me the school does it to 'teach manners' and 'to be kind', but the purpose is multi-faceted: yes, this simple handshake teaches social skills (shake with the right hand and give eye contact), but it also gives the adults a clear chance to verbally acknowledge something personal about the child. It is an intentional strategy to show students that they are held in high regard, they belong, and they are expected to display positive interpersonal skills. 'I love the red scarf you are wearing today,' I hear Zlata say to one student who has bundled up to head out into the cold to meet her grandmother.

At the end of every day, staff and students at Clapham Manor Primary School connect with a handshake.

Like many schools, Clapham Manor Primary School is strategic about making sure their staff connect with children and build a positive learning environment. They know that students have a greater chance of reaching their potential – and truly thriving – when they trust their teachers and believe their teachers want the best for them. This could be shown simply by a handshake or a smile at the door. We notice something new or remember a detail from an earlier conversation: 'How was the trip to the dentist?' These brief moments in the classroom, the hallways and the playground add up and lead to strong positive relationships over time. This is as true for our much older students as it is for their younger peers.

WHAT IS MEANT BY POSITIVE RELATIONSHIPS?

We all want to belong and be valued. We experience this through our relationships with others – through our positive relationships. **Positive relationships** happen when people connect emotionally and value each other's complex identities. As educators, we exhibit positive relationships through our actions, like those that clearly communicate high expectations and high regard. This can look like the following:

- A girl, aged 11, is struggling with reading aloud in class. Although she's intimidated by her seemingly confident peers, she tries reading aloud anyway because the teacher has taught her that practice is the best way to improve and that the teacher will not tolerate teasing by peers.

- A student accepts teacher feedback because they believe the teacher is trying to help them get better.

- A teacher calls home when a 16-year-old student is absent from class, asking them what prevented them from coming and expressing the expectation and hope that they return the next day.

- A young student chooses to tell the teacher that they are being bullied. They trust that this teacher will help.

- A teacher plans their lessons with a clear idea of their students' prior knowledge and learning

- A teacher abides by a 17-year-old student's wish to be referred to as 'them' instead of 'him'.

These brief moments in the classroom, the hallways and the playground add up and lead to strong positive relationships over time.

'It is teachers ... who have created positive student-teacher relationships that are more likely to have the above average effects on student achievement.'
(Hattie, 2009)

WHY DO RELATIONSHIPS MATTER?

Although many educators feel they may not have 'enough time' to focus on relationship building, all teachers can – and should – invest in relationships to maximise learning for young people.

RELATIONSHIPS MAKE TEACHING AND LEARNING BETTER

It turns out that one common folk saying that permeates teaching – 'Don't smile until Christmas' – is not sage advice. There is a large body of evidence, in fact, that shows that positive school-based relationships impact student success in significant ways. Contrary to advice often given to new teachers, smiles are OK and are fit for the first day of school. A positive, caring, and respectful classroom climate sets the foundation for learning to thrive. In this environment, students find a safe place to take risks and have the confidence to admit what they don't know. Research backs this finding. In 2009, John Hattie, professor and education researcher for nearly 30 years, published findings from over 800 meta-studies of more than 80 million students worldwide, examining what works best for students' learning and academic success. Hattie concluded that relationships are a key factor contributing to learning and creating environments where students take academic risks (Hattie, 2009). Relationships matter.

'Classroom climate' has been identified as one of the six components of great teaching, leading to student progress, according to the Sutton Trust's project report 'What makes great teaching? Review of the underpinning research' by Coe et al. (2014). Classroom climate refers to the 'quality of interactions between teachers and students, and teacher expectations: the need to create a classroom that is constantly demanding more, but still recognising students' self-worth.' Although strategies like effective feedback top the charts for impact (Education Endowment Foundation, 2011), Dylan Wiliam, British educationalist and Emeritus Professor of Educational Assessment at the UCL Institute of Education, reminds us that relationships are at the centre of effective feedback: 'Without that relationship, all the research in the world won't matter' (Wiliam, 2014). Mary Myatt (education advisor and author who also spends a lot of her time talking to different leaders, teachers and students) adamantly concurred when I interviewed her, saying, 'It's the teacher's role to extend that gift of a positive relationship first through their actions' (Myatt, 2019). Classroom climate and positive relationships stand tall in the ranks of content knowledge, instruction and feedback simply because, if students don't trust you, they aren't fully engaged. The impact of hours of marking or strategic lesson planning is reduced when a student does not feel they belong or feels the teacher expects less of them, despite your most well-intended feedback.

RECOMMENDED READING
'What makes great teaching? Review of the underpinning research' (Coe et al., 2014) by the Sutton Trust, a foundation which improves social mobility in the UK through evidence-based programmes, research and policy advocacy. The Trust produces a number of valuable research reports on topics such as education, employment and home life.

LEARNING TOGETHER AND THE IMPORTANCE OF PEERS

Peer relationships are critical to student success. 'Positive relationships can help a student develop socially,' according to the American Psychological Association, who compiled a comprehensive review of the power of developing positive relationships on both cognitive and noncognitive factors titled 'Improving students' relationships with teachers to provide essential supports for learning.' (Rimm-Kaufman and Sandilos, 2011) In their analysis, they report that improving relationships:

- Contributes to school adjustment and academic and social performance
- Results in better attendance, increased cooperation, enhanced engagement and more self-directed behaviours
- Reduces stress for both teachers and students

As much as we teachers might think we are the centre of attention – setting objectives and calling the shots – we have steep competition. Peer-to-peer relationships are especially salient for students during the years of adolescence, when 12- to 16-year-olds are more sensitive to peer scrutiny and exclusivity (Dweck et al., 2014). In the seminal book *The Hidden Lives of Learners*, Graham Nuthall, who recorded hundreds of hours of student conversations in the classroom, reminds his readers that 'social relationships determine learning' (Nuthall, 2007), mostly referring to peer culture that teachers just don't see. Nuthall's message, like that of others who work closely with young people, is that we must take into account all that a child is experiencing as they sit in our classrooms if we want to understand what works best in schools. The child's experience is determined more by the 25 or so young bodies in the room than by the teacher at the front. This impacts academics as well as behaviour and classroom management. 'When there is a clash between peer culture and the teacher's management procedures, the peer culture wins every time' (Nuthall, 2007, p. 37).

Systematic reviews of the research into 'teacher-student relationship quality' show that teachers can learn how to build better bonds with and between students. Rather than being strictly intuitive and 'natural', interventions can be learned and rehearsed in order to assist teachers to develop supportive, low-conflict relationships with students. Building positive relationships is particularly important for students who have experienced trauma, or those who demonstrate a lack of motivation: 'When children perceive social support in the form of affection, admiration, satisfaction, and strength of alliance, they develop academically-relevant self-views that promote motivated engagement in learning.' (Hughes, 2011) By no means are positive relationships a proxy for great teaching. They are part of a whole as we connect the dots between what matters the most and what we can actually control. Therefore we must be strategic in how we build relationships, which is the basis for the Classroom and Leadership sections in this chapter.

SCHOOL CONNECTEDNESS

When Andria Zafirakou, an associate deputy at a UK school, won the Global Teacher Prize in 2018, she told reporters, 'Build trust with your kids – then everything else can happen' (Aitkenhead, 2018). Zafirakou is referring to the art of intentionally creating a sense of belonging for all students who are not only disadvantaged economically, but also in other areas of their lives. 'If our school could open at 6 o'clock in the morning, there would be a queue of children waiting outside at 5 o'clock in the morning,' Zafirakou told the audience at the 2018 Global Teacher Prize. 'Our schools must be safe havens.' Positive, warm and caring relationships in the classroom, amongst peers and teachers, impact the entire school climate and increase the feeling of school connectedness (Bryk and Schneider, 2002). School connectedness leads to healthier and more responsible habits among students. According to the Center for Disease Control, 'Research has shown

RECOMMENDED READING
The Hidden Lives of Learners by Graham Nuthall is a fascinating and informative journey into what a child actually experiences in the classroom.

'The most important thing we can do as teachers is to ensure that our schools are safe havens' – Andria Zafirakou, Global Teacher Prize in 2018 (Zafirakou, 2018).

that young people who feel connected to their school are less likely to engage in many risky behaviours, including early sexual initiation, alcohol, tobacco, and other drug use, and violence and gang involvement' (Centers for Disease Control and Prevention, 2018). Studies based on 25,395 students aged 11 to 18, reported by Search Institute (Roehlkepartain et al., 2017), show that the number of strong relationships positively impacts academic motivation, socio-emotional skills and responsibility.

IN SUMMARY

Relationships matter. If we prioritise students and learning, we need to prioritise building positive relationships. In summary, positive school-based relationships lead to:

- Willingness to take academic risks, make mistakes
- Enhanced openness to feedback
- Higher self-expectations and willingness to set higher goals
- More perseverance and tenacity
- Self-control, less conflict prone
- Increased attendance (more present)

Negative school-based relationships lead to:

- Self-preservation dominating thoughts and behaviour
- Lack of trust and participation in learning activities and applying feedback
- Low self-image and internalised oppression

While it's clear the research shows that positive relationships affect learning, teachers know that creating and maintaining a positive relationship with a child is not a perfect science. Every teacher has their own approach and personality, and every child comes to us with a variety of prior experiences, beliefs and cognitive abilities. What we do when a student arrives at school makes a powerful difference. For most of the year, students spend a majority of their days and waking hours in schools. They are growing up in our care. The effects of the relationships they build with non-parental adults are long lasting and crucial to learning.

THE SCIENCE OF POSITIVE RELATIONSHIPS

When information enters the brain, the routing system determines how well we use it. Teachers influence the pathway to learning.

To better understand why positive relationships have such an impact, let's begin with what actually happens inside the brain on a basic level. 'Close supportive relationships stimulate positive emotions, neuroplasticity and learning,' writes psychologist and professor of psychology Louis Cozolino in *The Social Neuroscience of Education* (Cozolino, 2013). In short, the brain is highly influenced by our surroundings and interactions with others. Neuroscience research is just beginning to unravel the mysteries of our social and complex brains. We now know that any cognitive task employs multiple parts of the brain to work together, constantly changing our brains. Good relationships literally shape the brain, because good relationships create a situation that allows sensory input from our environments to be processed in what neuroscientist and educator Judy Willis calls 'the thinking reflective brain' rather than 'the reactive brain' (Willis, 2009).

The key players in this process are the amygdala, hippocampus and prefrontal cortex. Of course, the brain is much more complex and mysterious than presented in this chapter. We will describe the learning process more in depth in the Memory chapter. For now, let's look at the architecture of the brain to see how it receives and processes information. These basics about the brain will help us better understand and serve our students.

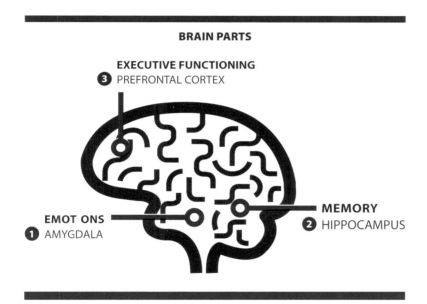

BRAIN PARTS

EXECUTIVE FUNCTIONING
3 PREFRONTAL CORTEX

EMOTIONS
1 AMYGDALA

MEMORY
2 HIPPOCAMPUS

KEY PLAYERS
The key players in processing information are the amygdala, hippocampus and prefrontal cortex. Understanding how they work will help us better serve our students.

THE BRAIN SEEKS SAFETY FIRST

The brain follows a 'safety first' policy, constantly at work scanning our surroundings to ensure nothing will harm us. Every second, about 11 million bits of information are absorbed through our **sensory nerves** (in our eyes, ears, mouth, face, skin, muscles and internal organs). (*Encyclopædia Britannica*, no date) This information reaches our brains through the limbic system, which is the emotional core where the (1) amygdala and hippocampus evaluate the information. The **amygdala** plays the main role here, acting like a routing system or air traffic control for information. It is sensitive to social and physical threat or even boredom and determines how information is channelled through the brain and whether it will be remembered or discarded. It is also at the ready to prepare our body to survive impending danger. The (2) **hippocampus** is our brain's **data storage unit**, the part of the brain responsible for higher cognitive memory consolidation and storing memories. It uses our past memories to help the amygdala decide if and how much information can move further into the brain and eventually to the **prefrontal cortex** (PFC).

Executive functioning, which includes reasoning, self-regulation and abstract thinking, allows us to consider and voluntarily control our thinking, emotional responses and behaviour.

RESPONSE TO STRESS
When the brain is in a positive emotional state, or 'relaxed-alert state', the amygdala, which is influenced by memories from the hippocampus, allows information to be processed in your prefrontal cortex (PFC).

OUR EMOTIONAL STATES HELP ROUTE INFORMATION

If the information processed by the amygdala is not seen as a threat, the brain is in a positive emotional state, or **relaxed-alert state**, and the amygdala allows information to be processed in the hippocampus and move to the PFC. The (3) PFC or thinking brain, is the control tower, in charge of higher-ordering processing and executive functioning such as reasoning, planning, self-regulation and abstract thinking. This kind of thinking helps us see different solutions to a problem, plan what needs to happen first in a task, react appropriately when angry or apply concepts to new learning. It is important for teachers to also be aware that the PFC is still forming in children's brains and will not be fully mature until around the age of 25. It will take young children and adolescents more time than adults to engage the PFC. This is a normal part of brain maturation.

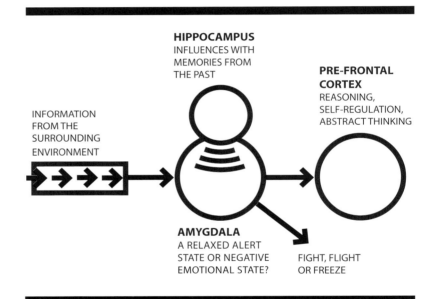

HIPPOCAMPUS
INFLUENCES WITH MEMORIES FROM THE PAST

PRE-FRONTAL CORTEX
REASONING, SELF-REGULATION, ABSTRACT THINKING

INFORMATION FROM THE SURROUNDING ENVIRONMENT

AMYGDALA
A RELAXED ALERT STATE OR NEGATIVE EMOTIONAL STATE?

FIGHT, FLIGHT OR FREEZE

When the brain is in a negative emotional state, caused, for example, by fear, anxiety or boredom, the amygdala sends distress signals to the adrenal glands which release extra cortisol, a stress hormone. In this state, information is less likely to move to the thinking brain, or prefrontal cortex, for higher-order thinking and judgement. Instead, the brain responds with a **fight**, **flight** or **freeze** stance, the body's strategy to survive life-threatening situations. Here's how it might play out during the school day for two different students: Jasmine's sensory nerves pick up the sound of whispering by her peers during science class. Jasmine feels certain they are gossiping about her and she is not able to focus on her work. Tom's teacher, Mr Ballard, unexpectedly touches his back. Tom's amygdala, already on chronic high alert because of a previous event in his life, initiates his 'freeze' stance, as it perceives this touch as a threat. The amygdala is reacting to the memories of Tom's sexual abuse by a relative when he was younger. His heart rate increases, and his body stiffens.

While situations like Tom's abuse happened long ago and outside of school, research shows that when children experience **adverse childhood experiences** (called ACEs) – such as homelessness, incarceration of a parent, abuse, neglect, mental illness in the home, domestic violence, war, or the stress of poverty and oppression – there is a long-term negative impact on learning, wellness and physical health (The National Child Traumatic Stress Network, no date). Alarmingly, approximately 47% of US children between 0–17 years old have experienced at least one ACE, according to a 2011–12 National Survey of Children's Health (Bethell et al., 2017).

These moments have made it more challenging for Jasmine's and Tom's brains to pass the teachers' instructions or content to the prefrontal cortex. Jasmine's and Tom's days are not necessarily so different from those of many of our students. Given that our brains function more efficiently in a positive emotion state, it is imperative that teachers adapt the learning environment to cultivate this state of being as much as possible.

TRIGGERS OF STUDENT STRESS

Stress impacts how brains work – in both positive and negative ways. Some stress is helpful to the brain as it increases alertness and cognitive clarity. A car tyre is a good metaphor for stress. A tyre needs a certain amount of air pressure or 'stress' to function best and keep the car moving – a perfect symbol for a relaxed-alert state. With too much stress, the tyre will burst; and with too little stress, the tyre is flat and can't go anywhere. Too much or too little stress will get in the way of students' learning and wellbeing. It's useful to teach students about these effects so that you can work with them to manage stress and set them up for successful learning experiences. In order to effectively teach about stress and the brain, adults should become familiar with the stress triggers their students face and how intense the triggers are on their particular stress levels.

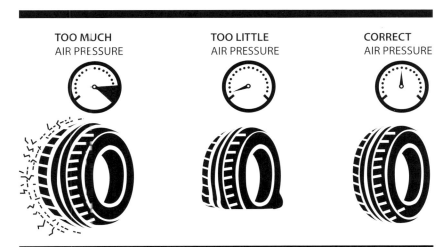

TOO MUCH AIR PRESSURE

TOO LITTLE AIR PRESSURE

CORRECT AIR PRESSURE

This tyre needs just the right amount of pressure to keep going. Too much and it will burst; not enough and it won't go anywhere.

In order to find the degree to which very young students may need strategies for stress, a colleague and I asked her Year 1 (kindergarten) students what they worried about.

Some of their responses are below:

- 'I worry about my family – if they are going to be OK when I am at school.'
- 'If I don't see my teacher in the morning.'
- 'When we were doing maths, people were talking so loudly and in my head I was saying, "STOP! STOP! STOP!"'
- 'Rushing for school makes me stressed.'
- 'I get worried when I don't get picked up on time.'
- 'I get worried when I get my spellings wrong.'

We shared this data with the other teachers and the children's parents, many of whom were struck by the impact of small daily stressors on children's emotional states. 'I forget that it's not just me who is stressed in the morning when we have to run to school,' said one parent. In fact, recent studies show that today's students are increasingly stressed out. In a 2018 survey by YouGov, 70% of British 16-year-olds and 48% of 12-year-olds report feeling sad or anxious at least once a week (Barnado's, 2018). The top causes of stress were school (65%), their future (43%) and problems at home (31%) (Barnado's, 2018). In the US, a poll of 35,000 teens put out by After School showed that 44% of teens feel stressed 'all the time' and the major causes were relationships (27%), teachers (24%) and parents (13%) (Collins, 2018). School leaders have also noticed this trend. Nearly 8 in 10 (78%) primary leaders and 9 in 10 (87%) secondary leaders have seen an increase in stress, anxiety or panic attacks among their students, according to a 2017 report by The Key. School leaders reported social media, examinations and school expectations to be the top stressors (The Key, 2017).

Stress can be triggered by a number of factors, such as transition, peer relationships, trauma, lack of self-regard, fear of failure or getting in trouble, chaotic environments or a student's anxiety that their teachers don't like them. Consider some typical daily experiences of a student:

- Your best friend is not in school today, and you are worried about who you will sit next to at lunch or hang out with at break time
- Your teacher mispronounces your name again and a few students laugh
- You got a negative message on social media
- English is your second language and you're afraid the teacher will speak too quickly
- You are new to the school and not sure about the routines
- You are gay and no one will change clothes next to you in PE. You have PE today
- You have experienced sexual abuse by a relative and no one knows
- You overheard your parents talking about how they can't afford rent this month

Stress is real and has a significant impact on learning. We can help reduce unwanted stress by creating a safe classroom climate and being aware of the triggers that cause student stress. Furthermore, building relationships allow students in crisis to confide in us. We can then point them to where to find support.

CONNECT TO MEMORY

In the Memory chapter, we address how stress and uncertainty impact cognitive load. In order to maximise memory, teachers need to be aware of triggers of student stress.

THE BENEFITS OF CONNECTION

Don't underestimate the power of school-based relationships. They open up a world of learning opportunities that would otherwise be closed to students who don't feel connected.

As adults, we know the uncomfortable feeling of entering an unfamiliar space, like the first day of a new job or a party where you know only the host. Yet, as adults, we are equipped to reason that this discomfort will pass. We find commonalities with others and share stories. We engage our more-developed prefrontal cortexes to reason and rationalise. Children's brains are different, however. We can tell a student not to worry; we may even think that their concerns are trivial; but it's more helpful for adults to step outside of ourselves and see the school experience from students' perspectives (Yeager et al., 2013). How might students feel when they walk through the front door in the morning, or as they enter the classroom and find their seat? Do they feel acknowledged and valued and fully included in this setting – with this teacher and these students? Negative classroom experiences can happen right under our noses. 'I feel like my teachers don't see me,' a Year 11 (10th grade) student told me during a focus group with low-performing students. We all know this girl: she is quiet and well-behaved, often falling off our radar. When students feel invisible or unimportant to teachers, they often disassociate themselves from being a 'learner'. School can become a stressful, cold and emotionally unsafe place where students' brains are primed to shift into fight, flight or freeze mode, or a place where they just don't like being. I'll never forget what one 10-year-old told me when I was in teacher training many years ago: 'School sucks eggs through a straw.'

ACCOUNTABILITY FOR ALL STUDENTS

Despite the best of intentions to connect with every student, children still get unintentionally overlooked in the busyness of the everyday. Interventions that specifically focus on accounting for each child help educators to systematically develop positive relationships across the whole school. Every child should be able to say that there is at least one adult in school who really knows them and cares about them.

In Cold Springs Middle School, located on the rural outskirts of Reno, Nevada, the school staff took this advice and devised a whole-school intervention. Principal Roberta Duvall took the names of every single student in the school and posted a chart with distinct columns titled 'Name/Face', 'Something Personal', 'Personal/Family Story', and 'Academic Standing' (Korbey, 2017). Duvall wanted to find out whether each child in school was known by name and face and how much more the adults knew about each child, including personal interests and family backgrounds. Teachers collectively indicated how much they knew about each student, making evident which students were less 'known'. This chart then grew into a system for ensuring that every student connected with at least one adult at school – every day. Teachers devised specific strategies like remembering a student collects stickers and asking about it or creating an in-class system whereby students anonymously complement each other via sticky notes the teacher reads out. It also served as a tool to share small and significant details about children. This initiative was part of a larger focus on social and emotional

> 'I feel like my teachers don't see me,' a Year 11 (10th grade) student told me during a recent focus group with low-performing students.

SPOTLIGHT

RECOMMENDED READING
The Washoe County district, Nevada implemented an SEL programme in the 2012–2013 school year and increasingly saw graduation rates improve. We recommend watching the video about this intervention. Go to 'The Power of Being Seen' by Holly Korbey: http://edut.to/2Gi3j1J

learning (SEL) at the middle school and more broadly within the 64,000-student Washoe County district (Korbey, 2017).

In the five years since adopting the SEL-oriented approach, according to Korbey, Washoe schools have seen higher rates of attendance and higher scores on state reading and maths tests and fewer disciplinary infractions and suspensions among students with higher social and emotional skills. Across the whole district, graduation rates have risen 18 percentage points.

THE PUZZLE GROUP

The connection between belonging and persistence is strong no matter the students' ages. For example, in one study (Master and Walton, 2013), four-year-olds, placed alone in a room, were faced with a challenging puzzle to complete. There were three conditions. In the first one, the children simply received a puzzle. In a second one, they wore a shirt with the number three on it and were told, 'You're child number 3. You are the puzzle child.' In a third condition, the children wore a blue T-shirt and were told, 'You are part of the blue group. The blue group is the puzzles group.' Those who heard they were in the 'puzzles group' persisted 29% longer than children in the 'child number 3' condition and 35% longer than children not allocated to a group or individual identity. All of the children worked on the puzzle alone, so there were no others to influence them. The researchers concluded that identifying with a group increased persistence even when the children never saw any other members of the group. This research is consistent with other studies across different ages, including adults. (Walton et al., 2012) The puzzle study speaks to the importance of creating a 'team' ethos in the classroom, with students working toward collective goals and a caring, supporting atmosphere where they celebrate each other's success and the success of the group.

BELONGING TO A GROUP
The researchers concluded that identifying with a group increased persistence even when the children never saw any other members of the group.

FIRST GROUP
The children simply received a puzzle.

SECOND GROUP
They wore a shirt with the number three on it and were told, 'You're child number 3. You are the puzzle child.'

THIRD GROUP
The children wore a blue T-shirt and were told, 'You are part of the blue group. The blue group is the puzzles group.'

THE POWER OF NEGOTIATING NORMS

We are often naturally more committed to something when we feel a part of a group. While it's essential to foster that hard-wired desire to form connections and follow group behaviour, we must also safeguard students against the more negative aspects of group behaviours, such as bullying, exclusion, unwanted peer pressure, cheating or even violence. In order to establish an equitable, inclusive and peaceful environment, educators can create structures that provide guidelines for wanted behaviours. It may seem obvious that the classroom needs rules (and students and teachers need to follow them); however, the research suggests taking it one step further and facilitating the creation of class norms. Students come to schools with some understanding of the way they are supposed to act as well as having their own desires about how they want the class to run. It's the teacher's job to work with students to negotiate shared classroom norms so that everyone has the same understanding and they can be more easily modelled, exemplified and practised.

THE BENEFITS OF NORMS

Norms are a set of agreements amongst members of a group that help guide how we socially interact. Merriam-Webster's definition of a norm is useful: 'a principle of right action binding upon the members of a group and serving to guide, control, or regulate proper and acceptable behaviour'. Researchers discuss norms in terms of spoken and unspoken guidelines. In this book we will focus on norms that are spoken, created collectively by the members of the class; they are explicit and concrete. Examples of classroom norms include: 'One person talks at a time' and 'We respect each others' possessions'.

Norms also produce a number of other psychological outcomes that benefit a group of learners.

1. Norms can help students feel safe. Students both want and need teachers to demonstrate authority by setting realistic academic and behavioural expectations (Brophy, 1998). For example, a student in a classroom with a norm such as 'We accept mistakes as an important part of the learning process and support each other in this process' may feel more comfortable openly taking academic risks.

2. Norms create a sense of belonging. Norms unite learning communities around common behaviours, which they hold each other accountable to.

3. Academic and social goals are more likely to be reached in a classroom with established norms (Schwartz et al., 2016a; Schmuck and Schmuck, 1992).

4. Students rise to the occasion: 'When teachers hold high expectations of students, the students typically meet higher standards of performance' (Good and Brophy, 2000).

To intentionally create a climate that maximises learning potential, a teacher sets the tone through her use of language and actions, maintaining zero tolerance for behaviours that don't support a positive classroom culture. She is providing a model for her students and their interactions with each other. Recall Nuthall, who spent several

> It's the teacher's job to work with students to negotiate shared classroom norms so that everyone has the same understanding and they can be more easily modelled, exemplified and practised.

 SPOTLIGHT

CLASSROOM
Find examples of norms and strategies to create and maintain them in Relationships: Classroom.

> The majority of interactions a student will have at school are with other students, not teachers. Teachers have the power – and the responsibility – to influence those interactions by establishing clear norms with their students.

years following the lives and interactions of students amongst their peers, reporting on how children experience school and how that relates to learning. He noted that peer interactions are central to students' attitudes towards – and achievement in – school (Nuthall, 2007). The majority of interactions a student will have at school are with other students, not teachers. Teachers have the power – and the responsibility – to influence those interactions by establishing clear norms with their students.

A teacher, therefore, must be keenly aware of student interactions and the prominence they have in the classroom. Nuthall writes, 'We need to know who, among our students, is friends with whom, who has status, what roles students adopt with respect to one another, the knowledge and beliefs students share about aspects of popular culture – music, television, clothes – and their ways of participating and working together' (Nuthall, 2007). This may sound like a tall order, especially for teachers of secondary students whom teachers see less often, but when a teacher uses intentional strategies (see Relationships: Classroom), connecting with students becomes routine and has a myriad of benefits. As mentioned earlier, aligning peer norms with teacher norms for the learning environment will yield the highest academic and social impact.

THE HIDDEN NATURE OF HIGH EXPECTATIONS
Our choice of which students we call on more, listen to a little longer and give more feedback to is influenced by the expectations we have for each learner.

We all aim to have high expectations for all our students. It's commonly embossed on banners hanging in school foyers or framing websites: 'Aim for the Stars', 'Excellence for all' and 'We are Lifelong Learners'. In reality, these sentiments are easier said than done. According to the research, our expectations are not always in our conscious awareness. We may be sending subtle messages that we have high expectations for Ioana but lower expectations for Mai Ly – without being aware of it. It is as if we have two minds – and indeed we do. We have 'the mind you know well and another mind you know about only indirectly … One mind is conscious, but the other is unconscious' (Hattie and Yates, 2014). Being members of society, we are constantly primed with information to think or act a certain way, and we will do so – without our conscious minds being aware of it, according to Kahneman (2012).

Classroom teachers are inundated with data about their students – their academic levels and targets, standardised test results over time, writing ability, special educational needs, disabilities, behaviour history, language acquisition, ethnicity, race, attendance rate, family socioeconomic status, etc. – and this information can unwittingly prime us to have lower expectations for some students than others. Consider this simple example: In *Thinking, Fast and Slow*, Nobel Prize winner Daniel Kahneman explains, 'If you have recently seen the word "eat", you are temporarily more likely to complete the word fragment SO-P as SOUP than as SOAP.' Or this one: the mere mention of the words 'Florida', 'forgetful', 'bald', 'grey' or 'wrinkly' made participants in one study walk slower. The key point of this 'Florida effect' was that the participants didn't recall any mention of words relating to age, or recall seeing the word 'eat' in the previous example. Their actions happened without awareness (Kahneman, 2012, p. 53). The **priming effect** refers to the way in which merely being presented with information unconsciously influences our decisions and actions. (We pick up this point later when we discuss implicit bias.) Kahneman warns: 'We must accept that (the findings) are true for you'(Kahneman, 2012). According to the Office for Standards in Education, Children's Services and Skills (Ofsted) *Education Inspection Framework: Overview of Research* (Ofsted, 2019), when a teacher expects less of particular students, these expectations manifest in many aspects of daily teaching practice: failing to give feedback to responses; criticising them more often and not waiting as long for their answers; calling on them less frequently; only asking lower-order questions; and giving them more seatwork (e.g. completing worksheets).

THE PYGMALION EFFECT

 SPOTLIGHT

According to numerous research studies, high expectations can drive high achievement, including for students who do not have a history of academic success (Lemov, 2010) and especially for students from 'stigmatised social groups' (Jussim and Harber, 2005). Let's take a look at a fascinating study that highlights the impact of the self-fulfilling prophecy, or Pygmalion effect (Rosenthal and Jacobson, 1968). A group of teachers in the study were given completely false 'data' that certain randomly selected students were 'growth spurters'. The researchers then observed the teachers and found that they treated the 'growth spurter' students as if they had more potential than their peers. When retested months later, that group of students performed better than the 'non-spurters'. Robert Rosenthal concluded, 'When we expect certain behaviours of others, we are likely to act in ways that make the expected behaviour more likely to occur' (Rosenthal and Babad, 1985). Imagine what might happen if we exhibited high expectations for all of our students?

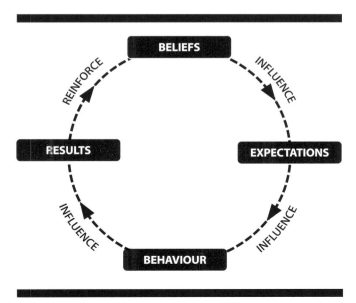

THE PYGMALION EFFECT
'When we expect certain behaviours of others, we are likely to act in ways that make the expected behaviour more likely to occur.' Robert Rosenthal (Rosenthal and Babad, 1985).

To further back up their claims, Rosenthal and Rubin (1978, cited in Goldenberg, 1992) co-authored a report summarising 345 experiments involving the influence of interpersonal expectations, which gave credence to the original study. Subsequent studies have shown that when teachers are deliberate about their interactions, they can learn to send messages of high expectations by developing better relationships based on an understanding of the students' cognitive and emotional development. More recently, Rosenthal has stated that there are four major areas in which teacher expectations influence students:

- Climate (warmer and friendlier behaviour toward students for whom they have high expectations)
- Input (the tendency for teachers to devote more energy to their special students)
- Output (the way teachers call on some students more often for answers)
- Feedback (giving generally more helpful responses to the students for whom teachers have the highest hopes) (Ellison, 2015)

If teachers are aware of these areas, they can intentionally self-correct for them, for example by actually tracking how often they call on certain students and how much wait time they give individuals. (Ellison, 2015)

HIGH EXPECTATIONS MEAN MORE TO MARGINALISED STUDENTS

Communicating high expectations when giving feedback to students is as much about the teacher's message as it about the student's interpretation. For students of disadvantaged backgrounds or those whose 'stress-response systems have been compromised by early experiences of adversity,' such as poverty, neglect or abuse (Tough, 2016, p. 83), messages get distorted or diminished since trust has been eroded over time or never developed. A student may ask themselves: Does this teacher believe in me? Do they respect me? Will my effort be worth it? 'This means that it's critical that when teachers set high expectations, they clearly communicate positive belief in the student's ability to reach them.'

STICKY NOTE MESSAGES

In 2006, Geoffrey Cohen and Julio Garcia designed an experiment with a group of underachieving Year 8 (7th grade) students of a variety of racial and ethnic groups (Cohen et al., 2006). The students were assigned to write an essay about their heroes. Each essay was marked by their teachers (all of whom were white in this study) with feedback for redrafting. The only difference was that one group of students received a message on a sticky note written in the teacher's handwriting saying, 'I'm giving you these comments so that you have feedback on your paper.' The other group received a similar message, stating, 'I'm giving you these comments because I have high expectations and I know that you can reach them.' Then the students were given the opportunity to improve the essay. The white students were slightly more likely to revise the essay if they received the 'high expectations' sticky note than the more general-sounding sticky note (87% vs 62% more likely, respectively). Results were much more poignant among the black students: 72% of those students who received the 'high expectations' sticky note redrafted, compared to just 17 % of the black students in the control group (with 'feedback only' message). The findings were even more significant

> A student may ask themselves: Does this teacher believe in me? Do they respect me? Will my effort be worth it?

SPOTLIGHT

for black students who had reported low trust in their teachers in surveys, with 82% revising their essays in the high-expectations group, compared to none in the control group. In a second, similar study in which all students were required to redraft their essays, 88% of those black recipients of the 'high expectations' sticky note earned better grades on their revised essays, compared to 34% of black students in the control group (Yeager et al., 2014).

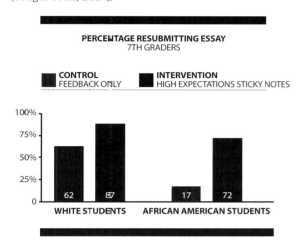

PERCENTAGE RESUBMITTING ESSAY
7TH GRADERS

■ **CONTROL**
FEEDBACK ONLY

■ **INTERVENTION**
HIGH EXPECTATIONS STICKY NOTES

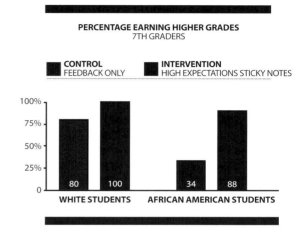

PERCENTAGE EARNING HIGHER GRADES
7TH GRADERS

■ **CONTROL**
FEEDBACK ONLY

■ **INTERVENTION**
HIGH EXPECTATIONS STICKY NOTES

According to Yeager, who helped Cohen to repeat the study, the message on the sticky note had the effect of switching off the fight-or-flight alarm at critical time when the student must decide what to do with the feedback. Instead of the message being a threat, the message posed an 'alternative' framing. The point here is not that high expectations will lead directly to a better essay, but that it is likely to lead students to invest more effort into using feedback from their teacher. Good teaching and quality feedback are still essential. An important point is that the strategy, as stated, does not have the same impact on all students. If we were to average the effect, it is moderate; but if we home in on students who are less likely to have a sense of belonging, we see that a simple intervention has a big impact on those students.

THE PRACTICE OF BEING PROPORTIONALLY MORE POSITIVE

When we set and exhibit high expectations for our students, we are sending them the message that we believe in them and that they can reach our expectations with our support. In order to trust this message and learn best, students need to feel that we respect and like them. To that end, we advocate straightforward, intentional strategies for cultivating positive relationships. One study counted on teachers being more positive – literally. The strategy is based on a **5:1 ratio**, insuring five positive interactions or comments to every one reprimanding or negative comment, to 'improve students' feelings of connectedness and positivity' to the classroom experience. A study, conducted in 4th, 5th, 7th and 8th grades (Years 5, 6, 8 and 9) required that teachers interact with students using a 5:1 positive to negative ratio (Cook et al., 2017). Teachers were instructed to:

RECOMMENDED READING
For a concise overview of recommendations and risks, see 'Addressing Achievement Gaps with Psychological Interventions' (Yeager et al., 2013).

- Focus attention on positive behaviours that lead to classroom success, rather than on problem behaviours.
- Deliver specific verbal praise and approval statements.
- Engage in verbal and non-verbal positive interactions (e.g. questions about students' interests, appropriate jokes, etc.).

One of the key components of the successful implementation of the intervention was a teacher checklist, used to keep track of the positive and negative teacher comments. For teachers in the study, a device was used to prompt them to give positive feedback about every five minutes. The researchers found that students in the intervention group exhibited a 'significant deduction in disruptive behaviour and increases in academic engaged time'. To be exact, the group increased their academic engagement by an average of 22%, which translates into an extra 13.2 minutes of engagement per instructional hour. Furthermore, the teachers found the strategy to be manageable and fair (Cook et al., 2017).

CLASSROOM
For tips on how to implement the 5:1 ratio, see the Connection Interaction Tracking Sheet in Relationships: Classroom.

Positivity is nice; intentional positivity is powerful. At one teacher training, the principal did something similar to the principal at Cold Springs Middle School, the school mentioned earlier. He posted the names of every student on the wall. He then asked teachers to place a green sticky note next to the names of students with whom they had had a positive encounter and a red one signifying a negative encounter or no encounter at all (Parr, 2018). Once the sticky note activity was completed, it became immediately clear which students experienced consistent negative interactions (or a lack of interactions altogether) with adults across different classrooms and contexts. As a consequence, the school put in place a plan aimed to make sure staff connected with all students in a positive way. (Earlier, we introduced you to another school that took a similar, more comprehensive approach.)

CONNECT TO MINDSET
See the Mindset: Research to learn more about what experts on feedback advise teachers to do to cultivate a learning mindset.

Positivity, however, does not mean praise for the sake of it. Students can see right through empty praise and it can lead to low expectations or low self-esteem. Praise must be authentic and suited for the age. Furthermore, it is more effective to praise publicly, and reprimand privately.

FIRM AND FRIENDLY, NOT BEST FRIENDS

Trust means that students feel that the adults at school 'have their back'. They feel like learners in this class, and feel that other students and teachers are working to help them succeed to their highest level. High expectations and trust are inextricably linked. When students feel trust, their brains feel safe and information makes it to their thinking brains, which we discussed earlier. In practical terms, they are able to listen to feedback and willing to have a go even when they aren't sure they are right. A teacher gains trust through effective and honest feedback, high expectations, an interest in students as individuals, and an approach to curriculum delivery that is considered and taught with passion and respect. My favourite teachers were always the ones who loved their subjects and were explicitly excited about bringing me along – like they wanted to share a gift. This is echoed in the research. Trust can be built by developing a high-performance relationship style.

There is plenty of research that identifies the characteristics of effective relationship styles or types. While the wording differs slightly, researchers generally agree that effective teacher-student relationships demonstrate **high expectations** and **high care**. At the Australian Society of Evidence Based Teaching (no date), research gathered from various studies led to the identification of two essential elements of a high-performance style relationship – **care** and **pressure**. Effective teachers, they claim, 'care about their kids, while also pressing them to do well'. In *Why Don't Students Like School?*, Daniel Willingham writes, 'Effective teachers … are able to connect personally with students, and they organise the material in a way that makes it interesting and easy to understand, thus placing the emphasis on both caring and curriculum delivery (Willingham, 2010). Doug Lemov in *Teach Like a Champion* coins this approach, **warm/strict** (Lemov, 2010). In *Culturally Responsive Teaching and the Brain*, Zaretta Hammond borrows the term **warm demander** from Judith Kleinfeld (1975, cited in Hammond, 2014, p. 97) and describes it as the right mix of care and push (Hammond, 2014). Therefore, when discussing positive relationships, it is useful to distinguish positive relationships from unwarranted praise and becoming 'friends' with students – a common mistake for teachers at the start of their teaching careers. High expectations should include three elements: 1) setting challenges that stretch students at their individual levels; 2) demonstrating a belief that students can succeed with proper strategies; and 3) maintaining support and guidance to help them achieve. It's about being firm and friendly, not best friends.

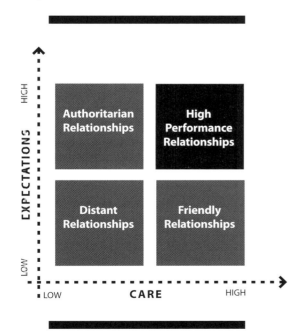

RELATIONSHIP STYLES
The most effective teachers practise high expectations and high care.

BARRIERS TO CONNECTION

Great teachers are self aware. At times, our daily thoughts and actions may be unintentional, yet potentially counter-productive.

While discussing this book with a British friend of mine, I told her I was writing a section on implicit bias. 'What?' she asked. I explained that a bias is a tendency to believe that some people, or ideas, are better than others and that usually results in treating some people unfairly. She looked dubious.

I shared some research. A pair of Columbia Business School professors, for example, took a Harvard Business School case study about a successful and outgoing venture capitalist named Heidi Roizen. Before sharing with students, the professors changed her name to 'Howard' in half of the classes taught (Routson, 2009). The students read the case study and the professors then surveyed the students about their impressions of Heidi or Howard. While both Heidi and Howard were rated as equally competent, students said they found 'Heidi' more power-hungry, self-promoting and disingenuous and not 'the type of person you would want to hire or work for', whereas 'Howard' was given positive attributes.

'The same is true for race,' I tell her and see that look of doubt again.

'Well racism is a case of nurture, not nature,' she said. 'Racism's an American thing.'

American-born, I am sensitive to this comment, especially during the Age of Donald Trump. I hear this a lot from non-Americans – that racism affects Americans, because Americans are more racist than Brits. This idea is played out in English schools during history lessons about American slavery and the American Civil Rights Movement, in the news and media. It's true that, in the US, racism and issues of race are deeply and uniquely entrenched in the soil of our nation. But racism also exists in Britain, as do classism, ageism, sexism, ableism and gender oppression etc. It's not easy getting people to talk about it. In my experience, it's hard getting leadership in particular to talk about race openly. Lola Okolosie, a writer for *The Guardian* newspaper frequently covering issues relating to race and equality in the UK, writes about a South Asian teacher who experiences racial slurs at school but is told by her well-meaning colleagues to just keep quiet (Okolosie, 2017), otherwise she'd be known in the area as a 'troublemaker'. These common suggestions to keep quiet or 'keep the peace' create a barrier to belonging and equity in both American and English schools and beyond. Racism is everyone's issue and responsibility (in particular white people) and it is vital to address it straight on by challenging social injustice when we see it.

I push back during the conversation with my friend: 'It's actually the way our brains work. We automatically have biases in favour of those we connect with. We are preconditioned.'

IMPLICIT BIAS

Humans are predisposed to having biases. As mentioned earlier in the book, millions of pieces of sensory information enter our brains in any given second. We can only consciously process a tiny fraction of this information (under a hundred pieces of data), sending the majority of it to the unconscious brain. There the brain looks for shortcuts, connecting new information to larger mental models or schemas. In milliseconds, and

RECOMMENDED READING
Unconscious Bias In Schools, by veteran educators Tracey A. Benson and Sarah E. Fiarman, offers a thoughtful and thorough examination of the negative impact of implicit racial bias on students and educators.

Implicit bias and **unconscious bias** are synonymous terms, both referring to our brain's tendency to process information based on unconscious associations and feelings, even when these are contrary to our conscious values and beliefs. Read more about bias in Memory: Research.

without being conscious of it, we judge whether or not people are like us – are they part of our ingroup? – and whether or not they pose a threat. These decisions are quick and often inaccurate. These are our **implicit, or unconscious, biases**.

Some examples of implicit bias in the classroom

Teachers may:

- Expect students who speak with certain accents to be poor writers.
- Tend to ask girls more often than boys to help tidy up after the lesson.
- Interpret loud voices as automatically aggressive or hostile.
- Call on boys more often than girls.
- Treat students with physical disabilities as if they also have a learning disability.
- Assume that parents from poorer socioeconomic backgrounds care less about their children's education than more affluent parents.
- See active students as 'troublemakers' and be more punitive with them.
- Perceive black girls to be older and less needing of care than they actually are.

Likewise, students might have implicit biases based on a peer's appearance, personality or background. They may also have a bias against a teacher. For example, a student may perceive a teacher as less intelligent if they speak with a foreign accent or less authoritative if female.

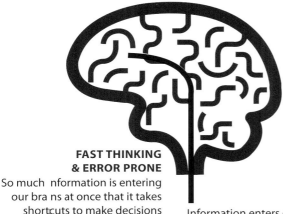

THINKING FAST, THINKING SLOW

SLOW THINKING & MORE RELIABLE
If we slow down and question these decisions in our conscious, thinking brain, we can self-correct

FAST THINKING & ERROR PRONE
So much information is entering our brains at once that it takes shortcuts to make decisions

Information enters our brains

CLASSROOM

In Relationships: Classroom, you can find a more detailed approach to Disrupt Your Unconscious Bias and practical strategies teachers can use.

RECOMMENDED READING

Culturally Responsive Teaching and the Brain by Zaretta Hammond (2014) is a thought-provoking and practical book that has influenced the writing of this chapter.

Whether we like it or not, bias guides our behaviours and actions. It's the way the brain works in an attempt to handle the large amounts of sensory input we get at any given moment. If we slow down and question our decisions in our conscious, thinking brain, we can self-correct. Importantly, the only way to counter our implicit biases is to be willing to admit that they exist, and to have the commitment and desire to counter them. This is especially important when teaching students who come from different cultures to our own – and when teaching students whose level of privilege may differ from ours.

BEYOND THE SURFACE OF WHAT WE SEE: LEVELS OF CULTURE

Zaretta Hammond writes that the layer of complexity is added to by one's culture, especially one's **deep culture**, which 'is made up of tacit knowledge and unconscious assumptions that govern our worldview' (Hammond, 2014, p. 23). 'Two people from different cultures can look at the same event and have very different reactions to it because the meaning they attached to the event is based on their deep culture.' Take this simple example of how directives, or ways of talking, are interpreted. Lisa Delpit explains in 'The Silenced Dialogue' how certain questions that are meant to be directives are interpreted differently (Delpit, 1988). A teacher, wanting a student to sit down, may say, 'Would you please return to your desk?' The student may interpret this as an actual question and respond, 'No, I'm not finished yet,' not realising that the teacher meant, 'Return to your seat now.' The teacher, in turn, interprets the child's response as defiance.

WHAT IS SAID	TEACHER THINKS	STUDENT THINKS
Teacher: *Would you please return to your desk?* **Student:** *No, I'm not finished yet.*	I just told this student to return to his desk and he refused. This student is defiant.	My teacher has asked me if I want to return to my desk. I don't want to. If she wanted me to return, she would say *"Return to your seat now".*

To utilise our understanding of culture, it's useful to consider cultural elements. Some cultural elements are evident on the **surface**: they are observable and when people disagree or contrast in this level of culture, it may carry low emotional charge (like food). Just below that are **shallow** elements (e.g. personal space) that may carry some emotional charge if challenged and lead to a lack of trust or belonging, according to Hammond (2014). Lastly, **deep** culture relates to our worldview (for example, spirituality). Challenges at this level can trigger fight, flight or freeze, inhibiting learning. Again, this deep culture is part of our schema, the mental model of the way things are that has formed throughout our lives and determines how we understand and read the world around us. Differences in deep culture show up in the classroom and can cause misunderstandings. For example, Nina recalls times as a new teacher that she'd tell students, 'Look at me!' when addressing unwanted behaviour with a student. Using her lens, she perceived avoided eye contact as either a sign of dishonesty, a manifestation of shame or a lack of interest. However, she later learned that for many of her students, direct eye contact with an adult during conflict was considered disrespectful.

LEVELS OF CULTURE

SURFACE

Concrete, observable features of culture: food, dress, music, holidays, games, hairstyles.

BACKGROUND

The unspoken rules of everyday social interactions and norms: concepts of time, appropraite touching and personal space, communication, rules about eye contact, attitudes towards elders and adolescents.

DEPTH

Conscious knowledge and unconscious assumptions that govern our worldview: good and bad, spirituality, interpretations of threat, cooperation v competition, problem-solving and decision-making.

POVERTY, LIKE CULTURE, AFFECTS OUR WORLDVIEW

Another important factor to consider as an educator is the impact of poverty and low socioeconomic status on behaviours, beliefs and thought processes. The effects of poverty, be they sudden or endemic in a children's family history, are often not taken into account when teachers are engaging with students. In an evidence-based review of over 200 studies examining the effect of poverty on key psychological, social and cultural processes underpinning decision making, the Joseph Rowntree Foundation reported some profoundly important findings that have implications in the classrooms (Sheehy-Skeffington and Rea, 2017). For example:

- Poverty makes people focus more on the present moment (Less focus on long-term goals)
- Community is more important to poor children.
- It's harder to trust people.
- People may experience lower sense of self-worth, which can dampen their motivation.
- There is a weaker sense of belonging at school.

For children from families who have lived in poverty for generations, these attitudes run deep and are often counter to those of university-educated teachers from a typically more middle-class background. Parents of these children may also have had a negative experience at school and therefore have a negative view of school or a distrust for the institution. I have heard this often from headteachers in schools with a large percentage

See 'Where I'm from' poems in Relationships: Classroom. There you'll find other creative ideas for learning more about your students' cultures.

RECOMMENDED READING

The Joseph Rowntree Foundation is an 'independent social change organisation working to solve UK poverty'. It produces a number of resources worth reading for educators, such as 'How Poverty affects people's decision-making processes' (Sheehy-Skeffington and Rea, 2007), found on their website.

of children from poor families. Outreach to these parents meant breaking down barriers (the use of multiple languages to advertise and promote events) and building trust (having many one-to-one conversations on the playground).

THE IMPACT OF BIAS
It's often surprising to learn the high price we pay when we don't address bias head on.

'It's an issue of social justice,' explained Becky Francis, speaking about bias at the 2018 National ResearchED Conference in London. Francis, Director of the University College London Institute of Education, led an extensive research project on the impact of setting (tracking) students. The study looked at data from 12,178 Year 7 (6th grade) students, 140 schools and discussion groups and individual interviews with 33 students (Archer et al., 2018). Researchers found that when they compared student exam results in maths with how students were set (tracked according to ability) when they moved to secondary school, there were shocking findings:

- Black students were 2.54 times more likely than white students to be placed in a lower ability group.
- Asian* students were 1.77 times more likely than white students to be placed in a lower ability group.
- Girls were 1.55 times more likely than boys to be placed in a lower ability group.
- 'Bottom-set students' (students tracked into lower level classes) were more likely to be working class and black.

*In Britain, the term 'Asian' is used to refer to people of South Asian ancestry (Pakistanis, Indians, Bangladeshis and Sri Lankans).

What the study reveals is that there is clear bias related to ethnicity, class and gender by teachers, based on 'perceived attitudes' and implicit bias, not on actual intelligence or outcomes. Furthermore, other research also found that 'teachers who are highly qualified in their subject are less likely to teach lower sets; some young people in lower sets feel limited or "babied" by their teachers; and those in lower sets have less self-confidence in the subject' (UCL Institute of Education, 2018). Studies like these are so important because they help bring to light what we cannot always see otherwise.

In a 2015 poll of 450 'Black, Asian and minority ethnic' (BAME) teachers, 62% stated that they did not believe that schools treat BAME pupils fairly (Haque and Elliott, 2015). This is worrying, especially in school systems where teachers from BAME backgrounds are underrepresented in both the UK and the US.

In the US, black students are nearly four times as likely to be suspended as white students, according to a 2016 US Department of Education data collection included in Ryan Felton's 2016 *Guardian* article 'Black Students in US nearly four times as likely to be suspended as white students' (Felton, 2016). In England, black Caribbean students are three times more likely to receive permanent exclusions, according to a Department of Education report on exclusions in 2015/2016. Similar disheartening statistics relate to factors such as socioeconomic status or gender. In the UK, for example, the lowest performing boys in GCSEs (final examinations) are white working class (Department

RECOMMENDED READING
The UCL team produced guidelines for grouping, Dos and don'ts of attainment grouping, which are applicable to all schools, not just English ones. You can find them here: www.bit.ly/2Sd4Evu

for Education, 2013). In the US, students in the lowest performing schools come from the communities with the highest poverty level. Compared to boys, a much smaller percentage of girls enter into STEM subjects that lead to higher-paying and more professional jobs. The reasons behind the lack of girls in STEM subjects are complex and various: lower expectations and less encouragement from teachers, lack of social belonging, positive role models and much lower rate of self-efficacy in maths and science subjects.

My own experience was similar. When I started high school, I followed the lead of my big brother who recommended I take mechanical drawing as an elective subject. I absolutely loved it, but I was the only girl and I didn't know anyone; it was a vocational class and I was in the college prep stream, so I had no other classes with these boys. I grew increasingly uncomfortable and quiet in this alien environment. I wasn't confident enough at the time to stick it out. After one year, I regrettably quit. I became another number. Each troublesome statistic has its own story, and, to compound the confusion, the data contributes to prime us to unconsciously expect particular attainment or completion levels from different individuals: girls don't perform well in technical subjects; boys don't behave well in general. As we discussed earlier with expectations, some teachers, armed with preconceived ideas mostly based on hard data, make vast (and often negative) assumptions about students' abilities, interests, and capacity.

◆ TEACHER MISJUDGEMENTS

A study by University College London's (UCL) Institute of Education which involved analysing nearly 5000 seven-year-olds in English state schools found that teachers perceive children from poorer homes as less able than their rich classmates who achieve similar scores (Campbell, 2015). Likewise, teachers are more likely to judge girls good at reading, not maths, and boys good at maths, not reading. Campbell found that boys, for example, are consistently given lower scores by teachers compared to their actual ability in English and reading. According to researchers, the reasons for this are characteristic of a world where gender is socially constructed in our classrooms, toy stores and media. Researcher Tammy Campbell compared pupils' performance on independent, survey-administered cognitive tests to teachers' judgements of those same pupils' capabilities. 'I found disparities according to gender, family income-level, diagnosis of special educational needs, the language children spoke, and their ethnicity: all characteristics long-reported as underpinning gaps in primary school achievement' (Campbell, 2015).

Similar research was conducted at Yale University (Gilliam et al., 2016). Researchers showed 135 educators videos of children in a classroom setting. Each video had a black boy and girl, and a white boy and girl. The teachers were told the following:

> We are interested in learning about how teachers detect challenging behaviour in the classroom. Sometimes this involves seeing behaviour before it becomes problematic. The video segments you are about to view are of preschoolers engaging in various activities. Some clips may or may not contain challenging behaviours. Your job is to press the enter key on the external keypad every time you see a behaviour that could become a potential challenge.

While the teachers were asked to detect 'challenging behaviour', no such behaviour existed in any of the videos. Yet when asked which children required the most attention, 42% of teachers identified the black boys, 34% for white boys, 13% for white girls and 10% for black girls. Referring to studies whereby we see these types of disparities, Campbell (author of the UCL study above) concluded: 'This is not a conscious thing. It's an unconscious stereotyping by teachers that's going on. It's down to the information they are bombarded with about which children are expected to perform at what levels' (Campbell, 2015).

Which students were teachers watching when expecting 'challenging behaviour'?

TEACHER BIAS STUDY
Preschool (reception) teachers tended to track black students more than white students and boys more than girls, when challenging behaviours are expected (Gilliam et al., 2016).

RECOMMENDED READING
For a closer look at how relationships, including expectations and bias, impact boys, we highly recommend *Boys Don't Try? Rethinking Masculinity in Schools* by Matt Pinkett and Mark Roberts.

Recall our earlier discussion about high expectations leading to higher outcomes. The same is true for low expectations – they increase the likelihood of low outcomes. The information we receive is compounded by confirmation bias, the tendency to interpret new evidence as confirmation of one's existing beliefs or theories. If I unconsciously think my student isn't very clever because of his accent or even tone of voice, later when he doesn't understand something in class, my previous bias will be 'confirmed' in my mind and my beliefs will be further fortified. And as discussed earlier, our brains evolved to make snap judgements, favouring people who look, sound and act like us. This can have a significant impact if most of our students don't look like us or come from a similar culture or background. As I've become a more reflective practitioner in light of the research into bias and effective strategies, I've been able to identity that one of my own triggers is the high volume of a student's voice. In the past, I caught myself viewing students who were particularly boisterous as less studious than their more subdued peers. I believe I must have even unconsciously judged their intelligence or aptitude on occasion. Using the Disrupt Your Bias strategy has helped me – and teachers I work with – to disrupt our biases.

THE STIGMA OF STEREOTYPES THREATEN BELONGING

Implicit bias is complex, contextual and pervasive and it stems from stereotypes that are culturally constructed by our family, friends, and society, as well as small comments we've heard in passing, toys we play with and the media we consume at a faster and faster pace. As young people grow up, they learn these stereotypes from a variety of sources and many experience **stereotype threat**, meaning that people internalise and often believe the stereotypes about themselves or are convinced others do. Being members of historically marginalised or stereotyped groups – based on race, gender, sexuality, class, language and physical ability – can affect their outlooks and outcomes because they feel they may conform to the negative stereotype. According to systematic reviews of research on stereotype threat, it also creates distractions that deplete working memory, making it more difficult to learn (Singletary et al., 2009; Pennington et al., 2016). Let's look at two landmark studies that reveal that even the mention of being part of a marginalised group can impact outcomes.

STEREOTYPE THREAT, RACE

Much of what has been written about stereotype threat begins with Steele and Aronson (1995) who gave black and white university students a half-hour test using difficult items from the verbal Graduate Record Exam, an aptitude exam for entry into graduate schools in the US. In the 'stereotype threat' condition, they told students the test diagnosed intellectual ability, thus potentially eliciting the stereotype that black students are less intelligent than white ones. In the 'no stereotype threat' condition, the researchers told students that the test was a problem-solving lab task that said nothing about ability, presumably rendering stereotypes irrelevant. In the 'stereotype threat' condition, black students, who were matched with white students in their group by SAT scores, did less well. In the 'no stereotype threat' condition, in which the exact same test was described as a lab task that did not indicate ability, black students' performance rose to match that of equally skilled white students. Additional experiments that minimised the stereotype threat endemic to standardised tests also resulted in equal performance. One study found that when students merely recorded their race (presumably making the stereotype salient) and were not told the test was diagnostic of their ability, black students still performed worse than white students.

STEREOTYPE THREAT, GENDER

In another study, researchers gave a maths test to men and women, telling half the women that the test had revealed gender differences but telling the rest of the study participants that the test results revealed no gender difference (Spencer et al., 1999). When test administrators told women that that tests showed no gender differences, the women performed equal to men. However, those who were told the test showed gender differences did significantly worse than men. Unfortunately, this was also the case when women were told nothing about the test. Spencer et al. concluded that unless women are told the test reveals no gender bias, women perform worse than men. Note that this experiment was conducted with women who were top performers in maths. An American study by Lin Bian, Sarah-Jane Leslie and Andrei Cimpian has shown that five-

CLASSROOM
In Relationships: Classroom, find a more detailed approach to Disrupt Your Bias.

 SPOTLIGHT

Stereotype threat is 'situational predicament in which people are or feel themselves to be at risk of conforming to stereotypes about their social group'. The term was coined by the researchers Claude Steele and Joshua Aronson.

year-old girls are as likely to say that girls can be 'really, really smart' as they are to say the same about boys, but from six up they think brilliance is much more likely to reside in boys (Bian et al., 2017).

PERCEPTIONS OF BRILLIANCE
Five-year-old girls are as likely to say that girls can be 'really, really smart' as they are to say the same about boys, but from age six and up they think brilliance is much more likely to reside in boys. This is reflected in these studies with two different groups of children.

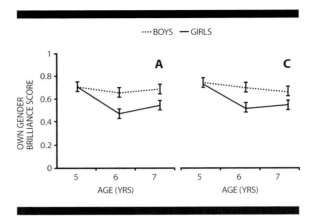

These are individual studies in varying contexts, contrived and outside of classrooms, yet as teachers they help us understand the thinking of different kinds of students. Furthermore, systematic studies lay bare similar results: stereotype threat affects people, in particular those in marginalised groups. Also, students don't need to believe the stereotype for it to have an affect (Steele and Aronson, 1995). For example, EAL (English as an additional language) students may personally know that people with limited English are still knowledgeable but might be affected by the belief that others feel otherwise. Although much of the research relating to stereotype threat has centred on women/girls and minorities, these groups are not the only ones negatively impacted. A sense of belonging is often elusive for students from different groups relating to class, ability, sexuality, etc. Furthermore, because stereotype threat is hidden or blurry, the mechanisms for triggering it are complex and varied and therefore hard to pinpoint (Pennington et al., 2016).

UNINTENTIONAL MICROAGGRESSIONS ALIENATE STUDENTS

In the classroom, young people may receive subtle messages that they do not belong to the larger group. Consider our previous discussion about culture and how factors such as ways of relating to people or group dynamics can vary as well as students' emotional response when there is cultural conflict. Students pick up on subtle social cues to determine whether or not they belong. These cues, or **microaggressions**, can be small verbal, behavioural or environmental signifiers that alienate students. Examples might include someone asking a mixed-race person, 'What are you?' or assuming that a person of Asian descent does not speak English. Sometimes people of a particular ethnicity are viewed as experts and asked to represent 'the perspective' of their ethnic group. A person who describes a TV show they don't like as 'gay' is therefore assigning a negative connotation to homosexuality – a microaggression that is often ignored but, in my experience, heard a lot in school corridors. In fact, in the Stonewall *School Report 2017* (Stonewall, 2017), 86% of LGBT pupils in British schools said they regularly hear phrases such as 'That's so gay' or 'You're so gay' in schools and only 32% report that teachers or school staff consistently challenge this language when they hear it. Alternatively, these subtle insults may take the form of a look, sound or seemingly innocuous comment during a normal routine, such as mispronouncing a name when taking attendance.

There are few things more personal than a first name. One's name is a badge given to us at birth that we wear each day, representing our culture, our family and our identity. Therefore, it is understandable that mispronouncing a student's name, which may seem innocuous and be unintentional, is a common microaggression. The teacher who mispronounces a student's name may laugh due to embarrassment or say 'Sorry, I'm so bad with names', but this is still harmful. Worse yet, the teacher may say, 'Your name is hard to pronounce', sending the message that the child's culture is difficult and 'outside' of what is considered the norm in the classroom. In a qualitative study of students from diverse backgrounds, this behaviour affected both the child's perception of self and of their culture and worldview (Kohli and Solórzano, 2012). Taking the time to learn and use a student's name properly is our first opportunity (outside of a smile) to connect with young people. And this step cannot be overlooked for its significance.

Other often-overlooked microaggressions exist in schools. When almost all the people in the pictures on the walls, in the textbooks or the lesson slides are of the same gender and race, for example, this sends a cue as to who belongs there and who does not. A quick flip through the latest anthology of English literature at GCSE (UK exams) reveals only one person of colour and one female. The remaining authors are white males. What kind of message does this send to anyone who doesn't fit into that mould? Likewise, how might a transgender or gender-fluid student feel when teachers automatically refer to them with pronouns aligned with their sex at birth? At my school, one student wanted to be called 'he', so the headteacher announced to the staff and we followed suit. Finally, who are we representing in our lesson presentations and lesson PowerPoints? Several years ago, a 14-year-old Black female student interrupted Nina's stress management session to thank her for including diverse faces her presentation. 'I hardly ever see images of people who look like me,' she said. The images we show our students send subtle messages about who belongs and who is othered.

If you are of the dominant culture in a setting, this goes easily unnoticed. In a study, researchers scrutinised 160 children's science books in two public libraries in England, counting the frequency of images of men, women, boys and girls relative to their roles, with specific attention to who the scientific professionals, astronauts and doctors were (Williams, 2018). With 26 of those books, they further examined what the professionals were doing, wearing and holding. 'We found that, overall, children's science books pictured males three times more often than females,' write the authors of the study, 'reinforcing the stereotype that science is a man's pursuit. The underrepresentation of females only worsened as the target age of the book increased. The women were generally depicted as passive, lower status and unskilled – or their presence was not acknowledged at all.' These representations matter to both males and females.

School prospectuses and websites often reflect a mix of ethnicity and gender, selling the school as inclusive but the true test is to walk the halls, look in the library and talk to

Microaggressions are small verbal, behavioural or environmental signifiers that alienate students.

CLASSROOM
See Relationships: Classroom for ideas on how to intentionally create an inclusive environment.

the students. Find out whose stories are being told. My friend and colleague Claire Hitchcock, an English teacher, told me about a conversation she had with her Year 10 (9th grade) girls – avid readers and enthusiastic students. Every year in primary school during World Book Day, when many English children go to school dressed as their favourite characters, the girls said they struggled to dress up as someone that looks like them. 'If you're not white, there are not that many lookalikes in books,' Claire explained. 'It can also be alienating to be told (explicitly or implicitly) that you can't be Hermione because she's not black or Harry Potter because he's a boy.'

It's not good enough to recognise that we have unconscious bias and that our students may struggle with stereotype threat; we need to take actions so that biases and stereotypes do not inform our perspectives, our practice or our pupils. Although the primitive part of our brain seeks out biases and uses stereotypes to work more efficiently, the more developed prefrontal cortex needs to be in charge.

SCHOOLS WITH STRONG RELATIONSHIPS
In our rush to figure out how to make schools better, we don't see what is right in front of us – people. And that connection between people builds trust and better schools.

TRUST IN SCHOOLS

After a workshop with the whole staff of a large primary school, I asked them to write down on a sticky note one small change they were going to make to build better relationships in the school. My favourite response came from one of the secretaries at the front desk: 'I'm going to smile when people come into the office'. The assistant principal stated that she was going to be more present in hallways and learn more names. Playground staff pledged to have more conversations with students about the things they like to do on the weekend. Teachers pointed to strategies they wanted to try (many of which are in the Relationships: Classroom section). Building connections means noticing the quiet students too and seeking them out. Teaching and learning are not individual but rather social endeavours involving all members of the school community and, as such, they are best achieved by working together on the big stuff and the little things. In schools, research has found that student performance increases dramatically when teachers have frequent and instructionally focused conversations with colleagues.

RELATIONAL TRUST IN SCHOOLS

In a seminal study, Bryk and Schneider conducted a seven-year analysis of 400 elementary (primary) schools about relational trust, representing 12 different school communities (Bryk and Schneider, 2003). Through a variety of methods – such as interviews, focus groups, observations and surveys with teachers, students, leadership, parents and community members – they determined a school's degree of relational trust, referring to the interpersonal social exchanges that take place in a school community. Bryk and Schneider found that higher levels of relational trust meant higher academic outcomes. They identified four criteria for building relational trust:

1. Mutual respect and genuinely listening to the views of others
2. Competence in the carrying-out of the role
3. Personal regard for others beyond what is required
4. Integrity, meaning consistency between what people say and what they do (Bryk and Schneider, 2002)

'Relational trust entails much more than just making school staff feel good about their work environment and colleagues. A school cannot achieve relational trust simply through a few workshops, a retreat, or form of sensitivity training, although all of these activities can help. Rather, schools build relational trust in day-to-day social exchanges' (Bryk and Schneider, 2003).

Bryk and Schneider found, unsurprisingly, that schools that find ways to reach out to parents, who may otherwise be disconnected or disenfranchised from the school, developed higher levels of relational trust and were more effective. The school community obviously goes beyond the school walls. Ongoing research shows that family engagement in schools improves student achievement, reduces absenteeism, and restores parents' confidence in their children's education. Students with involved parents or other caregivers earn higher grades and test scores, have better social skills, and show improved behaviour. Again, schools must be strategic about finding ways to connect with families, especially families from culturally diverse backgrounds or parents who may have endured negative educational experiences growing up.

CONNECTEDNESS AND TEACHER COLLABORATION

To get a more global perspective on the importance of relationships, I tracked down Lucy Crehan, author of *Cleverlands: the secrets behind the success of the world's education superpowers*. In her book, Crehan, a former UK teacher and now education consultant, documented her time when she immersed herself in the daily lives of five of the world's top-performing education systems to discover lessons we can glean from them (Crehan, 2017). The recount of her experiences is interwoven with research and links to US and UK schools. Crehan told me that relationships and collaboration are key elements that lead to success in school. We begin with the Canadian example, which, according to Crehan, is more similar to the US and UK context. '[Relationships] was something that came up a lot. It was important to find an entry point for every child,' she told me. Successful schools made sure that, from each child's perspective, 'there was something they came to school for'. Therefore, the structure of the day included opportunities outside the timetable that attracted children, such as extracurricular activities. Related to that, every child had at least one adult with whom they had a strong relationship.

Schools that prioritise relationships, teacher collaboration and mastery for all children create systems and school cultures that best allow that to happen. In the UK, Crehan says, 'we've become a culture in which teachers are in their individual classrooms, doing their individual planning as opposed to planning done collaboratively. Schools take up a lot of meeting time looking at dates, tracking, talking about school policies, preparing for Ofsted, as opposed to teaching and learning.' Many schools in the UK create teaching timetables that hinder collaboration. I recalled my early teaching experiences in the

Schools build relational trust in day-to-day social exchanges.'
Anthony Bryk and Barbara Schneider

RECOMMENDED READING
Cleverlands: the secrets behind the success of the world's education superpowers by Lucy Crehan.

UK and finding out I had to teach five different year groups (grades) of English. At the time, it seemed impossible; but it was soon normalised, leaving little time for teacher collaboration. Crehan echoed my frustration: 'The way we organise teacher time in the UK is punitive – and teachers have come to expect it.' It is clear that schools that are intentional about relationships and investing in social capital outperform those who don't, she said. It's about prioritising (Crehan, 2018a).

COLLABORATION YIELDS MORE IMPACT

Research into what causes schools to be most effective makes a persuasive case that strong relationships are an important factor leading to success for students. Carrie Leana studied 130 elementary schools in NYC, following 1000 fourth and fifth graders (Years 5 and 6) and their teachers between 2005 to 2007 (Leana, 2011). Leana measured the staff's **human capital** (qualifications and subject knowledge) and the staff's **social capital** (trust and collaboration amongst staff). She then compared these teacher factors to student maths achievement by measuring the amount of knowledge of maths advanced in a year with a particular teacher. The researchers took other factors into account, such as the socioeconomics and academic needs of the children. Schools with strong social and human capital together did the best in terms of knowledge acquisition, but what made social capital so important was its influence on others. High social capital – measured by asking questions such as 'To what extent do teachers in this school work in a trusting, collaborative way to focus on learning and the engagement and improvement of students achievement?' – raised the bar and expertise of the whole school, rather than just the individual. Leana writes, 'The effects of teachers' social capital on student performance were powerful. If a teacher's social capital was just one standard deviation higher than the average, her students' math scores increased by 5.7 percent' (Leana, 2011). 'In other words, teacher social capital was a significant predictor of student achievement gains above and beyond teacher experience or ability in the classroom.'

The teachers in Leana's research collaborated, observed each other's lessons and sought feedback. Leadership prioritised this to happen. This type of intentional and focused teacher collaboration evident in Leana's research is also referred to as professional capital and is a leading indicator of improved student performance according to the University of Chicago Consortium on School Research (University of Chicago, 2011). In my interview with Mary Myatt, she passionately recounted a recent visit to a primary school. In a Year 3 (2nd grade) classroom, she found the reception (kindergarten) teacher modelling a maths problem as the classroom teacher observed. This type of shared learning was commonplace in this school – teachers collaborating and learning from each other. This all happened without any input from senior leadership, Myatt explained. The headteacher got a request for cover and trusted the teachers' professionalism. 'This is a great example of trust and relationships at work … No wonder this school is number one in their local authority, yet serving one the most deprived catchment areas' (Myatt, 2019).

SPOTLIGHT

'The effects of teacher social capital on student performance were powerful. If a teacher's social capital was just one standard deviation higher than the average, her students' math scores increased by 5.7 percent.'
Carrie Leana,
University of Pittsburgh

TIME TO TAKE THE NEXT STEP

A strong relationship is not proxy for great teaching, but it is an essential part of the whole package. Teachers who can form strong, positive relationships but who lack the understanding of how to instruct will have little impact on learning. Teachers with strong subject knowledge and training in how to teach, but whom students dislike or fear, will also find limited learning in the classroom. We must do both. In Relationships: Classroom, we offer tools good teachers use to build positive relationships.

RELATIONSHIPS: CLASSROOM

Relationships:
in the **Classroom**

It's the small stuff, like remembering a detail told to you in passing…and the big stuff, like challenging bias, that creates a climate where every child belongs.

The research on relationships is compelling. Relationships matter. Therefore, we begin Relationships: Classroom with some approaches for directly teaching young people about the importance of positive relationships and encouraging discussion and debate. Then for most of this section, we present a selection of strategies to use at the start of the year and then throughout – all based on research and from our classroom experiences.

BE EXPLICIT ABOUT HOW POSITIVE RELATIONSHIPS WORK

Following a half-day workshop about learning with Year 9 (8th grade) students, I asked them to reflect on one thing they would do as a result of the workshop. One student said, 'I'm going to be nicer. I didn't know how much my attitude actually helped others learn.' Inspired by comments like these and the positive effect of teaching students about relationships, we start with some suggestions for teaching young people about the importance of positive relationships.

DIRECT TEACH: SHARE STORIES OF DIVERSITY, BELONGING AND SOCIAL INTERACTION

For **younger students:** use the children's books below to introduce aspects of positive relationships. If age appropriate, ask students to create their own stories about belonging. Consider pairing students with slightly younger children to share their stories. Here are some books recommended by teacher colleagues from both the US and England:

Celebrating differences and individuality

- *Elmer*, David McKee (diversity and uniqueness)
- *Whoever You Are*, Mem Fox (differences and similarities)
- *It's Okay to be Different*, Todd Parr (individuality and self-acceptance)
- *I Like Myself!* Karen Beaumont (self-love and acceptance despite what others might say/think)
- *Chrysanthemum*, Kevin Henkes (names, effects of teasing, peer support)
- *Stand Tall, Molly Lou Melon*, Patty Lovell (the power of confidence)
- *Bein' With You This Way*, W. Nikola-Lisa (differences and similarities)
- *One*, Kathryn Otoshi (bullying and taking a stand against it)
- 'The Sneetches', Dr Seuss (discrimination and how differences should not divide people)
- *You Be You*, Linda Kranz (self-acceptance, acceptance of others and ways to navigate the world)
- *Max the Champion*, Sean Stockdale and Alex Strick (inclusivity and diversity)

Family-specific

- *A Family Is a Family Is a Family*, Sara O'Leary (celebrates the wide diversity of families)
- *Families, Families, Families*, Suzanne Lang (diversity of families)
- *Mommy, Mama and Me*, Lesléa Newman (diversity of family: two mums)

Positive behaviours and relationships

- *The Invisible Boy*, Trudy Ludwig (belonging and inclusivity)
- *My Mouth is a Volcano*, Julia Cook (strategies to limit interrupting; part of a series about prosocial behaviours)
- *Share and Take Turns*, Cheri J. Meiners (sharing; part of a recommended series)
- *How Do Dinosaurs Play With Their Friends?* Jane Yolen and Mark Teague (friendships; part of a recommended series)
- *Swimmy*, Leo Lionni (teamwork)

DIRECT TEACH: USE RESEARCH STUDIES TO TEACH ABOUT POSITIVE RELATIONSHIPS

For **older students**: below are two variations for teaching older students about the research relating to relationships. Each of the activities utilises the resource Research Studies on pages 53 and 59, which is a selection of extracts from studies relating to relationships. Alternatively, create your own extracts from the sources from interesting articles you would like to share with students.

Variation one: USE A RESEARCH STUDY TO KICK OFF DISCUSSION

Explain to students that some scientists study people and how they behave in different situations. Then read one of the **Research Studies**. Clarify that students understand the main points. Then choose some of the following questions for a Think, Pair, Share (see Mindset: Classroom on page 281), Listening Lab or Two Minute Interviews (detailed later in this section). Suggestions for discussion questions:

- What is the main point of the research?
- Is this research important? Why or why not?

RECOMMENDED READING
The Greater Good Magazine: The Science for a Meaningful Life (greatergood.berkeley.edu) is a great resource for articles about positive relationships.

- Describe a situation when you've noticed this.
- Describe a situation when this research might not be true.
- How could we use this research to help us as a class?
- After reading this research, what is something you will do more often and why?
- How could you teach this to someone else?

Variation two: USE THE JIGSAW METHOD

The **Jigsaw Method** is a teaching strategy that has been shown to have a high-effect impact (Hattie, 2011) because students work together to ensure that all group members understand, can re-teach and apply the content to a new situation. This strategy is also an opportunity for students to work together toward common goals. Nina and I have been using this since our Brooklyn days.

1. **Prepare** by figuring out how many expert groups you will have. Take the number of people in the whole group (class) and divide this by the number of topics to equal the number of people in each expert group. Any remaining people should be added to the expert groups. *For example: 27 people in the whole group (class) ÷ 5 topics = 5 people in each group with 2 people remaining. So 3 groups of 5 and 2 groups of 6.* Copy and cut the Research Studies on pages 58 and 59 into strips so that each person in the expert group gets a copy of the same study.

2. **Introduce the Research Studies by telling** students that some scientists study people and how they behave in different situations and that students will use the Jigsaw Method to learn more and teach each others about their findings.

3. **Explain** the Jigsaw Method: 'There are two stages to this activity. During the first stage, you will be in expert groups. You will be given a research topic relating to relationships. You must read it, discuss it with the group and decide how to teach it to a new group. The second stage is when you will move to a jigsaw group, independent of anyone in your expert group, and you will teach the jigsaw group members about your research topic.'

4. **Review:** Show students the diagram on the next page to reinforce the structure.

5. **Start the Jigsaw Method**

   First stage: the expert group
   Put students into expert groups. Each expert group gets a different topic. They need to read the text and summarise in their own words what the study is about. They should then prepare to teach the research to their jigsaw group, including explaining how their topic relates to positive relationships.

   Second stage: the jigsaw group
   Put students into jigsaw groups made up of one person from each expert group. Participants take turns teaching about their research while the other students take notes. Decide on three actions the class could take to support a sense of belonging and positivity in the class.

6. **Debrief:** Discuss the jigsaw groups' recommended actions, prioritise one or more as a class, and then identify a simple action plan (tasks and roles) for classroom application. See talking points at the top of the next page.

Talking points:

- When discussing issues of belonging with students, be clear that we all experience feelings of not belonging at times. It's normal.

- Remind students that it's the responsibility of all of us to ensure that everyone feels they belong. Discuss the importance of looking out for peers.

CONNECT TO MINDSET
See Looking Back: Letters to Younger Peers on page 293 in Mindset: Classroom. These cross-age letters can include some essential tips and further address the fact that being nervous or wondering if they'll belong is a normal part of starting a new year.

THE JIGSAW METHOD
HOW IT WORKS

1 GET INTO EXPERT GROUPS

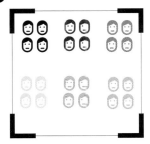

4 BACK INTO WHOLE GROUP

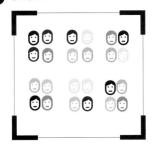

DISCUSSION
Discuss the groups' recommended actions, prioritise one or more as a class, and then create a simple action plan with specific tasks and roles.

2 EXPERT GROUPS RECEIVE DIFFERENT TOPICS

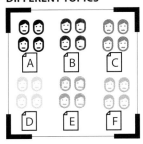

GROUP TASK
■ Read the text
■ Summarise in your own words what the study is about. It may help to create an illustration to explain the research
■ Prepare to summarise the research to your Jigsaw Group, including explaining how your topic relates to positive relationships

3 THE JIGSAW GROUP

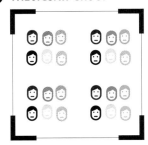

MAKE UP OF GROUP
One person from each Expert Group is in a Jigsaw Group

GROUP TASK
■ Each member of the Jigsaw Group teaches their topic and discusses actions that could be taken.

RESOURCE: RESEARCH EXCERPTS to be used with Jigsaw Method

DIVERSITY AND PROFIT
(From Hunt et al., 2018)

A business is likely to perform better financially if its workforce is more diverse. McKinsey and Company, a global consulting firm, examined more than 1000 companies across 12 countries and found that firms with the highest gender diversity at the executive level were 21% more likely to have above-average profitability than companies that lack diversity. Companies with the highest ethnic and cultural diversity were 33% more likely to outperform on profitability. The least diverse companies are 29% more likely to underperform. Some of the reasons diverse companies may outperform others is that by having a diverse workforce they attract top talent, improve decision-making and send a message to employees and other stakeholders that the company values the community and customers that they serve, according to the consultants.

Hunt, V., Prince, S., Dixon-Fyle, S. and Yee, L. (2018) *Delivering through diversity*. New York, NY: McKinsey & Company.

DOLLS AND THE TEA KETTLE
(From Marsh, 2010)

In a 2008 study, sixty 18-month-old children were shown photos of household objects, like a tea kettle. Each photo was slightly different. In one of the sets, the background of every photo had two dolls facing each other; another set showed one of those dolls standing alone in the background; a third set replaced the dolls with two stacks of colourful blocks; and the final set had the two dolls standing back to back. After the children viewed all the photos in their set, the experimenter left the room and in walked another experimenter who 'accidentally' dropped a bundle of sticks. The researchers observed how many of the kids in each of the four conditions spontaneously tried to help pick up the sticks. The infants who saw the dolls facing each other were three times more likely than the infants who saw the other background images to spontaneously help a person in need. Researchers concluded that the children were influenced by the images of people connecting with each other.

SOURCE: Over, H. and Carpenter, M. (2009) 'Eighteen-month-old infants show increased helping following priming with affiliation', *Psychological Science* 20 (10) pp. 1189–1193.

THE PUZZLE GROUP
(From Schwartz et al., 2016a)

The importance of belonging starts at a very young age. In one study (Master and Walton, 2013), four-year-old children who were alone in a room received a very challenging puzzle to complete. In one condition, pre-schoolers simply received the puzzle. In another, they wore a shirt with the number three on it. They were told, 'You're child number 3. You are the puzzle child.' In a third condition, they wore a blue T-shirt and were told, 'You are part of the blue group. The blue group is the puzzles group.' Although all children worked on the puzzle alone, those who heard they were in the 'puzzles group' persisted about 40% longer than the other two groups.

Researchers concluded that identifying with a group increased persistence even when the children never saw any other members of the group.

SOURCE: Extract from: Schwartz, D. L., Tsang, J. M. and Blair, K. P. (2016a) *The ABCs of how we learn: 26 scientifically proven approaches, how they work, and when to use them*. New York, NY: W. W. Norton & Company.

Master, A. and Walton, G. M. (2013) 'Minimal groups increase young children's motivation and learning on group-relevant tasks', *Child Development* 84 (2) pp. 737–751.

COVER LETTERS
(From Gino, 2013)

In one study, participants edited a student's cover letter and then received either a neutral message from the student (i.e., 'Dear [name], I just wanted to let you know that I received your feedback on my cover letter.') or a grateful one ('Dear [name], I just wanted to let you know that I received your feedback on my cover letter. Thank you so much! I am really grateful'). The student sending the message then asked for help on another cover letter – long after the experiment had ended and participants had no obvious reason to help. Among the participants who were thanked, 66% were willing to provide further help, as compared to just 32% of those who had not been thanked. [Researchers concluded that] expressions of gratitude increase prosocial behaviour by enabling people to feel socially valued.

SOURCE: Gino, F. (2013) 'Be grateful more often', *Harvard Business Review* [Online], 26 November. Available at: www.bit.ly/2LWGx2I (Accessed 3 November 2018).

COUNT YOUR BLESSINGS
(From Gino, 2013)

In a series of well-known studies, psychologists asked participants to keep weekly journals for ten weeks. Some were asked to write about five things or people they were grateful for each week, some were asked to write about five hassles that they experienced during the week, and a third group was asked to write about any five events that occurred during the week. Participants who listed what they were grateful for mentioned experiences such as the generosity of their friends, learning something interesting, and seeing the sunset through the clouds. Those who were asked to list hassles included the following: hard-to-find parking, spending their money too quickly, and burned macaroni and cheese. At the end of the study, those in the gratitude group scored higher on measures of positive emotions, self-reported symptoms of their physical and mental health, and they also felt more connected to others as compared to those who made routine notes about their days or wrote about hassles. In short, gratitude appears to build friendships and other social bonds.

SOURCE: Gino, F. (2013) 'Be grateful more often', *Harvard Business Review* [Online], 26 November. Available at: www.bit.ly/2LWGx2I (Accessed 3 November 2018).

Emmons, R. A. and McCullough, M. E. (2003) 'Counting blessings versus burdens: an experimental investigation of gratitude and subjective well-being in daily life', *Journal of Personality and Social Psychology* 84 (2) pp. 377–389.

ESTABLISH CLASSROOM NORMS

Teachers who invest in establishing **class norms** and routines from the start create a place where kids want to learn, saving hours of wasted time managing behaviours.

What is meant by class norms?

In contrast to rules, which are (usually) teacher- or school-generated and work best with **younger students**, **norms** are a set of agreements among members of a classroom or school. They are collectively created guidelines of behaviour that describe the desired culture and climate of the learning environment and are most appropriate for **older students**.

WHY ARE THEY IMPORTANT?
▪ Help students feel safe and protected
▪ Help define the desired climate and identify wanted behaviours
▪ Create an inclusive environment: all voices and needs are important
▪ Support children to practise collaboration and social awareness
▪ Provide common language to refer to when holding peers accountable

 AT THE START

 AAA STRATEGY

DIRECT TEACH: INTRODUCE RULES OR NORMS STEP BY STEP

Different approaches work for different developmental stages and school contexts. In many primary schools, teachers tend to use rules. We see value in that. With **young students**, it's important for them to understand the importance of rules and know that they will have adults setting limits for them to keep them safe and happy. However, as students get older and their critical thinking ability is more developed, they are able to – and should – help in the creation of classroom guidelines. In that case, they are to be considered 'norms' rather than 'rules'.

For **older students**:

1. **Brainstorm** with students as many school rules as possible within two minutes. Ask students which rules they think are the most important/beneficial and why. Explain that these rules are decided by the people in charge of schools. As school community members, we are bound to these rules.

2. **Explain** that the class will create norms. **Norms** are a set of agreements amongst members of a group that help guide how we socially interact. They are set by the class to help guide how we act in order to keep people happy, safe

and productive. Share some real-world examples of norms (e.g. the unspoken agreement about the ways we behave in a fancy restaurant).

3. **Ask:** 'What are some examples of behaviours (by peers and by the teacher) we want for our class?' Appeal to students' drive to be respected, their sense of fairness and their desire to learn from others while still having their say: 'What kinds of environments and behaviours make you feel most engaged and feel like your time and participation are respected in class?'

4. **Help** students negotiate a list of about five norms and use the guidelines in 'Norms should be' to help with the wording. Refer back to the list of school rules to avoid redundancies.

5. **Be explicit** about what norms look and sound like. Ask, 'What does this specific norm look like and sound like between students, from student to teacher, from teacher to student?' Secondary school teachers should be assured that the investment in time to set classroom norms will pay off and save time in the future because they reduce unwanted behaviours. Stick with it.

For **young students**, the teacher sets the rules, and engages students in setting a few norms for the classroom. Show the students the school or classroom rules and then discuss what other things might help the class feel fun, safe and welcoming. Use this chart as a template during a class discussion:

> Class norms should be aligned with school norms. When students walk into different classes with different norms all day long, it's confusing and increases cognitive load, which we explain later in the Memory chapter.

What are OUR SCHOOL RULES?	What does it look like when we follow the rules and norms?
	(Draw or write here):
Classroom norms What other ways of acting do we want to add?	

For **very young students**, the teacher then writes up the rules on a classroom display and creates pictures that align with them. Students and the teacher can then act them out and give them a title. The teacher should be explicit about when they see norms being adhered to (or not) and use non-verbal redirective prompts, such as pointing to the poster (see below) to remind students of the rules.

NON VERBALS

Some schools teach all students sign language – a visual means of communicating using gestures, facial expression, and body language – to provide a more inclusive environment for those with speech, language and communication challenges. Also, check out the Makaton language programme, whereby signs are used alongside speech: www. makaton.org.

CONNECT TO MINDSET

For non-verbals that students can use alongside accountable talk, see page 285 in Mindset: Classroom.

IN OUR CLASS, WE USE...

Looking eyes

Listening ears

Quiet mouth

Helping hands

Walking feet

Norms should be:

- Specific to the setting (e.g. the classroom)
- Aligned with whole-school norms, rules, and core values (If your school already has 'rules' that are publicly shared, discuss with your students what additional norms would be useful for the classroom.)
- Written in positive language (about desired behaviours)
- Limited to about five to eight norms for the classroom
- Created by young people or inclusive of youth voice as much as possible to increase ownership
- Consistently taught, modelled, practised and assessed

Examples of norms:

- One person talks at a time.
- We respect each other's possessions.
- We agree to respectfully disagree.
- We use respectful language with each other.
- Everybody gets a chance to participate.
- Outside technology is put away.
- We accept mistakes as part of the learning process and respect when peers make mistakes.
- We arrive to class on time and immediately get out equipment/materials.
- When we need help, we ask for it.

 KEEP IT GOING

HOW TO GET NORMS BACK ON TRACK

It's normal for students to deviate from norms, so openly discuss how to get back on track. This strategy is especially appropriate at the start of the year or with an established group to refocus them. Use it with the whole class or in groups.

1. **Prepare** by creating a T-chart to identify obstacles that might interfere – or have interfered – with learning and then elicit solutions. If in groups, put the T-charts on big paper so they can be posted for all to see during the class discussion.

2. **Elicit** ideas for the left-hand side of the T-chart. Introduce a few other potential obstacles or issues that have not yet been addressed with the existing norms that relate to your classroom and age group. (See 'Other potential obstacles to choose from' list below.)

3. **Ask** the students to work in groups to develop specific norms that will help minimise these obstacles.

WHAT OBSTACLES GET IN THE WAY OF LEARNING?	WHAT NORMS COULD GET US BACK ON TRACK?
Example: Someone laughs when a person gets an answer wrong.	*Example: Respect the speaker's right to get it wrong. (It's more important to have a go than to get it right.)*

4. **Debrief:** After students finish developing the norms in groups, post the T-charts on the walls or in sight for all to see. Look for commonalities and suggest (or elicit) suggestions to create one phrase or sentence. Then vote on which the class wants to adopt. You may wish to suggest these **student sentence stems**.

- 'I agree with _____ because _____ (e.g. it promotes learning/it addresses a common problem or obstacle, etc.).'

- 'Although I can see why ___ is important, I think this norm is too similar to _____.'

- 'I would like to hear more about why you've listed _____.'

- 'I'm not sure this norm is realistic because _____ (e.g. "Stay in your seat" is not a good norm since students are often asked to come to the board, etc.).'

Other potential obstacles to choose from:

- Limited work space in the classroom

- Chaotic transition (entering and exiting the classroom, getting into groups, moving desks, etc.)

- Concern about personal property

RECOMMENDED READING
You can find a number of articles about creating classroom norms on edutopia.org. The T-chart strategy was inspired by *Edutopia* blogger and author Todd Finley.

- Discomfort with sensitive topics
- Stress which makes it hard to focus
- Intolerance or bias
- Challenge focusing during silent reading/thinking times or transitions
- Smartphones or use of technology
- Difficulty sharing materials
- Interrupting each other
- Not keeping hands to oneself

STUDENT RUBRICS TO EVALUATE THEIR NORMS

Use a **single-point rubric** to help students identify how they are doing at adhering to the norms they created. Students may refer back to that rubric when reflecting on their own, group or classroom interactions.

Example of norms using a single point rubric:

1 = Never 2 = Sometimes 3 = Usually 4 = All the time

NORM	RATING	EVIDENCE IN ACTION	RECOMMENDATIONS
One person talks at a time.	1 2 3 4		
We respect each other's possessions.	1 2 3 4		
We agree to respectfully disagree.	1 2 3 4		
Outside technology is put away.	1 2 3 4		

'SPOT IT, SHARE IT' BOARD

This is a display in the classroom where teachers can provide students with real-life examples of how classroom norms look and sound in action. We suggest selecting one norm or classroom routine as a focus, such as 'We respect each other's opinions and property'. Then when students or the teacher observe the norm in action, they post the details of what they see/hear, which students are enacting that norm, and photos of those students in action. This acts as a visual recognition of wanted behaviours and offers concrete examples of how norms are enacted on a daily basis. For **older students**: allow opportunities for whole-class discussions on how well the class behaviours are aligned with the norms they've set. Elicit examples of norms in action.

RECOMMENDED READING
Spot it, Share it, inspired by Paul Dix's 'Recognition Board', outlined in When The Adults Change, Everything Changes (2017), which we recommend for more about behaviour.

REFLECTION TOOLS

Use these activities as a tool to reflect on norms: Exit Tickets, classroom meetings and circle time for **younger students**. These can be done at a specific time (last Friday of the month for older students or after break time for young students) to ritualize them. Some discussion questions:

- What's one norm that the group should focus on this week and why?
- What's one norm the group adhered to really well and what's one way we can continue to work on this norm?
- Please shout out (or name) one person who contributed to a positive class environment today.

EXIT TICKET
Exit tickets, completed in the last few minutes of class, contain questions related to content or norms. Create a stack of Exit Tickets so they are ready to use if you need them.

TEACHER TALK TO FOSTER COMMUNITY

- Encourage students to use the language of the norms when holding each other accountable
  - 'You didn't adhere to norm 3, John. We said we'd agree to disagree, but you just told Malik to "shut up".'

- Use inclusive language that refers to norms and the importance of community.
  - 'This is the way **we** do it.' vs. 'In **my** classroom you need to…'
  - '**Our** classroom' vs '**this** classroom'
  - '**We** are learners, scholars, mathematicians, etc.'
- Offer individual feedback to make explicit that you noticed when a norm was being used. Encourage this with peer-to-peer feedback.
  - 'I noticed that you…'
  - 'Naomi, what did you notice about how Felix responded? That was a great example of enacting our norm about respecting each other.'

 KEEP IN MIND:

BE PREPARED FOR SOME COMMON CHALLENGES TO PRACTISING NORMS

1. **Challenge:** Students have been given rules so often that they aren't sure that norms are something other than rules with a fancy name.

   Strategy: The more you support individual and group reflection of norms in a low-stakes setting, the more students will value norms as a blueprint for how the class will function best. They will understand them as a learning tool, not a device to catch them misbehaving. They also need to see you adhere to the norms.

   Teacher Talk: 'Pardon, I just realised that I interrupted Ruby before she finished talking. Sorry for not following the norms.'

2. **Challenge:** Students push the limits.

   Strategy: Don't take it personally when students don't adhere to the norms. Keep in mind that the adolescent brain is geared towards immediate gratification, risk taking and scant contemplation of consequences. In other words, some norm breaking is par for the course. Firmly and patiently use minor unwanted behaviours as an opportunity to foster a community where all classroom members support their peers to uphold the norms through peer- and self-talk.

   Teacher Talk

   - 'Let's think back to why we thought these norms were important in the first place. What could you do right now to get back on track?'
   - 'Sometimes it feels difficult to follow the norms. Pause and think. Remember you have a choice.' You can also ask the class to consider what self-talk would be helpful here: 'What could you say to yourself when you don't want to follow a norm?' Some examples: 'I believe I can do this', 'This is in my control' or 'I don't feel like doing this, but it's important to the group.'

TEACHER TIP

Introduce your students to Bruce Tuckman's four stages of group development: forming, storming, norming and performing to help normalise the struggle groups initially face when making strong connections and exhibiting wanted behaviours.

SET HIGH EXPECTATIONS

When high expectations are intentional and authentic, students see their own potential rather than their limits.

What is meant by high expectations?

High expectations refers to the belief that someone can and will achieve something. When an adult has high regard and expectations for students, they care about the students and give the student the benefit of the doubt – assuming positive intention and the possibility for a high-quality outcome. Expectations are wrapped in our prior knowledge about someone and the context of our own biases and prior experience. High expectations lead students to feel valued, respected and included.

WHY ARE THEY IMPORTANT?
▪ Stronger sense of self-efficacy ('I believe I can do this') and agency ('This is in my control')
▪ Increased motivation and engagement/interest in the task
▪ Students better prepared for careers that will expect tasks to be completed to their highest standard before moving on

 AT THE START

FRAME THE LEARNING FOR HIGH EXPECTATIONS

Establish high expectations at the beginning of the year and connect them to norms. Be explicit and consistent about what you expect.

- 'I expect that you will finish your work in our class.'
- 'Everyone in this class is capable of the work we are about to do.'
- 'Completed work in this class may/will take several goes or drafts.'
- 'In this class when you get a test back, you will be expected to analyse why some answers were not correct and then correct them.'
- 'You will be expected to put your best effort into your assignments.'

INTENTIONALLY **PRACTISE PROCEDURES**

One of the most effective ways to set high expectations and also manage good behaviour is to ensure that students consistently follow the procedures you set. Teachers sometimes assume students will understand and be able to follow procedures after they are taught just once, but procedures need to be clearly and repeatedly explained and modelled. Also, although teachers may explain a procedure, in the hustle and bustle of the day, they let them slide. Use the steps and chart below to keep track, so that you are intentional and consistent.

1. Start by **making a list** of all procedures in the class that help it run effectively, such as:

   - What students should do immediately when they walk in
   - The procedure for using the toilet during the lesson
   - How they get into groups/move the chairs
   - How they circle up or line up
   - How they get and use materials (e.g. computers, art supplies)
   - How they hand in homework

   Obviously, these should be age-appropriate. The main idea is that teachers expect students to get it right.

2. Set aside lesson time for **modelling, practising and assessing** these procedures. Continue practising them until the class has done them correctly twice and is able to repeat them in ensuing class sessions. Point out when you **notice** procedures are being adhered to. Ask students to periodically assess how the procedures are going and where they struggle. Invite suggestions from students for how to do it right.

3. **Self-assess**. Are you keeping high standards for your students? Are you using a tone that sends the message that 1) you expect these procedures to stick; 2) you are aware that it takes practice and sometimes students will not get it right; and 3) these procedures have a purpose that benefits the whole class?

A PROCEDURE OR STUDENT ROUTINE	WHAT DOES THIS LOOK LIKE? WHAT DO I WANT TO MODEL?	HOW WILL I ASSESS THAT STUDENTS ARE CONSISTENTLY FOLLOWING THE PROCEDURE?
EXAMPLE		
Classroom entry procedure	*Coats and bags on chairs, equipment out*	*Weekly spot check right before taking attendance*

 KEEP IT GOING

 AAA STRATEGY

HIGH EXPECTATION QUESTIONING

1. ASK and WAIT

Sometimes teachers feel uncomfortable when a student struggles or takes a long time to answer a question, leading teachers to quickly call on someone else or provide the answer themselves. However, providing **wait time** and offering students the time to really work through a question until they get it promotes long-term learning (and memory) and sends a signal that you expect students to try their hardest. Here are a few things you can say before asking another student for the answer:

Teacher talk, if needed:

- 'I know you can get this and we're here to help you. What do you already understand? Now show us where you are stuck'.
- 'You are almost there. Talk more about... (provide a hint).'
- 'I know this is challenging AND I know you can do this with effort and the right strategies.'
- 'Take your time. Feel free to think aloud so we can hear your process.'

2. CHECK and CORRECT

The teacher or another student provides the correct answers or models how to solve the problem with a concrete example.

Teacher talk

- 'I will model for you how I would think through this problem. I would like you to use the same strategy when you solve a similar problem. Here is another one. Now you solve this.'
- 'That's OK. I see you really thought about it (if they did). I'm going to see if someone else knows the correct answer. I will come back to you to repeat it. This will help you remember the answer.' See the Mindset chapter to learn more about metacognitive modelling.

3. GO BACK

When students don't get the answer right, give them a chance to retry or practise the correct answer after you or another student has modelled it. Ask the student to paraphrase or repeat the correct answer or ask a relevant question. This allows the teacher to check for student understanding and builds confidence.

4. STRETCH and CHALLENGE

Encourage use of sophisticated and precise language when responding, even to younger students.

Teacher talk

- 'How can you restate that using vocabulary we've learned?' (more scientific language, literary terms, etc.)
- 'What is another way of saying that?' or 'Another way of saying it is _____. Repeat that back to me.'

Wait time is what the teacher does in order to give students a chance to think. **Think time** is what students do when they are trying to figure out a problem or think of an idea. Both terms should be used explicitly to show we value time to think. Both benefit memory and metacognition.

CONNECT TO MEMORY
For a more detailed look at this strategy as part of regular retrieval practice, see Cold Call Recall on page 170.

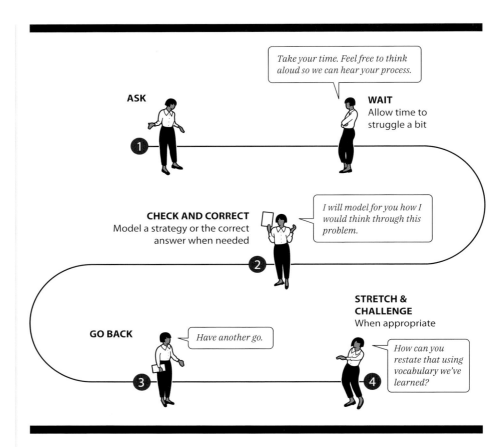

A FEW MORE GOOD IDEAS

PERSONALISED STICKY NOTE

MESSAGE: Use individualised signs or sticky notes to send students a personal message. Post individualised messages on desks or books. Messages might acknowledge students' perseverance with a problem until it was solved, or compliment a student for helping a peer. Welcome students back to school at the beginning of the year with a personal, handwritten message framing the year with high expectations.

RESEARCH
This strategy is inspired by the sticky note study in Relationships: Research on page 34. Use sparingly and authentically.

OPPORTUNITY TO SHARE AN ASSET: Find out which students would like to contribute to the classroom. This could be something they are already good at, such as counting in Mandarin, or simply something they would like to help out with, like passing out the supplies.

OPPORTUNITY TO TAKE ON CLASSROOM JOBS: Examples include: line leaders, artistic director (co-creates display boards), materials manager, homework collector, student ambassador (gives tours, welcomes visitors), liaison (brings messages to administration or other teachers), 'We missed you' manager (brings students who have been absent up to date with assignments), etc.

 KEEP IN MIND:

- Authenticity is paramount when establishing high expectations. Students of all ages will quickly pick up on teachers who overpraise for little effort or set goals that are way too challenging.
- High expectations are not in lieu of appropriate scaffolding. It's not as simple as, 'You can do this.' The message is: 'I believe you can do this and I am going to support you to get there.'
- Focus on the process of learning rather than the final outcome or the person.

Authenticity is important: Don't say it if you don't mean it. Students can sense when you're being real – and when you really don't mean it.

USE STUDENTS' NAMES TO BUILD CONNECTIONS – AND HAVE FUN

Using everyday strategies to learn and integrate names shows we value each child and all cultures.

Our names are incredibly personal, yet also represent culture, family and/or identity. Dedicating time to supporting the classroom community to learn and properly pronounce all students' names helps foster connection, a sense of dignity and social awareness. Below are a variety of suggestions and strategies for using names effectively to build positive relationships.

 AT THE START

LEARN TO PRONOUNCE ALL NAMES CORRECTLY

 AAA STRATEGY

Before you meet your students, review all of the names in your class. For primary, this goes without saying; but at secondary, where you have several classes with many different students, this may seem onerous. Rest assured: **the effort will pay off**. Highlight any student names you are unsure how to pronounce and check with colleagues who may already know the student. Ask students to pronounce their names and note it (phonetic spelling helps!) on your register (roster).

SOME STRATEGIES FOR LEARNING AND USING NAMES

NAME TENTS: Have students create name tents on folded cardstock or paper, writing their name on both sides. Use the name tents for the first week or two until you and the students know every name.

Save the **NAME TENTS** to use for guest speakers, cover (substitute) teachers or if a new student joins the class. Or create laminated NAME PLATES for students' desks with a pronunciation key. Nina saw one particularly great name plate made by Domonique Glover at The Riverside Avenue Community School in Brooklyn, NY. In addition to the student's name and phonetic pronunciation, it included the times tables to support memory, accountable talk prompts (which we introduce in Mindset: Classroom) and even featured an affirming statement about the student. Connect the dots!

NAME TENT TOSS by collecting all of the tents (or, if space allows, asking students to toss them into the centre) and asking two volunteers to return all of the name tents to their proper owners. Make it into a game by timing students or mixing up where people are sitting before the name tents are returned.

HELLO MY NAME IS... At the start of the year, instruct students to say their names before speaking when called on. Have students introduce themselves to their peers when they do pair or group work and use each other's names during discussions and collaborative work.

THE STORY OF MY NAME: Start by sharing the origins of your name and an anecdote that reveals some aspect of your personality or connects to your youth. Students then brainstorm all the things they know about their names, including stories related to their name and/or feeling associated with their name. They pick one aspect and write about it in brief. They share the story or a few lines from their writing with the class. You may also wish to ask students to interview their parents about their names or research the meaning of their names.

NAME MOVES: Ask the students to think of a simple movement that describes something they like to do. For younger students, ask them to first think of a hobby or interest. Brainstorm some examples, such as reading, a sport or even listening to music. Then ask them to think of a motion or gesture that represents that hobby or interest. In this game, each person will be asked to say their name, and say the hobby/interest while making a related motion.

Explain that each student will repeat the previous three student's names and motions before stating their own name, hobby and making the related motion. If you are limited by space, students can stay at their desks and use their arms and head and torso. The movements can be very simple. The teacher should model this with their own name to start.

TEACHER TIP
Show students the BBC video *Never Forget a Face* (available on BBC and also YouTube www.youtu.be/cJK9KcD2ABU) to help them memorise names.

LETTERS OF INTRODUCTION

At the start of the year, write a letter to your students for them to read during class. Introduce yourself, including interesting facts, academic history, hobbies, interests, and your love for teaching. For subject teachers, include your passion for the content you teach and why you are excited to teach other about it.

In the same letter, prompt students to share with you their goals for the class, feelings about the topic, hobbies, interests, strengths and something else they'd like you to know about them. If you are a subject teacher, ask them how they feel about your subject or about their favourite topic. You may also choose to ask what they think makes a great teacher.

Give students an option to end the letter with a question for you. When they are finished, ask them to underline one sentence, phrase or word that they can share with the class. Let each student share. Collect the letters. You can answer the questions to the whole class once you've read the letters. I've saved them. It is fun to look back at them at the end of the year or midway through.

Include parents: Nina also wrote brief notes to parents, asking them to write back about their goals for their students and anything she should know about the student. She received important information including that some students had vision problems, struggled with anxiety, or about particular issues at home. She also learned of students' hobbies, quirks and interests from parents. This is also really useful for younger students who cannot read or write yet or who lack the confidence to do so in front of peers. The parents of one five-year-old boy Tricia worked with, Mohammed, made a point to explain that he tried writing at home, but he was embarrassed to write in front of his peers at school. As a result, his classroom teacher worked on developing his mindset, showing examples of things that were once hard but now easy, like learning to walk, hold a fork etc. The boy grew in confidence and persisted to be a better writer. You'll hear more about Mohammed in Mindset: Research.

STUDENT QUESTIONNAIRES

For **older students:**

Similar to letters of introduction, simple questionnaires, handouts or digital surveys can be given to students at the start of the year and augmented as you learn or request more information. Here are some questions to get you started. Amend based on age and what you want to know.

- What is your name? (Include any nicknames you would like me to use)
- What do you most look forward to when you wake up in the morning and why?
- What do you like to do in your free time and why?
- What is your favourite poem, short story or novel? (or film, TV show, music, etc.)
- What are three things you would like to learn more about?
- What do you think are three qualities of an excellent teacher?
- What's really important to you? Name three things.

TEACHER TIP
There are many great platforms for creating online surveys. I use Google Forms. You can create a survey, send students the link and then export the responses to a spreadsheet that you can update throughout the year.

- What is something you think I should know about you?
- What would you like to accomplish in this class?

For **younger students:** Adapt the questionnaire by encouraging students to draw pictures or by asking the students questions in an interview or check-in format.

'WHERE I'M FROM' POEMS

'Where I'm From' is a poem by George Ella Lyon. It provides a fun and structured format for exploring identity. The following steps can be easily spread out over different time slots and differentiated for different age groups.

1. **Prepare** by copying the poems. There are some words that will likely not be familiar so we recommend you use the glossary below to annotate the poem, writing the definitions on the side. For younger students, just copy the first stanza.

2. **Read** the poem aloud or have students read individually. Tell students not to get hung up on words they don't know. Pay attention to the flow of the poem.

3. **Class discussion:**
   - What is this poem talking about?
   - What patterns or repeated words stood out to you?
   - This poem was written by a woman. What did you learn about her from this poem? (Students can make inferences about who she is and what her life was like growing up.)

4. **Students brainstorm** things in their lives like objects that have meaning to them, foods they love, expressions they commonly hear and other sounds, smells, things in their area, cultural traditions, etc. Encourage them to use words or phrases in a language specific to their background. For **younger students**, do the brainstorm as a group.

5. Then they **decide on a refrain**, such as 'Where I'm from...', 'I am...' or 'I am from...'

6. **Create the poem**, filling in the words from the brainstorm. For **younger students**, create a fill-in-the-blank template or use the one below. Provide the template for **older students** as an option, but encourage students to experiment with their own ideas.

7. **Poem share:** Students take turns sharing their poems.

'The activity ("Where I'm From" poems) let us celebrate all of our different cultures, heritages, and experiences. Still one of my favourite Advisory experiences, 13 years later' – Sarah Kaplan, former assistant principal, KECSS.

Where I'm From

by George Ella Lyon

I am from clothespins,
from Clorox and carbon-tetrachloride.
I am from the dirt under the back porch.
(Black, glistening,
it tasted like beets.)
I am from the forsythia bush
the Dutch elm
whose long-gone limbs I remember
as if they were my own.

I'm from fudge and eyeglasses,
   from Imogene and Alafair.
I'm from the know-it-alls
   and the pass-it-ons,
from Perk up! and Pipe down!
I'm from He restoreth my soul
   with a cotton ball lamb
   and ten verses I can say myself.

I'm from Artemus and Billie's Branch,
fried corn and strong coffee.
From the finger my grandfather lost
   to the auger,
the eye my father shut to keep his sight.

Under my bed was a dress box
spilling old pictures
a sift of lost faces
to drift beneath my dreams.
I am from those moments--
snapped before I budded --
leaf-fall from the family tree.

Glossary for poem

Clorox – bleach
Carbon tetrafluoride – a chemical for dry cleaning. Her father ran a dry cleaning shop.
forsythia bush – a bush with yellow flowers
Dutch elm – a kind of tree
Imogene and Alafair – relatives, perhaps grandparents
Pipe down! – a common expression in her house
Artemus and Billie's Branch – towns/places in Kentucky, in the United States, where she grew up
auger – a drill for making holes in the ground

TEACHER TIP
If you have less time with your students, such as a 20-minute form time session or 30-minute Advisory, break it up over a few sessions.

Where I'm From   By _____

I am from _____,

(something in your flat(apartment)/house)

from _____and _____.

              (food)   (food)

I am from _____.

              (something about the area where you live)

I am from _____

              (something about your culture/homeland) (Describe that thing)

I'm from _____and _____,

              (relative)   (relative)

from _____and _____.

              (tradition)   (food)

I'm from _____,

              (expression you or a family member say often)

and _____,

              (another expression)

from _____ and _____!

(something about your neighbourhood)   (something about your culture)

I'm from _____.

              (one of your favourite things in your room or a place you keep memories)

You will find _____.

         (what you find there or a feeling you'll have)

I am from _____.

(an emotion, anything from your room, flat/house, block, street, culture, expressions or relatives)

USE FOOD METAPHORS TO CREATE FUN FAMILY AND FRIEND POETRY

Metaphor poems are personal, fun and easy to create.

1. Ask students to make a list of people who are important to them, such as parents, carers, siblings and extended family. They may also want to include friends – anyone close whom they share a meal with.

2. Start with one person. List their favourite foods, using adjectives to describe the foods (and therefore the people), and then link each person to the food as a metaphor

   My mum is warm toast with lots of soft butter

   Hot cakes just out of the oven

   Roast dinners and golden Yorkshire puddings

   My sister is salad, green and calorie counted

   Ripe red tomatoes with cucumber crunch

   Celery garnish and a sprinkle of wild rocket

3. Share some of these and model your own.

4. Add more people to the poem until it is a few stanzas long.

🌀 KEEP IT GOING

This strategy was by English teacher and friend, Clare Hitchcock, whose students wrote these poems in her Key Stage 3 (11- to 14-year-olds) creative writing club. Claire says her students really enjoy this strategy and she loves that it's so personal.

ESTABLISH A PEER WELCOMING COMMITTEE

Students discuss how they might feel if they were to join an already established class, and what they might need in order to feel welcome and included. Students then design the roles, responsibilities and activities of a peer welcoming committee, consisting of several students in charge of supporting incoming peers during the year. Peer welcoming committee members might, for example, explain and model the classroom norms and procedures, introduce new students to others and sit next to them during lunch. They can also ensure that when a student is absent, they gather and give them all of the resources, notes and homework.

Allowing students to design the role and actions of the committee will add a layer of sensitivity to age appropriateness. Older students might not welcome overt attention, but might nevertheless appreciate the information and the chance to connect with others.

TEACHER TIP
The name tents you created at the start of the new year will come in handy as part of the welcoming committee's toolkit

SILENT LINE UP TO BUILD CLASSROOM COMMUNITY

This activity is a great way for students to learn something new about their class, while at the same time practise self-regulation and awareness. Start by explaining that they must line up in a particular order, such as alphabetically by first name, without speaking. They may – and are encouraged to – use gestures. Indicate where the start and finish points are. I have seen the noisiest classes do this in complete silence. It's fun to watch. Throughout the year, give them different criteria, such as lining up alphabetically according to:

- Last names or middle names
- The name of the street you live on (if appropriate)

- The name of their favourite food, book, song, etc. (These can be acted out too!)
- A career they are interested in pursuing

Or chronologically from youngest to oldest.

AAA STRATEGY

KEEP UP WITH YOUR CLASSROOM CONNECTIONS CHECK-IN – ONGOING

Similar to the Classroom Connections chart for the start of the year, this strategy can be used to maintain intentional connections with students over time. Create a new chart each term or semester. Adapt it for your school context. Use the **Wild Card** column to identify a particular topic you want to know about each of your students. Examples include:

- Siblings/extended family nearby
- Their aspirations or personal values
- Their favourite sport or leisure activity
- A good book they recently read
- What they're watching on TV or online right now
- What stresses them out and how they handle stress
- Something they are passionate about (the environment, animals, comic books)

STUDENT NAME	I HAVE HAD A POSITIVE ONE-ON-ONE CONVERSATION WITH THIS STUDENT WITHIN THE PAST _____ (E.G. A WEEK FOR PRIMARY AND A MONTH FOR SECONDARY)	I CAN RECALL AT LEAST TWO NEW THINGS ABOUT THIS STUDENT'S PERSONAL LIFE (HOBBIES, LIKES, CULTURAL BACKGROUND, FAMILY)	I KNOW ABOUT THIS STUDENT'S ACADEMIC PROGRESS OR I HAVE NOTICED SOMETHING ABOUT THEIR LEARNING MINDSET.	WILD CARD:

BUILD QUALITY CONNECTIONS BETWEEN PEERS

No matter what we want to believe, students are paying more attention to their peers than to us. Prioritise positive student-to-student interactions.

Below are three strategies teachers can use to help peers connect with each other. Although most of the activities throughout Relationships: Classroom are great for connecting with peers, these strategies, in addition to fostering connections between classmates, also have other academic and social benefits. They help to set expectations for speaking and listening and reinforce and model norms. The structure of these strategies supports more introverted students to share ideas freely and without interruption. It also aids more frequent speakers to practise listening quietly. These can easily be adapted for use in content subjects and differentiated for ages and abilities.

Use these strategies throughout the year. The more you and your students practise them, the better students will get at the process (the more automatic it becomes) and the more working memory they can devote to deep thinking and developing social-emotional skills. Incorporate different content. Repeat these activities when new students join the classes. We'll explore more about the working memory in the Memory chapter.

LISTENING LAB

This is a simple strategy whereby students practise listening to each other without interruption as they learn more about their classmates and hear varying opinions.

1. **Prepare** some questions for student discussion, such as:
   - 'What is one of your earliest, happiest memories?'
   - 'How would you describe your perfect day?'
   - 'If you were famous for something, what would you like to be famous for?'
   - 'What do you value most in a friendship?'

   Note: These could also be related to a content area, such as: 'Why do you think the protagonist made the decision to...' or 'Explain the steps you took to solve that maths problem.'

2. **Create student trios**.

3. **Explain Listening Lab:** 'The entire class will be asked one question. Each person in the trio will have a one minute to respond to the question, taking turns. To start, two people in the group will act as listeners while the third person speaks. Then when you hear me say 'Switch!', the next person in the trio will speak. This will repeat until all students have spoken. The group will then have two minutes to discuss (commonalities, responses, asking clarifying and probing questions, etc.) with each other.'

4. **Show** students the diagram on the next page to reinforce the structure. For **younger students**, take time to model what good listening looks like and practise it with them by speaking for 30 seconds and asking students to actively listen, using the elements (e.g. nodding) you modelled.

5. **Ask the class one question, explaining** that everyone should think silently of their response for 15 seconds of think time, or have them jot down some thoughts.

6. **Start the Listening Lab:** Time students, saying 'Switch!' after each minute until all students have had their turn to talk. Then allow discussion within the trio for two minutes.

7. **Debrief the content:** Invite students to share with the whole class something new they learned about their peers or what they all have in common.

8. **Debrief the process:**
   - How did it feel to speak in the trio? How could you tell that the listeners were listening? How did it feel to listen without interrupting or losing focus?

CONNECT TO MINDSET
See Mindset: Classroom for a list of different types of accountable talk on page 285.

TEACHER TIP
Ask students what active listening looks like and what might be difficult or easy about being the speaker or the listener. Ask them to think about strategies they could use. For example: active listeners will nod their heads or offer a simple 'uh huh' and ask questions at the right time.

- What strategies did you use or could you use to improve your listening skills?
- What are some things you learned about your peers during this activity?

Additional/optional debrief questions:

- What did you like about this activity?
- What did you do well at and what could your trio do to improve at Listening Lab?
- What are some questions you'd like to ask the class?

VARIATIONS

- Give students a list of questions they can choose from.
- Have students write a response first and then discuss.
- Use this strategy for content-specific questions.

In short:

Prompt

Think time (15 secs)

Person A shares for 1 minute while others listen

Person B shares for 1 minute while others listen

Person C shares for 1 minute while others listen

Discuss for 2 minutes

Debrief the content

Debrief the process

ROTATING INTERVIEWS

This strategy, like Listening Lab, helps students practise listening to each other without interruption as they learn more about their classmates and hear varying opinions. The added benefit is that students get a chance to interact with more peers.

1. **Prepare** by asking students to come up with a list of (school-appropriate) questions they would like to ask their classmates. (See examples in Listening Lab.) Post their questions so that they are visible.

2. **Then divide the class in half:** create a group A and group B. Push desks to the side and place chairs in two long rows: row A and row B, so that students sit facing each other. You may need to create two sets of rows, depending on the

number of students in your class or room size. You also might choose to use a different configuration like a horseshoe of two rows facing each other.

3. **Explain Rotating Interviews:** Students in row A will ask the person in row B across from them a question. Row B students will have one minute to answer their partner. Row A must listen carefully, without interrupting. After one minute, you will say, 'Switch!' and the roles will be reversed. Row B will ask a question to their partner in row A and row A students speak for a minute. Model the activity with a volunteer, using a different question.

4. **Review:** Show students the diagram below to reinforce the structure. For **younger students**, take time to model what good listening looks like. Model how to rotate seats.

5. **Start with the first question:** Follow the structure of step 3.

6. **Rotate and repeat with a new question:** When both A and B have finished, direct the students in Row A to **shift down one seat** on the count of 3. All row A students move down in the same direction to face a new partner. The row B students stay where they are. You may choose to have them shift down more seats to sit with someone further away. Continue as time and interest allows.

7. **Debrief the content:** What did you learn that was interesting or unique? What are some questions that still remain? What differences did you appreciate between you and your partner? What did you learn about someone during this activity?

8. **Debrief the process:**

   - For speakers: how did it feel to speak without interruption? How could you tell that the listeners were listening?

   - For listeners: how difficult or easy was it to listen and not interrupt?

   - For both: what strategies did you or could you use to improve your listening skills? Why might this be a good activity for practising listening skills and creating a sense of community?

   - Use student responses to create a list of strong listening habits that you display in your classroom.

Variations

- Use as a strategy to access prior knowledge about a topic. (See the Memory chapter for some notes about the importance of accessing prior knowledge.)

- Use this strategy with content-specific questions to facilitate deeper discussions.

In short:

Prompt

Think time

Share: Student A

Share: Student B

Student A shifts down the row

Repeat a few times

Debrief the content

Debrief the process

SAVE THE LAST WORD

This strategy for **older students** is designed to build on each other's thinking and requires students to be strategic and active speakers and listeners in a structured conversation. An added bonus is that the strategy provides more opportunities for students to build on each other's ideas, and the structured roles allow more introverted students to speak and respond without interruptions. Frequent speakers are encouraged to listen.

Recommended for Key Stages 3, 4 and 5 (middle and high school students)

1. **Prepare** by identifying a piece of text you want students to respond to. Some suggestions for text include: a newspaper article, short narrative or poem or one of the Research Statements on pages 58 and 59 as part of the Jigsaw Method.

2. **Students** read text on their own and, if useful, annotate the text. Then each person will identify an excerpt from the text (a few lines) that they think is significant. Give the students a few minutes to write an independent response about why they chose those lines. Suggested sentence starters:

   - 'I noticed that...'
   - 'This reminds me of...'
   - 'This part makes me wonder about...'
   - 'I'm unclear about...'
   - 'I found it a bit confusing because...'
   - 'I would like to know more about...'

3. When everyone is finished, create trios and decide which group members will be A, B and C.

4. **Explain Save the Last Word:**

   - Student A reads aloud the excerpt they chose but does not read their responses aloud yet. Students B and C have about 30 seconds each to respond to the excerpt student A chose. (Extend the time after the first round if you think students may need more time.) If needed, suggest student sentence stems from number 2.

   - Once students B and C have talked, student A has about two minutes to respond, sharing why they chose those lines and building on what they heard the others in their group say. Examples of student sentence stems:

     - 'I agree/disagree with…, because…'
     - 'After listening to you, I…'
     - 'At first I thought…and now…'

5. **Review:** Show students the diagram below to reinforce the structure. For **younger students**, take time to model what good listening looks like. Role-play how to rotate seats.

6. **Start.** 'I will give B and C about 30 seconds each to respond. A gets two minutes.'

7. **Repeat** this process, giving the other students in the group a chance to have the 'last word'.

8. **Debrief the content:** Depending on text, devise some questions related to student understanding.

9. **Debrief the process:**

   - For speakers: how did it feel to speak without interruption? How could you tell that the listeners were listening?

   - For listeners: how difficult or easy was it to listen and not interrupt?

   - For both: what strategies did you use or could you use to improve your listening skills? Why might this be a good activity for practising listening skills and creating a sense of community?

Variations:

   - In step 4, have students B and C discuss their responses together while A listens.

   - Use a fishbowl model, in which two students conduct a dialogue and the rest of the class observes and takes notes (ideally in response to specific prompts). Then, the students lead a discussion about what they noticed and draw conclusions about strong listening habits.

   - Rather than using text, use inspirational quotes or strategies. Instruct the students to choose a quote and respond to it. Some examples:

     I've learned that people will forget what you said, people will forget what you did, but people will never forget how you made them feel. – Maya Angelou

     You must be the change you wish to see in the world. – Mahatma Gandhi

TEACHER TIP
Don't forget to remind students to use each other's names during these activities.

Stress is not what happens. It's our response to what happens. And response is something we can choose at any moment. – Maureen Killoran

TEACHER TIP
There are many other opportunities throughout the book that are great for building peer connections, such as Self Talk Scenarios on pages 298 and 299, Counting to 20 and class discussions about goal setting from page 262.

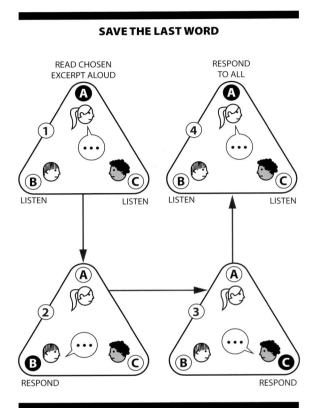

SAVE THE LAST WORD

In short:

All read and annotate

Student A reads aloud chosen excerpt

Student B responds to A's excerpt for two minutes

Student C responds to A's excerpt for two minutes

Student A responds and builds on comments for three minutes

Repeat the process for B and C

Debrief the content

Debrief the process

CREATE AN INCLUSIVE ENVIRONMENT

Students spend most of their waking hours within these walls. Make it a place where they want to be.

What is meant by environment?

School and classroom environments typically describe the physical condition, level of safety, procedures and climate in those spaces. The focus here is on the physical space and what educators can do to encourage more positive environments.

Each school and classroom has its own character. Environments vary depending on the teacher, the ages of the students and the school culture. Some classrooms radiate energy with bright colours and textures; clotheslines are draped with artwork and writing. There might be a sofa in the corner for private reading. Other classrooms at a different school with older students may adhere to a more orderly arrangement – matching backing paper on each board highlighting student work or providing key terminology, neatly typed and laminated. Students can thrive in either environment, but there are some basics that each setting should provide to help children really feel they belong and can flourish.

 AT THE START

WELCOME YOUR STUDENTS

Post a welcome sign from you and/or any other support staff, greeting students on the first day with a special message. The welcome sign can be used each time a new student arrives during the year. The sign should be changed periodically to refresh the message and maintain interest.

 AAA STRATEGY

Leaders, use a combination of strategies in Create an Inclusive Environment, as a AAA strategy.

ARRANGE SEATING WITH STUDENT EXPERIENCE IN MIND

Different types of instruction will require different seating arrangements, so be flexible. Setting the room up to allow students to work together – such as by making group tables – shows you value interaction and trust them. We also recommend setting the room in a horseshoe shape, if possible. As a rule, however, consider the student's experience at their chairs. Students should be able to see their classmates when they speak. A classroom set up in rows, for example, implies that the most important and frequent conversations are between teacher and students only. Also, the students in the front can't see the students behind them and the students in the back can only see the backs of heads of those in front.

A word about seating plans: Many schools require that teachers create seating plans at the start of the year. Be explicit with students about why you are creating the seating plan – in order to help you remember their names. **Keep in mind** that seating plans can communicate low expectations for students, because they imply that students cannot control their own behaviour or that they belong to a particular ability group. However, an advantage, especially at the start of the year, is that they can reduce anxiety for students. Figuring out where to sit in a classroom can be a stressful experience, especially for adolescents who are hypersensitive to peer attitudes and friendship groups. If you choose to use a seating plan, be sure to move students around, so that students can have a chance to work more closely with other peers.

COMFORT, NOT CLUTTER

In one classroom I visited, the teacher used floor lamps and banned the overhead fluorescent lights. It created a warm, comfortable atmosphere for students to learn.

Small additions to a classroom create a friendlier, more welcoming space. Some suggestions include adding: plants; pieces of art from a variety of cultures; bean bag chairs and sofas; lamps instead of overhead lights; or framed photographs. Create quiet reading and writing spaces. Allow students to use dry erase markers on desks. Comfortable learning environments find the right balance. Avoid too much clutter on walls. This can be distracting and decrease learning potential. Learn more in Memory: Classroom starting with cognitive load on page 164.

MAKE DIVERSITY and INCLUSIVITY VISIBLE

Books and other resources used (including prescribed textbooks, books on display in the library, chosen literature) should reflect the diversity in your classroom and in society at large based on gender, sexual orientation, race, ethnicity and ability. They should also reflect the variety of cultures and languages spoken in the classroom. Studies show that regardless of race/ethnicity, students benefit from seeing a positive, wide range of racial and ethnic diversity visuals. White boys need to and deserve to see images of black female scientists and male caregivers too.

DISPLAY USEFUL REMINDERS

Displays can also help students become familiar with the **norms, procedures and rules of a classroom**. We encourage teachers to post class norms, homework policies and examples of non-verbal signs (for primary classrooms).

Other useful reminders included in Mindset: Classroom include: Accountable Talk stems and Metacognitive Questioning. From Memory: Classroom, we suggest displaying worked examples and learning protocols that relate specifically to your subject.

 KEEP IT GOING

KEEP ON TOP OF PRESENTATIONS (e.g. smartboard presentations and PowerPoints) As you create new presentations and resources, make an effort to select images of people with a variety of skin tones, genders, religions, levels of physical ability, age, etc.

CREATE A 'SPOT IT, SHARE IT' BOARD, which is a display in the classroom where teachers can provide students with real life examples of how classroom norms look and sound in action. See more details on page 64.

COLLECT QUOTES that empower students, or invite students to bring some favourite quotes. I love this one that I found on the *Teaching Channel* website: 'Young people aren't bottles to be filled, but candles to be lit' (Robert Schaffer). Nina really likes: 'One of the lessons that I grew up with was to always stay true to yourself and never let what somebody else says distract you from your goals. And so when I hear about negative and false attacks, I really don't invest any energy in them, because I know who I am' (Michelle Obama).

DISPLAY THE LEARNING PROCESS: There are several examples in Mindset: Classroom that we also recommend, such as displaying the Learning Journey (a visual showing the ups and downs of learning on page 257) as well as displaying work that illustrates the process of learning, not just the final outcome. On page 162, we recommend displaying a KWNL chart – but we also remind you not to clutter your walls.

 KEEP IN MIND

- **Make sure examples of diversity are varied, positive and often the everyday**. Although it is important to celebrate the successes of marginalised groups of people who had to fight to be recognised as full citizens or even humans (Martin Luther King, Women's Suffrage), children need examples that go beyond heroes, holidays, and 'the Hall of Firsts' (e.g. The first woman...).

- Ensure displays are at a **reasonable height and readable for your students**. If they are too high or too small, they will only act as clutter, creating cognitive overload.

- Include displays that are **student-created**, not just teacher- or professionally created.

- The brain loves novelty, so **change the artwork**, patterns and pictures periodically, so walls don't feel wallpapered.

CONTINUALLY REFLECT ON YOUR TEACHING

Bias is unintentional; intuition is uncertain. We need an intentional, evidence-informed approach.

What is meant by reflection?

When we **reflect**, we deeply consider something that we might not otherwise have given much thought to. This helps us to learn. In this section we are referring to the educator's reflection on their practice and the impact on students.

Much of the day-to-day work life of an educator is managing what is immediately in front of us. It is the nature of working in schools and the reality of caring for children. A teacher committed to creating positive relationships must also be a committed lifelong learner – continually seeking information about their students and reflecting on their practice, biases and learning. Use the tools below to be intentional about how you reflect on your pedagogy with regards to relationships.

 AT THE START

IDENTIFY CONNECTION BUILDERS

AAA STRATEGY

Connection Builders are ways we can build trust with students and help create positive relationships. Use the table below based on Connection Builders to reflect on how you have demonstrated these components and then identify an area of focus at the end.

CONNECTION BUILDER	WHAT IT MEANS	WHAT IT LOOKS LIKE FOR EDUCATORS	HOW CAN I/HAVE I DEMONSTRATED THIS?
Openness	People connect to others who are open and honest, sharing appropriate stories of their lives and examples of error, such as being willing to make mistakes in front of others.	Sharing a new skill you are learning or have learned and what is hard about it. Model things you had to say to yourself along the way.	
Familiarity	People develop connections with people whom they see consistently in a particular setting, such as at the school gate every day or in hallways on a regular basis.	Making a concerted effort to be where students are – for example, visiting the lunchroom weekly to say hi to students. Finding commonalities and making reference to familiar places in the community.	
Personal interest	People connect when they see that the other person shows concern for issues and events important to them, such as births, birthdays and illnesses, or notice things that may be important such as a new haircut or interest in music.	Remembering details and experiences, demonstrated by asking follow-up questions about recent events. Creating opportunities to ask students about their lives so that you can know and respond (e.g. weekly reflections, family journals, 'Show and Tell')	
Competence	People tend to connect to others who demonstrate that they have the skill and knowledge, as well as the desire, to help and support them. This builds trust and leads to confidence.	Demonstrating the ability to teach effectively or make learning less confusing. Explaining why they are being taught something, what the point is.	

Table based on *Culturally Responsive Teaching and the Brain*, Zaretta Hammond (Hammond, 2014) and *Click: The Power of Instant Connections* by Ori and Rom Brafman (Brafman and Brafman, 2011)

Once you have completed the 'How can I/have I demonstrated this' column, pick at least one of the Connection Builders to focus on for a few weeks. Decide on a specific action you will take to connect with your students. (For ideas, see 'What it looks like for educators' above.) Keep a journal to reflect on impact with students. Ask yourself which Connection Builder you'd like to work on and what your next steps are.

INTENTIONALLY TACKLE IMPLICIT BIAS

Teachers have to make fast decisions all day long; time is limited. And these decisions – how we treat one student over another – are based on a combination of teacher experience and expertise as well as one's own ingrained biases. The unintentional nature of bias needs a very intentional approach that, over time, forms into habit.

TEST YOUR BIAS

- **Take** the Implicit Association Test (IAT), as a way to identify your own implicit bias. Devised by Harvard University, the test 'measures the strength of associations between concepts (e.g. black people, white people, gay people) and evaluations (e.g. good, bad) or stereotypes (e.g. athletic, clumsy)'. Go to www.bit. ly/2NZVmEE. The test takes about 30 minutes and you can choose a particular assessment category, such as gender, weight, race or skin tone. We know that taking the test can make one feel vulnerable, but it's a great step towards being more aware of our own biases. Nina told me she was really surprised by some of her results. Since then, she's been more aware of when she needs to 'slow down her thinking' and not let her biases influence her thinking or actions.

- **MTV's 'Look Different' campaign**, with the help of **Project Explicit**, also offers a shorter implicit bias test that would be more appropriate and easier to use with older students for discussion at www.bit.ly/2YZDlqM. Young people and teachers will also find other useful resources for discussion on the site.

DISRUPT YOUR IMPLICIT BIAS

1. **Be aware** of research about bias. The first step to mitigating implicit or unintentional bias is being aware that bias exists and we all have it. Re-read the section on implicit bias in the Research section of this book.

2. **Make a personal commitment.** It is possible to minimise your biases, but that is dependent on the belief that you can change and your commitment to do so. It's up to you!

3. **Identify your triggers.** Are there student behaviours that simply annoy you or that conflict with your own culture reference? It's good to know what these are, be prepared for them and reflect on why they trigger you.

4. **Use strategies** to minimise bias. The Stop and Refocus strategy gives you steps to do this.

RESEARCH
For more on the research about and examples of implicit bias and levels of culture, go to Barriers to Connection in Relationships: Research on page 38

Authenticity is key. Look for real connections that show you care and are interested.

STOP AND REFOCUS

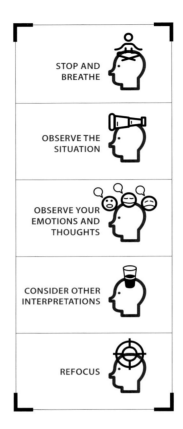

- Stop and breathe.
- Observe the situation: What is actually happening here (The details of the situation)?
- Observe your emotions and interpretations: What am I feeling and might these feelings/interpretation be caused by bias? Am I responding to this student the same way I would respond to someone else?
- Consider other interpretations: What other interpretations could I have in this situation? What other ways could I respond?
- Re-focus and change course.

 KEEP IT GOING

Once you've done the work of identifying some of your biases and further noted which of your students you might hold a bias against, use a strategy to examine your interactions with these students. This can help you see how your biases play out in the classroom and ultimately shift your practice.

DISRUPT YOUR BIAS: Closer look

1. **START BY IDENTIFYING ONE STUDENT YOU MAY HAVE A BIAS AGAINST.** (A difficult but brave move.) Use this confidential tracker below to evaluate your interactions on a daily basis, marking each either + (positive), / (neutral) or − (negative). This document, based on Zarrieta Hammond's 'Rapport Interaction Tally Tracking', can illuminate the percentage of positive vs negative interactions you have with these students and in what contexts. It will also highlight if you lack interaction. You may also wish to complete the tracker for a student you may have a bias towards (feel positively about) for comparison.

STUDENT INITIALS:

DATE	CONTEXT (LOCATION)	INTERACTION + (POSITIVE) / (NEUTRAL) − (NEGATIVE)	NOTES

Once you have completed the Tracking Sheet, reflect on what patterns you notice. Then identify an action you can take to begin to improve that relationship. Suggestions:

2. **REFER BACK THE CONNECTION BUILDERS** on page 90 to identify ways you can connect positively with the student. Recall the categories:

   - Openness
   - Familiarity
   - Personal interest
   - Competence

3. **BE INTENTIONALLY MORE POSITIVE.** Use the 5:1 Ratio Feedback. For every 1 corrective comment, make 5 positive ones.

   - Focus attention on positive behaviours that lead to classroom success rather than on problem behaviours: 'Thanks for getting to class on time.'
   - Deliver specific and authentic verbal praise and approval statements: 'I see you worked really hard on that.'
   - Engage in verbal and non-verbal positive interactions (e.g. questions about students' interests, empathy statements, appropriate jokes, etc.): 'How was your weekend?'; 'Have you seen any good films lately?' Make a point of smiling. Or just welcome them to the lesson!
   - Praise publicly; reprimand privately.

RESEARCH
See Relationships: Research for more on the 5:1 study.

TEACHER TIP
Create a non-descript sign or even a sticky note that reads, '5:1'. Put it in a spot where you look a lot. Switch it up so that it doesn't become part of the paint. Eventually, it will become a habit.

A FEW MORE GOOD IDEAS

ELICIT FEEDBACK FROM A COLLEAGUE: Ask a teacher to observe student-teacher and student-student interactions during your lesson. Make sure that you act as normal as possible. Some schools permit teachers to video record their lessons. (Obviously, ask students for permission.) An even simpler approach would be to record your voice, play it back and tally positive and negative comments. This will also encourage you to use the names of students, so you can identify them when listening.

SOLICIT STUDENT FEEDBACK: Show students that you value their opinions and can learn from them by creating student feedback forms at the end of units, semesters and/ or the school year so that students can evaluate your teaching practices, behaviours, content delivery and the classroom culture.

 KEEP IN MIND

At times, the teacher may feel that a relationship with a particular student is so fractured that there is no way back. In these moments, we have some suggestions that have worked for other teachers:

- **Be open:** Tell the student that you would like to find a way to improve the relationship. However, a teacher should NEVER say something like, 'I think our relationship is broken beyond repair.' Depersonalise the student's behaviour. Most disrespectful behaviour is NOT because the student doesn't like the teacher but because they are lashing out for lack of the prefrontal cortex support to know how to deal with issues in a more complex and thoughtful way.

- **Get feedback:** Ask the students if they see the relationship as strained and why they think this is the case. Tell them that you are just going to listen while they speak.

- **Offer a fresh start and make a plan:** This does not have to mean overly compromising. It means that expectations are reset.

- **Seek a mediator:** Ask the student to recommend an adult they trust to help you two navigate the conflict and develop a plan to make it better.

- **Be consistent and fair.**

- Review the **class norms.**

- **Observe other teachers** with the same students. Notice strategies, body posture, feedback used as well as seat positioning and adjacent peers.

RESEARCH

Remember the prefrontal cortex, which helps us to think and see different solutions to a problem and react appropriately when angry – is still forming in children's brains and will take longer to engage.

RELATIONSHIPS: LEADERSHIP

Relationships: Leadership
and professional learning

Good leaders put their money where their mouths are. Not only do they value positive relationships with their staff and students, they model how it's done.

No matter one's leadership style, years on the job, school size or ages of the students, there are key points that all educators should know about the ways positive relationships help us serve our students better now and tomorrow. Our message to teachers and staff must be clear and consistent: **positive relationships matter**. Putting that into action takes the whole school, every day throughout the year.

This section includes two parts to help you support your staff. The first part is called **Professional learning: at the start**, which includes suggestions to help you turnkey the research and model classroom application strategies. The second part is called **Professional learning: keep it going**, which outlines suggestions for maintaining and developing relationships throughout the year.

 PROFESSIONAL LEARNING: AT THE START

RESEARCH into RELATIONSHIPS

THE JIGSAW METHOD

The **Jigsaw Method** is a teaching strategy we introduced in Relationships: Classroom. The Jigsaw Method has been shown to have a high-effect impact (Hattie, 2011) because participants work together to ensure that all group members understand, can re-teach and apply the content to a new situation. This strategy is also an opportunity for participants to work together toward common goals.

3. Start the Jigsaw Method

    First stage: the expert group

    Put students into expert groups. Each expert group gets a different topic. They need to read the text and summarise in their own words what the study is about. They should then prepare to teach the research to their jigsaw group, including explaining how their topic relates to positive relationships.

    Second stage: the jigsaw group

    Put students into jigsaw groups made up of one person from each expert group. Participants take turns teaching about their research while the other students take notes. Decide on three actions the class could take to support a sense of belonging and positivity in the class.

4. **Debrief:** Share the responses to the final question(s) and then make a connection to the research. Elicit next steps and implementation ideas from teachers and staff. For Talking Points, see 'facilitator talking points' in the Jigsaw Method content guide above.

CLASSROOM
There is a jigsaw activity for students to do in Relationships: Classroom. This activity can be easily adapted using different content.

THE HAND AS BRAIN – BOTH A MODEL AND A METHOD

When the brain is in a positive emotional state, information is processed more efficiently and the learner can better utilise their thinking brain, or prefrontal cortex (PFC). In other words, when children are in a relaxed alert state they learn better. This is an important point for teachers to understand. (For more on this topic, see The Science of Positive Relationships in Relationships: Research.)

If explaining the brain to your staff, use the **Hand Model**, developed by Dan Siegel, clinical professor of psychiatry and author of *Mindsight: The New Science of Personal Transformation* (Siegel, 2010). This useful tool uses your hand to represent three parts of the brain: the spinal cord, the limbic system (including the amygdala) and the prefrontal cortex. Educators can also use this model as an effective self-regulation strategy to use with students by taking them through the steps in the diagram on the next page.

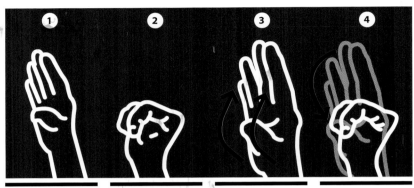

The wrist represents the spinal cord where information enters the brain. The thumb represents the amygdala in the limbic system.	Fold the fingers over. The fingers represent the prefrontal cortex (PFC). This is your brain.	If incoming information triggers a 'fight, flight, freeze' response, you 'flip your lid'. The PFC is disengaged and you can't think clearly.	Slowly re-engage the PFC by folding your fingers over the thumb. The engaged PFC helps us respond more calmly and rationally.

The amount of time it takes them to fold their fingers back over their hand can be enough time to calm down (re-engage the PFC). I have used Siegel's 'handy' brain as a model for teaching and a method for self-regulating across all ages – primary, secondary, parents and teachers. I have used it myself sometimes when I've 'flipped my lid'. Try it.

Debrief: What triggers stress for our students? When might the hand model be useful?

Talking points:

- Stress can be triggered by a number of factors, such as transition, peer relationships, lack of self-regard, fear of failure or getting in trouble, poor student-teacher relationships, chaotic environments or anxiety that their teachers don't like them.

- Students also report anxiety-producing factors outside of school such as family issues, systemic oppression (racism, sexism, homophobia), poverty, neighbourhood violence and even world issues – the news! Stress is real and has a significant impact on learning.

CLASSROOM APPLICATIONS THAT BUILD RELATIONSHIPS

ADOPT, ADAPT OR ADD

In Adopt, Adapt or Add (AAA), staff are asked to engage with classroom strategies and decide whether they would like to either **Adopt** a strategy *as is* for their classrooms, **Adapt** it to better fit their classroom context or **Add** a different, related strategy they could share with the group.

RECOMMENDED READING
You can easily find videos of Dan Siegel demonstrating a hand model of brain on his YouTube channel. Here is one: www.bit. ly/2JE6dzJ

1. **Decide on strategies:** For this section, pick about four or five strategies or a group of strategies from the Classroom section. Some strategies that we have found are liked by teachers and work well with Adopt, Adapt, Add have been marked using this icon . We will call these our AAA (for Adopt, Adapt, Add) strategies. Facilitators may decide to use some of their own ideas or strategies from other parts of Classroom to better match the school context. There are three different variations delivering Adopt, Adapt and Add. Choose the one that works best for you!

2. **Prepare:** On chart paper, copy and paste one AAA strategy on the left-hand side and leave space for Adopt, Adapt or Add on the right.

STRATEGY	ADOPT, ADAPT OR ADD?
AAA Strategy goes here	

3. **Explain Rotation Station**

   a. 'Each table or group will get one AAA strategy or group of strategies.'

   b. 'Read the strategy. Then decide what you would do: Adopt, Adapt and/or Add to enhance or customise the strategy and list the ideas on the right-hand side.'

   c. 'Groups then rotate from chart to chart (or table to table), so you get a chance to look at each different strategy. When you get to a chart, you must read the strategies and pay particular attention to what the previous groups thought were the best ideas to Adopt, Adapt or Add.'

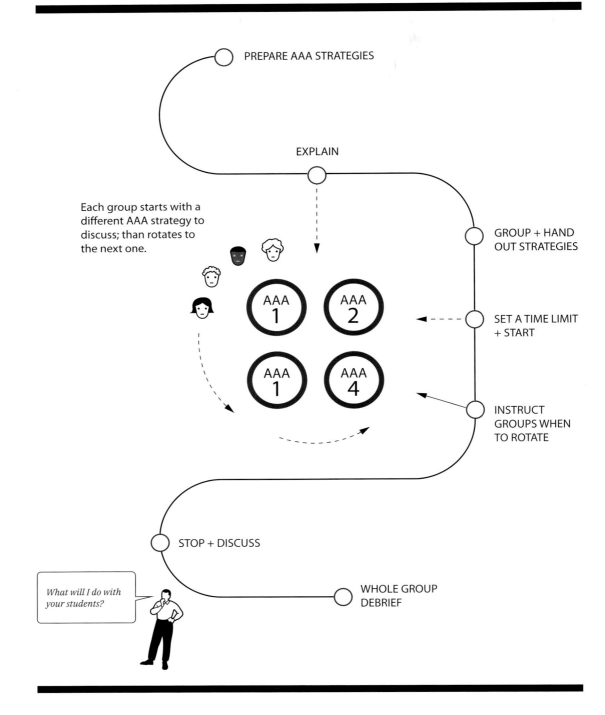

PREPARE AAA STRATEGIES

EXPLAIN

Each group starts with a different AAA strategy to discuss; than rotates to the next one.

AAA 1

AAA 2

AAA 1

AAA 4

GROUP + HAND OUT STRATEGIES

SET A TIME LIMIT + START

INSTRUCT GROUPS WHEN TO ROTATE

STOP + DISCUSS

WHOLE GROUP DEBRIEF

What will I do with your students?

4. **Put the participants into groups and give each group** a different AAA strategy. (For large groups, repeat strategies).

5. **Give participants a time limit** and **start Rotation Station**.

6. **Instruct groups to rotate to the next station when time is up.** (Give them a two-minute warning.) Continue until each group has been to each station.

7. **Stop groups, instruct them to return to their original station and discuss:** Read the comments and suggestions. Discuss what strategies each person would like to implement in their own teaching.

8. **Debrief:** Share some of the immediate, individual ideas participants committed to doing. Option to have participants commit on paper to doing the strategy by a certain date, and pair up with an 'accountability partner' to check in on their progress and hear how things went.

Variations:

Individual group stations: This variation is like the above, but participants stay at their table rather than rotate. As a group, they prepare what they want to share with the whole group. After all groups have shared, participants have **time to reflect** on their individual next steps. What will you start to do immediately? Again, option for participants to set specific goals and check in with an 'accountability partner'.

Facilitator-led instruction

The facilitator shares ideas from the Classroom section with the whole group. Then gives pairs, small groups or individuals time to reflect on what they would Adopt, Adapt or Add.

 KEEP IT GOING **Professional learning**

SHARE PROGRESS AND NEW IDEAS
School leaders create the culture and climate of a school. Walk the talk throughout the whole journey.

TEACHER FEATURES

Teacher features are 10- to 15-minute presentations in which staff share a classroom strategy they have implemented. They can be done during morning briefings, the start of staff meetings or any other time when the whole staff convenes.

Guiding questions for staff:

- What strategy did I implement?

- Why did I do it? 'I wanted students to…'

- How did I evaluate it? 'I noticed that…'; 'Student surveys showed…'

- What did I learn? 'I learned that I should…'; 'Next time, I would change…'

Remember that this is an opportunity for staff to share what they have learned. Encourage staff to share challenges, misconceptions and mistakes as well as successes.

CLASSROOM
The Story of My Name on page 72 and Classroom Connection Check-in on page 74 are great teacher features for the start of the year.

SHORT SHARES FOR BREAKTHROUGH MOMENTS

Throughout the year, try to capture some of the day-to-day connections we make with students or even those breakthrough moments we have with children, especially those who are hard to reach. For a Short Share, ask staff to briefly note something they did that connected with a student or something they noticed or learned about a student. For example, 'This week, I decided to eat lunch with my students and I learned that Albert loves to make cakes' or 'During a Listening Lab yesterday, it was a pleasure to see Shabina speaking confidently without anyone interrupting her. The other students were really listening.'

'KEEP IT GOING' STRATEGIES

Use the **Keep it Going** strategies (see Classroom) to periodically reinforce positive relationships and build on previous professional learning. Provide handouts for staff or templates so that the resources are easy to use and/or adapt. Follow this up by asking teachers if you can visit their classrooms while they do the activity.

EDUCATOR STUDY GROUPS

Study groups are made up of a group of staff members who meet regularly to discuss a topic. Leadership can help support staff in forming study groups by providing space, a format and resources, such as short articles or videos that can drive discussion. You can find a list of resources in Recommended Readings and Resources on page 318.

CREATE A CULTURE WHERE ALL STAFF ARE KNOWN

Select from these seven strategies to foster a sense of belonging and community amongst staff.

TEATIME WITH LEADERSHIP

Set aside time to have ten-minute meetings with **all** members of your staff in order to learn more about them. Use this as an opportunity to find out their work style as well as interests outside of school.

SCHOOL SOCIALS AND OUTREACH

Organise social connections or events throughout the year to connect staff. At one school where I taught, we had a variety of these, such as Friday 'bake-off' competitions at lunchtime in the staffroom and termly quiz nights. Someone was in charge of making sure there was a venture organised for all staff to meet on the last day of term to celebrate. In the US, many schools have what is called the **Sunshine Committee**, set up to collect donations and organise small tokens of our esteem and consideration to colleagues who are either celebrating a happy occasion or facing a challenging time in their lives.

TEACHER TIP

Make Short Shares easy to implement by creating small cards that are kept somewhere where staff congregate or entrance tickets that are handed out at the start of a meeting.

STAFFROOM BUDDY

At the start of year, match up new members of staff with current members of staff, so they have somebody to check in with, to sit with at lunch and to show them the ropes. Ideally, this person is not the new staff member's supervisor; they are a friendly face who is dependable, helpful and enthusiastic. Likewise, if someone joins later in the year, ensure that they have a buddy, and check in with them periodically to make sure that everything is OK. The buddy system helped me enormously – and I am still good friends with my staffroom buddy from 14 years ago.

COMMUNICATION AND FOLLOW-THROUGH

Keep on top of the little things to show you value the time and opinions or all members of staff. For example:

- Reply to a letter or email within a day or two of it being sent.
- Arrive on time to meetings and meet deadlines that all staff are asked to meet.
- Keep colleagues in the loop regarding issues and decisions.
- Follow through with agreements.
- Stay in the room during professional learning sessions to show your interest and investment.
- Ask for feedback after the event and acknowledge how the feedback was used.

RECOMMEND READING
These suggestions are adapted from Andy Buck's *Leadership Matters: How Leaders at all Levels Can Create Great Schools* (Buck, 2016).

SHOUT-OUTS TO STAFF

Create a system whereby leadership can easily acknowledge the contribution or hard work of a member of staff. At one school I worked at, the principal had postcards he used for such occasions. These handwritten messages, placed in staff pigeon holes (mailboxes), were a simple way to say thank you. At another school, one senior member of the team was in charge of sending out a brief email on Friday acknowledging different members of the team.

STUDENT SHOUT-OUTS AND THANK-YOUS

Distribute thank-you card templates to students once every few weeks. On it, they can write a short thank-you or appreciation to a member of staff. Collect them and read them at the next staff meeting.

Try this method used by the Urban Assembly Maker Academy in NYC – students **publicly offer 'shout-outs'** to their peers or educators for demonstrating alignment with the school's core values (therefore promoting a positive school climate). An example would be 'I want to give a shout out to Nile for exhibiting COURAGE this week by presenting her essay at Open School Night.'

For **younger students**, use the book *Have You Filled a Bucket Today?* by Carol McCloud as a prompt for introducing acts of daily kindness, gratefulness and appreciation. In the book, bucket filling and bucket dipping are metaphors for how our actions and words impact others and ourselves (McCloud, 2015). Some schools we work with have bucket-filling slips and a real bucket in the room. Students randomly (and sometimes collectively) appreciate peers and adults by completing the slip and putting it in the bucket to be read aloud at a set time.

STAFF MEETING STARTER: TEMPERATURE CHECKS

A quick or extended warm-up activity that is easy to use and fosters self-awareness as well as social awareness.

Directions:

1. Explain: 'Silently reflect for about 30 seconds on how you are feeling today. What is your emotional 'temperature?' What number they would rate themselves on a scale of 1–10, with a 1 being 'feeling stressed, low energy or just not my day', and a 10 being 'feeling excited, energised and alert'.

TEMPERATURE CHECK THERMOSTAT POSTER

2. Then ask: 'Hands up: Who is a 1 in the room? A 2? etc...' Notice the 'temperatures' in the room. You can also ask them to put up all hands at once, but it is less easy to see the range.

Variation: Temperature Check: (7–10 minutes)

Materials and set up: Use big chart paper to create a number line drawn with numbers 1, 5 and 10. Post it on the wall with space in between for sticky notes (see figure at the top of the next page) – one poster per 30 people. Have at least one sticky note per participant.

NUMBER LINE ON WALL

Directions:

Same start as above, but instead of sharing with a 'Hands up', participants write down their number on a sticky note. They then place their sticky on the thermometer or number line posted on the wall.

Discuss with participants:

- What patterns do you notice?
- What can this activity teach/remind us?
- Why might this activity be helpful to use in your classroom?
- What strategies do you use when energy is low in your classroom?

Talking points:

- This warm-up reminds staff that a group of individuals will have individual energy levels, moods, backgrounds and attitudes that may vary from day to day. 'The first step in building good relationships is recognising that everyone is different.'
- It also can be used with students to raise the level of self-awareness, discern energy level of class, identify patterns of low energy from specific students and support social-awareness.
- This is a great activity to do with students because it allows them to share their emotional status in a low-risk way.
- This can lead to a discussion (individually) of what students might need in order to feel engaged. If a teacher notices that a large number of students have a low number, it might be a good idea to conduct a short icebreaker to lift the mood or evaluate which students might need checking in with after class.

MEMORY

MEMORY: RESEARCH

Memory: Research
worth knowing

Memory and learning are inseparable. A better understanding of memory makes us better teachers and builds long-term learners – across all ages.

PRACTICE, PROGRESS, PERMANENCE

In a classroom in London, I asked the students what they remembered about the brain. There was a buzz in the room. A few students recalled neurons and synapses, pulling from earlier lessons about how the brain learns. One girl said, 'We learn when we think hard about something.' Perfect set-up. I wanted to move the conversation to memory. I then asked the students to recall information about plants, a topic covered earlier in the year with their classroom teacher. The teacher posted words such as 'reproduction' and 'parts' to scaffold the recall. We then asked them to write down on blank paper what they remembered. 'You have time to think about it.' Then we waited.

Most students didn't write for the first minute or so. Then we gave them some questions that related to some of the prompts we had posted, like 'How do plants reproduce?' and 'Which part of the plant carries minerals to the leaves?' The students started to write down some information, but in general we weren't seeing a lot of success. I reminded students of an earlier discussion: 'It's OK to forget.' Together with the students, we checked their responses.

'I learned it; why can't I remember it?' asked one girl during our follow-up discussion when we asked students what it was like to try to recall information they learned. 'I thought it was going to be easy, but it was hard,' said a boy. We ended the lesson by telling them we'd be back to teach them about memory and together we'd learn some ways to help them remember better. They were eager to learn about learning. Although these students were Year 3 (2nd grade), their interest is ageless. One of the most common questions older

One of the most common questions older students ask when I teach them ways to maximise memory is 'Why didn't we learn this when we were younger?'

students ask when I teach them ways to maximise memory is 'Why didn't we learn this when we were younger?'

WHAT IS MEANT BY MEMORY?

In those talks with Year 3 (2nd grade), we unravelled the meaning of memory and how it works. The wisdom of the students is reflected in my favourite Year 3 response to my question, 'What is memory?' Ruby said, 'Remembering is like when you've lost something in the back of your wardrobe (or closet) and you have to keep looking for it until you find it.'

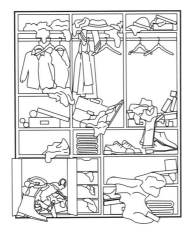

Although in reality it's a bit different because memory is **reconstructive** (which we get to later in this section), this metaphor is a good starting point because it represents how people typically see memory, like a holding bin for information you need to search for. Actually, memory is more than 'memorising' or thinking back on something. We don't remember everything we experience and if we do remember it, our memory is rarely exactly as it happened. It's not a video recorder that captures each moment exactly as it was. We don't hold information in some library of memories to pull out later. 'Memory is the residue of thought,' according to cognitive scientist Daniel Willingham. We remember what is left after we have thought about it and what's left varies considerably. 'Memory is the label we use for cognitive processes that are central to our lives and sense of who we are, and they cross the boundaries of all types of activities of our lives' (Bailey and Pransky, 2014). In short, memory shapes who we are and how we see the world.

WHAT DOES MEMORY LOOK LIKE?

Thinking is based on a complex web of experiences remembered and forgotten. When we think, we use our memory. Examples of how we use memory in our daily life include:

- Explaining how to get somewhere
- Knowing how to drive a car or ride a bike

RECOMMENDED READING
In *Why Don't Students Like School?* Daniel Willingham masterfully unpacks how memory works and what this looks like in the classroom. A must read.

- Remembering the name of that film you saw
- Being able to shop for a friend's birthday gift
- Counting change after buying something
- Remembering that you must pick up your child early from school to bring her to the dentist
- Recalling a story from your youth
- Making decisions that require reasoning and insight

Peel each of these examples apart and you have layers and layers of other associated memories of different types of knowledge. Explaining to someone how to get somewhere requires an understanding of language, space, direction and body language. You may weigh different options based on your knowledge of the time of day, suggest different modes of transport, and unconsciously your memory is making judgements about this person based facial expression, voice and appearance. The whole experience is being added to your memory, altering it in some way.

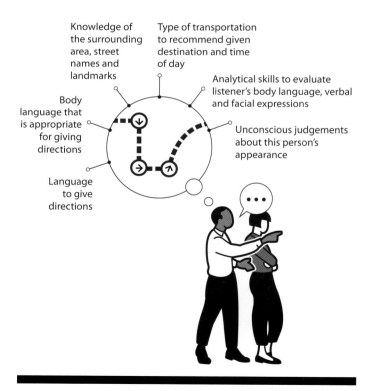

GIVING DIRECTIONS

Knowledge of the surrounding area, street names and landmarks

Type of transportation to recommend given destination and time of day

Analytical skills to evaluate listener's body language, verbal and facial expressions

Body language that is appropriate for giving directions

Unconscious judgements about this person's appearance

Language to give directions

WHY DOES MEMORY MATTER (SO MUCH IN TEACHING)?

Who we are now and who we'll become in the future is shaped in large part by memory.

Everything we learn is based on our prior memories, what is stored in long-term memory. Learning is connecting new experiences to existing ones. 'Learning is a process that leads to change, which occurs as a result of experience and increases the potential for improved performance and future learning,' according to Susan Ambrose (2014), Professor of Education and History at Northeastern University. Two of our biggest challenges as teachers are 1) figuring out what our students have stored in their long-term memory; and 2) managing instruction in order to maximise memory potential to make new learning permanent and transferable.

Understanding memory matters because educators who have a better understanding of memory can be better teachers and better leaders. Using what we know about memory, we can organise instruction better, build curriculum that is more efficient and educate students to be independent learners. Likewise, students who have an understanding of memory become more motivated to persist through the struggle of thinking hard. 'Students come to understand that learning is not something done to them, but something they themselves do' (Ambrose, 2014).

Knowing about the role of memory is also a social justice issue. Helping students to have the tools to learn and build knowledge is a levelling of the playing field. Students who come to us with less of a variety of life experiences or knowledge gained – from wider travel or reading of books, for example – find it harder to gain more knowledge. The more students have in their memories (or knowledge from prior experiences), the more information they have available to recall and use to learn new information. Known as the **Matthew effect** of accumulated advantage, this theory essentially means that the rich get richer and the poor get poorer in terms of knowledge acquisition. Children with restricted vocabulary at five years old are more likely to be poor readers later (Law et al., 2009, cited in Quigley, 2018, p. 6). Learning vocabulary significantly improves comprehension which in turn leads to future learning of new content.

To illustrate this point, take a moment to read the following paragraph from Doug Lemov's article 'How knowledge powers reading' (Lemov, 2017) and then answer the comprehension questions below.

> Rick Porcello has been the anchor of the Red Sox rotation all year, and tonight, he showed why. He was perfect through the first 11 outs. Then he hit Manny Machado. Porcello shouted 'I'm not trying to hit you, Bro,' to remind the slugger that it would make no sense to have plunked him with a perfect game still on the table, but Machado took apparent issue. Then, after he scored on Mark Trumbo's double, he stared down Porcello. So Porcello proceeded to strike Machado out on three pitches in the sixth, and then fanned him on four in the ninth.

- Describe the conflict between Rick Porcello and Machado.
- What does the author mean by 'Porcelo fanned Machado on four in the ninth'?

If you are knowledgeable about baseball, you would have understood most of it. If not, then this short paragraph may have been difficult to read and comprehend. As

'Students come to understand that learning is not something done to them, but something they themselves do' (Ambrose, 2014).

RECOMMENDED READING

Closing the Vocabulary Gap by Alex Quigley is an evidence-informed guide to closing the gap between the 'word poor' and 'word rich'.

Lemov explains in the article, you'd have to have knowledge of baseball to follow the central conflict between Rick Porcello and Machado (and the tension that ensues) by understanding words and phrases such as 'anchor', 'rotation' (with reference to baseball), 'perfect' (which doesn't mean what you think it means), what it means to get hit in baseball and the meaning of 'fanned him on four in the ninth'. Lemov further explains that if you did understand the conflict, it wasn't due to inference, but due to prior knowledge. Another reader who is unfamiliar with baseball may feel like they comprehended what was written because they know a lot of words and recognise a narrative structure, but in reality they would not have fully understood the meaning of the paragraph. That's what it's like for students in our classroom who lack prior knowledge. In fact, to comfortably comprehend text, readers should know 95% of the words (Quigley, 2018, pp. 7–8). Dr Sean H. K. Kang explains that 'acquiring fundamental knowledge and being able to quickly access relevant information from memory are prerequisites for higher order learning and reasoning' (Kang, 2016).

TYPES OF MEMORY: EXPLICIT AND IMPLICIT

Not all memories are the same. This is an important point that teachers need to know. Some are **explicit**; some are **implicit**. **Explicit memories** are what we normally think of when we think of memories and include things like remembering someone's name or an address or what happened on your 16th birthday.

Explicit memory can be further broken down into **episodic** and **semantic** memory. As the name implies, **episodic memory** refers to episodes of our lives and personal stories that are rooted in time and place, like that trip last year to the museum that had huge dinosaurs or to a local farm where you saw a pig race. 'It's like a movie we are starring in, filled with sounds, images, emotions and physical sensations' (Bailey and Pransky, 2014). We create **episodic memories** without trying. According to Bailey and Pransky, many children benefit from experiencing a concrete, episodic experience prior to learning more abstract concepts. This helps to contextualise their new learning. In a science lesson I observed, a teacher used a recent visit to Chislehurst Caves in England to discuss whether or not light travels in a straight line. She brilliantly used an episodic memory (a visit to dark caves) to frame the learning of the properties of light. Episodic memories, however, are not enough for academic learning because they are tied up in our experience from a particular time and place. We want students to be able to recall information outside of context. The teacher wanted the students to know the properties of light and this is why **semantic memory** is also important.

Semantic memory refers to things we learn – information stored in the form of general facts and knowledge. These memories take some effort to form and can be recalled without having to also recall the experience of, for example, sitting in Mr Ahmed's drama class or that visit to Chislehurst Caves. That means this information is easily transferable. These memories are ones we are conscious of, and we can name and describe. So semantic memory is crucial because it is the foundation of knowledge. Episodic memory is important because it contextualises knowledge acquisition for novice learners, and, importantly, is responsible for forming positive relationships with other humans by creating shared positive experiences and piquing the interests of our students.

EPISODIC VS SEMANTIC

Episodic Memory

Semantic Memory

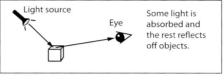

Related to events in context

Connected to a time and place; personal

Fades and is not reliable

General knowledge and facts

Can be recalled any time and any place, not attached to an event or self

This graphic was inspired by Clare Sealy's blog post called 'Memory, No Memories: Teaching for Long-Term Learning'. Clare blogs at primarytimery.com.

Other memories are implicit (unconscious), aptly referred to as **implicit memory**. These are mostly **procedural**, like remembering how to ride a bike. We know how to do it, but it's hard to explain what we are doing because it has become so automatic. These memories are difficult to articulate (for example, exactly how we ride a bike – understanding what pressure to use or how to balance ourselves). Implicit memories can also be emotional and misleading, like how we unconsciously judge people based on race, gender or other factors without being aware. A familiar riddle that illustrates this point is:

> A father and son have a car accident and are both badly hurt. They are both taken to separate hospitals. When the boy is taken in for an operation, the surgeon says, 'I cannot do the surgery because this is my son.' How is this possible?

If it took you a few seconds to find the answer, that makes sense. It's likely based on your past experiences and associations. If every time you go to the doctor, the physician is a man, and if most of the representations of surgeons in the media are men, then when you think of 'surgeon', an image of a man will come to mind (rather than a woman). This is called **priming**. (See Relationships: Research for more about unconscious bias and the impact of priming.) Implicit memory is slow to acquire and it takes a lot of exposure and practice in order to fully learn something. Once these memories are formed, however, they can be recalled automatically and unconsciously. If fact, they are resistant to change (Bailey and Pransky, 2014, p. 122). This is why unconscious bias is so hard to unlearn and why – no matter how long it has been – you can still ride that bike.

There is one more twist in this surgeon riddle, however, which is that it is entirely possible that the son could have two dads, making it possible for the surgeon to also be a man. We are primed to assume that parents must be a man and a woman. This is not the case.

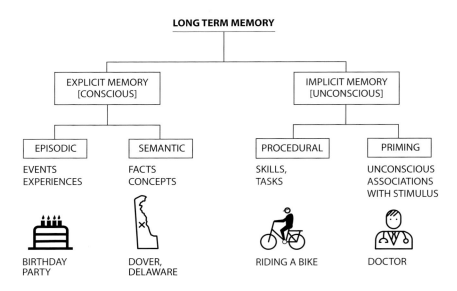

LONG TERM MEMORY

EXPLICIT MEMORY [CONSCIOUS]

IMPLICIT MEMORY [UNCONSCIOUS]

EPISODIC — EVENTS EXPERIENCES — BIRTHDAY PARTY

SEMANTIC — FACTS CONCEPTS — DOVER, DELAWARE

PROCEDURAL — SKILLS, TASKS — RIDING A BIKE

PRIMING — UNCONSCIOUS ASSOCIATIONS WITH STIMULUS — DOCTOR

Both implicit (procedural and priming) and explicit (episodic and semantic) memories are stored in long-term memory. As teachers, the distinction between the types of memory is important:

- A student might remember an experience (episodic memory), but ultimately we want them to remember the concepts or information (semantic memory) for the learning to be transferable.

- Because semantic memory takes effort, we must build in opportunities to teach the concepts and information explicitly.

- We gain procedural knowledge through lots of practice and exposure.

- We need to be aware of implicit (unconscious) bias and the fact that it is resistant to change.

AN ESSENTIAL MODEL FOR HOW MEMORY WORKS

This practical model of memory takes the highly complex process of learning and simplifies it so we can put to use what's most important for the classroom.

Automaticity is the ability to do things without occupying the mind with the low-level details required, allowing it to become an automatic response pattern or habit. It is usually the result of repetition and practice.

The brain is constantly changing, shaped by our experiences. Learning is a physical change in the brain, as we discuss in Relationships and Mindset. 'If you repeat the same thought-demanding task again and again, it will eventually become automatic; your brain will change so that you can complete the task without thinking about it' (Willingham, 2009). Automaticity is essential to learning.

To understand memory, it's useful to explain it as a model of how memory is processed and stored. First conceived by Atkinson and Shiffrin in 1968, the model has been tweaked along the way each time, adding important findings that help us understand how we learn. There are several players we must consider: **sensory memory,**

working memory and **long-term memory** and how these all work together within the surrounding **environment** (Atkinson and Shiffrin, 1968; Atkinson and Shiffrin, 1971; Baddeley and Hitch, 1974). We only briefly address short-term memory, because while it is often referred to when one learns about memory, it's actually less important. Later in our discussion, we will add the role of verbal and visual processing to this model as we build the full picture.

MEMORY MODEL: KEY PLAYERS

SURROUNDING
ENVIRONMENT

SENSORY
MEMORY

Let's begin with the **environment**. This is our surrounding physical area. In schools, it's typically the classroom. As we discussed in Relationships: Research, there is a barrage of information in classrooms – noises and sounds, for instance – that reside for a very short period of time in our sensory memory. What we end up paying attention to has the potential to be learned, but it's not that simple.

PAYING ATTENTION

In *Understanding How We Learn*, Weinstein and Sumeracki (2018) use money as an analogy to explain **attention**. Let's say a teenager has a certain amount of pocket money (allowance) each week. She wants to buy new school supplies, but she also wants to purchase a pizza with friends and doesn't have enough money for both. Attention works the same way. We have a certain amount of attention to spend on different tasks and our brain is continuously deciding what to pay attention to. Attention is limited and it varies from person to person. It also varies depending on the task at hand. If you are doing a difficult task, this will take more attention. Something less difficult means you might have attention left over.

In the classroom, two students can have vastly different experiences. Let's imagine two separate students during a lesson while the teacher is explaining something. Alice is attending to what the teacher says and is taking down some notes. Another student, Zain, is distracted by a nearby conversation between two of his peers. Both are attending to something and both are processing incoming information, utilising their long-term memories, but only one is potentially learning what the teacher is aiming to teach. So attention to what is actually being taught (and this will be obvious to teachers) is crucial.

Although many factors influence how long a person can pay attention to one thing, Bailey and Pranksy suggest using a convenient rule of thumb: 'Age plus 2' (Bailey and Pranksy, 2014, p. 87). So an 8-year-old child would have an attention span of 10 minutes and a 10-year-old's would be 12 minutes. Adults' attention spans can last about 20

RECOMMENDED READING
Understanding How We Learn by Yana Weinstein and Megan Sumeracki (and illustrated by our very own Oliver Caviglioli) beautifully weaves real-life examples into complex concepts of cognitive science.

minutes. '**Attention span**', for the purposes of this book, refers to maintaining focus on activities students are directed to do. Motivation and interest also play a role. If a child is highly motivated, attention will increase; and if they are bored, it can drop to zero. Sound familiar? In order to 'reset their timer', researchers suggest that students have a break. Teachers should plan breaks every 10 minutes by doing something to alter the flow of the lesson, according to John Medina, author of *Brain Rules: 12 Principles for Surviving and Thriving at Work, Home, and School*. Medina and others point out that the brain seeks novelty; it was crucial throughout our evolution to notice changes in our environment in order to remain safe from threats (Medina, 2008). Likewise, our interests are picked by predictions. Again, we are hardwired with a need to know, according to neuroscientist and author Judy Willis, so predictions and teasers of what is to come increase attention. It's also important to note that we tend to pay attention to information that fits with what we already know (Sorden, 2013), which explains the importance of material being relevant to students.

CLASSROOM
See Memory: Classroom for ways to grab students' attention, such as using prediction, adding novelty and suggestions for taking breaks.

SHORT-TERM MEMORY AND WORKING MEMORY

The sensory information we pay attention to is held briefly (a few seconds) by our senses – just long enough to make it into our **short-term memory (STM)**. Short-term memory is capable of holding that small amount of information for roughly 15 to 30 seconds (Weinstein and Sumeracki, 2018). A simple example of this is when you remember a telephone number just long enough to dial the number. If I was to show you a five-digit number, how long do you think you could remember it? Let's experiment. Read this five-digit number below for three seconds. Then see if you can recall all five numbers right away, 15 seconds later, 30 seconds later and a minute later. Or after you check your phone for a message.

85247

Most people can remember only a handful of pieces of information in short-term memory for only a few seconds until the knowledge fades (unless you use a strategy). If I showed a really long number it would be very hard, if not impossible, to hold all of this in your short-term memory. Want to give it a try?

8524730894652345

So STM is determined by attention and limited by capacity – how much we can hold at once.

Holding information in your STM is not enough. Even if a student is paying attention, it is still not guaranteed that they have learned. Students can be attentive and look engaged, but if information doesn't get processed in the STM, it's lost!

Processing happens in the working memory, and for the purposes of teaching, it is the working memory we should focus on. **Working memory** is when you hold some information in your STM (we can hold about four pieces (Cowan, 2010) and manipulate it some way. So if you take the same number we just tried to memorise above (85247) and add one to each digit, for example, it will likely feel a lot different, a lot harder. 'It's in working memory where we do our thinking, decision-making, problem-solving, reasoning, and just plain making sense of the world around us, both in terms of incoming sensory information and what we retrieve from long-term memory' (EdX, 2018). It's our mental workshop.

Working memory is where we hold information for shorts period of time, manipulate it and then transfer it to long-term memory. It's our mental workshop.

Based on Baddeley and Hitch's (1974) Working Memory Model, a robust theory about how working memory works, we know that working memory and long-term memory work together to process new information. It's ingenious teamwork. Working memory relies on what is in **long-term memory (LTM)** in order to process information. It's like a dialogue between the two storage units. In the example above, for instance, where I asked you to add up the numbers, you would automatically integrate what you already know from your LTM – such as what numbers mean, what it means to add and how to do it. Whenever you are using your working memory, or thinking, you are also using your LTM to some extent. Learners construct meaning by actively building relationships between stimuli (materials they are working with) and their stored information, such as knowledge and experiences (Wittrock, 1989, p. 349).

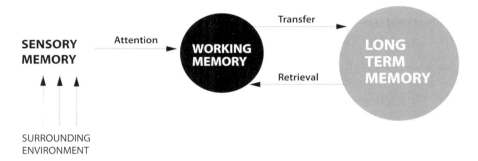

MEMORY MODEL
This simplified memory model illustrates how we learn. Information we pay attention to in the environment is processed in the working memory by retrieving, and making connections with, the vast storage of knowledge in the our long-term memory. New information is then transferred long-term memory.

MENTAL MODELS RESIDE IN LONG-TERM MEMORY

The information in LTM is stored as **schemas**, interconnected networks of concepts that are sorted according to their relationships with each other. In other words, a mental model. One such schema could relate to turkeys, for example. For most Americans, the mention of the word 'turkey' conjures up an array of related images associated with Thanksgiving – stuffing, mashed potatoes, extended family. It may also include emotions related to enjoying football on TV, the stress of a meal or a set of expectations about how to behave. You may also have other associations of turkeys in the larger context of animals or birds: they're like chicken or geese (that we eat); they lay eggs (which we don't eat), etc. For a Brit, 'turkey' will have a similar schema, only relating to Christmas rather than Thanksgiving; any relation to the latter will mostly be from films or TV (and a long way down the list of associations!). Everyone has their own unique schema – and it can be triggered by a word.

Schema is an interconnected network of concepts that are sorted according to their relationships with each other. In other words, a mental model.

A common example used to explain how schemas relate to the classroom is the process of learning to write (Sweller et al., 1998, pp. 255–258). Letters are basically squiggles on a page; these combine to create words, which become sentences. 'This process of ever more complex **schema construction** eventually allows readers to scan a page filled with squiggles and deduce meaning from it' (Centre for Education Statistics and Evaluation, 2017a, p. 3). Another important factor in schema construction is automation, whereby information can be processed automatically without lots of effort. As we mentioned, automation occurs after extensive practice; so in this case, after a lot of reading of little squiggles, our brains automatically processes these shapes as letters and their combinations as words and so on. When we teach, we are guiding students to link information we present to them to existing mental models, forming new schemas with this information. Although it may seem removed from the everyday practicalities, understanding schemas is fundamental to understanding the rationale behind recommended strategies in Memory: Classroom that aim to tap into students' prior knowledge or existing schemas. These are powerful strategies for maximising working memory.

WORKING MEMORY CAPACITY

Everybody has a personal **working memory capacity** that is relatively fixed and different from others. You can think of working memory like a bucket. Each person has their own bucket, and they can only put so much information into that bucket until it is too full and overflows.

This capacity affects how well someone can do an activity, learn to read, solve maths problems or even follow directions. Even students of the same age can have a wide range of working memory capacities. According to Gathercole and Alloway (2007), 'in a typical class of 30 children aged 7 to 8 years, we could expect at least three of them to have the working capacity of the average 4-year-old child and three others to have the capacity of the average 11-year-old child, which is quite close to adult levels'. Working memory increases with age; yet, as the figure below indicates, children with poor working memories do not catch up with those who have better working memories.

CHANGES IN WORKING MEMORY

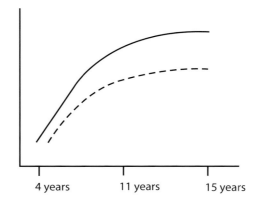

4 years   11 years   15 years

SPOTLIGHT

> "
> it is more useful to help children to maximise the efficiency of their working memory through learning and teaching strategies than to compare students, which only further alienates those with low working memory capacities.

(Gathercole and Alloway, 2007)

'The changes in working memory capacity with age for an average child are shown by the solid line. Scores of a child with low working memory capacity are represented by the broken line' (Gathercole and Alloway, 2007).

POOR WORKING MEMORY

A student with a **poor working memory** compared to their peers may quickly lose track of the lesson, giving the impression that they are disengaged or distracted, when merely experiencing cognitive overload. For example, by the time a teacher has said the end of this sentence, the beginning may have been forgotten: 'I want everyone to get out their books, turn to page 120 and start answering the questions at the bottom of the page.' According to Gathercole and Alloway (2007), working memory failures can be detected by looking out for: incomplete recall; failing to following directions; place-keeping errors; and task abandonment.

Typically, children with poor working memory:

- are well-adjusted socially.
- are reserved in group activities in the classroom, rarely volunteering answers and sometimes not answering direct questions.
- behave as though they have not paid attention, for example forgetting part or all of the instructions or messages, or not seeing tasks through to completion.
- frequently lose their place in complicated tasks that they may eventually abandon.
- forget the content of messages and instructions.
- make poor academic progress during the school years, particularly in the areas of reading and mathematics.
- are considered by their teachers to have short attention spans and also to be easily distracted.

(Gathercole and Alloway, 2007, p. 10)

Although working memory capacity is relatively fixed for individuals at any given time, there are things educators can do to improve the efficiency of memory.

UNDERSTANDING COGNITIVE LOAD CAN MAXIMISE MEMORY

For at least four decades, research has revealed ways to keep a cap on cognitive load.

Our role as teachers, or cognitive coaches, is to help maximise the working memories of all students. To do this, it is useful to have an understanding of **cognitive load** and its impact on learning. In a now often-quoted 2017 tweet, Dylan Wiliam, professor and author, wrote: 'I've come to the conclusion Sweller's Cognitive Load Theory is the single most important thing for teachers to know.' Immediately, interest in **cognitive load theory (CLT)** became the subject of blogs and workshops for schools. It plays a prominent role in the new Ofsted framework as part of their focus on evidence-informed practice (Muijs, 2019) (For our non-British readers, Ofsted is a regulatory body that inspects services like schools, so this focus will draw attention).

RECOMMENDED READING
Understanding Working Memory: A Classroom Guide by Professor Susan E. Gathercole & Dr Tracy Packiam Alloway. This is a free, downloadable resource.

 SPOTLIGHT

Working memory failures can be detected by looking out for incomplete recall; failing to following direction; place-keeping errors and task abandonment (Gathercole and Alloway, 2007).

SPOTLIGHT

COGNITIVE LOAD THEORY

Cognitive load theory states that our brains can only process a certain amount of information (load) at once, as we demonstrate with the bucket analogy for working memory. Because our memories have a limited capacity, too much information – or to be more precise, the mental effort needed to process that information – leads to an overload. The bucket overflows. CLT asserts that educators can use teaching techniques to optimise working memory and therefore maximise learning. The theory defines three types of load: **intrinsic**, **extraneous** and **germane** (Sweller et al., 1998). For the purposes of this book, and to be more aligned with recent discourse relating to CLT (Sweller et al., 2019), we have reframed the types of load into two categories: **relevant** and **irrelevant**. **Relevant load** is necessary for learning; and irrelevant load, as you might imagine, gets in the way of it. There are other contextual factors, often overlooked when in discussion about cognitive load, that relate to the social and emotional barriers that impact cognitive load.

COGNITIVE LOAD:
FILLING THE BUCKET
Using a simple analogy, our working memories are like buckets with a limited capacity. The watering pails represent the different types of load that can take up space before the bucket potentially gets overloaded.

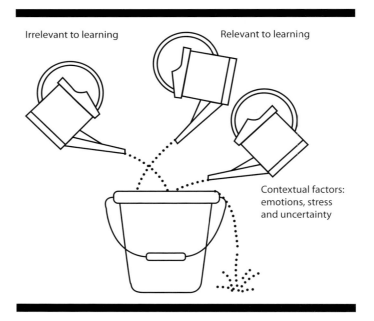

Let's start with what's irrelevant.

IRRELEVANT (TO LEARNING) LOAD

Irrelevant load on working memory occurs when too much cognitive effort is wasted due to the way information is presented. For example, when we organise our instruction so that students have to split their attention between multiple sources of information, we waste precious working memory capacity as students switch back and forth (Chandler and Sweller, 1992). If we talk to our class while they have been asked to read something else, we also risk overload. How many times have we asked students to read directions, yet proceeded to also explain them aloud with every intent to be helpful? We want to reduce this unnecessary, irrelevant load as much as possible and cognitive load theory states that this possible (Chandler and Sweller, 1991). It is up to us. In fact, small tweaks to how we present information can reduce cognitive load for our students and boost their memory retention.

Irrelevant load is also caused by such things as multi-step instructions, lists of unconnected facts, chains of logic longer than two or three steps, and the application of just-learned concepts to new material (unless the concept is quite simple) (Willingham, 2010, p. 20). In these situations, students have too many new elements of information that they must interact with at once, referred to as **element interactivity**. Another example is when a student is faced with a problem that they simply do not have enough background knowledge to solve. These are the times when the teacher needs to slow it down or even back up: 'What does my student need in order to access my teaching?' Put yourself in the place of the learner. What is often not obvious to us as teachers is that we already know a lot of information about what we are teaching, often referred to as the **curse of knowledge**. As experts, we have a solid grasp of what we are teaching; the information is already in our long-term memories, so it doesn't need processing space in the working memory. We teachers can easily lose sight of the fact that our students are processing new information; the buckets quickly fill up.

A BALANCING ACT

Adapting your teaching to individual working memories and optimising cognitive load is a sophisticated balancing act. Take, for instance, the **worked example effect**, a widely replicated finding which shows that novice learners greatly benefit from having a problem solved or modelled for them, with each step outlined along the way. According to the Centre for Education Statistics and Evidence (whose report on cognitive load is a must-read), 'unguided problem solving places a heavy burden on working memory, inhibiting the ability of a learner to transfer the information into their long-term memory' (Centre for Education Statistics and Evaluation, 2017a). In effect, the students may solve the problem on their own, but in the process, their working memory becomes so overwhelmed trying to figure out what to do that they may not be able to recall how to do it again with a subsequent similar problem. There are too many elements interacting with each other. However, there is a balance – like almost all things. Heavy use of worked examples becomes less and less effective as learners' expertise increases, eventually becoming redundant or even counterproductive to the learning outcomes. This is called the **expertise reversal effect** (Kalyuga et al., 2003). This is another reminder of the importance of assessing prior knowledge. Prior knowledge reduces the element interactivity; it reduces cognitive load.

> We teachers can easily lose sight of the fact that our students are processing new information; the buckets quickly fill up.

WORKED EXAMPLES AND EXPERTISE REVERSAL

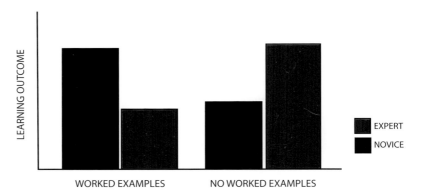

CONTEXTUAL FACTORS: EMOTIONS, STRESS AND UNCERTAINTY

Cognitive load theory defines three types of load: intrinsic, extraneous and germane (Sweller et al., 1998). To simplify and be more aligned with recent discussion relating to research on CLT (Sweller et al., 2019) we have reframed the types of load into two categories: irrelevant and relevant.

CONNECT TO RELATIONSHIPS
See Relationships: Research for our discussion on the science of positive relationship (page 24) and barriers to forming connections with students (page 38).

CONTEXTUAL FACTORS: EMOTIONS, STRESS AND UNCERTAINTY

Other factors influence cognitive load, such as stress, anxiety, poor health and lack of nutrition or sleep. Students may come to class feeling sad or worried about a difficult home experience. Maybe they didn't have breakfast. Perhaps they've experienced trauma. In these cases, building relationships with students and learning more about their stressors can help (see suggestions for building connections throughout Relationships: Classroom). The classroom climate may be another factor in creating cognitive load. For example, in classes where peers are allowed to tease each other for wrong answers or the teacher does not express care and high regard, students' working memories may be taxed by **contextual factors** relating to stress and anxiety (Sweller et al., 2019).

Sweller et al. (2019) explore the contribution of contextual factors to cognitive load, and recognise that some tasks will carry a certain degree of stress, emotion and uncertainty for some learners. They argue that students need opportunities to hone strategies to overcome these factors since stressors constantly surround us. For example, public speaking is widely recognised as an activity that creates anxiety. This obviously doesn't mean we avoid providing students these opportunities; but coupled with the opportunities, we must offer strategies for coping and opportunities to practise for presentations. Sweller points out that research by Arora et al. in 2011 looked at the successful use of imagination or mental practice prior to performing the task and found that this may lower the load during the actual task performance, counterbalancing the high load resulting from stress, emotion or uncertainty of the task (Arora et al., 2011, cited in Sweller et al., 2019).

RELEVANT LOAD FOR LEARNING

Relevant load describes the cognitive effort of acquiring and automating essential information in long-term memory. In other words, it's the repetitive deep thinking we do in order to learn something and be able to use the information again. This type of load, also termed 'germane load' (Sweller et al., 2019), is essential to learning, even though it also increases cognitive load and contributes to filling up the bucket, or working memory. This is akin to 'desirable difficulties', which we discuss later in this section. Once working memory is overloaded, regardless of what type of load (relevant or irrelevant), learning diminishes. Teachers should aim to reduce the negative, irrelevant load while increasing relevant load as much as possible without overflowing.

An indirect way of increasing relevant load is by helping students to understand the best strategies and cues for learning. For example, students often associate actual learning with long hours studying or the ease of processing when re-reading material; however, a better cue would be attempting to generate key concepts from the text at a future point or self-explaining the concepts, both of which would require more cognitive effort but would lead to more learning. (This is why there is a section in Memory: Classroom dedicated to teaching students about memory.) Likewise, teaching learners self-regulation and metacognitive skills can potentially reduce unnecessary load created from feeling uncertainty about learning or their own abilities.

The key is to be conscientious about the cognitive load so that students are thinking hard about what we want them to learn without overloading the working memory. The aim is to maximise mental effort to process essential information (while not exceeding cognitive capacity) and minimise cognitive effort to process irrelevant information. We address specific strategies later in this section and they are outlined for use in Memory: Classroom.

In summary, in order to reduce irrelevant and unnecessary load and increase relevant load, we should be asking ourselves these questions:

- In what ways can I present information more efficiently (avoid split attention) to reduce unnecessary load?
- What do I know about students' prior knowledge? Is there anything I need to do to make the task more accessible (worked example) or more challenging (remove scaffolding)?
- Is there anything I can do to increase deep thinking (processing) (e.g. vary conditions, use retrieval practice, etc.)?
- What do I know about this student's social and emotional state and level of self-efficacy for this task?

As much as we understand that cognitive load theory is an essential component of effective teaching, it is, as Sweller has aptly noted, not the theory of everything (Sweller, 2012). It is, nonetheless, an important piece in connecting the dots between memory, relationships and mindset. Now that we understand the flow of information from working memory to long-term memory, let's take a closer look into information-processing potential of information in the working memory.

THE POWER RELATIONSHIP BETWEEN WORDS AND IMAGES IN WORKING MEMORY

When humans process information, it is essentially done through two separate systems – one for processing verbal information and the other for processing visual information (Paivio, 1971). **Verbal** refers to language, either written text or spoken language that is organised sequentially (one word comes after the next to make sense). **Visual** is what we

RECOMMENDED READING
Cognitive Load Theory: Research that Teachers Really Need to Understand (Centre for Education Statistics and Evaluation, 2017a). The Centre for Education Statistics and Evaluation have taken the lead on providing more background information and practical suggestions, pulling from decades of research on cognitive load theory.

see, which includes pictures or objects on a page. Visual information is simultaneously organised, so that the eye can take in many elements at once. Although verbal and visual information are processed separately, words and images work together, with connections forming between them. As a result, they leave more memory traces (physical changes in the brain) and make information easier to recall. For example, if two forms (words and images) of the same information (let's say a picture of a cat and the word 'cat') are presented together, when we recall the word 'cat' later, an image comes to mind as well and vice versa. This dual processing power of the brain is referred to as **dual coding theory** (Paivio, 1971).

DUAL CODING
Pictures and words from the environment are processed separately, yet form connections, making memories more powerful. (Graphic part based on Kirschner and Neelen, 2017)

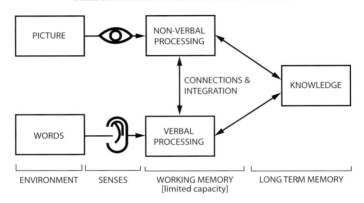

ALLAN PAIVIO'S DUAL CODING THEORY

As you can see in the figure above, information from the environment comes, via our senses (eyes and ears), into our working memories for processing, visual and verbal information connect with each other and integrate with **prior knowledge** (schemas in the long-term memory). By processing the information verbally and visually together, we reduce the load on working memory (Kirschner and Neelen, 2017). Although words and images work well together as one triggers a connection to the other, adding more of the same impedes processing. For example, if we are reading something, we can't also process what someone is saying. These two pieces of information are both verbal and therefore redundant. However, we can watch a video (visual) and listen to someone narrating an explanation and retain information. This has obvious classroom implications, which we address later in this chapter in Memory: Classroom.

HOW DURABLE AND FLEXIBLE MEMORIES ARE MADE
Memory goes on a journey before it sticks – but once it sticks, it stays. The key is finding it when you need it.

THE IMPORTANCE OF RETRIEVAL

SPOTLIGHT

One of the best ways to explain the relationship between working memory and long-term memory is the analogy introduced earlier – the wardrobe (or closet). Recall that

Year 3 (2nd grade) student who said that remembering something is like going into your wardrobe and finding a piece of clothing. From the grimace on Ruby's face that day, I think she was imagining a very messy wardrobe, which works best for our analogy, because that's the way memory really works. When you first learn something, memories can be hard to find, like finding something in a messy wardrobe. So if we use the analogy of tidying your wardrobe, each time we go back to our memories (or the wardrobe), we are tidying them up – we are stacking the trousers together, hanging the shirts, putting the shoes on shelves, etc. That's because each time we retrieve a memory, we actually reconstruct it (Schacter, 2015). A memory is not a literal account of what happened; it's a reconstruction. When we recall something, we pull up (or retrieve) a combination of specific traces of what actually happened along with other information, expectations and beliefs. Recalling a memory often creates secondary retrieval pathways to that memory and makes it easier to retrieve later (Klingenstein Center, 2018). Also, by searching for a memory, we frequently activate information connected to that memory and link it in a more networked context, or schema, for easier future access. Recalling memories makes them stronger, more durable (lasting) and flexible (transferrable) as they are modified, reorganised and consolidated better in our long-term storage.

Students love the wardrobe analogy and they can easily visualise and remember it. Often when I am teaching and we recall previously learned content, I remind students that they are tidying their wardrobes. Or if we learn something for the first time, I tell them that their wardrobes are messy now, but that we'll keep coming back to this and their wardrobes will become more tidy. In an exam or when solving a difficult problem, we will want to go to a tidy wardrobe to find the facts about an event or the steps for solving a problem. To stretch the metaphor further, we can't tidy our wardrobes in one day. Building durable and flexible memories takes time and effort – and a degree of forgetting.

THE WARDROBE

Memory is like tidying a messy wardrobe. Each time you go into the wardrobe, you tidy it up a bit so it becomes easier to find what you are looking for the next time. Each time you recall information, you make that information easier to find again in your brain.

SPOTLIGHT

THE POWER OF FORGETTING IN ORDER TO REMEMBER

Almost all of what we experience is forgotten. This forgetting serves an important purpose: forgetting allows us to get rid of useless information. The brain does not need to recall every house you passed on the way to school today, each word you heard spoken during the day. This is inefficient and would likely drive you crazy. Paradoxically, forgetting also serves another function, which is to help to provide moments whereby memories can become stronger. When a person is taught something and asked to recall it immediately, they are typically able to do so, provided they paid attention long enough for it to have been processed in their working memory. Time passes, however, and we quickly forget. Our brains are made in such a way that we even forget stuff that we thought we'd learned just hours or days ago. For both students and teachers, this rate of forgetting can be discouraging. 'An uncomfortable truth is that, however "great" our teaching of a lesson, our pupils will forget much (if not most) of the new learning,' according to Nick Rose (2018), Fellow in Learning Design at the Ambition Institute.

Starting with Hermann Ebbinghaus in the late 1800s, psychologists have been plotting how quickly humans forget on what has been termed **the forgetting curve**, which is simply a graph of what happens to memory over time. No surprise: if nothing is done to retain specific information, such as consciously reviewing the new material, a memory will fade. This happens quickly. In fact, in a matter of hours and days we lose most of what we were taught (Brown et al., 2014, p. 28). The speed of forgetting depends on a number of factors too, such as the difficulty of learned material, how meaningful it is to the learner, associated cues, and factors like stress, fatigue and emotional safety. The good news is that when we recall that information later – before we've forgotten it completely – we make that memory stronger. This is illustrated in the graph on the next page. Forgetting (or almost forgetting) has created a situation in which recall is a bit more difficult but in which that difficulty actually aids making the memory stronger each time we do it, gradually building a more durable memory.

Robert and Elizabeth Bjork, professors at the University of California, Los Angeles and experts in the field of learning and memory, refer to this optimal level of effortful recall as **desirable difficulty**, an important concept first coined in 1992 (Bjork and Bjork, 1992). They found that when students were put into a situation in which retrieval was difficult, they remembered the information better when they recalled it later. 'Learning happens when people have to think hard,' according to Robert Coe, Professor in the School of Education and Director of the Centre for Evaluation and Monitoring (CEM), Durham University (Coe, 2015). Thinking hard means having to recall information (rather than just looking at the material), ideally several weeks after information is presented (or at whatever time retrieval strength fades nearly completely and you have almost forgotten the information). Eventually the recalling of the material will become easier, less time will be needed and it will become automatic if it is recalled again and again. 'It's a bit like learning how to write your name,' I tell students. 'At first, it takes a lot of concentration; but with practice, it gets easier.'

> The good news is that when we recall that information later – before we've forgotten it completely – we make that memory stronger.

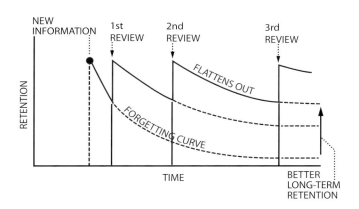

THE FORGETTING CURVE
The forgetting curve shows that the first time we learn something, we forget most of it quite quickly; but each time we review it, we forget less. Forgetting and review helps us build strong memories. In Classrooms, see how you can use this graph to teach students.

RETRIEVAL VS STORAGE STRENGTH: STORAGE IS UNLIMITED BUT NOT ALWAYS RETRIEVABLE

Nonetheless, we've all had that feeling of something being on the tip of our tongue, but we can't recall it until something (a cue) triggers our memory. This phenomenon is explained in part by **the new theory of disuse** – another theory of the Bjorks' but built on the shoulders of many researchers before them – which states that memory has two different strengths. **Retrieval strength** refers to how easily it can be recalled at a particular time; and a memory's **storage strength** refers to how durable it is or how embedded it is (Bjork and Bjork, 1992). Immediately after being introduced to information, retrieval strength is high, as we discussed with the forgetting curve. This is due to the surrounding context and other cues that prompt the learner to easily remember. In a classroom, there may be notes on the board or the teacher may have just reviewed the information. Retrieval strength is fleeting. Storage strength, however, is potentially unlimited. Examples of information with typically strong storage strength include our multiplication tables, the spelling of words, our address and the date of our mother's birthday. These things have been built up over the years, mostly because they have been drilled into us over repeated practice. Unfortunately they too can fade with time. Storage strength has little use if we can't retrieve the memory. That's why retrieval strength is also important. Without going back to the information again, retrieval strength drops off quickly. For example, I won't remember what I had for breakfast a year ago, because I haven't had to pull up that memory many times. Why would I? It's not important to the brain (although eating breakfast is!). It's important that I remember my mother's birthday. This has both strong storage strength and strong retrieval strength. (See figure on the next page.)

MEMORY STRENGTH
Long-term memories that are durable and flexible must have both high storage and high retrieval strengths.

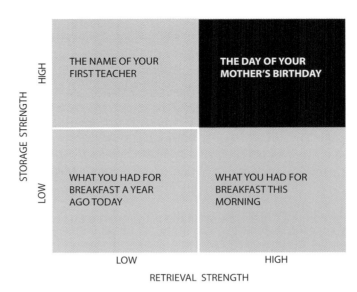

IN THE CLASSROOM

For practical real-classroom reasons, learners need to be able to use that information when they need it; it must have strong storage strength and strong retrieval strength. For example, a student I was coaching thought she knew her physics formulas for an impending exam. 'I learned this in Year 9. I got it covered,' she told me. When I quizzed her, she recalled each one, but only after some considerable thought and a few hints. I explained to her that she had learned the formulas in the past and developed a level of storage strength to recall them then, but in order to do well on her exam, she needed to improve her retrieval strength by revising (studying). 'During the exam,' I explained, 'you won't have time to ponder. These formulas need to be automatic. You want to access them from a tidy wardrobe.' And then we set out a plan to revisit the formulas in a few weeks' time. The good news for this student is that each time she recalls these physics formulas, it will be easier.

The most optimal time for the greatest learning gains is when retrieval strength is low, when that information is on the tip of your tongue. And although I've read several blogs from educators trying to pinpoint exactly when that is, in reality the maximum potential point is too elusive and varied to be practically applied to the typical classroom setting. It depends on each student's prior knowledge, context cues and content. The two most important takeaways for teachers to remember from the new theory of disuse are: 1) Just because you learned something in the past, doesn't mean you will know it in the future; and (2) **Performance** (displaying knowledge in the present) is not the same as actually **learning** (a permanent change in long-term memory). We cannot measure learning immediately after it has been taught. A review quiz at the end of the lesson is not an accurate measurement of what was learned. 'Be suspicious of your current performance,' says Robert Bjork. 'If you want long-term learning you must revisit things – in different contexts' (Bjork, 2017). This is an important lesson for students, who may suffer from an illusion of knowing and therefore fail to return to review the material.

THE ILLUSION OF KNOWING

It will come as no surprise by now to know that there is a negative correlation between a learner's notion of what the best strategies for learning are and what the research says. In other words, study after study shows that we are bad at predicting what works best for us. This is called the **illusion of knowing**, a situation in which the learner thinks they know more than they do, because the material is familiar or because they put a lot of (ineffective) effort into study. The illusion also occurs when we think we learned something immediately after it's been taught (learning vs performing) and when we think we know something because the cues in the classroom give us the answer (posters on the wall, notes or even the way a teacher typically frames questions.) This happens at all ages, but it's particularly poignant when children start to do more independent study. The disparity between what learners think works versus what actually works is a major problem for both teachers and students. In 2018, at Columbia University's SOLER symposium, Robert Bjork used the graphs on the next page to explain this negative correlation (Bjork, 2018). In fact, Bjork explains that 'conditions of instruction that make performance improve rapidly' – such as cramming, which we discuss later – 'often fail to support long-term retention and transfer, whereas conditions of instruction that appear to create difficulties for the learner, slowing the rate of apparent learning, often optimise long-term retention and transfer'. These, as we have mentioned, are desirable difficulties, created by such factors as:

- Distributing or spacing (rather than massing) study or practice sessions
- Using tests as learning strategies rather than just presenting the information again
- Varying the conditions of learning (rather than keeping them constant and predictable)
- Interleaving (rather than blocking) study or practice of the components of to-be-learned knowledge skills (Bjork, 2018)

SPOTLIGHT

CLASSROOM

One way of addressing the illusion of knowing is through spaced retrieval practice (testing to see what you know) over time and metacognitive practices (such as reflection), which we'll cover in the Mindset chapter. See Memory: Classroom for lots of ideas on how to do this.

NEGATIVE CORRELATION.
There is negative correlation between people's judgement of their learning (or judgement of the best way to learn) versus their actual learning. Graph adapted from Robert Bjork presentation at Columbia University's SOLER Symposium (2018)

'Generation' (as mentioned in the graph to the right) refers to generating words, rather than simply reading them, making them more memorable. This can be achieved for single words through the use of a letter-stem cue (e.g. 'fl____' for 'flower') or by unscrambling an anagram (e.g. 'rolwfe' for 'flower') (Bjork Learning and Forgetting Lab, no date). This is called the **generation effect**.

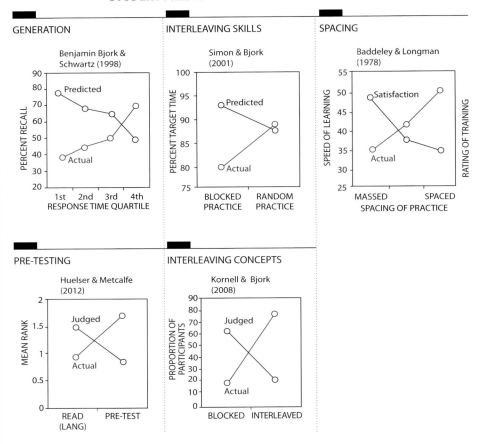

STUDENT PREDICTIONS VS. ACTUAL OUTCOMES

STRUGGLE ISN'T ALWAYS GOOD FOR LEARNING

Not all types of difficulty or struggle are the same. Kornell and Finn make the distinction between 'struggling while thinking' and 'struggling to think'. 'Struggling while thinking, meaning thinking hard about the information one is trying to learn, is productive and desirable,' they write (e.g. quizzing yourself). 'Struggling to think, which means struggling to dedicate one's mental resources to thinking hard, is neither productive nor desirable' (Kornell and Finn, 2016). For example, if a student is trying to think hard while other students are being distracting, this means the student unnecessarily has to struggle to understand and remember the material. 'Making bad choices about how to study can be akin to pedalling a stationary bike: when you put in effort but you go nowhere,' according to researchers Kornell and Finn (2016). Recall the two students Zain and Alice in the classroom, both paying attention to someone. Zain is focused on a conversation next to him; Alice is attending to the teacher. Alice may be struggling while thinking, or thinking hard, to understand a concept the teaching is talking about (which as we know is called desirable difficulty). Zain will likely be struggling to listen to his peers as well as struggling to think about what the teacher is saying (or trying to look like he is anyway). Zain is multitasking.

MULTITASKING IS ACTUALLY MULTI-SWITCHING

Although originally popularised to describe computer processing, multitasking is in many ways human nature. **Multitasking** refers to doing more than one task at a time. Life would be very difficult if we couldn't walk and talk at the same time. In this book, however, when referring to multitasking, we typically are referring to cognitive tasks (e.g. problem solving) rather than physical tasks (walking or driving), which are procedural and have become automated. When doing more than one thing at a time – especially more than one complex, cognitive task – you are less productive, because you have to switch your attention between different things.

New tasks equal new rules. As we switch from task to task, new goals and rules have to be brought into working memory to re-engage with the task (Rubinstein et al., 2001). There is a cost: efficiency decreases and response time slows down. Depending on the complexity of the tasks involved and the time available to complete them, performance can also suffer. Research shows that even having the TV on in the background produces less effective homework. According to some studies, multitasking can reduce our productivity by 40% (Meyer and Kieras, 1997a; Meyer and Kieras, 1997b). To do something well – to optimise working memory – it is best for your brain to focus on one task at a time. Since our brains weren't designed to 'multitask' cognitive tasks, a more accurate term would be 'multi-switching'.

Young people have many more things to pay attention to compared with older generations, so temptations and potential addictions are heightened. A 'like' notification on your smartphone can lead the brain to release dopamine (a pleasure-inducing chemical that seeks more rewards once its gets a taste), pulling your attention toward the phone and away from anything else (Haynes, 2018). The phone is basically a switchboard of attention grabbers. Adolescent brains, which are much more sensitive to pleasure and peer acceptance than adult brains, are forming habits of mind that will be difficult to unlearn once taken into adulthood. (We address this in Memory: Classroom with strategies to bring students on board through directly teaching them about memory and modelling the best strategies. Putting our money where our mouths are.)

LEADERSHIP
In Memory: Leadership, find a fun and illuminating task that will help staff and older students experience first-hand that multitasking is a myth.

EVIDENCE BEHIND LEARNING STRATEGIES

And now for the bad news and the good news. Learners need to know that some of the best strategies feel like the worst. Fortunately there are also plenty of strategies that make learning easier – and even more fun.

One summer, I visited a friend whose 15-year-old son (we'll call him Sam) was about to take his exams. We found ourselves in one of those familiar conversations you get into as a teacher-friend. 'So, tell Tricia what you are doing to revise for your exams.'

Sam replied, 'We had an assembly about how to test ourselves and plan revision.' Our heads nod in approval. Further probing led me to conclude that he had also learned about robust evidence-informed strategies. 'And,' he added, 'we got a workbook.'

'Oh,' my friend lamented, 'I found that crumpled in your bag. I'm not sure what I did with it.'

Sam said, 'Doesn't matter. I won't use it.'

One-off assemblies and lessons about revision are wasted opportunities if no effort is put into following up with students. I wondered if Sam's teachers were reinforcing the strategies by using them in their lessons, so I asked Sam. 'No,' he said – and then he was off to find more interesting conversation.

PUTTING POPULAR TECHNIQUES TO THE TEST

Often the teaching of how to learn, study or revise is presented as a one-off lesson or assembly when it needs to be explicitly and repeatedly modelled and practised with students. Armed with a strong understanding of the efficacy of evidence-informed learning strategies, teachers can be more convincing salespeople – and better teachers. The clear drawback to using the best strategies is that they take more effort to execute. Students need to understand the rationale behind them as they – as any normal teenager would – balance value for effort. 'Is this worth my time?'

In a quest to find out what works best for students, Professor John Dunlosky and his team at Kent State University put together a list of learning techniques for closer scrutiny in an extremely important study, called 'Improving Students' Learning with Effective Learning Techniques: Promising Directions from Cognitive and Educational Psychology' (Dunlosky et al., 2013). The team chose to include learning strategies that were relatively easy to use and therefore could be adopted by students. They also included strategies that they knew students already use such as highlighting, rewriting notes and rereading. It was important, they reported, to examine how well these frequently used strategies work alongside others. Below is a table that indicates the strategies they analysed and their definitions.

RECOMMENDED READING
For an abridged and reader-friendly version of Dunlosky et al. 2013, see 'Strengthening the Student Toolbox: Study Strategies to Boost Learning' by John Dunlosky (2013a).

TECHNIQUES AND DEFINITIONS

1. **Elaborative interrogation:** generating an explanation for why an explicitly stated fact or concept is true
2. **Self-explanation:** explaining how new information is related to known information, or explaining steps taken during problem solving
3. **Summarization:** writing summaries (of various lengths) of to-be-learned texts
4. **Highlighting/underlining:** marking potentially important portions of to-be-learned materials while reading
5. **Keyword mnemonic:** using keywords and mental imagery to associate verbal materials
6. **Imagery for text:** attempting to form mental images of text materials while reading or listening
7. **Rereading:** restudying text material again after an initial reading
8. **Practice testing (retrieval practice):** self-testing or taking practice tests over to-be-learned material
9. **Distributed practice (spaced practice):** implementing a schedule of practice that spreads out study activities over time Interleaved practice: implementing a schedule of practice that mixes different kinds of problems, or a schedule of study that mixes different kinds of material, within a single study session
10. **Interleaved practice:** implementing a schedule of practice that mixes different kinds of problems, or a schedule of study that mixes different kinds of material, within a single study session

(Dunlosky et al., 2013)

Practice testing (or retrieval practice) and **distributed practice** (spaced practice) got the highest ratings for effectiveness because they 'can enhance learning and comprehension of a large range of materials, and, most important, they can boost student achievement' (Dunlosky et al., 2013) – see the figure below. It's important to note that the utility, or effectiveness, of the learning techniques below was based on what strategies had the broadest impact. Keep in mind that context is king! Strategies like **mnemonics** and '**imagery for text**' (attempting to form mental imagery of text materials while reading or listening) work well for core concepts or facts whereas **self-explanation** may work better for comprehension (Dunlosky et al., 2013). Highlighting got low marks, but that doesn't mean students need to throw out their highlighters; it just means that they must realise that the highlighter is the prep work (identifying key material) and the learning starts when that step is done and the deep thinking begins.

TECHNIQUES	EFFICACY
1. Elaborative interrogation	Moderate
2. Self-explanation	Moderate
3. Summarization	Low
4. Highlighting/underlining	Low
5. Keyword mnemonic	Low
6. Imagery for text	Low
7. Rereading	Low
8. Practice testing	High
9. Distributed practice	High
10. Interleaved practice	Moderate

(Dunlosky et al., 2013)

Since the high-ranking strategies are the winners, we'll begin with **retrieval practice** and **spaced practice**, the merits of which have about 100 years of research behind them.

Then we'll proceed to examine varying the conditions of practice and interleaving, because of their natural link to retrieval practice and spaced practice. After that, we'll look at a number of other learning strategies that have great promise, because their merits have also been pointed out in Dunlosky et al. 2013 and beyond – including *Make it Stick: The Science of Successful Learning* (Brown et al., 2014), Susan's Ambrose's *7 Research-Based Principles for Smart Teaching* (Ambrose, 2014) and the Learning Scientists' and Daniel Willingham's extensive writing on how we learn. Below is a list of strategies we'll cover.

1. Retrieval practice
2. Spaced practice
3. Varying conditions and Interleaving
4. Dual coding/visuals
5. Chunking
6. Mnemonics
7. Elaboration
8. Storytelling

 SPOTLIGHT

RETRIEVAL PRACTICE

Retrieval practice is the act of bringing something to mind that you've learned before. It typically comes in the form of low-stakes quizzes, but can range from the effective use of wait time to practice tests. On a basic level, retrieval practice benefits learning because when learners put effort into retrieving information, they remember it better. Recall desirable difficulties. It is widely accepted by cognitive scientists that retrieval practice is the most powerful tool for cementing learning over the long term. In a review of the impact of **practice testing**, analysing different features and outcomes of 118 articles (involving 15,427 participants), the authors conclude that there is an overwhelming amount of evidence to suggest that retrieval practice increases achievement (Adesope et al., 2017). The authors of this meta-analysis write, 'The benefits of retrieval practice persist across the wide array of educational levels, settings and testing formats and procedures. Therefore, students should be taught how to use retrieval practice during self-directed learning activities, and teachers should incorporate retrieval practice into structured classroom activities that students practise first-hand.' Hear, hear!

The benefits of retrieval practice happen in two ways. One is cognitive: retrieval practice simply creates that desirable difficulty we discussed earlier. Additionally, we know (recall the wardrobe analogy) that every time we bring something to mind, we are making that memory more durable and easier to find, thus flexible. The other benefit is **metacognitive**: retrieval practice helps students to regulate their learning, by informing them what they actually do and don't know and what they need to spend more time on. For example, take two students who are reading a text. Each reads it once. Then the first student reads it again while the second student quizzes themself, covering parts of the text, thinking about the answers and then checking the text for accuracy. The second student will remember more than the first. And that's not the only benefit: the second

CONNECT TO MINDSET

Retrieval practice is a metacognitive tool that helps students reflect on their learning and the impact of their effort, fostering a learning mindset. Learn more about metacognition in Mindset: Research.

student will also have more awareness of what they actually know and don't know. If retrieval practice is used in the classroom, then obviously it will also give the teacher more feedback on what the student already knows.

It is important to note that although much of the research on retrieval practice has been focused on secondary and university students, results from studies measuring the impact of retrieval practice on primary (elementary) school children have similar and promising results (Karpicke et al., 2016). With younger students, it is essential to build in regular feedback and experiences of success. Younger students will also need more scaffolding, so very-short-answer questions and partially completed concept maps, for example, are more appropriate (Karpicke et al., 2014). Lastly, it is also important to dispel the notion that retrieval practice is solely for rote memorisation. In *Understanding How We Learn*, the authors write, 'What makes retrieval practice such a valuable strategy is that it helps promote meaningful learning, and it's not just for memorisation of facts' (Weinstein and Sumeracki, 2018, p. 120). Retrieval-based learning helps students use information more flexibly in the future and in the real world.

Although there are countless studies, one by Karpicke and Roediger (2008) is often cited to show the benefits of testing over studying of Swahili-English translations (e.g. 'zabibu' means grapes). One group repeatedly 'studied' while another group integrated testing to recall translations. The latter group did significantly better on the final recall. Performance on a final test one week later was substantially greater after continued testing (80%) than after continued study (36%). In further studies by Butler (2010), not only was retrieval beneficial for fact-based learning, it also improved retention of more complex concepts as well as their transfer to new situations.)

> 'What makes retrieval practice such a valuable strategy is that it helps promote meaningful learning, and it's not just for memorisation of facts.' (Weinstein and Sumeracki, 2018)

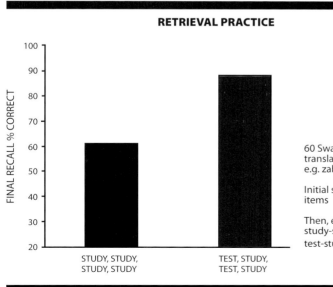

RETRIEVAL PRACTICE

60 Swahili—English translations
e.g. zabibu = grapes

Initial study trials for all items

Then, either:
study-study-study-study or
test-study-test-study

Karpicke and Roediger (2008)

⟡ SPOTLIGHT

SPACED PRACTICE

Spaced practice, sometimes referred to as **distributed practice**, is a method where the learner is presented with a concept or information and then time passes before the learner reviews the same information again. Spaced practice can include several repetitions, spaced at different intervals depending on the complexity of the material and the student's understanding. In other words, it's the opposite of cramming. In Dunlosky et al. (2013), this practice is given one of the highest utility ratings. Likewise, 'hundreds of studies in cognitive and educational psychology have demonstrated that spacing out repeated encounters with the material over time produces superior long-term learning, compared with repetitions that are massed together' (Kang, 2016).

SPACED BEATS BLOCKED
Spaced practice has greater impact on retention than the equivalent amount of time if practice is blocked.

The efficacy of spaced practice can be explained by what we know about the power of forgetting and storage and retrieval strength discussed earlier in this section. When we space out our recall of information, we create a condition of desirable difficulty. The spacing between recall requires extra cognitive effort, creating stronger memory traces. Not only does spaced practice improve the memorisation of information, it also enhances memory, problem solving and transfer of learning to new concepts (Kang, 2016). Like retrieval practice, spaced practice also provides a second indirect benefit of prompting the learner to be more metacognitive about their learning. Recall my discussion with Year 3 (2nd grade) after I asked them what they remembered about plants – and their shock and disappointment that they could remember very little of what they had just learned a few months ago. This realisation, along with our guidance and reassurances, helped them to understand that memory is built over time and we need to practise recalling it. 'I feel happy because I'm getting better at what I learnt a long time ago,' wrote one student on her Exit Ticket after my second visit.

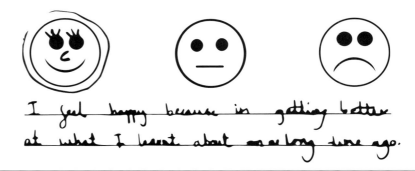

SPACED RETRIEVAL PRACTICE

Retrieval practice and spaced practice go hand in hand, and I often refer to them as one strategy – **spaced retrieval practice**. Retrieval practice is what to do and spaced practice is when to do it. This is one of the most powerful ways to boost the effectiveness of revision. One approach, termed successive relearning (Bahrick, 1979) involves retrieval practice until the learner correctly recalls the target information from memory over several, spaced sessions. In one study, Rawson et al. (2013) put this strategy to the test in a real class setting. The researchers wanted to find out the impact of the following:

- Spaced retrieval (quizzing participants on terms until they got the answer correct (three times) over several spaced sessions
- Restudy (reading the words and definitions over again several times) over several spaced sessions
- Business as usual (participants left on their own to learn the terms, thus most likely cramming)

In order to do this, they split up the students into two groups. In each group a strategy was used on half of the vocabulary words, and for the other half, students were allowed to 'do their own thing'. One group did spaced retrieval and the other group did restudy, but they only used the strategies for half of the terms they had to learn. For the other half of these terms, they could do whatever they liked (business as usual, which would likely be cramming, according to Dunlosky). The students were informed that all of the terms would be on the exam two days after the practice sessions.

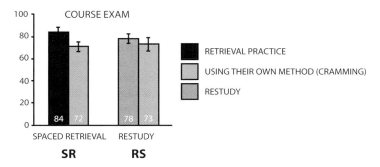

When they assessed the students via a real exam two days later, they found that those who used spaced practice outperformed restudy and business as usual. The more poignant result, however, showed up days and weeks later when they assessed the students again (without additional practice sessions). In the figure on the next page, it is clear to see not only that spaced retrieval practice is the more potent strategy, but that long-term retention is significantly improved simply by spacing out review (be it retrieval or restudy).

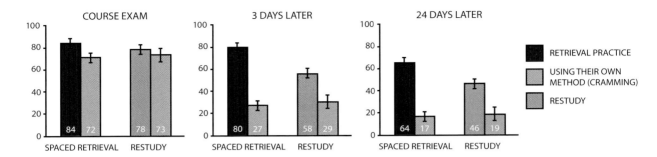

SPACED RETRIEVAL PRACTICE
This study by Rawson et al. (2013) shows the power of spaced retrieval practice which outperformed restudy and one's own method.

For a closer look at this study and similar ones, including clear graphics to illustrate key points about cognitive science, see Efrat Furst's website, *Bridging (Neuro) Science & Education* at www.bit.ly/2JRDiZd

Note, in the graph above, that after 24 days, students could only recall 17% of materials while those who used a spaced retrieval strategy performed 47% better over the long term. Anecdotally, the researchers write, 'We even had students in the laboratory tell us that they were shocked about how well they could learn all the definitions and asked whether their friends could be part of the experiment!'

USE SPACED RETRIEVAL PRACTICE FOR WHAT'S MOST IMPORTANT TO KNOW

Although this study was conducted with undergraduate students, similar and robust results can be found with younger students. One study by McDaniel et al. (2011), incorporating spaced retrieval practice in an 8th grade (Year 9) science class, demonstrated that spaced quizzing significantly improves performance over time. The research also noted that the low-stakes quizzing also improved metacognition (because the 8th graders were more aware of what they did and did not know) and motivation (because students experienced success on the quizzes after feedback).

The evidence for incorporating spaced practice and retrieval practice into the school curriculum is overwhelmingly positive, yet it can sometimes feel like a Herculean task to organise, because it means purposefully planning moments to come back to previously studied content. Furthermore, some teachers and curriculum leaders fear that if they incorporate spaced retrieval practice into the curriculum, they will not have time to cover all of the necessary class content. This is a real concern in both the UK and US. The key aspect to remember (which will come back to in Memory: Classroom), however, is that cognitive scientists aren't advocating the near-impossible task of recalling *all* content as part of your practice; they recommend that educators pinpoint the key knowledge learners need to know to access the wider curriculum. Automaticity of the key knowledge will enable the acquisition of new information more easily – a point we hope has been made by now.

From the perspective based on sturdy empirical evidence, it seems a disservice not to incorporate retrieval practice and spaced practice into the day-to-day and long-term teaching of students. What is the point in teaching students content on top of content if learners are remembering so little of it? If you don't take the time to at least incorporate retrieval of foundational knowledge (the stuff you want students to know quickly and automatically), then you are essentially piling information that will be forgotten on top of information that will be forgotten. 'You could regard a lesson series as a sequence of things to be forgotten,' De Bruyckere (2018) mischievously writes. 'Of course, no one worth his or her salt wants to look at his or her lessons in this way.'

VARYING CONDITIONS AND INTERLEAVING

As with retrieval and spaced practice, teachers and learners can manipulate instruction and revision in order to create desirable difficulties. In general, when we mix up how students study, this benefits learning, according to research. One way of mixing up learning is to vary the conditions under which material is practised. 'When instruction occurs under conditions that are constrained and predictable, learning tends to become contextualized. Material is easily retrieved in that context, but the learning does not support later performance if tested at a delay, in a different context, or both' (Bjork and Bjork, 2011). By varying conditions, learning is enhanced. This is evident with regards to motor skills. In one study, for example, 8- and 12-year-olds who practised throwing bean bags at targets at varying distances (for example, three feet for the 8-year-olds) outperformed those who practised throwing to the same distance when later tested (Kerr and Booth, 1978, cited in Bjork and Bjork, 2011). Similar research into varying conditions for learning physical skills reaches the same result. Likewise, varying the place of study or revision from one consistent place to two separate rooms showed better recall (Smith et al., 1978, cited in Bjork and Bjork, 2011).

Furthermore, even when it comes to the highly effective technique of retrieval practice, the impact will plateau if the questions are not varied because they become predictable. Teachers, for example, tend to ask questions in characteristic ways, so students learn how to respond accordingly rather than deeply thinking about the material. To avoid this, it's useful to vary the routes by which semantic memory is accessed – by 'varying the conditions of practice', write David Didau and Nick Rose in *What Every Teacher Needs to Know about Psychology* (Didau and Rose, 2016, p. 57). According to the variability effect (Sweller et al., 2019), variability can increase cognitive load during practice, but it also tends to increase transfer of learning. For learners who have working memory capacity (room in the bucket), varying practice has benefits. Variability can also overburden students and cause cognitive overload. Teachers need to find the balance.

INTERLEAVE RELATED TOPICS

Another way to mix up practice is to interleave. **Interleaving** is a technique that refers to reviewing material from different (but related) topics. (This differs from sticking with only one topic before moving to the next, commonly referred to as **blocked** or **massed practice**.) Interleaving is similar to spaced practice because practice is broken up over time, but it is its own strategy because the emphasis is more on mixing up the items of practice. Roediger and Pyc (2012) offer the following concrete example of how this might look as students review maths operations:

> **If M = multiplication; A = Addition; S = Subtraction; D = Division**
> **Blocked practice: MMMM AAAA SSSS DDDD**
> **Interleaved practice: MASD MASD MASD**

RECOMMENDED READING
Spacing out your practice also allows for the learner to consolidate their learning with sleep. For a brief article on the importance of sleep for consolidation, see 'The Importance of Sleep for Memory and Cognition' (Wooldridge, 2016).

The authors proposed, based on the research, that interleaving these maths problems will produce better results, in part because interleaving forces the learner to identify a problem type and identify how to solve that problem rather than robotically applying the same strategy from the previous problem. In our example, if you were doing a series of maths problems that were all the same (e.g. division), after a few problems you would just begin to do them all without having to consider which strategy to use – business as usual. A key skill for successful learners is knowing procedural knowledge (knowing how to solve a problem) as well as knowing when to use what strategy. According to Weinstein et al. (2018), this is helpful because interleaving mirrors real life (where we do not typically get to answer a lot of similar questions in a row) and because it allows the learner to select incorrect strategies and make errors that can then be corrected. This helps students to understand which strategy to use in which situation.

Interleaving has shown benefits particularly in domains such as motor-skill acquisition (like learning to play basketball), category learning (like categorising different painting styles with artists' names) (Zulkiply and Burt, 2013) and mathematics problem solving (Rohrer and Taylor, 2007; Taylor and Rohrer, 2010; Mayfield & Chase, 2002). Interleaving may be best used as a revision or independent study strategy, or as a review strategy for homework, such as giving students assignments that require the review or retrieval of different types of problems. However, it is important to note that researchers have recommended that interleaving be done with related but not too similar topics – like different types of maths problems, not completely different subjects. The research on interleaving as a strategy is not as extensive as that of retrieval practice and spaced practice, yet it is very compelling.

MEASURE LEARNING OVER TIME

Interleaving – like varying conditions, retrieval practice and spaced practice – produces desirable difficulties which lead to long-term learning. Keep in mind, however, that when students are tested immediately after interleaving topics versus blocked practice, they will likely perform better on the latter. However, only one week later the results will be quite different. Take, for example, one study below, where students learned to compute the volume of four different geometric solids either through massed practice or interleaved practice. You can see in the figure on the next page that interleaving, in the longer term, had more benefit. (Rohrer and Taylor, 2007). Taylor and Rohrer (2010) have had similar results with 4th grade (Year 5) students interleaving and blocking of maths problems and their application to novel questions.

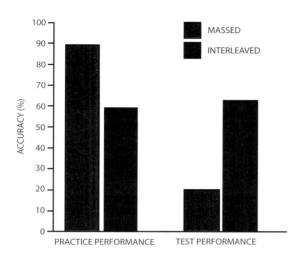

INTERLEAVING
Massed practice may have immediate retention impact, but over the long term (only one week later) interleaving is much more effective. (From Dunlosky et al., 2013, cited in Taylor and Rohrer, 2010)

So far it may feel like it's all bad news for students and teachers: learning is tough (desirable difficulties); we forget most of what we are taught (the forgetting curve) and we are often clueless about what how much we actually know (the illusion of knowing) – to name a few. Time for some good news. There are a number of teaching and learning strategies that make recall and learning much easier – and in some cases, more enjoyable. Let's begin with pictures.

DUAL CODING AND VISUAL METAPHORS

The saying that a picture is worth a thousand words has stood the test of time. Scientists agree and there is also a wealth of evidence to back up this expression. Put simply, visuals matter – a lot. One picture can capture a lot of information. If a friend is reminding you of a conversation with somebody the two of you met on a trip, you may struggle to recall it, explain the authors of *Make it Stick*. 'She tells you where the discussion happened and you picture the place. Ah, yes, it comes flooding back. Images cue memories' (Brown et al., 2014, pp. 186–187).

According to neuroscientist John Medina, if you hear information, you are likely to remember about 10% three days later. The recall rate, however, will shoot up to 65% if you pair it with an image. That's 6.5 times as much information remembered as listening to the words alone (Medina, 2008, p. 233). This makes sense based on our earlier discussion of **dual coding**. Co-locating visuals with verbal material can help students maximise the capacity of thinking, or working memory, during instruction (Paivio, 1971). When information is presented in this way it means we can access it from both our visual and verbal memories, thus allowing more room in our working memory. In other words, when we use dual coding, we help the information go in better (to long-term memory) and come out more easily (to use in working memory), as has been shown in numerous studies (Weinstein et al., 2018). In fact, it is one of the Learning Scientists' top recommended learning strategies for students (Smith and Weinstein, 2016a).

THE SCIENCE OF INSTRUCTION

The exploration of dual coding instruction is increasingly more exciting, and salient, given that many classrooms are now equipped with some form of digital device for screening information. As our understanding of working memory evolved, Richard Mayer and other colleagues, including Roxana Morena, homed in on how dual processing works more specifically with multimedia presentations (i.e. presentations that have both words and pictures). Aligned with the findings of Paivio and Sweller, Mayer produced a series of practical recommendations (Mayer, 2009), which are integrated throughout the Memory: Classroom section. For example: (1) People learn better from graphics and narration than from graphics, narration and on-screen text (the redundancy principle) and (2) People learn better when extraneous words, pictures and sounds (e.g. on a Powerpoint) are minimised (the coherence principle). Researchers warn that overly complicated or detailed images may actually deter student learning. When presented with complex images, the learner can be confused and have to use working memory to figure out the image's connection to the concept, or the learner can get lost in thinking too much about irrelevant information in the image. (We cover the dual coding 'dos and don'ts' in Memory: Classroom.)

REDUNDANCY EFFECT
In the example, verbal information is presented two ways (through text on the screen and orally from the teacher), which is redundant and difficult to process. On the right, the teacher has removed the text as she explains the images. This is more efficient.

INEFFICIENT

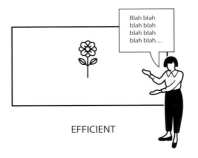

EFFICIENT

A number of related studies of the impact of drawing on retention and learning by Fernandes et al. (2018) found not only that drawing helped with the recall of words, but that it also worked for remembering more complex things like concepts and definitions. These researchers state that drawing (e.g. drawing vs repeatedly writing a word or definition) is a 'reliable, replicable means of boosting performance' requiring no more than 'four seconds to provide benefit' (Fernandes et al., 2018) and this was true for participants over a range of ages. Not only does drawing benefit from the advances of the power of picture, the act also incorporates elaboration of the meaning of a word in order to create the drawing as well as the physical hand movements (motor action).

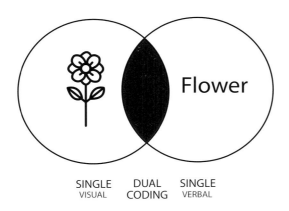

Flower

SINGLE
VISUAL

DUAL
CODING

SINGLE
VERBAL

DUAL CODING VENN DIAGRAM
A simple diagram for explaining that 'dual' in dual coding refers to two ways of processing information.

CHUNKING: TURNING MANY INTO ONE

We have established that our working memory is limited, but just how much information can it hold? Although this question is still a mystery and working memory capacity varies from person to person, researchers agree it's not a lot. In the 1950s, George Miller argued that the 'magic number' of items that we can hold is 7, plus or minus 2 (Miller, 1956), but more recent findings from Cowan (2010) and others show that the number of items one can hold in our working memory is likely to be closer to four. The point is that the number of items of information, often referred to as **chunks**, that we can hold at once is not a lot, and that is something teachers should know and plan around (Awh, no date). Each item or chunk of information is defined as the largest unit of meaning and this depends on what the person already knows. For example, take the word 'petrichor'. If you don't know the word, it may feel like a string of random letters consisting of 5 to 9 items (p e t r i c h o r), depending on how you group them. In contrast, the word 'fragrance', which readers will know, is only one item. (By the way, 'petrichor' is a noun that means 'a pleasant smell that frequently accompanies the first rain after a long period of warm, dry weather'.) When we gain new knowledge or an understanding of something, we can group items together to remember more. This sentence you are reading is a number of items you have grouped for meaning, a chunking strategy you have been using since you were a child, starting with squiggles on a page. Novice learners chunk to improve reading from word families ('cat' and 'rat') to phrases ('under the table') to whole sentences. Chunking is used in maths when working out how many groups of a number fit into another number. In fact, chunking is used in almost everything we learn.

DECREASE COGNITIVE LOAD, INCREASE RECALL

Grouping items helps us to handle more information in our working memory, so we free up room to do other tasks. The term cognitive scientists use for this is **chunking**, but teachers have been using terms like grouping, categorising, classifying, etc. for years. The science helps explain it. When we chunk, each (chunked) group of information is viewed by the brain as a schema, which explains why prior knowledge is important. If we can attach new information to an existing schema, we're in!

CHUNKING

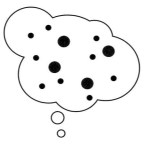

Our brains can hold about four bits of information at a time while thinking.

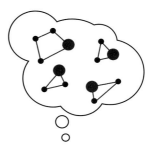

If we group the items together, each chunk counts as one. That means we can hold more information!

Without linking new items to existing ones, information can feel random and unwieldy to hold on to. Take this string of letters for example:

WLNGCSADXLWSRHYLYA

This is too hard to recall without a strategy. If we chunked it, it would be easier to remember:

WAS NYC LAX LGW LHR SYD.

Chunking depends on background knowledge. If you didn't recognise these groups of letters as airport codes (NYC = New York City, LGW = London Gatwick Airport, etc.), it would be much more challenging – if not impossible – for you to remember them. If you did know them, your brain would consider each group of three letters as a single item because you've given them meaning. We use knowledge stored in the LTM to chunk so we can hold it in working memory.

CHUNKING KNOWLEDGE FOR COMPREHENSION

Not only does chunking reduce cognitive load, it also helps to make the items easier to recall later on, and this in turn helps with comprehension. One study by Recht and Leslie (1988) tested 624 seventh and eighth grade (Years 8 and 9) students on how well they could comprehend a passage about the events in a particular baseball game. Prior to this, students were tested on their prior knowledge of baseball and also evaluated on their reading level. The authors wanted to find out which has the most impact on comprehension: prior knowledge of baseball or reading ability. They found that reading ability had little impact on how the students comprehended the passage; knowledge of baseball had much more. In fact, those who were weaker readers yet had knowledge of baseball did as well as strong readers. The reason behind this is because having knowledge allows the learners to chunk information. 'WIthout being able to chunk, the students with little based knowledge simply didn't have enough free space in the working memory to simultaneously remember all of the actions, keep track of their order, do the enactment, and describe it,' explains Daniel Willingham, who cites the study in 'How Knowledge Helps' (Willingham, 2006).

MNEMONIC DEVICES

Mnemonic devices are shortcuts or mental tools used to help hold a large volume of new material in memory, cued up and ready for recall. Imagine: it's like having someone offstage during a performance, poised and ready to tell you the start of your lines if you forget them.

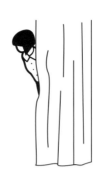

THE CUE: MNEMONIC DEVICES
Mnemonic devices are like having someone offstage during a performance. They are poised and ready to tell you the start of your lines if you forget them.

The Ancient Greeks even used mnemonic devices ('mnemonic' comes from the Greek word meaning 'to remember') to help them remember long speeches. In fact, mnemonic devices are useful any time the learner is trying to memorise information by rote and the information does not connect to one's prior knowledge. Mnemonics take a variety of forms. In UK English classes, one common mnemonic is the acronym 'PEEL', which cues the writer to follow a standard paragraph structure: point, evidence, explain, and link. Rhymes such as '30 days has September...' are also helpful to teach younger students to what may seem like random information about how many days are in each month. Research has shown that mnemonics also work well with visual imagery and locations. In these examples, we can see that mnemonic devices provide a familiar framework for unfamiliar material. That framework can look like a number of different things, such as a poem, sentence, acronym or route home from school.

ELABORATION

Elaboration means connecting new information to prior knowledge, typically by asking yourself questions which you attempt to answer. 'Elaboration' is an umbrella term, referring to either elaborative interrogation or self-explanation. **Elaborative interrogation** is when learners ask themselves why an explicitly stated fact or concept is true or how something works. For example, if you are learning about the castles in England, you may ask yourself how they were made or why we stopped using them. If you are studying the order of operations in maths, you might ask yourself what would happen if you didn't follow the correct order to solve a problem. In the figure on the next page, Weinstein et al. (2018) suggest that physics students, for example, could independently think of 'how' and 'why' questions (presumably after learning this strategy) and then also attempt to answer them. The teacher's crucial role here is to check for accuracy. Uncertainty primes our memory, but the right answer is the goal.

CONCRETE EXAMPLES
Elaboration lends itself to encouraging students to come up with concrete examples of their learning. We learn better from concrete examples than abstract concepts, so this goes further to fortify memories (Paivio, 1971).

ELABORATIVE INTERROGATION

Here's an example from Weinstein et al. (2018) explaining elaborative interrogation. These 'how' and 'why' questions help students make connections and delve deeper into their learning.

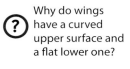  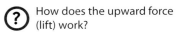

Why do wings have a curved upper surface and a flat lower one?

Why is there a downwash behind the wings?

How does the upward force (lift) work?

How does a plane take off?

Why does a plane need an engine?

The other type of elaboration learners can use is called **self-explanation**. With self-explanation, the learner relates the new learning to themselves either by thinking about how it relates to what they already know or how it relates to the world outside of the classroom. Self-explanation also refers to when the learner explains the new information to someone else, giving concrete examples. Finding a metaphor or a visual image that represents new material – such as the example of tidying the wardrobe to explain how recall improves memory – is another powerful example of elaboration (Brown, 2014). In fact, even if you don't know the answer to the question, merely asking prompts you to retrieve information from long-term memories, which in itself is beneficial. (See generation effect on p. 134.)

Since whenever we learn new information, it is based on prior knowledge, these linking and self-explanation questions are powerful. As we have discussed, pieces of information are not isolated, but rather they are held in schemas, complex architectures of knowledge stored in long-term memory. Elaboration helps make sense of new things by placing them somehow within these representations. Not only does elaboration require the learner to retrieve information to make a connection, it is prompting the reader to connect directly to the schema. It helps you to locate that schema, like the pin on a map app on your smartphone.

In Dunlosky et al. (2013), elaboration does not receive the highest mark, because the research is still limited. However, Dunlosky writes that other cognitive scientists who have studied elaboration 'enthusiastically promote' elaboration and therefore also recommends that teachers use it as part of their pedagogy (Dunlosky, 2013a). Dunlosky et al. (2013) also point to one study that found that students who self-explained were three times more likely to do better on the final assessment (Berry, 1983). Other research from McDaniel and Donnelly (1996) found that elaborative interrogation produced potent effects for learners and 'it produced robust gains in both factual and inference learning regardless of whether it was combined with another technique'. Elaborative interrogation works best when studying general facts about a topic, whereas self-explanation works best when reading or solving problems – for example, in maths or science. Dunlosky warns that elaborative interrogation, or asking why and how, can be daunting and frustrating for students with little background knowledge, so it may be best used once students gain more knowledge. For all types of questioning, if there is little or no response from the learner, it is likely time to directly teach the content and come back to elaboration later.

STORYTELLING

Humans love a good story. Stories entertain us and help us make sense of the world. Stories are 'psychologically privileged', according to Daniel Willingham (2004), 'meaning that our minds treat stories differently than other types of material'. In short, stories are interesting, easy to understand and memorable, thus learning through stories can improve attention, comprehension and memory.

The secret to the story's success is its narrative structure. There is a beginning ('Once upon a time...'), a middle (a conflict of some sort) and an end or resolution ('and they all lived happily ever after...'). Although not all stories follow that traditional structure, it's a familiar pattern that is frequently mirrored in our own lives. Stories help memory, because they provide a framework we can relate to, according to education consultant and former classroom teacher Judy Willis, who also happens to be a neurologist specialising in brain research regarding learning and the brain. Because all new learning is related to previous learning or understanding, stories give us a hook, 'a way in', when learning information. They also help with recall because stories provide cues. If we remember the first bit of a story, we are likely to remember the rest. Even the presentation of a story aids memory. Since stories are not step-by-step accounts but rather pieces of information that are moderately related, they force the reader to think hard about the connections between story elements, but in a way that is pleasurable.

RECOMMENDED READING
'Ask the Cognitive Scientist: The Privileged Status of Story' by Daniel Willingham (2004).

ONCE UPON A TIME.
Using storytelling as a teaching tool has many memory-enhancing advantages.

Pleasure reward
Stories create prediction and hightened awareness to know the answer.

Once upon a time...

Picture power
Stories create images that aid memory.

Mnemonics
Stories provide cues. Once you recall a part of the story, the rest is easier to retrieve.

Prior knowledge
Stories have a familiar narrative; provivde context.

Connection
The listener is more engaged to the speaker.

In school, students are often asked to read expository texts, such as extracts from textbooks, reports, which are less memorable than narrative structures. In one study (Graesser et al., 1994, cited in Willingham, 2004), participants remembered 50% more from stories than expository text. This same study concluded that stories are easier to understand and remember than expository text because we know the format, thus aiding comprehension. The structure of a narrative text is more familiar, more frequently encountered and easier to comprehend than expository text (Britton et al., 1983, cited in Willingham, 2004).

Below is a comparison between expository text (nonfiction or informational text usually found in textbooks or informational articles) and narrative (text found in storytelling). The narrative structure will take some creative storytelling from the teacher or students, but students are more likely to remember the information.

EXPOSITORY TEXT	NARRATIVE STRUCTURE
All stars begin life in the same way. A star forms from massive clouds of dust and gas in space, also known as a nebula. A **nebula** becomes a protostar, which goes on to become a **main sequence** star, which is a stable period for a star that lasts many years. Following this, stars develop in different ways depending on their size. (from BBC Bitesize, 'The Life Cycle of Stars')	All stars in the universe begin the same way, but can have very different endings. It all begins with the tale of Nebula. Once upon a time, there lived Nebula, a massive cloud of dust and gas. Imagine: just dust and gas! In time, however, Nebula formed into a young star called Protostar. As Protostar grew up, it began to settle down to a Main Sequence star. For many years, it lived a stable and happy life. What happened next would change its life forever…

'Stories are data with soul,' writes Carmen Gallo, author of *Talk Like TED* (2014). It's that soul factor that also aids memory as well as boosting engagement. Stories are emotive and allow us to make predictions and connections. This reward-pleasure response when we predict what will happen next sends our brains a boost of dopamine, according to Willis (2017). There is also a connection between the storyteller and the listener (versus expository text). Another study (Stephens et al., 2010) recorded the brain activity of a woman telling a personal story along with the brain activity of the audience members. It found that brains sync up: 'When her frontal cortex lit up, so did theirs.' By simply telling a story, the instructor could plant ideas, thoughts, and emotions into the listeners' brains, reported neuroscientist Uri Hasson (Gallo, 2014, cited in Smith and Evans, 2018, p. 106). Stories create pictures in our minds, drawing on the powers of visuals for memory.

NEXT STOP

The mechanics of memory are fascinating. Now it's time to move onto Memory: Classroom to better understand how to teach what we know about memory and how to put the more effective learning strategies into practice, so that our students are more efficient learners – not only now, but into the future.

MEMORY: CLASSROOM

Memory:
in the **Classroom**

Memory and learning are inextricably connected. Understanding how they work together makes us better teachers.

In an era of evidence-informed practice, research into memory and cognitive science is at the forefront, helping educators to learn more about how the human brain learns best. However, a controlled setting – which is where research usually starts – is a different kettle of fish from a real classroom. Real classrooms require both the teacher and the learners to understand what works best from the science of learning as well as what works best across ages, subjects and varying degrees of prior knowledge – and levels of motivation. This is why the Memory: Classroom section integrates teaching students about learning and explicitly modelling the methodology of strategies. We begin this section with a case for starting this process with young students.

EXPLICITLY TEACH HOW WE LEARN

What if evidence-informed learning techniques were gradually integrated into teaching as part of 'how we do things' right from the start of schooling? And what if students also learned the rationale behind these techniques and that memory itself, like the learning journey we discuss in the Mindset chapter, involves a process. Better than teaching children to work hard, we should teach them to work smart. This approach not only helps students become better learners, it also empowers them and helps close the existing educational gap between students of privilege and those who have been historically under-resourced. It helps to level the playing field.

DIRECT TEACH: WHAT MAKES MEMORIES STICK

Below is a two-part lesson to introduce memory to students, particularly appropriate for **Key Stage 2** (2nd to 3rd grade) and **older students**. Following that, we've included a guide for how to integrate the teaching of memory across all ages. Using your own teaching expertise and your understanding of your students, use the suggestions to integrate *how* we learn into *what* we learn. Throughout the section there are other suggestions for directly teaching students about different aspects of memory.

PART ONE: MEANING HELPS MEMORIES STICK

1. **Prepare the memory task** (see the task in step 5) on slips of paper.

2. **Ask whole class:** What do you know about MEMORY?

    a. Take responses. For **younger students**, ask further questions, such as: 'What is something you know? A street name, someone's birthday, the name of a friend. Why do you think memory is important?'

    b. Start with a basic definition of memory by saying to students: 'A student gave this definition for memory: "Remembering is like when you've lost something in the back of your wardrobe and you have to keep looking for it until you find it." It's the way that the brain stores things you have experienced and learned. You have to think to find them.'

3. **Explain:** 'Today we are going to do a task to learn more about memory. There are three things you'll need to do. (1) Circle words that begin with a capital letter; (2) Circle things you own; and (3) Circle things that rhyme with "cat".'

4. **For younger students**, demonstrate how to do this with the whole class in a practice round:

    Read the instructions and then words aloud, followed by the question.

    1. Circle words that begin with a capital letter: Tissue   fork

        Ask, 'Which would you circle?'

    2. Circle things you own: hat   clouds

        Ask, 'Which would you circle?'

    3. Circle things that rhyme with 'cat':   Rat   door

        Ask, 'Which would you circle?'

5. **Hand out the memory task and start**. Everyone should begin at the same time and turn over their papers when done. Reassure students that it's not a test or competition. No one will mark it.

Better than teaching children to work hard, we should teach them to work smart.

Table adapted from De Bruyckere (2018) and Craik and Tulving (1975).

1. Circle words that begin with a capital letter.				
Apple	jacket	plant	House	diamond

2. Circle the things you own.				
shoes	lemon	spoon	ball	water

3. Circle things that rhyme with 'cat'.				
pat	car	steps	sat	slide

6. When students finish, instruct them: 'With the sheet turned over, write down all of the words you remember. It doesn't matter how many. Just see what you recall.'

7. After about two minutes, display the following list of terms. 'Look at the different categories.'

1	2	3
apple	shoes	pat
jacket	lemon	car
plant	spoon	steps
house	ball	sat
diamond	water	slide

8. **Ask students** in which category they remembered the most words. Most students will remember more words in column 2.

9. **Explain:** 'When we have to think hard about something, we are more likely to remember it. For the items in column two, we needed to think about the meaning of the words in order to know if we own any of them. That extra effort helped us remember the information.'

RECOMMENDED READING
There are similar demonstrations like the one above in Daniel Willingham's article 'What Will Improve a Student's Memory?' (Willingham, 2008).

Teacher talk: 'To remember something, you need to think hard about its meaning. This is why things like quizzing and self-testing help you remember information – because you need to think hard about it.' (For teachers: This also explains why tapping into prior knowledge is important for retention. We remember new learning that is attached to what we already know, like things we own. It is also easier to recall something that we have pictured in our minds, which we discuss later in this chapter.)

PART TWO: MEMORIES STICK BETTER EACH TIME THEY ARE RECALLED

1. **Transition:** 'Although we remember the items in column 2 now, we will forget them quickly. How do we make information stick in our memory?'

2. Recall the memory analogy 'Memory is like a wardrobe, etc.' and show the picture at the top of page 157.

Explain that Ruby's definition of memory being like a wardrobe that you look through is right (sort of), but it's not the whole story. It's more like this: memory is like a wardrobe that gets tidied. Each time you go into the wardrobe, you tidy it up a bit so it becomes easier to find what you are looking for. You hang up the shirts, stack the shoes and fold the trousers. Each time you recall something, you make the memory easier to find in the brain.

- **Explain:** 'To remember something, you should practise recalling it, going back and tidying your brain's wardrobe. Each time you go back, you organise the wardrobe, making it easier to find the clothes. You hang up the shirts and stack things neatly.'

- **Debrief the content:**
  - What did you learn about memory today?
  - How could you make sure you space out recalling information days, weeks, months after you learned it?

Teacher Talk:

- 'To remember something, you need to think hard about its meaning and you need to practise recalling it over time.'

- 'Recall learning how to count, multiply or spell your name. When you first started, it would have been difficult, but the more you stuck with it, the easier it got and now you probably do it automatically!'

For older students: SURVEY SAYS...WHAT WE THINK WORKS BEST OFTEN DOESN'T

Comparing what the research says with what students believe about what works best is an eye-opener for students and teachers.

1. Start by asking students what strategies they already use during revision (studying).

2. Then compare this to the research. Most students think that the best strategies are rereading information, highlighting text or recopying their notes. These strategies may actually be the least impactful, because they create the illusion that one has studied hard. The reality is that there is generally low impact from these strategies mentioned above. Check out this table below to see which strategies were marked as highly effective according to research:

REVISION STRATEGY	Level of effectiveness (according to research)
Rewriting notes	LOW
Highlighting	LOW
Re-reading notes	LOW
Retrieval practice, such as flashcards	HIGH
Spaced practice	HIGH

Based on Dunlosky et al., 2013.

3. Ask students why they think some strategies – rewriting notes, highlighting and re-reading notes – were given such low marks while others – retrieval practice and flashcards – received high marks. Based on what they have learned about memory and thinking hard, students may be quick to recognise the reason, which is that the last two require deeper thought or 'desirable difficulty'.

4. Share these tips for turning low-impact strategies into memory boosters.

TEACHER TIP
This is an opportune time to explain to students about the forgetting curve on page 131. This is a powerful graphic I use with older students to make the point that we need time to forget in order to remember.

RESEARCH
'The illusion of knowing' means believing you know more than you do. This can be a result of working hard, yet using a low-impact strategy; or the result of feeling like you know something immediately after you were taught, yet you haven't practised it enough for it to be in your long-term memory.

REVISION STRATEGY	Would have more impact if you...
Rewriting notes	Pull out key terms or concepts and then try to rewrite your notes without peeking. Or create questions to recall, or try to reconstruct your notes into a graphic organiser.
Highlighting	Use highlighters to identify key terms you will later aim to recall.
Re-reading notes	Use sticky notes, cover up a part of your notes and try to recall the answer. (This is a bit like fill-in-the-blank.)

Teacher Talk

When teaching students about the importance of retrieval practice, it is all about the framing: 'I'm teaching you a strategy that is going to save you time even though it might not feel that way at first.'

AGE BY AGE GUIDE: HOW TO INTRODUCE MEMORY

The following two tables can be used to guide teachers and leaders to integrate memory concepts and strategies across different ages.

FOR EARLY YEARS AND YOUNGER STUDENTS

Introduce the concept of memory through conversation:
- Ask simple questions that require recalling something from the past or something they remember about one of their peers.
- Think aloud how you remembered something.
- After you've read a book, ask questions that elicit recall (about the characters, plot, scene) or make predictions.

YEARS 1 and 2 (K and 1st grade)

Explain that there are ways we can remember things. 'To remember where my keys are, I always put my keys in the same spot.'; 'To remember, the alphabet, I sing it.'
Tap into prior knowledge
Ask students: 'What do you already know about this topic?'

YEARS 3 and 4 (2nd and 3rd grade)

Explicitly teach about memory
- The importance of retrieval practice and spaced practice
- How to use paired peer quizzing
Use elaboration (self-explanation)
When explaining a concept or process, ask:
- 'How does this relate to what I already know?'
- 'How does it relate to my life or things I know outside of the classroom?'
- 'What metaphor or visual could I use to explain this?'
Tell students to explain the new learning to someone else or themselves, incorporating concrete examples.

'Making bad choices about how to study can be akin to pedaling a stationary bike: you put in effort but you go nowhere' (Kornell and Finn, 2016).

FOR OLDER STUDENTS

YEARS 5 and 6 (4th and 5th grade)

Teach other learning strategies and when to use them
- **Dual coding** (what it is and how to use visuals with text)
- **Chunking** (what it is and how to group information)

Model using other strategies like **storytelling** and **mnemonics**

Use elaboration (elaborative interrogation)
When students are reviewing explicitly stated facts or concepts, tell them to ask themselves:
- 'Why is this happening? Why is this true?'
- 'How does that work?'

KEY STAGE 3 (Middle school)

Tap into prior knowledge
Ask students: 'What do already know about this topic?' and teach them to ask that question to themselves at the start of all new learning.

Explicitly teach about memory
- The importance of **retrieval practice** and **spaced practice**
- How to use paired peer quizzing, independently
- **Managing cognitive load** and the **memory drain of distractions**

Teach and model the use of other learning strategies and when to use them
- **Dual coding** (What it is and how to use visuals with text)
- **Chunking** (What it is and how to group information) and the use of **visual maps**
- **Storytelling** and **mnemonics** as learning strategies

Use elaboration (self-explanation)
When explaining a concept or process, ask:
- 'How does this relate to what you already know or experience?'
- 'What metaphor or visual could be used to explain this?'
- Tell students to explain their new learning to someone else or yourself, incorporating concrete examples.

Use elaboration (elaborative interrogation)
When students are reviewing explicitly stated facts or concepts, ask:
- 'Why is this happening? Why is this true?'
- 'How does this work?'

KEY STAGES 4 and 5 (High school)

Support a plan for independent learning
- **Review and reinforce the strategies** above while supporting more independent revision. Focus on how students can independently manage **retrieval practice, spaced practice** and **interleaving**.
- Expose the myth of multitasking and the illusion of knowing (page 133 in Memory: Research)
- See the Mindset: Classroom section for suggestions on how to do teach goal setting

Teach and model a more sophisticated use of:
- **Elaboration techniques** and **note taking** (independently during lessons and at home)
- **Chunking** (using more complex graphic organisers and independent concept mapping)

RECOMMENDED READING
The online course *Learning How to Learn: Powerful mental tools to help you master tough subjects* (Oakley and Sejnowski, no date) and its related book – *Learning How to Learn: How to Succeed in School Without Spending All Your Time Studying; A Guide for Kids and Teens* (Oakley et al., 2018) – are aimed at students and are incredibly useful for teachers. Oakley uses science, metaphor and personal experience to help us learn better.

PRIOR KNOWLEDGE: FIND OUT WHAT STUDENTS ALREADY KNOW

It may seem obvious, but finding out what students already know is one of the easiest, most efficient ways to help them acquire new knowledge.

All new learning is based on prior learning, so a crucial first step is to find out what knowledge and skills students already have in order to both plan your teaching and address any misconceptions. Tapping into prior knowledge is also a good idea because it helps students to relate new learning to their experiences (or existing schema), making learning more relevant. As we've said, it's like putting the pin on a map app on your smartphone.

 AT THE START

TAP INTO PRIOR KNOWLEDGE AT THE START OF NEW LEARNING

Step one: identify key information:

- What students should know as a result of learning a topic/the success criteria
- What would be useful to know in order to engage with this new topic – the basics. This will help you to figure out if there are any terms you want to pre-teach.

When you ask students what they already know, they will say a range of things. It's important for you to be aware that there will likely be some knowledge gaps between students' experiences that pre-teaching could resolve and that some information (vocabulary, places, etc.) needs to be pre-taught directly. It's also, of course, essential that you are clear about what you want students to grasp by the end of the lesson/unit.

Step two: Next, use one of the strategies below (or one of your own) to elicit from students what they already know:

- **Brain dump** (see instructions on page 171): For **younger students**, include prompts or cues, such as subtopics or questions. Remind students that it's OK if they don't have any prior knowledge. That's why we are in school!
- **Visual maps** such as simple mind maps or graphic organisers provide a structure for recall. Include only the subtopics and let students attempt to fill in the rest. (For more information about visual maps, see **chunking** on page 180.)

CONNECT TO MINDSET
Check our guidelines for giving feedback based on prior knowledge on page 301 in Mindset: Classroom.

SHAKESPEARE MAP

Plays

Time period

SHAKESPEARE

The person
(who was
shakespeare)

Characters

The
language

- **Scale or questionnaire:** Use the template below to design a simple way of finding out how familiar students are with upcoming terminology and content.

PRIOR KNOWLEDGE CHART
Adapt the columns to make sense for your age group and subject. For younger students, use traffic light colours or thumbs up, sideways and down.

Here list the subtopics, vocabulary or prompt questions for the topics. Or give them a separate list and ask them to fill in the chart. As they learn new information, they can start to cross off items in the columns to the left and populate the other column.		Never heard (about) it	Sounds familiar, but i'm not completely sure what it means.	I know this! I can tell you about it and give you an example.

- **KWNL charts**
  - Use the KWNL chart to find out what students already know. At the beginning of each unit of study, create a **KWNL** chart (what I **K**now, what I **W**ant to know, what I **N**eed to know, what I **L**earned) to elicit from students what they know (or think they know) and what they want to know. The teacher inserts the knowledge that students need to know in the third column. This is the core information students need to know to access the curriculum.

What do you know?	What do you want to know?	What do you need to know? (From the teacher)	What did you learn?

- Evaluate students' prior knowledge to inform what you will need to pre-teach, based on what you identified in the 'What do you know?' column. Pre-teach specific information and any other key information (e.g. vocabulary) that would help students to understand and engage more with the topic.

- Keep the chart up throughout the unit so that students can complete the last column ('What did you learn?') and correct some misunderstandings from the 'What do you know?' column. They may also choose to write a check mark next to any 'What do you want/need to know' topics that have been taught in the unit. Alternatively, have students keep individual copies so they can see their own progress.

 KEEP IT GOING

REGULARLY ACCESS PRIOR KNOWLEDGE AT THE START OF YOUR LESSONS

- Start lessons with a short review or **Entry Tickets** (just like an Exit Ticket on page 287, but given out as students enter class) of the previous lesson or students' prior knowledge. (You could also use this time to pick up on common errors or struggles.)

- Use **free recall** or **cued recall** (recall with some hints). See Brain Dump and other retrieval practice strategies on page 168.

- **Word scramble**. Display key terms from the previous lesson and ask students to write sentences using these words. The sentences should relate to the previous lesson. (This also takes advantage of the benefits of elaboration, because students can make links between concepts.)

- **Pre-test students** using questions related to upcoming content. Explain to students that this is just to get them thinking. For **older students**, explain the generation effect (see SIDE NOTE on page 134.)

Ensure that the knowledge you want students to recall relates to the semantic knowledge. It should be the most relevant information you want them to learn.

ASK QUESTIONS THAT PROBE UNDERSTANDING AND UNCOVER MISCONCEPTIONS:

For clarification:

- 'That's interesting; what makes you say that?'
- 'That's true, but why do you think that is?'

For more explanation:

- 'Can you give an example of where/when that happens?'
- 'Can you explain how you worked that out?'
- 'How would you justify that answer?'

For deeper thought:

- 'Is there a different way to say the same thing?'
- 'Which of those things makes the biggest impact?'
- 'What is the theme that links all those ideas together?'

RESEARCH
Children with restricted vocabulary at five years old are more likely to be poor readers later (Law et al., 2009, cited in Quigley, 2018, p. 6). Learning vocabulary significantly improves comprehension and future learning of new content.

RECOMMENDED READING
Most of the recommendations presented here coincide with Barak Rosenshine's excellent collection of best practices, 'Principles of Instruction: Research-based Strategies that All Teachers Should Know' (Rosenshine, 2012). This is a free downloadable resource.

For different perspectives:

- 'Does anyone agree/disagree? Why? What would you say instead/add to it?'
- 'Is that always true or just in this example?'
- 'What would be the opposite of that?'

For misconceptions or lack of clarity:

- 'Not sure if that's quite right. Have another go...Is that what you meant?'
- 'That's the gist of it, but could you say that more fluently?'

 KEEP IN MIND:

Ensure you get responses from all students, using a 'no hands up' policy. Otherwise, you hear from just the students who are the most confident or who know the right answer. Questioning is not about finding the right answer; it's about finding out how much your students know and what your next steps are.

Avoid questions that are vague or too general, such as the following:

- Does everyone understand?
- Does anyone have any questions?
- Is everyone OK with that?

TEACHER TIP
See 'cold call recall' in this section when we discuss retrieval practice for a closer look at how to question the whole class, ensuring you hear from all students.

COGNITIVE LOAD
Conserve the precious capacity of working memory by being more aware of factors that contribute to cognitive load.

Cognitive load is the total amount of mental activity the working memory can hold at one time. **Cognitive load theory** states that instruction design can help reduce cognitive load.

The brain, or more accurately our working memory, is a lot like a bucket that gets filled up while we think. For the brain to work its best, we need to avoid filling it with things that distract us (like noise, notifications on our phones, etc.) and fill it up with things that help us learn, like challenging problems to solve.

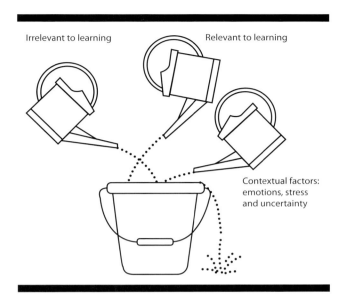

Irrelevant to learning

Relevant to learning

Contextual factors:
emotions, stress
and uncertainty

COGNITIVE LOAD
Working memory is like a bucket
that can easily overflow with too
much input. Instruction should
minimise irrelevant load, maximise
relevant load and manage
contextual factors.

ORGANISE YOUR INSTRUCTION with COGNITIVE LOAD IN MIND

In short, when we start to consider our cognitive load, we become more aware of the small things that crowd our memories but serve little purpose. Below is a list of recommendations for teachers, adapted from the Centre for Education Statistics and Evaluation and the research of educational psychologist John Sweller and his colleagues to help students be more memory efficient.

1. Use concrete examples to explain abstract ideas: Abstract concepts are harder to remember than those that are concrete because abstract ideas are not easily relatable to what we already know and are difficult to visualise. For example, the concept of kindness would be more easily understood and remembered by relating it to a concrete example of kindness, such as offering someone your seat if they look tired. Likewise, explaining gravity by showing a ball thrown up in the air, and then coming down versus only giving the abstract definition: 'the force that attracts a body towards the centre of the earth, or towards any other physical body having mass'. Additionally, aim to use more than one concrete example.

Make the link: Due to the **curse of knowledge**, we, as teachers, might feel that it is obvious how the examples connect to the abstract ideas. It's important for us to also make the link between the concrete examples and abstract ideas, explaining why and how the examples illustrate those abstract concepts. We can also point out which specific features of the examples match up to the abstract concept. Otherwise, we risk the students only remembering the concrete example itself, and not how it relates to the abstract idea (The Learning Scientists, 2018).

Use familiar **analogies** and **metaphors** when teaching. Don't worry if the metaphor isn't perfect. You can adapt as you go. For example, 'The brain is like a muscle' is a simplistic – yet meaningful – way of explaining the impact of effort on learning. In truth, the brain is much more complex than a muscle.

RECOMMEND READING
For more information about
cognitive load strategies,
see *Cognitive Load In Practice:
Examples for the Classroom* (Centre
for Education Statistics and
Evaluation, 2017b).

2. Provide worked (solved) examples: A **worked example** is a step-by-step guide for how to do a task or solve a problem, which is especially important for novice learners. 'The presentation of worked examples begins with the teacher modelling and explaining the steps that can be taken to solve a specific problem' (Rosenshine, 2012). This is commonly used in maths and science, but can be used across a variety of subjects, such as the arts, PE and writing. As learners gain expertise, guided instruction becomes less impactful and may even hinder learning because students are unnecessarily processing redundant information. Make sure you allow students to gradually increase independent problem solving as they grasp concepts by providing less information in the worked examples (see figure below). Furthermore, if students have a strong knowledge base about a topic, they will not need worked examples.

FADING OF WORKED EXAMPLE

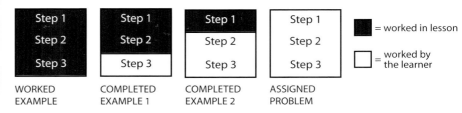

Fading of worked example, from Koedinger (no date)

CREATE A MEMORY-FRIENDLY CLASSROOM ENVIRONMENT

1. Display visible memory aids, such as:

- Writing on the board during discussion to save students from keeping too much information in working memory. For example, during class discussion, the teacher may want to write the key points students make as they speak so others can refer back to them.

- On-going vocabulary clearly posted with student-friendly definitions and/or defining images.

- Resources in the classroom, such as number lines, times table grids, calculators, fact sheets, writing prompts, grammar rules, etc. (Avoid resource overload. Be sure, however, that these resources do not replace actually first trying to have students recall the information. They will provide cues for the learner and therefore may not be an accurate measure of knowing the material. Gradually remove resources as expertise increases.)

2. Cut out all nonessential or redundant information

- **Simplify and focus slide presentations.** Remove extra photos, words, colours and shapes that are not necessary or relevant to the main point. In an attempt to give as much information as possible on one slide, we can actually detract from the main learning. If there is a lot of information to communicate, break it up.

- **Keep the clutter away.** Make sure to organise displays and posters so that at least 20% of your wall space is clear. Regularly change displays instead of just adding more and more things on the walls (Terada, 2018).

RECOMMENDED READING
For a closer look into understanding the rules of multimedia instruction, see Richard Mayer's *Multimedia Learning* (Mayer, 2009) or search online for Mayer's 12 Principles of Multimedia Learning.

- **Be aware of when you're talking while they are doing.** Don't talk over students when they are trying to read/do something else. This will overload students' memories and prevent retention because talk and text are both verbal and can't be processed at the same time. This includes reducing unnecessary background music with lyrics.

🐧 KEEP IN MIND:

- The list above is limited. In fact, all of the strategies in Memory: Classroom help reduce irrelevant load (the bad stuff) and increase relevant load – that's the good stuff, such as desirable difficulty, which (as we discussed in Memory: Research) is essential when moving information to long-term memory.

- Dual coding is closely linked to cognitive load, so check out the teaching strategies from page 176 in that part for quick tips, such as co-locating words and visuals to avoid the split-attention effect.

- Find the balance: expert learners do not need problems to be broken down. If the lesson is simple, increase the complexity of the task and look for ways to increase independence.

ATTEND TO LIMITED ATTENTION SPAN

Attention is a limited commodity and there are many things happening in the classroom that can distract students. Based on what we know about the brain's limited attention span and what it's attracted to, use the following strategies to grab students' attention:

Prediction: Prediction is an attention grabber. Ask students to predict answers or what will come next.

- **Start** the lesson with a hook or questions about upcoming content.
- **Ask** students how a mystery/unfamiliar object is related to the topic.
- **Conclude** with a cliffhanger. Pose an interesting question, but wait until the next lesson, or 'episode', to reveal the answer.

Switch it up: Use signposting, novelty and following-up on predictions as strategies to break up the lesson.

- Take breaks: Give your students' brains a chance to recharge, especially after deep processing, problem solving or a direct teach. Students might stand up and stretch; put heads on the desk; talk to a friend, etc.

- Follow-up on predictions: Provide new predictions or the answers to earlier prediction questions.

- Signpost: Intermittently, remind students of where you are in the learning and where you are going, using phrases such as 'Let's think back: so far we have covered ___, ___, and ____. Now let's look at ____'; 'Now, where are we?'; or 'Today's objective was to _____. Where have we got to so far?'

- Novelty: Insert something that is distinctly different, such as:
    - Put on a funny hat when emphasising a point (novelty)

- Turn to a student and spontaneously ask their opinion on the lesson or the topic you are learning (novelty)
- Insert a silly image into your slides to spike attention and bring humour to the class (novelty)

KEEP IN MIND:

- Novelty attention-grabbers should be used sparingly in order to maintain their impact and to avoid adding unnecessary distractions.
- See storytelling and visual metaphors for additional ideas to engage students.

RECOMMENDED READING
This video by Judy Willis (2012) offers creative and fun ways to help students focus: www.bit.ly/2Zzprvc

Retrieval practice also supports metacognition, because the learner will be more aware of what they do and don't know.

LEARNING STRATEGIES to MAXIMISE MEMORY

RETRIEVAL PRACTICE

Most cognitive scientists agree that retrieval practice scores the highest marks for making memory stick.

What is meant by retrieval practice?

Retrieval practice is the act of deliberately bringing something to mind that you've learned before. It typically comes in the form of low-stakes quizzes and then checking for accuracy.

 AT THE START

DIRECT TEACH: RETRIEVAL PRACTICE

Remind students of the memory task on page 155. 'During the task, we remembered things better when we had to think hard about the meaning, such as whether or not we owned an item versus if it was capitalised. That extra effort helped us keep the information in our memory. This is why things like quizzing and self-testing help you remember information – because you need to think hard about it.'

MODEL RETRIEVAL PRACTICE IN THE CLASSROOM

There's a myriad of different ways to incorporate retrieval practice into your lesson. It's important to remember that retrieval practice refers to **low-stakes recall strategies, such as quizzes**, done in an emotionally safe environment, and should not be used for formal assessment or high-stakes competition. Remember, students are simply using retrieval to 'tidy their wardrobe'.

For younger students: Find opportunities to integrate retrieval practice during the day:

- Daily reviews or any questions that focus attention on the details of the day or the learning:
  - 'Remember the time when…? Tell me about it.'
  - 'Name three things you learned about insects today.'

- Have students retell an event that happened in the past.

- Use flashcards with pictures or simple definitions.

- Photograph a learning event and then ask students to help write captions about what happened.

- Ask students to recall what they know about their peers. This also helps to build relationships between students.

- After you've read a book, ask questions that elicit recall (about the characters, plot, scene) or make predictions. Return to previous learned vocabulary from, for example, picture books. Use the following strategies, found in *Bringing Words to Life: Robust Vocabulary Instruction* (Beck et al., 2013):

  Give examples:

  - 'If there were an emergency on the playground, what might happen?'

  - 'I'll say some things and you tell me how they might protect you: a pot holder; shoes; seat belt.'

  Making choices:

  - 'If any of the things I say might be examples of people clutching something, say "clutching". If they aren't examples of clutching, don't say anything.

    - Holding on tightly to a handbag

    - Holding a fistful of money

    - Softly petting a cat's fur

    - Holding onto branches when climbing a tree

    - Blowing bubbles and trying to catch them'

For Key Stage 2 (2nd–5th grade) and older students:

PAIRED PEER QUIZ

This flowchart makes explicit what students should be doing when they quiz each other. It's a great opportunity to model 'thinking hard' and building independent learning. And students like it!

1. **Prepare** by having some information that students can use to quiz each other. For example, a list of vocabulary with definitions, formulas in maths or science or short-answer questions with answers. When you first introduce quizzing, make sure students understand how to turn information into questions as needed. This may require modelling. Where developmentally appropriate, they may be able to pick their own questions from notes or a textbook. If you use knowledge organisers, this is a creative opportunity for students to engage independently with them, using them to create questions for each other.

2. **Explain** the flowchart by breaking it down. Take students through each pathway as you model the flowchart first. Point out that when quizzing each other, it's important to let their partner think hard about the answer before giving a hint or the answer itself.

RECOMMENDED READING
Bringing Words to Life: Robust Vocabulary Instruction (Beck et al., 2013) is full of loads of suggestions to help teachers of all ages to teach vocabulary.

3. **Put students into pairs** and let them get to work.

4. Things to look out for:

  ▪ Are they giving each other think time?

  ▪ Are they supportive and using encouraging language (accountable talk)?

  ▪ Are they spending too much time giving hints when they should just give the answer if their partner is getting it wrong? (One or two quick hints is enough.)

  ▪ Are the questions too easy? Are they too hard?

TEACHER TIP
Once students learn the paired peer quiz flowchart, encourage them to study together or get someone to quiz them. For **younger students**, this is a perfect opportunity to get parents on board. Students can even teach parents the flowchart.

PAIRED PEER QUIZZING FLOWCHART

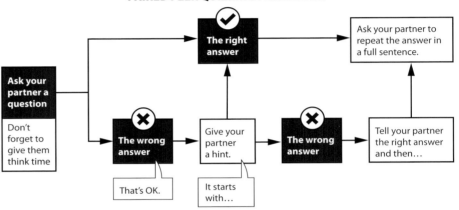

Teacher Talk

  ▪ 'It's OK to forget. That's an important part of making memories last.'

  ▪ 'I'm giving you this quiz/test because I want to strengthen your recall of key information. That's how memory works.'

  ▪ 'You are thinking hard about this question. You are creating a stronger pathway to those memories, making it easier to recall next time.'

 KEEP IT GOING

AAA STRATEGY

COLD CALL RECALL

Use this traditional questioning technique whereby the teacher calls on students to recall previously taught content. This is a 'no hands up' technique, inspired by Doug Lemov's Cold Call (Lemov, 2014).

1. Have a list of questions from previously learned content you can easily pull from for Cold Call Recall.

2. Announce that you will not be calling on students by name and remind students that it is OK if they get the answer wrong and to pay attention to the correct answer. Say 'No hands up' or use another strategy like lollipop/popsicle sticks, whereby each student in class is assigned a number that corresponds to a stick. Students know their individual numbers. Keep the sticks in a cup and pull one out after a question.

3. Say the question. Silent pause. Then say the student's name. 'What is the answer to number 4?', pause, 'Alex, what is the answer?'

KEEP IN MIND:

- Make sure all notes are away, so that students are not simply re-reading or looking up answers.
- If you make Cold Call Recall a regular practice, it will be normalised and expected, reducing the anxiety some students may experience at first.

Teacher Talk

For Cold Call Recall and other retrieval practice strategies, it's essential to create a supportive classroom where students feel comfortable making mistakes when called on. These Teacher Talk examples aim to reduce stress and ensure that all children are included in the recall.

If the question is hard and you expect many might get it wrong:

- 'This is a tough question. Let's see what you come up with…'
- Offer a hint: 'For the next question, tell me if you want a hint. The question is…'

If you suspect a student is feeling anxious at first about Cold Call Recall:

- Start with a simple question, such as, 'Did you have a go at number 5? Did you find it difficult? Let's hear what you came up with.'
- Pre-call, meaning quietly tell the student (while you are circulating) that you will call on them for an answer. (Make sure you are confident they will get it correct.) This is a scaffolding approach to give more reluctant students some practice answering questions aloud in the class. After a few times, include them in the cold call list to answer a random question.)

To ensure that students are listening to each other: Ask students to develop/add to a peer's response or repeat what another student said in a full sentence: 'Lola, Albert just gave an excellent response to my question. Please repeat what he said in a full sentence.'

To build confidence and later success if a student gets an answer wrong: When the correct answer is revealed, return to the student who got it wrong so that they can practise the right answer. 'Let's see if someone can help us find the correct answer. Listen for it and I'll come back to you to repeat it.'

BRAIN DUMP

Ask students to write down everything they already know or remember about a topic or previously learned content. This **Brain Dump** activity, sometimes called a **free recall**, also works well in pairs or threes where each student takes a turn listing as many things as they can recall about a topic or previous learning until they cannot name any more details.

RECOMMENDED READING
Teach Like a Champion 2.0 (2014) by Doug Lemov is an encyclopaedia of powerful teaching strategies for all ages. Lemov's blog is also a great resource and often features videos of teachers using these strategies. See teachlikeachampion.com/blog

CONNECT TO RELATIONSHIPS
See Relationships: Classrooms for ideas on how to build a positive classroom community that values supporting each other and thinking hard. This is essential for full participation in Cold Call Recall and other retrieval practice strategies.

BRAIN DUMP
Ask students to write down what they remember and then reveal suggestions, based on previously learned content.

BRAIN DUMP

Put your notes and book away.
Write down everything you can recall about…

YOU COULD HAVE WRITTEN…

Some key information about the topic goes here for students to compare responses.

- ....
- ....
- ....
- ....
- ....
- ....
- ....
- ....
- ....

🐧 KEEP IN MIND:

For **younger students**, brain dump may be too challenging. In this case, use cued recall. In other words, include prompts like sentence starters, key words or images from previous lessons to scaffold free recall.

TEACHER TIP
There are several online applications for students and teachers to utilise retrieval practice. Kate Jones, a secondary school teacher, author and blogger in the UK, recommends Plickers, Kahoot! and Quizizz. You can read more about Kate's ideas on her blog at www.lovetoteach87.com

EXIT TICKETS

Exit Tickets can take the shape of a short quiz. They are a great way to incorporate retrieval practice into your lessons. Students are given an Exit Ticket with a short quiz on it and they hand it to the teacher as they leave. You can review these quizzes quickly and they can be used to expose misconceptions and patterns of mistakes which will inform the need for future and specific teaching or retrieval practice. Make sure you give the students the correct answer in the next lesson. Feedback is essential.

Students can also create Exit Tickets for class quizzes, but you must check that they are relevant and rigorous enough. And *make sure, along with a quiz question, they write the answer too!*

PAIR SWAP

This technique allows students to experience the benefits of recalling the same information twice – first with a partner and then independently. Think pub quiz.

1. The teacher conducts an **oral quiz** by calling out a series of questions. In pairs, students confer to answer each question.

2. When the quiz is over, **each pair swaps** with another pair who will mark the answers. To keep the pace quick, the **teacher provides the answers** by calling them out or displaying them.

3. Students **return the answer sheet to the original pair**, who take a few minutes to review the ones they got wrong. Tell them they will take an individual quiz on the same content the next day.

4. **The next day**: give students an individual quiz. Review and give them the correct answers again.

5. **The next week or so**: give students another quiz with the same information to access long-term memory.

Teacher talk

- 'If your partner knows the answer but you don't, that's OK. Take some time to think hard about it so you both remember it next time.'

- 'This is not a competition. We are all supporting each other to "organise our wardrobes".'

 KEEP IN MIND

- **Wait time and think time** are essential if you are quizzing students in a whole-class situation.

- Use a **variety of questions**, including both short-answer and multiple-choice questions. Vary the wording.

- **Scaffold** by giving hints to help students remember the answer if they are struggling beyond the level of 'desired difficulty'.

- Be sure to give the **correct answer** in the end.

- **Check** for understanding with **all students**. Retrieval practice is about each child having opportunities to practise recall, not about finding who knows the correct answer. Below are a few suggestions for ensuring you hear from all students.

  - Think, Pair, Share

  - Individual whiteboards

  - Cold Call Recall

  - Choral responses (make sure all students start at the same time)

- Ensure that students experience **success**. This is essential to secure for **younger students** from the start, so include questions you are confident they will know. This also fosters a learning mindset.

- Gradually **vary the wording of questions and conditions**, so that learners don't rely on external cues and predictable question formats.

- Keep it **positive**. Retrieval practice is neither a class behaviour tool nor a 'gotcha' strategy to catch students not paying attention. Likewise, avoid rewards for correct answers.

Retrieval practice is most effective when there are repeated opportunities to recall previously learned content. See ideas for spacing out retrieval practice on page 193.

FOR INDEPENDENT PRACTICE

SHOW STUDENTS HOW TO GET THE MOST FROM FLASHCARDS

For older students: Once you have explained memory, retrieval practice and the importance of learning over time, model creating flashcards in your lesson. **Flashcards** are a highly effective way to self-quiz, provided they are used correctly. Students like flashcards, but need guidance to get the most out of them. Some common mistakes include:

- Writing all of the information on one side of the card, rather than a question and answer on different sides
- Spending too much time making them look pretty rather than thinking hard about them, creating an illusion that the work has been done
- Making them, but only using them once
- Looking at the answers too quickly
- Losing them or failing to keep them organised

Use these instructions to explain to students how to effectively use flashcards.

- You must think hard about the answer before checking to see if you are right.
- If you're wrong, use a strategy to remember the information. (See other strategies.) If there is time, test yourself again at the end of your review session.
- If you get it right, come back to it later – in a few weeks and again in a few months, depending on when your formal assessment is or how soon you want to know the information automatically. Give yourself time to forget it a little.
- If you keep getting it right, rewrite the question to make it trickier. You'll learn it better if you have to answer it in different ways or apply it to a problem.
- As an option, try the flashcard-plus method by rephrasing definitions or questions/answers to put into your own words and/or generating a realistic example of the term from your life (Senzaki et al., 2017).

TRAIN STUDENTS TO TAKE INTERACTIVE NOTES THAT SAVE TIME AND AID MEMORY

For older students: Explain that taking notes is an important skill and students who take better notes do better in school. One of the most well-known note-taking strategies is called The Cornell Notetaking System, created for university students in the 1940s by Walter Pauk at Cornell University. Below is a simplified version for secondary students (middle and high school).

Show students how to organise their notes.

- **Fold your page** into three sections. (See illustration)
- In the Notes column, **write down notes** during the lesson.
- In the Recall column, after class (or in the last few minutes of class, if the teacher chooses) **write questions** to self-test, list terms to be recalled or create simple drawings that represent concepts in the notes section.

TEACHER TIP

Offer strategies for keeping up with flashcards. They can take a long time to create, so if a few are done each day, it's manageable. We recommend ritualising this practice by leaving a few minutes at the end of the lesson to do this. Support students to have a flashcard holder (such as a plastic baggies, small boxes or just a few rubber bands) so that their flashcards stay organised and in good shape. (See note taking below for more ideas.)

 AAA STRATEGY

- At the end of the lesson or later for homework, use the summary row to **write a summary** of the notes.

- Fold the paper so that the notes section is hidden and **ask yourself the questions** listed on the Recall column, writing the answer in full sentences on a different sheet of paper.

- **Regularly return** to these questions as a retrieval tool.

Title	Date
Recall **After class** *Write questions to self-test, list terms to be recalled or simple drawings that represents concepts.*	**Notes** **During class** *Main point and detail from class.*

Summary
After class *or the end of class, write a summary. You may also include any connections to other content/concepts.*

INTERACTIVE NOTETAKING
Adapt the layout of the template so that it works best for your subject and your students' development level. Encourage students to use simple drawings and symbols.

Build in reflection time. Ritualise this practice by setting aside several minutes at the end of the lesson for pairs or groups of students to compare notes. As an option, ask students to fill in the recall section of the notes, which they then share with the class, building their skills to create self-test questions and allowing them to learn from their peers' work.

Variation: Prepare **skeleton notes** (an outline of some of the information to be taught) or an advanced organiser based on the visual maps later in this section. This is particularly useful for **younger students** and novice learners.

🐧 KEEP IN MIND:

- Adapt the layout of the template so that it works best for your subject and your students' development levels. Aim to stick with a consistent template (same font, column width, headings each time) so that the process becomes habit for students and they don't use up memory capacity trying to figure out a different format each time.

RECOMMENDED READING.
Read more about notetaking in 'A Note on Note-Taking' (Kuepper-Tetzel, 2018) and 'Note-taking: A Research Roundup' (Gonzales, 2018).

- If students are taking notes and listening to you at the same time, their working memories are working double and they may not be paying as much attention to the actual meaning of what you are saying. Slow down, allow for silence while they write and no writing when you explain complex concepts.

DUAL CODING and VISUAL METAPHORS

When it comes to memory, pictures pack power. Combine pictures with words to supercharge the capacity to recall even more.

What is meant by dual coding and visual metaphors?

Visuals, or **visual metaphors**, are simply pictures that represent something else, like a word or concept or process. Dual coding is combining verbal information with visuals to maximise retention and minimise cognitive load.

 AT THE START

DIRECT TEACH: THE POWER OF PICTURES AND WORDS WITH DUAL CODING

- Recall prior experience: Ask: 'Have you ever noticed that when you hear or read a story, you can picture it in your head? That's because our brain likes pictures. Pictures help us remember information.'

- Explain dual coding: **Dual coding** is combining verbal information, like words or speech, with visuals, such as pictures, drawings or diagrams, to help learning. Our brains learn better this way. There is one part of our brain that processes (makes sense of) things we see. This includes pictures. Another part of our brain makes sense of what we hear or read. When it's time to remember the information later, we have two ways of finding that information. This includes written words or someone's voice. This works best with things we can visualise, like a chair, and less well with a concept like 'truth' which is hard to visualise.

  a. Give examples: 'For example, if I want you to remember the word "flower", I can show you a flower and say, "flower" – or show you the word.'

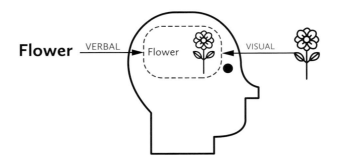

  b. Find your own: Look in your own environment for examples, such as labelled pictures in books, especially science books, or signs around school.

TEACHER TIP
Dual coding can also easily be combined with other tools, such as retrieval practice and chunking, to further boost its effectiveness.

 KEEP IT GOING

DUAL CODING AS A TEACHING TOOL

- **Use simple drawings and illustrative photographs** in your handouts, presentations and displays that explain important concepts, processes or vocabulary (as we've done in this book).

- **Visually organise information** using infographics, timelines, diagrams, sketchnotes and graphic organisers. (See chunking next for further examples.)

- **Avoid split attention**. When labelling the visuals, place descriptions next to the specific things represented, rather than separating them below or in another document. The exception to this would be if the text obfuscates the actual drawing because there is simply too much of it. Too much text will also overload the learner.

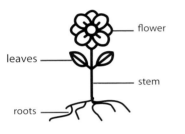

Effective use of Dual Coding

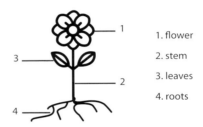

Less Effective use of Dual Coding

SPLIT ATTENTION
The drawing on the left above is more effective because the words are next to the image. The one on the right makes the learner switch attention back and forth. This is known as the split attention effect.

- **Choose talk over text**. When possible, orally explain the image or diagram, for example, rather than including a lot of text. Talk trumps written text for retention and managing cognitive load so it's better to explain the image alone. For novice learners and students with English as an additional language (EAL), however, it is still helpful to include keywords or some resources for reference. It may be the case that the pace of the instruction needs to slow down (Oberfoell and Correia, 2016).

OKAY

BETTER

- **Use signalling.** When including text, indicate the most important information with cues, such as keywords, arrows and marks or step-by-step compilations of a diagram, such as the flowchart used throughout the book. Or use a zoom-in on key elements.

◉ AAA STRATEGY

QUESTION, DRAW, EXPLAIN AND LABEL

This is a step-by-step process that students can follow to use dual coding when learning new vocabulary. It incorporates other learning strategies that we want to model for our students, such as tapping into prior knowledge, elaboration and retrieval practice. It also takes advantage of the benefit of drawing. The whole process reinforces metacognition, because students are thinking more about their learning.

1. Prepare a list of words and definitions on a handout. (Optional)
2. Ask students: 'What do you already know?' If this is a whole-class activity with a set group of words, I may use a form like this one below, to see how familiar students are with the words by rating them according to how much they already know:

   1. Never heard (about) it
   2. Sounds familiar, but I'm not sure what it means
   3. I know this! Here's the definition…

WHAT DO YOU ALREADY KNOW?
Year 5 students at Julian's Primary School in London use this template to assess prior knowledge of WWII vocabulary.

Cavalry	2	
Frontline	1	
Trenches	3	The muddy place where soldiers lived.
Saddle	3	The leather seat on a horse.
Barrage	1	

3. Tell students to pick one of the level 1 or 2 words to start with and hand out the definitions.
   Start Question, Draw, Explain, Label

   1. **Draw:** Once students understand the definition, they can start to illustrate that word. You may choose to prepare a few Google image search screen grabs for them to help them visualise the definition, but the challenge for them is to make a simple drawing, not an intricate one!
   2. **Explain**. Students pair up and explain their drawing to a peer and then give a concrete example of the definition. Teachers can use this time to give examples of how the word can be used differently in different contexts. For example, in wartime, 'trenches' were dug for protection. 'In the trenches' can also mean to be involved in something that's onerous or difficult.
   3. **Label**. Students label the picture using the word and definition.
   4. Students can use retrieval practice by trying to reproduce the image or the definition without looking at the answer.

QUESTION, DRAW, EXPLAIN, LABEL

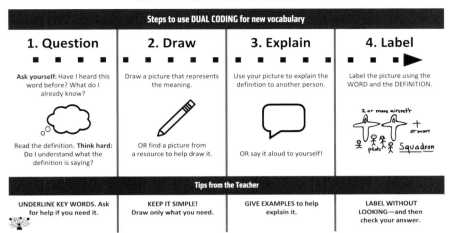

Steps to use DUAL CODING for new vocabulary

1. Question	2. Draw	3. Explain	4. Label
Ask yourself: Have I heard this word before? What do I already know?	Draw a picture that represents the meaning.	Use your picture to explain the definition to another person.	Label the picture using the WORD and the DEFINITION.
Read the definition. **Think hard:** Do I understand what the definition is saying?	OR find a picture from a resource to help draw it.	OR say it aloud to yourself!	

Tips from the Teacher

UNDERLINE KEY WORDS. Ask for help if you need it.	KEEP IT SIMPLE! Draw only what you need.	GIVE EXAMPLES to help explain it.	LABEL WITHOUT LOOKING—and then check your answer.

TEACHER TIP
Display student examples using a visualiser or by photographing them and projecting examples to share with the class. Use your own examples as well.

A FEW MORE GOOD IDEAS

There are plenty of ways you can put dual coding into the hands of students so that they have more independence.

- **Picture it:** Create dual coding classwork and homework assignments. For example, have students come up with different ways to represent information from the lesson through simple drawings or graphic organisation.

- **Recall it:** Students recall visuals as a retrieval practice strategy. For example, ask students to recall the diagram used to explain a concept and recreate it without looking at the original.

- **Quick Draw Exit Tickets:** Ask students to quickly create an image that represents a key element they learned in the lesson – or several key elements. *Use a visualiser or photograph the next day to display clear examples or dispel misconceptions.*

- Encourage students to **visualise** concepts and procedures that they have learned. This may take modelling at first: 'I am going to visualise how to multiply 10 by 20 in my head' or 'Let's visualize how to (give a speech).'

RECOMMENDED READING
Here is an excellent blog that offers more dual coding ideas with examples: The Learning Scientists' 'Learn How to Study Using…Dual Coding' (Smith and Weinstein, 2016a). For an even closer look, read *Dual Coding with Teachers* by Oliver Caviglioli (2019). It's an informative and beautifully illustrated gem. Psst: I'm featured on page 194.

KEEP IN MIND:

Dual coding does not work with all content. Concepts that are too complex may be better suited to other strategies. Likewise, information that is too simple may not require dual coding.

- Dual coding for comprehension may work best for beginners who lack knowledge about a topic and are therefore not able to form images as they read, whereas experts can (Mayer, 2019).

- This will take practice. Students, especially the artists in the group, will want to create elaborate drawings. As mentioned above, have them keep it simple or you lose the educational benefits – students will have a pretty picture but won't remember the information. Likewise, those who feel less competent in art may be hesitant to draw.

- Also, teachers: keep visuals simple. If the image doesn't pop into your head as a good illustration, it won't pop into theirs.

- Share your images with your colleagues so that your students see the same images (used to refer to the same concept) in multiple classes or year to year.

CHUNKING

Chunking makes the most of our memory by turning many items into a manageable few.

What is meant by chunking?

Chunking is the grouping of lots of small pieces of information into large, more meaningful pieces of information that can be held more easily in working memory. Chunking can also refer to breaking down larger units into smaller, more memorable bits of information.

 AT THE START

DIRECT TEACH: WHY AND HOW TO CHUNK

1. Explain chunking to students

- Recall prior learning: Remind students of the example of the wardrobe (when learning about memory) and how it was easier to find clothing if it was grouped together (e.g. all of the trousers were folded together). 'This is called chunking.'

- Explain that chunking is a word that scientists use for grouping of small pieces of information into large, more meaningful pieces of information that we can hold more easily in working memory. Chunking helps to hold more information in our brains while we are thinking and makes it easier to recall information later.

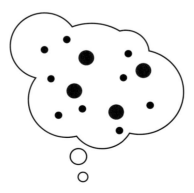

Our brains can hold about four bits of information at a time while thinking.

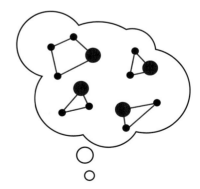

If we group the items together, each chunk counts as one. That means we can hold more information!

CONNECT TO MINDSET
Teaching how to chunk is particularly useful for novice learners and aids metacognition by providing a framework for organising thoughts and ideas.

CHUNKING
When we group, or 'chunk' similar items, we can retain more information. This also makes the information easier to recall.

2. Give examples:

- Start by using letters or number combinations that your children will know. Below are two examples that show how chunking would help the memory of these.

Show this: **YMIASTESATPCE** and then compare it with this: MY CAT EATS PIES

Or make your own by mixing up four familiar 3-letter combos, such as BBC CIA FBI ABC NBA CNN PHD ITV NYC.

- Give more concrete examples: We constantly group information such as language, maths, grocery lists, sentences and words. This makes it easier to understand and to remember – or find that information, like the wardrobe. If we had a big list of items to pick up from the shop, for example, we could remember the items more easily if we grouped them by aisle or type. Or if we have a big task to do or remember, we might 'un-chunk' to break it down into more memorable stages, such remembering a dance routine or how to change a tyre.

2. Teach different approaches to chunking

Small to big: How to chunk when you have a large number of items:

- Gather all of your items
- Look for patterns/similarities
- Group like items

For example, with a list of things you want to memorise about fission in chemistry you would write down all of the important pieces of information you recall and then group into cause, effect, dangers, benefits, etc. When writing an essay or report, you could brainstorm the information you want to include and then look for common points to chunk into paragraph order so that one flows into the next.

Big to small: How to (un-)chunk when you have a big topic or task that would be more memorable and manageable if you worked with smaller chunks:

- Break down the main topic into smaller topics.
- Group information into manageable units or subtopics. Should any of the smaller topics be grouped together because they are similar?
- Break each subtopic down to include important details about each.

For example, when reviewing a topic: If you are revising *Macbeth*, you may choose to break it down into smaller categories, like themes, characters, setting, key quotes etc. Then identify topics that are related. Characters and quotes might get chunked together, putting quotes with related characters. Lastly, break down your subtopics and important details you'll want to remember.

 KEEP IT GOING

VISUAL MAPS: PULLING TOGETHER THE BENEFITS OF DUAL CODING AND CHUNKING

Visual Mapping combines the benefits of both dual coding and chunking and can be used in a variety of contexts. Here we look at concept maps and graphic organisers, which are similar but have different starting points.

GRAPHIC ORGANISER TEMPLATES

A graphic organiser is a diagram that visually depicts an abstract concept in pre-defined category boxes with specified relationships, such as: cause and effect; compare and contrast; story structures; venn diagrams; and simple listings like fact vs fiction. (See example below.) They are based on a tried-and-tested analytical frameworks. Use graphic organisers to help students organise their thinking or use them as an advanced organiser (e.g. filling in the compare-and-contrast graphic organiser to organise thinking relating the similarities and differences of butterflies and frogs). Model how to use graphic organisers when you introduce them.

COMPARE AND CONTRAST

| Life cycle of a frog | Life cycle of a butterfly |

HOW ALIKE?

Goes through metamorphosis, lays eggs …

HOW DIFFERENT WITH REGARD TO...

| Anywhere where there is a water source, like in ponds or marshes | Habitat | Places where there are flowers that produce nectar. They need warm weather |

FINAL THOUGHTS: WHAT DID YOU NOTICE?

Compare and contrast graphic organiser from *Infusing the Teaching of Critical and Creative Thinking into Content Instruction* by Swartz and Parks (1994)

Flow Chart, Venn Diagram and Fishbone diagram from *Dual Coding with Teachers* by Oliver Caviglioli (2019)

Flow Chart
The simplest way to show the flow of a process by a series of factors or events joined by arrows. Too many such nodes makes understanding more difficult.

Venn Diagram
The visual depiction of set theory. Agreed attributes determine inclusion in a set. An overlap of circles highlights the similarities.

Fishbone Diagram
Situations are rarely explained by a simple line of causes. In such cases, causes are chunked into similar themes to indicate a more subtle sphere of influence.

C = Cause **E** = Effect

Students can use information to first fill in a graphic organiser template (or concept map on the next page) that already has the topics or main ideas filled in by the teacher. The students must fill in the supporting details. Once complete and checked, students are given a new blank or partially blank graphic organiser to fill in by recalling (from memory) the completed one. The teacher can also give a word bank of the missing information if it needs more scaffolding.

CONCEPT MAPS

A concept map is a visual tool for organising or grouping knowledge into similar characteristics and visually displaying links between concepts. Concept maps begin with a main topic and then branch out to related subtopics; they are typically hierarchical. What makes them different from other visual maps is that concepts are linked together by words or phrases that show the connections between two concepts, as evident in the figure on the next page.

How to create a concept map

For younger students: Concept maps work best when the teacher creates them to explain relationships. Include pictures. Otherwise, they can be very challenging and overload students' working memories because there are a lot of things to think about at the same time that you are learning the strategy.

For older students, concept maps are an excellent way to reinforce relationships between concepts. Start by modelling.

- Start with a main topic or idea.
- Break it down: List all of the elements, such as concepts, subtopics and key terminology that relate to the main topic. (Sticky notes work well here.)
- Get organised: Group similar elements and organise in hierarchical order. Give bigger concepts more space and a higher position.
- Draw arrows or lines to connect the boxes that contain related knowledge. Words or phrases can be written along these lines to explain the relationship between the elements in the boxes and circle.

TEACHER TIP

Graphic organisers and concept maps can easily be used alongside other powerful strategies such as retrieval practice. Once students have filled in the visual map, give them a blank one (or partially blank) and ask them to recall what was in each box.

CONCEPT MAP

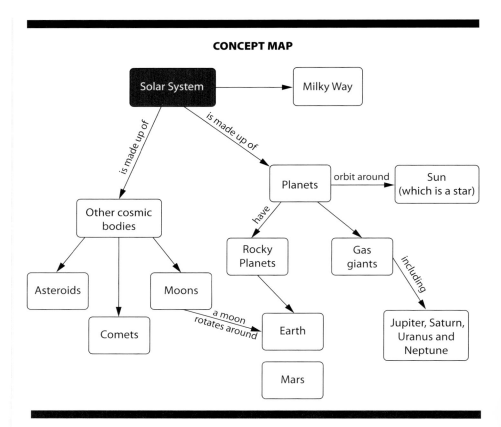

TEACHER TIP
Concept maps are useful as note-taking tools while a student reads a textbook or article. Teachers and students can construct concept maps together during a lesson to better chunk ideas and show relationships.

MIND MAPS

Mind maps tend to be used at the start of new learning as a brainstorming activity, but they are best used as a review or to help organise previously learned content. Information is usually presented visually (with images and colour), with a central idea placed in the middle and associated ideas arranged around it.

MIND MAP

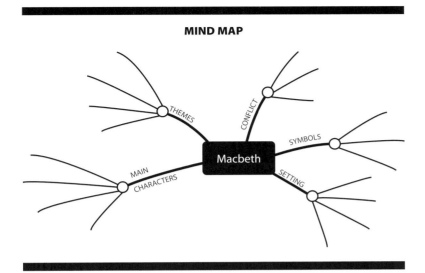

 KEEP IN MIND

- Although different subjects and concepts require different graphic organisers, it's best to adopt a school-wide approach to using them. Switching between different styles unnecessarily uses up working memory capacity.

- Model how to use the graphic organisers and concept maps using familiar understandings, such as a graphic organiser comparison between crisps (potato chips) and chocolate, or a concept map about food production, for instance. This is an especially important step for **younger students**.

For more clarification on visual mapping, use the following table for comparison between visual maps in order to decide which is a better fit for your teaching goals.

TABLE FOR VISUAL MAPS
(Adapted from Eppler (2006).)

	Concept Map	Mind Map	Graphic organiser templates
Example representations			
Purpose	Shows systematic relationships among sub-concepts relating to one main concept	Shows sub-topics of a domain in a creative and seamless manner	Analyses a topic or situation through a proven analytical framework
Best when	Classroom teaching, self-study and revision	Personal note taking and reviewing	Slide presentations, self-study, planning document for essay writing
Guidelines	Start with the main concept (at the top), and end with examples (on the bottom); boxes/bubbles designate concepts, arrows represent relationships between elements. Put words or phrases on arrows to explain the connections	Start with the main topic (center) and branch out to sub-topics, employ pictograms and colours to add additional meaning. Write text above the branches	Label all boxes. Fill all boxes with corresponding text. Larger boxes designate more important information
Level of difficulty	Medium to high	Low	Low to high

MNEMONIC DEVICES

Mnemonic devices are mental tools that are used to help hold a large volume of new material in memory so it is cued up and ready for recall. Imagine: it's like being on stage and having a friend offstage during a performance. They are poised, ready to give you the start of your lines if you forget them.

DIRECT TEACH: Explain to students that mnemonic devices are a great tool to memorise information that may seem random or difficult to recall. Remind them of some specific mnemonic devices they likely used when younger: a song to remember the alphabet or the number of days in each month.

MNEMONIC DEVICES AS TEACHING TOOLS

AAA STRATEGY

Mnemonic devices come in many forms. Below are the ones we've found to be the most useful. The related examples below can be used to illustrate how the mnemonic devices work, but coming up with your own examples is the best bet. Encourage students to make up their own as well.

Acronyms: Use the first letter of each target word to create a new word or acronym. For example: A very common one used in English schools for writing paragraphs is PEEL, which stands for 'point, evidence, explain, link'. Another common one is Roy G Biv to remember the colours of the rainbow.

Acrostic: Create a sentence by using the same first letter of the things you want to remember. For example:

Mercury	My
Venus	Very
Earth	Excellent
Mars	Mother
Jupiter	Just
Saturn	Served
Uranus	Us
Neptune	Nachos

Method of Loci (or Memory Palace): This is a more complex mnemonic device. Imagine a space that you're familiar with, like your walk home from school or the inside of your home. You then imagine the items you need to remember in the location you are visualising. For example if you need to pick up milk, eggs, bread and bananas from the store you might imagine your living room, with milk spilled on the coach, eggs on the side table, a huge piece of bread where the chair cushion would be, and bananas hanging from the lamp.

This strategy combines the power of pictures with the power of associations. Method of Loci works best when the images you visualise are exaggerated (such as the huge piece of bread where the chair cushion should be). The only challenge is that if you have a lot to remember, you'll run out of places. Tell students to reserve this for tricky, really important information they want to remember.

Rhymes and songs: Making up a rhyme or adding rhythm to something you want to remember helps you to recall it later – such as the alphabet song.

STORYTELLING

The brain likes stories and we remember information better if it has a story structure with a beginning (Once upon a time...), rising action, conflict and resolution. Humans

RECOMMENDED READING
These two videos are great examples of how to use mnemonic devices. Show older students Joshua Feor's Feats of memory anyone can do (Feor, 2012); For younger students, check out the BBC's *Take a Walk in Your Mind* (BBC, 2010).

naturally want to create and hear stories; stories prompt us to visualise what is happening, which also helps make the memory stronger.

DIRECT TEACH: STORYTELLING

Encourage students to use stories to remember information, adding characters and details. Use the diagram below to recap on all the reasons stories enhance our learning.

Pleasure reward
Stories create prediction and hightened awareness to know the answer.

Once upon a time…

Picture power
Stories create images that aid memory.

Mnemonics
Stories provide cues. Once you recall a part of the story, the rest is easier to retrieve.

Prior knowledge
Stories have a familiar narrative; provivde context.

Connection
The listener is more engaged to the speaker.

AAA STRATEGY

STORIES AS A TEACHING TOOL

You can utilise the power of stories by incorporating them into your teaching. Here are two suggestions:

1. **Relate content to a story:** Look for times when you can relate the content you are teaching to a story. When teaching about the periodic table, tell the fascinating story of Dmitri Mendeleev, his poor upbringing, determined mother and a dream that came to him at night about how to position the elements.

2. **Make content sound like a story:**
   - The beginning: establish location, characters, time: 'Once upon a time…'
   - Rising action: the plot thickens, there are complications, suspense builds 'Until one day…'
   - Climax: the point of highest tension, the turning point: 'Suddenly…'
   - Falling action: the quick pace to the end
   - Resolution: And they all live happily ever after…or not.

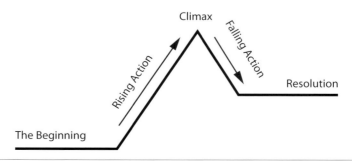

 KEEP IN MIND

Avoid adding too much embellishment in your stories. Although we encourage exaggeration when using stories to memorise, you don't want students to remember unnecessary or inaccurate details.

TEACHER TIP
Daniel Willingham (2004) recommends using the 4 Cs of stories when lesson planning: Causality, Conflict, Complications and Character.

ELABORATION

Elaboration is the process of finding additional layers of meaning in new material, usually through questioning: 'Would you please elaborate on that?' Elaboration helps students to relate new learning to existing learning in long-term memory, thus helping to make that new learning stick. There are two common approaches to elaboration – elaborative interrogation and self-explanation. (See Memory: Research for a more detailed discussion of each approach.)

DIRECT TEACH: ELABORATION

For elaboration, the key to direct teaching is to explain that by asking ourselves questions, we can help our brain make better connections in our long-term memory. Teach students to use all the elaboration-type questions below when working independently. Elaborative interrogation is especially useful for **older students**.

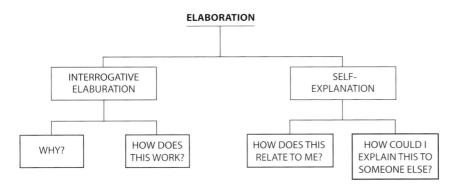

ELABORATION AS A TEACHING TOOL

 AAA STRATEGY

1. Self-explanation

When explaining a concept or process, ask students:

- How does this relate to what you already know?
- How does it relate to your life or things you know outside of the classroom?

Then ask students to explain their learning to someone else or themselves, incorporating concrete examples. Have them consider what metaphor or visual they might use to explain this.

For example, in a geography lesson about locating countries in Europe, ask: 'What do you already about maps?'; 'What do you know about the countries in Europe?'; 'Have you been to any countries or have you seen them in movies or on TV?'; and 'Can you teach someone how to use geographical coordinates to explain where Romania is located?'

EACH ONE, TEACH ONE: For this strategy, give each student a few different concepts or terms you want them to learn or recall from a previous lesson. Put terms/concepts on small strips of paper. Give students time to read and understand the information on their strip of paper. Then instruct them to get out of their seats, find a partner and teach their concept/term to that person. Repeat as desired. At the end, use Cold Call Recall to see what the class remembers.

🐧 KEEP IN MIND

As a rule, teachers and students should routinely ask themselves, 'What do I already know about this topic?' and 'How does it relate to me?'

2. Elaborative interrogation

When students are reviewing explicitly stated facts or concepts, ask why- and how-related questions:

- 'Why is this happening?'; 'Why is this true?'
- 'How does that work?'; 'How is this related to other topics?'

For example, if students are studying an art movement like Cubism, they may ask themselves these questions to better understand the motive behind Cubism and to better understand how Cubist paintings are created: 'Why did the artist paint in geometric shapes?'; 'How did they start the painting?'

RECOMMENDED READING for students about how to use elaborative interrogation: Smith and Weinstein, 2016b.

The human memory remembers concrete information better than abstract information because it relates concrete examples to existing schema, or mental representations we already have in our memories.

Why did the artist paint in geometric shapes?

How did they start the painting?

🐧 KEEP IN MIND:

- When using elaborative interrogation strategy, it is important that students check their responses with their teacher for accuracy.
- Elaboration can be used with students of all ages; however, asking why and how something works can be frustrating for students with little background knowledge, so elaboration should only be used once students have gained some basic knowledge.

CONCEPT MIX AND MINGLE: Identify key information students should know about a topic, enough facts or concepts for each student (or most students if your class is large) to have a different piece of information. Give each student one of the pieces of information. For example, if they are learning about plants in science, you could give them words like 'roots', 'flowers', 'bees', 'food', etc. Then instruct the students to mingle around the room and meet as many people as possible, one at a time, with their information. With each new person, they must figure out why the two pieces of information are important to the topic, what they have in common, and how they differ. For this activity you could also include information from previously learned topics, when appropriate.

THE FINAL STEP: SPACING OUT THE LEARNING STRATEGIES

Here we combine the research behind retrieval practice and learning strategies with the memory benefits of spaced practice to create a plan that maximises memory over the long term.

What is meant by spaced practice?

Spaced practice is when you spread your review of material out over time, so that there are opportunities to forget and recall previously learned content.

 AT THE START

DIRECT TEACH: HELP STUDENTS SPACE IT OUT AND MIX IT UP

1. Explain spaced practice: Ask students to recall the wardrobe analogy and the importance of returning to the wardrobe (or previously learned content) to tidy it. This serves to move knowledge (behaviours and ways of thinking) to long-term memory from the working memory. Reviewing information is a way to return to the wardrobe. Each time we return, we remember things better, but we need to leave a gap in time. That's why revising (studying) something for eight hours over two weeks is more powerful than revising for eight hours in one block of time. Spaced practice is when you spread your learning out over time (rather than cramming). The power of spaced practice can also be explained using the forgetting curve.

2. Explain the forgetting curve to students. The forgetting curve demonstrates how memory is lost over time if it is not recalled. The best time to recall information is after it has been partially forgotten. In the graph below, you can see that when something is recalled, there is a forgetting curve that lessens a bit more each time, meaning that students remember more.

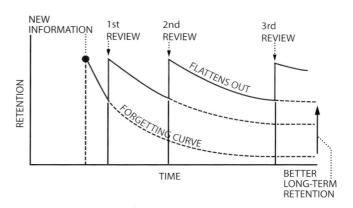

RESEARCH
The forgetting curve, which dates back to the 1880s, shows that the first time we learn something, we forget most of it quite quickly; but each time we review it, we forget less. Learn more from The Power of Forgetting in Order to Remember on page 130 of Memory: Research.

3. Mix it up: Interleaving is the process of mixing up topics while you study in order to improve recall of all material over the long term and transfer of knowledge to different contexts like new situations or problems. This is opposite to blocked practice (or cramming) whereby you study one topic thoroughly before moving on to another topic. It is recommended that the student interleave similar topics, such as chemistry with biology, various poems or different types of maths problems.

DIRECT TEACH: SETTING THE STAGE FOR INDEPENDENT LEARNING

When surveying students about the biggest obstacles they face when revising (studying), they consistently report 'distractions'. The pull, particularly of social media, is incredibly strong. One student told me, 'But even if I turn off notifications, I'll still know they are there. I'll be missing something.'

Advice for students:

1. **Put down the phone and avoid other distractions:** Share some of your own strategies, but ultimately get students to come up with their own ways to avoid distractions. Smartphones are obviously a main attention-eating culprit. I loved one student's idea to give his phone to his mum. Another student said that when she gets the urge to check for notifications, she just takes a deep breath and says, 'They're not going anywhere.' Other strategies include:

   - Turn off all notifications, put your phone on aeroplane mode or activate the 'Do Not Disturb' mode.
   - Close tabs if working on a computer.
   - Tell people that you do not want to be disturbed. (Wear headphones as a sign that you don't want company.)
   - Find a quiet place to work, preferably away from your family and friends. (For some students, this may encourage them to stay after school if home life is chaotic.) They can vary the places they revise – this helps to create desirable difficulty – but the places should be shielded from distractions.
   - Set a timer so you know when you will get to check your phone.

2. **Plan breaks:** Research shows that our brains were not meant for long periods of concentration. According to neurologist and teacher Judy Willis, our brains need breaks in order to replenish brain chemicals (neurotransmitters that carry messages from one nerve to the next as we learn) (Willis, 2016). Depending on students' ages and 'focus development', brain break frequency will vary. According to Willis: 'As a general rule, concentrated study of 10 to 15 minutes for elementary (primary) school and 20 to 30 minutes for middle and high school (secondary school) students calls for a three- to five-minute break.'

3. **Time yourself:** Encourage students to use a timer, preferably one that is not on a phone. But if they must use the phone, there are some apps for timing your productivity. Just search online for 'Pomodoro technique apps'. One that I recommend is called Focus Keeper.

What about music? Many students claim that they work better with music playing. The jury is still out on this one, but anything that draws their attention is a distraction. When I taught A level photography, I often played music or let students listen using headphones while they were working on their books. It helped them avoid unpredictable distractions (these are the worst) like other students talking. However, music is a major distraction when they spend too much time trying to find the right song or sing along with the lyrics. If they are going to listen, advise them to create a long playlist (so no finding the right song every few minutes) and include instrumental songs. For deep thought processing, though, quiet is king.

🐧 KEEP IN MIND:

Commonly used strategies like rereading or rewriting notes may have quicker returns and feel like less effort. However, research shows that with these strategies, you will remember less in the long term. **Spaced practice** and **interleaving** are worth the effort; over time, you'll remember more.

TEACHERS: SPACE IT OUT AND MIX IT UP TO PRACTISE RETRIEVAL

5-A-DAY STARTER

Begin every lesson with five questions that students must immediately answer without referring to their notes. Use a mix of recall (fill-in-the blank, name it), comprehension, analysis questions and/or process questions, such as 'If solving the following problem, what is the first thing you should consider?' Find questions from previously learned content from several months ago, weeks ago and recently. (See figure on next page.) Use previous exams, textbooks or class notes to build a bank of questions. This can also be used as a **Do Now**, a short activity always found in the same location (e.g. on the top left-hand side of the board) when students enter. *Don't make the questions too long. It's a starter.*

TEACHER TIP
For older students (secondary and high school), use the multitasking task in the Leadership section of this chapter. It's a great way to demonstrate the myth of multitasking.

'I first learned about 5-a-day from Rebecca Foster, Head of English and Associate Senior Leader at a secondary school in England, who wrote about it in her blog, *The Learning Profession* (Foster, 2016).

 AAA STRATEGY

TEACHER TIP
Be sure to vary the conditions on which to use retrieval practice, especially for other students. Ask the question in a different way or apply learning to a different context.

5-a-day

1	from MONTHS ago
2	
3	from a WEEK ago
4	from a RECENT lesson
5	

RETRIEVAL PRACTICE CHALLENGE GRID

This grid is based on a template that you make with boxes. Colour-code the boxes to represent different time periods. As you can see, this one has spaced out the retrieval questions for science over several months, leaving the oldest category (right column) open by calling it 'a long time ago'. Tailor this to your topics, ensuring to give even coverage. First inspired by teacher and writer Kate Jones, examples of challenge grids can be found online by searching 'retrieval practice challenge grid'.

RETRIEVAL PRACTICE CHALLENGE GRID

Name the different types of teeth humans have.	Why is water so important to humans?	Name the main steps of the digestive process?	What are the 4 main food groups?
How do animals get energy?	What happens to sugar left on your teeth?	Are plants producers, consumers or decomposers?	Name 3 ways we can take care of our teeth?
What is the system called that removes unnecessary waste?	Give 2 examples of a carbohydrate.	What happens in the stomach?	Why do humans sweat?

Last lesson (1 point)	Last week (2 points)	1 month ago (3 points)	Along time ago (4 points)

A FEW MORE GOOD IDEAS

- Create **assignments that incorporate learning from earlier in the course**, requiring students to recall the information rather than just look it up.
- Design **homework assignments** that test students on current content as well as content from weeks or months ago.
- Utilise the strategies in Spaced Retrieval Practice (see page 193) that space review such as 5-a-Day, Retrieval Practice Challenge and Cold Call Recall. Mix up knowledge from different topics within the same subject.

ORGANISE KEY KNOWLEDGE: EASY TO ACCESS, USE AND SHARE

A knowledge organiser (KO) is a document containing key information your students need to know to have a foundational understanding of a particular topic, including the specific details like the full definitions of terminology, dates and important diagrams. In other words, it's what you want students to be able to recall automatically in order to use their working memory for more complex tasks such as writing an essay or solving a difficult word problem. Not only are KOs an important tool for students, they are equally valuable for teachers as a planning tool because they help clarify what core knowledge the teacher wants every student to master so they can fully access the curriculum. One of the biggest mistakes is to overcrowd knowledge organisers with too much information.

What to include

Each topic should have its own knowledge organiser and each KO is usually no more than two sides of A4 (or US letter size) paper and should be clearly labelled and organised so that is easy to follow. Utilise dual coding by including labelled visuals. In maths, you may want to include mathematical processes like how to factor numbers. In English, the KO may be used to organise quotes, key characters or details about historical context.

Summary of types of information to include in knowledge organisers:

- Key ideas
- Key quotes
- Important themes
- Simple diagrams explaining a process
- Simple pictures
- Formulas
- Examples/real-world application
- Key dates or a timeline

Topic	Subject:	Year/Grade:
Prior learning: (Links to knowledge already covered)		**Curriculum links** (Links to other subjects outside this domain)
Important people (Name and what they did)		**Key vocabulary** (Word: definition next to it)
Timeline of events (Years and some details)		

EXAMPLE OF A KNOWLEDGE ORGANISER TEMPLATE
Create a template for knowledge organisers that can be adapted. A template will ensure that all knowledge organisers look the same and that information is easy to find. This also reduces irrelevant cognitive load.

EXAMPLE OF A KNOWLEDGE ORGANISER

based on template designed for Julian's Primary School. All knowledge organisers use the template.

Topics: States of Matter	Subject: Science	Year 5	Summer 1
What we learned before: Measuring temperatures; classifying materials; rocks and organic			

KEY KNOWLEDGE

States of Matter
- There are three states of matter: solids, liquids and gases. Nearly everything exists as solids, liquids or gases.

SOLID	**LIQUID**	**GAS**

• rigid	• not rigid	• not rigid
• fixed shape	• no fixed shape	• no fixed shape
• fixed volume	• fixed volume	• no fixed volume
cannot be squashed	cannot be squashed	can be squashed

Key facts
Materials can be changed from one state to another by heating or cooling.
If ice (solid) is heated, it changes to water liquid. This is called melting.
If liquid is heated, it changes to (water) vapour gas. This is called evaporation.

The water cycle
The water cycle is the complete journey that water makes, from one place to the other and from one state to the other.

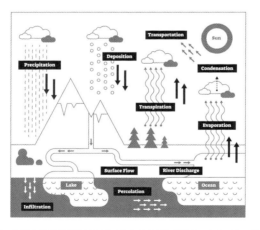

KEY VOCABULARY

Dissolve: the process of becoming a liquid from being a solid.

Exaporate: the process of becoming a gas from a liquid.

Condense: the process of becoming a liquid from gas.

Expand: to make larger or more extensive.

Soluble: able to be dissolved.

Material: the matter on which a thing can be made.

Temperature: the degree or intensity of heat present in a substance or object and shown by a thermometer or perceived by touch.

Molecules: the very tiny particles that make matter.

Chemical reaction: the process that involves the change of state.

Cycle: beginning at any point and following a path until it gets to where we started again.

Hypothesis: proposed explanation that guides further explanation.

Method: a way of doing something.

Variable: the part that changes in an experiment.

Conclusion: a summary linking back to the hypothesis.

Ways to interact with knowledge organisers

The biggest benefit is that KOs make using powerful strategies like retrieval practice and spaced practice much more manageable. Have a regular routine using KOs for recall of material covered two weeks ago, months ago, in past years. (See **5-a-day** above) Use your knowledge of the content and your understanding of your students to gauge how long the gaps should be between returning to previous content.

To utilise the research on elaboration, use how and why questions relating to the information in the knowledge organiser. Ask students to connect information in one KO to the information in another, identifying common themes and/or difference.

🐧 KEEP IN MIND:

- KOs work best when planned and created as a whole-school or whole-department initiative. Then you can easily use them to recall content learned in previous years or across subjects. Teachers in English, for example, may find it useful to refer to a KO from history or science to better understand the events in a novel.

- Make KOs student-friendly, so the learner can take advantage of using them independently or during paired peer quizzing.

- Do not allow students to access their knowledge organiser when they are tested. Retrieval practice requires that they think hard to find the answer in their long-term memory. No peeking!

- There are a lot of free downloadable KOs online, but the quality varies significantly. I often use them for ideas, but it's best to start from scratch.

SUMMARY OF CLASSROOM APPLICATION

The recommendations in this section are based on the research we've discussed in this chapter. These are general recommendations and ultimately should be coupled with your teacher expertise customised to your school context. See the following two pages for a summary of the classroom application.

PLANNING WITH MEMORY IN MIND

Prior knowledge: Tap into prior learning that relates to new learning in order to help students connect to long-term memory and help teachers plan appropriate entry points while addressing any misconceptions.

Best when:
- Used at the start of new learning
- Used daily (briefly) or regularly as a bridge between previous learning and current learning

For example: Entry Tickets; familiarity scale; KWNL charts; word scramble; Free/Cued Recall

Cognitive load: Maximise cognitive effort to process relevant information and minimise cognitive effort to process irrelevant information, all while not exceeding cognitive capacity.

Best when:
- Presenting complex concepts or new learning
- Using multimedia presentations
- Considered alongside the task difficulty and student prior knowledge

For example: Concrete examples; worked examples; visible memory aids; cutting out nonessential information; taking breaks

Attention: Prepare for limited attention spans.

Best when:
- The lesson includes lengthy teacher explanation or complex problem solving

For example: Plan prediction questions; take a break or pause the lesson, using signposting, novelty and following up with answers on prediction questions

Spaced practice: Breaking up practice or review of material of a topic into a number of short sessions – over a longer period of time, rather than massed practice.

Best when:
- There is a wide range of material that requires information from memory
- There is adequate time to recall previously learned content several times
- Used alongside retrieval practice

For example: 5-a-day, challenge quizzes

Interleaving: Mix up topics during retrieval in order to improve recall of all material over the long term

Best when:
- Mixing up different but similar items
- Working on motor skill acquisition (like learning to play basketball)
- Problem solving, such as in maths and science
- Used as a review technique (mixing up types of problems for homework)

For example: Review similar topics together

Varied conditions: Altering the conditions under which practice happens, thus removing cues that aid surface-level recall

Best when:
- Students become more expert in particular content

For example: Change the wording of questions, modality of teaching (e.g. discussion then debate), seating arrangements or even location. Varying conditions also relates to spaced practice because you are typically varying time of day and place when students are practising retrieval.

HIGH IMPACT LEARNING STRATEGIES

Retrieval practice: Recall previous learning information from long-term memory

Best when:
- Working with a wide range of material that requires information from memory (facts, concepts, and skills)
- Younger students may require more scaffolding and more opportunities for success
- Used alongside spaced practice

For example: Low-stakes quizzes, Brain Dump, Cold Call Recall, flashcards, interactive note-taking

Dual coding: Combine verbal information with visuals to maximise retention and minimise cognitive load. Visuals, or visual metaphors, are also useful; they are pictures that represent something else, like a word or concept or process.

Best when:
- Images are simple, helping to illustrate a point (rather than decorative)
- Used with image-friendly text, such as vocabulary or processes
- Focused on comprehension when reading, especially for beginners

For example: Co-locate pictures and text. Use visual information like diagrams and infographics; Question, Draw, Explain and Label strategy

Chunking: Group small pieces of information into large, more meaningful pieces of information that can be held more easily in working memory. Or create multiple subgroups of a large body of information.

Best when:
- Brainstorming, planning, reviewing previously learned content
- Information can utilise compare/contrast; sequencing; cause/effect and hierarchies

For example: Model different approaches; visual mapping (graphic organisers, concepts maps and mind maps)

Mnemonic devices: Use shortcuts or mental tools to help hold a large volume of new material in memory, queuing it up ready for recall.

Best when:
- Trying to memorise information by rote when the information does not connect to our prior knowledge
- Using visual imagery and locations

For example: acronyms, method of loci, acrostics, rhymes and songs

Storytelling: Using the narrative structure of a story to teach or review information

Best when:
- Used for comprehension of material that lends itself (with some creative license) to a narrative structure
- It complements the content of the lesson
- Students need a break from routine

For example: Relate content to stories; make content sound like a story (with a story structure)

Elaboration: Adding details to memories and integrating new information with prior knowledge

Best used when:
- Studying general facts about a topic
- Reading or solving problems, for example in maths or science

Examples: Asking how the material relates to life experience; Each One, Teach One; asking why and how questions; Mix and Mingle

MEMORY: LEADERSHIP

Memory: Leadership
and professional learning

When leaders teach teachers about memory, the benefits are exponential.

Good leaders know the value of understanding memory – the foundation of learning that shapes how one sees and interacts with the world. Not only should it inform classroom practice, but the understanding of how humans learn should guide professional learning and long term planning.

Educators of learners from across different age groups will take a slightly different approach to utilising memory strategies, yet all learners benefit when their teachers have a solid understanding of this fascinating field of learning.

CONNECT TO RESEARCH
See Why Does Memory Matter (So Much in Teaching) on page 115 for more talking points about the importance of memory and knowledge.

As with Relationships and Memory, this section includes **Professional learning: at the start** for ideas on how to introduce concepts and research to your staff and **Professional learning: keep it going**, which outlines suggestions for maintaining and developing educators' capacity to implement these strategies throughout the year. Together these two parts provide multiple experiences for leaders to model, practise and share the research and application of cognitive science.

PROFESSIONAL LEARNING: AT THE START

HOW MEMORY WORKS

Our cognitive architecture is complex. We explain it here with models and metaphors.

HOW MEMORY WORKS: THE KEY PLAYERS

Over the past several decades, cognitive scientists have developed simple models of memory that help explain how memory works. Since memory is central to learning, it's important for teachers to understand how we can maximise the memory potential for our students.

1. **Prepare** by making copies of the Memory Task (page 156) on slips of paper (one per participant) and copies or a projection of the Memory Model (below) and the wardrobe (page 157).

2. **Explain** the key players of the Memory Model; use the prompts below to point to the specific key players in the Memory Model:

   - Cognitive scientists see learning as moving information from your working memory (WM) to your long-term memory (LTM), where it is stored for future use.

   - First, we have the environment, where there is a lot of sensory information (information from our senses) that is briefly stored in sensory memory. We pay attention to a small part of that. That part goes into short-term memory.

   - Our WM processes that information. This is what we do when we are thinking. Working memory can hold information for a short period of time.

   - Lastly, we have our long-term memory, which has potentially unlimited capacity. The WM will retrieve information from the LTM when it needs it to think, as shown below. The working memory also transfers some information into the LTM.

   - So...one way of thinking about learning is that it is the moving of information from our WM to LTM.

3. **Debrief:** How might understanding the key players in memory benefit your teaching practice?

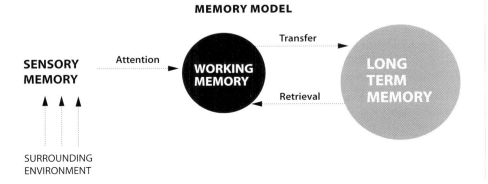

MEMORY MODEL

SENSORY MEMORY → Attention → WORKING MEMORY → Transfer → LONG TERM MEMORY

Retrieval

SURROUNDING ENVIRONMENT

CONNECT TO RESEARCH
Understanding the difference between episodic and semantic memory helps teachers to distinguish memories that are tied to an event (episodic) and memories that can be recalled and transferred (semantic). We suggest coming back to this at a later point in the year. See page 116 for a closer look.

Talking points:

- 'Let's consider the example (discussed in Memory: Research earlier) of a person receiving the directions for a journey. They will have used their working memory to follow along as directions were given, retrieving information from long-term memory to help them with directions, knowledge of streets and places and the concept of distance.'

- 'If a person has to do the same journey again and again, they will remember it well (it will move to the LTM). Otherwise, it will quickly fade.'

- 'Furthermore, if too many directions are given at once, the working memory will become overloaded, but we'll get to that later.'

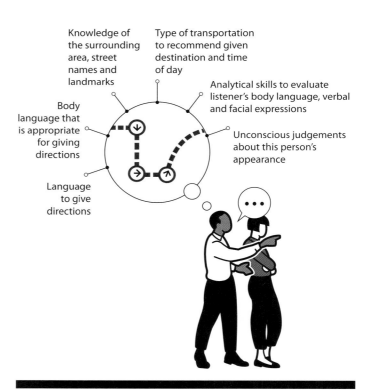

GIVING DIRECTIONS

Knowledge of the surrounding area, street names and landmarks

Type of transportation to recommend given destination and time of day

Analytical skills to evaluate listener's body language, verbal and facial expressions

Body language that is appropriate for giving directions

Unconscious judgements about this person's appearance

Language to give directions

EXTENSION: We outline steps for teaching students about Memory in Direct Teach: What Makes Memories Stick in the Memory: Classroom section on page 155. This strategy could be easily adapted for staff, providing a great opportunity to model how teachers could teach it to students.

THE JIGSAW METHOD

Since the Jigsaw Method has such a high effect rating (Hattie, 2011), we recommend you use it when turnkeying research to your staff. This is a great way to model the strategy so that educators feel more comfortable using with their students. Please refer to Relationships: Leadership on page 96 for instructions on how to facilitate it. Use the Jigsaw Method Content Guide below to adapt the Jigsaw Method to the teaching of memory.

Please refer to Relationships: Leadership on page 96 for instructions on how to facilitate it.

  SPOTLIGHT

FACILITATOR TIP
Don't forget to look for the spotlight icon to find our suggestions for expert group topics.

JIGSAW METHOD CONTENT GUIDE

TOPIC: RELATIONSHIPS	
EXPERT GROUP TOPICS	**FACILITATOR TALKING POINTS**
Choose approximately five from the list: • Working memory capacity • Poor working memory • Cognitive load theory and irrelevant load • The importance of retrieval • The power of forgetting • The illusion of knowing* • Retrieval practice* • Spaced practice* *Especially relevant for older students	• Cognitive load theory is not a perfect science, but a reminder of the importance of the working memory's limited capacity. • All of our students have different working memories. The goal is not to increase working capacity. (We can't.) The goal is to maximise memory by using effective teaching and learning strategies, such as retrieval practice and spaced practice. • When we have to think hard about something, we are more likely to remember it. That extra effort helps us to retain the information. This is why things like quizzing and self-testing help you remember information – because you need to think hard about it.
GUIDING QUESTIONS FOR JIGSAW GROUP	
Choose a relevant question, based on your Expert Group Topics. Or make up your own. • What are the three most important things we learned about working memory and cognitive load? • In what way will this research inform your teaching? What actions will you take? • Based on what you have learned, what information about memory do you think students also need to know? How would you teach this?	• Getting students to recall what they already know taps into their prior knowledge and this makes the new learning stick better. • This information will quickly fade, however, if we don't have to recall it again. Additionally, you can give staff the Planning With Memory in Mind on page 198 as a handout. This is a summary of the practical application of cognitive load.

PUTTING MULTITASKING TO THE TEST

This is a great strategy to help people feel the effects of cognitive overload from 'multitasking' (which is actually task switching) and staying focused on a task. The

> Don't confuse the effort it takes to multitask, which is inefficient and doesn't lead to learning, with the effort required for desirable difficulties, as occurs during retrieval practice and interleaving, which does lead to learning.

activity also helps to simulate what split-attention effect feels like. **Split attention** is a common occurrence in classrooms, where students are often requested to process information from two or more sources at the same time in order to solve a problem.

1. **Prepare** by gathering a piece of paper for each participant and a few extra pens, available if needed. Hand out a piece of paper to all participants.

2. **Explain the multitasking activity:** participants will take part in a brief experiment to demonstrate cognitive load theory.

3. **Round 1:**

   a. **Explain** that participants will write down the numbers 1 to 21 horizontally and then, underneath that, write WE ALL LOVE MULTITASKING. See 'Round 1' below. You will time them, counting the seconds aloud when you notice people finishing. Ask them to look up at you when they are finished and jot down their time.

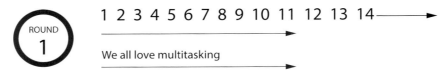

   b. **Start Round 1** and set the stopwatch. As participants look up, start to count aloud so they are aware of how long it took them. Remind participants to write down their number of seconds when done.

4. **Round 2:** Participants write down the same numbers and letters, but this time alternating between the two so they will write 1, then W underneath it, then 2, then E underneath the 2, etc. The final result will look the same.

   a. Tell them to look at you when they are finished. Do the same as above with the timing.

5. **Debrief:** What did that feel like? Which task took longer or seemed more challenging? Why might the second one have been harder?

Talking points:

- As we switch from task to task, new goals and rules have to be brought into the working memory to re-engage with each task. Depending on the complexity of the tasks involved and the time available to complete them, performance can suffer.

- Research shows that even having the TV on in the background produces less effective homework. According to some studies, multitasking can reduce our productivity by 40% (American Psychological Association, 2006).

- To do something well, it is best for your brain to focus on one task at a time. Our brains just weren't designed to 'multitask' cognitive tasks. (A more accurate term to describe what our brains are doing would be 'multi-switching'.)
- Multitasking is most depleting to our productivity when we are completing higher order tasks, such as writing a persuasive essay, completing complex maths problems or rehearsing lines for drama.

Transition: 'Now that we have explored how memory works, let's move on to putting that understanding into practice.'

CLASSROOM APPLICATIONS THAT MAXIMISE MEMORY

ADOPT, ADAPT OR ADD

In Adopt, Adapt or Add (AAA) staff are asked to engage with classroom strategies and decide whether they would like to either **Adopt** a strategy *as is* for their classrooms, **Adapt** it to better fit their classroom context or **Add** a different, related strategy they could share with the group. For consistency and practice, we use the same strategy for the Leadership sections in Relationships, Memory and Mindset. See Relationships: Leadership on page 100 for detailed steps to facilitate this. There are three different ways to facilitate Adopt, Adapt and Add. Choose the one that works best for you!

Materials and setup:

For this section, pick about four or five strategies from the Memory: Classroom section. Some strategies that we have found are liked by teachers and work well with Adopt, Adapt or Add have been marked using this symbol ◉. We will call these our AAA (for Adopt, Adapt or Add) strategies. Facilitators may decide to use some of their own ideas or strategies from other parts of Memory: Classroom to better match the school context. (There is a summary of the high-impact learning strategies on page 199 of Memory: Classroom. Give this to staff as resource.)

FACILITATOR TIP
Don't forget to look for the AAA icon to find our suggestions for this activity.

RECOMMENDED READING
For a series of student-friendly videos and teacher blogs explaining learning strategies, see The Learning Scientists at www.learningscientists.org

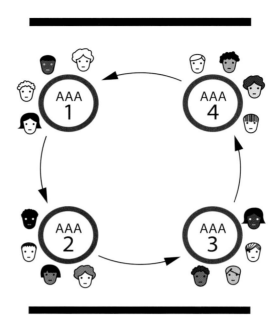

PROFESSIONAL LEARNING: KEEP IT GOING

SHARE PROGRESS AND NEW IDEAS

TEACHER FEATURES

Teacher features are 10- to 15-minute presentations by staff who share a classroom strategy they have implemented. They can be done during morning briefings, at the start of staff meetings or any other time when the whole staff convenes.

Guiding questions for staff:

- What strategy did I implement?
- Why did I do it? 'I wanted students to...'
- How did I evaluate it? 'I noticed that...'; 'Student surveys showed...'
- What did I learn? 'I learned that I should...'; 'Next time, I would change...'

Remember that this is an opportunity for staff to share what they have learned. Encourage staff to share challenges, misconceptions and mistakes as well as successes. Acknowledge that these strategies take practice and that you encourage staff members' continued professional risk-taking and perseverance, even when the strategies don't go as planned at first.

MODEL SPACED RETRIEVAL PRACTICE

Use the content from this professional learning session and other relevant content (other aspects of professional learning at your school) to create short quizzes based on previously covered topics. Be explicit that you are modelling a highly effective learning strategy. 5-a-day and Challenges Quizzes (on page 194) work well for this. Throw in a funny one from time to time from an event that happened at school or in the news.

LEARNING STRATEGIES

Use learning strategies in Memory: Classroom to introduce new ideas to teachers. Provide handouts or templates for staff so that the resources are easy to use and/or adapt. Follow this up by asking teachers if you can visit their classroom while they do the activity.

EDUCATOR STUDY GROUPS

Teacher study groups are made up of staff members who meet regularly to discuss a topic. Leadership can help support staff in forming study groups by providing space, a format and resources, such as short articles or videos that can drive discussion. You can find a list of resources in Recommended Readings and Resources on page 318.

 KEEP IN MIND:

As you share progress and new ideas, help teachers manage their own memory efficiency and cognitive load:

- Be aware of the number of new initiatives and processes staff need to learn, especially novice teachers and those new to the school.
- Create systems that are consistent and resources that are easy to find.
- Use the guidelines in Memory: Classroom to reduce irrelevant information in presentation slides and documents.
- Use spaced retrieval practice to help staff remember the key concepts and strategies introduced in the professional learning session. (See suggestions above.)
- Encourage lots of practice!

→ MINDSET

MINDSET: RESEARCH

Mindset: Research
worth knowing

Our attitude to learning is informed by experience, empowered by reflection and focused on setting us up for success.

AUTHENTIC, EXPLICIT AND INCREMENTAL

In a French class at Dunraven School in south London, the teacher greets students as they enter the room and stand directly behind their desks. 'Bonjour la classe,' says Jennie Prescott to her Year 7 (6th grade) students. They know the routine: before they sit down, they must ask a question in French, a daily practice in Jennie's class. Some students struggle at first to remember how to start; some ask for a word in French to keep the conversation going when Jennie adds a follow-up question. There are pauses; students wait for their peers as they try out this new language. Jennie happily supports with hints to help them recall phrases or with new words that she scribes on the board. One by one, each student earns the right to sit down – not by providing a perfect question or correct response to Jennie's follow-up questions, but by having a go.

To ultimately learn French, Jennie knows that her students, many of whom may have feared making a mistake in front of peers, need to practise taking risks and confidently 'playing with' their knowledge of this new language. 'It's no coincidence that many of these Year 7 students went on to achieve very successful outcomes at GCSE (exams),' says Jennie. The entire department adopted a new approach to teaching that encouraged students to see the classroom as a safe and secure environment which fostered spontaneous talk and the confidence to respond, even if they did not fully understand the question or have all the requisite vocabulary to provide an answer. This shift necessitated that teachers and students explicitly talked about how we learn and they practised routines (such as this one) that could be repeated and normalised, Jennie explains, 'and this provided a structure students needed'.

Like many schools, this one has inspirational quotes adorning the corridors and posters reminding students to embrace challenge and work hard. While visible reminders of values are an element of creating a school-wide culture, Jennie recognises that any message the school sends needs to connect to classroom content. She finds moments during her lesson to point to a poster she created with her class – a brainstorm of what it takes to learn a new language. They came up with 'lots of practice; getting it wrong and knowing it's OK; looking for connections'. Students are practising these habits of learning every day. Jennie says her lessons are part and parcel of our whole-school approach to developing a learning mindset.

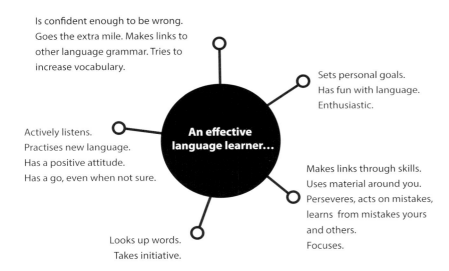

Is confident enough to be wrong. Goes the extra mile. Makes links to other language grammar. Tries to increase vocabulary.

An effective language learner...

Sets personal goals. Has fun with language. Enthusiastic.

Actively listens. Practises new language. Has a positive attitude. Has a go, even when not sure.

Makes links through skills. Uses material around you. Perseveres, acts on mistakes, learns from mistakes yours and others. Focuses.

Looks up words. Takes initiative.

CLASS BRAINSTORM
Re-created using the same words and phrases Jennie and her students used to create a mind map of 'What an effective language learner is.'

WHAT IS MEANT BY LEARNING MINDSET?

According to the Merriam-Webster dictionary, a mindset is 'a particular way of thinking: a person's attitude or set of opinions about something'. A mindset about learning, therefore, is a particular way of thinking about learning. Students who have what we call a **learning mindset** have an understanding that learning is a process (it takes time and effort, for example) and a belief that they have control over their own learning ('If this doesn't work, I'll try another way'). Learning is something they do, not something that is done to them. In the classroom, then, when one practises a learning mindset, they recognise that to get better at something necessitates perseverance, practice, effort and awareness that we make decisions throughout the learning process as we plan, monitor and evaluate.

Just as we don't jump from the bottom of the stairs to the top, learning is a step-by-step journey. We can explain this to children, showing them videos of famous failures and putting up posters as reminders, but that's not good enough. A learning mindset means that you have experienced and reflected on your own learning journey and the steps you've taken along the way. As educators, we play a pivotal role in cultivating our students' learning mindsets. It's up to us to educate students about the process of

> Bandura found that people with high self-efficacy viewed difficult tasks as challenges to be mastered, set challenging goals, sustained their efforts and attributed failure to insufficient effort.

learning in general, teach them strategies that put them in the driver's seat of their own learning experiences and ensure opportunities for reflection.

HISTORY OF MINDSET

The concept of mindsets has its roots in a long history of educationalists examining self-beliefs and how these beliefs impact our learning. One of the first researchers to gain prominence in this arena was Albert Bandura, Professor Emeritus at Stanford University, who is widely regarded as one of the greatest living psychologists. In the 1970s, Bandura (1977) used the term **self-efficacy** to refer to one's belief or personal judgement about the likelihood that they can reach task-specific goals. ('Do I think I can learn to ride a bike? Yes.') Based on decades of robust research into self-belief, Bandura found that a person with high self-efficacy approached tasks differently than someone with low self-efficacy, or doubts in their capabilities (Bandura, 1994).

Bandura found that people with high self-efficacy viewed difficult tasks as challenges to be mastered, set challenging goals, sustained their efforts and attributed failure to insufficient effort. Those with low self-efficacy, on the other hand, shied away from tasks that they saw as difficult, set low aspirational goals, dwelled on personal deficiencies when faced with obstacles and gave up quickly. Another key difference between high and low self-efficacy learners was a person's approach to threatening situations: when one had high self-efficacy, they would approach a threatening situation with assurance that they could exercise control over it whereas they were slow to recover from setbacks if they had low self-efficacy (Bandura, 1994). Bandura (1997) reminds us, 'Self-belief does not necessarily ensure success, but self-disbelief assuredly spawns failure.'

Self-efficacy is one's belief or personal judgement about the likelihood that they can reach task-specific goals.

Carol Dweck, Professor of Psychology at Stanford University, is another major player in understanding mindsets, with research spanning over four decades across numerous ages, socioeconomic status and institutions, sport, education and business (Dweck and Yeager, 2019). Dweck popularised the terms **growth mindset** and **fixed mindset** in her book *Mindset: The New Psychology of Success* (Dweck, 2016a) to help explain two different attitudes a person can have toward learning (believing – or not – that capabilities can change). Like Bandura, Dweck asserts that our belief about our abilities influences how we approach learning. She further argues that a growth mindset helps students persevere when faced with challenges. Having a growth mindset involves decision making and coping skills when learning specific tasks. In contrast, a fixed mindset – believing that we are born with a fixed amount of ability or intelligence – leads people to easily give up, or settle for tasks that are too easy (Dweck, 2016a).

Recently, there's been controversy surrounding the growth mindset concept, as many schools have oversimplified its application, reducing their efforts to posting catchy quotes, over-emphasising praise for effort or insinuating that one only need to chant 'I can do it' to *'become growth mindset'*. Amongst other misapplications, what got lost in the mix was the crucial role of decision making and monitoring one's learning during a specific learning experience, often referred to as 'metacognition', which we discuss in more detail later in this chapter. Cera et al. (2013), in their research into the connection between self-efficacy and metacognition, state, 'The relationships between self-efficacy and metacognitive skills allow students to foster a high level of confidence in their own abilities, encouraging them to have a positive approach to learning and to consider the difficulties as challenges rather than threats to be avoided.' With more practical advice available, educators have begun to implement more metacognitive strategies alongside mindset initiatives. Additionally, the long-standing and extensive research on the powerful impact of goal attainment by Edwin A Locke and Gary P Latham (2002) and deliberate and purposeful practice by Anders Ericsson (Ericsson, 2006; Ericsson and Pool, 2016) have enriched more recent conversations.

WHAT DOES A LEARNING MINDSET LOOK LIKE?

Below are examples of how students practise a learning mindset in the classroom setting, based on real experiences:

- Mohammed, age five, did not like to write when he came to school. His parents told his teacher that he just found it hard and was embarrassed and frustrated in class when his peers could hold a pencil without a problem. His teacher started to talk during circle time about the importance of **practice** using real-life examples. Mohammed started to try a **little harder** and used a writing guide to **check** his letters. His teacher pointed out his **effort** toward the small improvements he was making. Mohammed started to practise more and can now write his name.

- Leah's history teacher had asked the class to prepare a report on the of the key events of the American Civil Rights Movement. To plan this, Leah **reflected** on what she already knew about the topic and what she'd need to find out to write the report. She **decided** to go back to her notes twice and highlight key information, knowing that sometimes she struggles to organise her writing. Then Leah **remembered** that her teacher gave them a graphic organiser to sequence events. She **used this to organise** herself. When she finished, she **read through her work again** and reflected on the experience. Leah noticed she's getting better at report writing.

- In maths, Jamal was asked to explain to the class how he solved a problem. He got toward the end of his explanation and **realised** he got the wrong answer. **He thought to himself**, 'I can do this. Let's go back and check.' He **re-checked his steps** and compared it to a worked example on the wall. Aha. Jamal **realised** where he had made a mistake. The teacher asked the class, 'How many of you made the same mistake?' Ten hands went up. Jamal explained what he'd **do differently** next time. The teacher thanked him for sharing this learning opportunity to the class.

MINDSETS VARY
A learning mindset will look different depending on the developmental stage of the students and learning episode. However, students that develop such a mindset share a common understanding that their behaviours and decisions can improve their learning.

Mohammed   Leah   Jamal

WHY DOES A LEARNING MINDSET MATTER?

Does an attitude toward learning really have a significant impact on student success? The answer is yes...and no.

IMPACT ON LEARNING

An attitude to learning, or mindset, has an impact when it leads to certain behaviours, actions and strategies needed for successful learning. (I may really want to get good at tennis, but it's to no avail if I keep holding the wrong end of the racket.) As we've already stated, a learning mindset is not simply an 'I can do it' attitude; it's an understanding of the process of learning itself.

Mindset matters because learning takes time. All students, regardless of level of achievement, typically need to be exposed to any new skill or concept at least three to five times before it has a high probability of being learned (Nuthall and Alton-Lee, 1997; Nuthall, 2007, p. 155). Students will need a variety of learning experiences and feedback over those instances of exposure. **A learning mindset helps them to persevere**.

Mindset matters because learning is tough. In our discussion of memory we recognise that the best learning strategies take the most struggle; difficulty is inevitable and, in fact, essential in order to maximise memory. The process to move information from working memory to long-term memory is repetitive and effortful, so in order to do so, learners must be able to associate effort with learning. **A learning mindset helps learners maximise memory**.

According to The University of Chicago Consortium on School Research, 'Mindsets are closely linked to perseverance and academic behaviors, which have the most direct effect on academic performance' (The University of Chicago, 2018).

A mindset matters because learning is active. Learners must make decisions and reflect on those choices. When we practise a learning mindset, we use metacognitive strategies that evidence has clearly shown have more impact on school success than intelligence (Muijs et al., 2014). **A learning mindset puts metacognition centre stage**.

The chart on the next page outlines how practising a learning mindset may lead to decisions that impact learning and how we learn to associate certain characteristics with learning.

WHEN FACED WITH	WE CHOOSE TO:	AND ASSOCIATE LEARNING WITH:
Challenges	Embrace challenges; set high goals, break down tasks	Challenge
New learning	Engage in effective effort, purposeful practice and self-talk	Effort, Practice
Prolonged difficulty	Persist through difficulty; try new strategies, take a break	Perseverance
Lack of understanding	Seek help; ask questions; start again	Resourcefulness
Mistakes	Use mistakes as an opportunity to learn; evaluate what went wrong	Resilience
Critical feedback	Listen and learn from feedback	Feedback
With all tasks, learners use metacognitive skills of planning, monitoring and evaluation and adapt their learning behaviours and strategies		Metacognition

IT'S AN ISSUE OF SOCIAL JUSTICE...

Cultivating a learning mindset for young people is an issue of social justice. Much of the research on mindset shows that socio-cognitive (or social psychological) interventions (those that aim to change beliefs or teach non-cognitive skills) have the highest impact on disadvantaged groups. In one recent US study looking at a large sample of 12,500 9th grade (Year 8) students transitioning to high school, Yeager et al. (2019) found that the most significant impact was found with students who were lower achieving. Students who underperform during this key transition period often do not recover academically, which has significant long-term effects. In a review of a number of socio-cognitive interventions (Schwartz et al., 2016b), the authors found that some groups benefited the most, such as Latinos; lowest achieving 9th graders (Year 10); black and Latino 9th graders; and lower achieving 9th graders. Likewise, systematic long-scale studies with a focus on metacognition, an important component of mindset, get high marks for impact, particularly for 'low achieving pupils' (Quigley et al., 2018). Other large scale studies have shown mindset interventions have impact across socio-economic status (Claro et al., 2016). Yeager et al. (2019) show that both low- and high-performing students were more likely to enrol in advanced placement courses if they participated in a mindset intervention that taught students how trying hard helps the brain learn. In this study, students were also asked to write letters to peers, reflecting on the strategies and hard work they used to learn new information.

Every learner is different and no single approach is a silver bullet. While research shows that mindset interventions can have a positive impact on students, particularly disadvantaged youth, addressing larger systems of oppression (racism, poverty, housing stability, etc.) is needed to fully support and gain equity for all of our students. Many of our students navigate the challenges of poverty, racism and unstable housing conditions on a daily basis. We must recognise their resilience and their range of assets that already support perseverance. Likewise, there is no substitute for creating a safe learning environment and offering effective teaching. Schools that implement mindset interventions without these elements see little or no impact (Yeager and Walton, 2011).

IT'S OUR JOB TO HELP STUDENTS TO PRACTISE A LEARNING MINDSET MORE OFTEN

There would be little point in outlining what learning mindset means if we had no influence as educators to help students develop it. The good news is that we do have an impact. Mindsets are malleable, but not through platitudes about effort and posters selling sound bites. We can't tell students to have a learning mindset; we need to show them. We can build a repertoire for how to talk about effective learning habits and create a positive classroom culture. Following on from that, we give students specific experiences that help them develop a learning mindset. For this, we take on specific strategies like getting goal-setting right and giving the most effective feedback. We take on board Bandura's call to create experiences of mastery and opportunities for our students to see people similar to them succeed through effort; we teach coping mechanisms for when learning is hard. Lastly, a learning mindset encompasses metacognitive skills which we can explicitly teach to children and they can practise and improve upon. If we incorporate these strategies into our pedagogy we can teach students how to have a learning mindset more often. Let's begin by looking at how our brain works and why this is important to developing a learning mindset.

THE NEUROSCIENCE OF LEARNING

Understanding a bit about the brain helps students to reframe how they feel about the effort they put into learning.

OUR CONSTANTLY CHANGING BRAINS

Your brain is made up of about 100 billion interconnected **nerve cells**, or neurons, that – as you learn and experience the world – are constantly firing chemical and electrical signals to each other across a gap, called a synapse. Two important things happen the more a signal fires across the synapse: (1) the pathway between those neurons becomes stronger; and (2) the signals can travel faster.

Let's take a closer look. Each neuron has three parts: dendrites, a cell body and an axon. When a student has a learning experience (like learning how to paint or read a map), neurons are activated and a signal is sent from the dendrites of one neuron down the axon, eventually reaching the end (the axon terminal) where the signal is sent to a dendrite on another neuron. In this way, information is sent from neuron to neuron, creating a pathway across the brain. As neurons fire repeatedly over time, the myelin sheath (which acts as an insulation) becomes thicker around the axon, helping the electrical signals travel faster. The more frequently these signals fire, the stronger the pathway becomes between the two neurons.

THE BASIC ANATOMY OF A NEURON

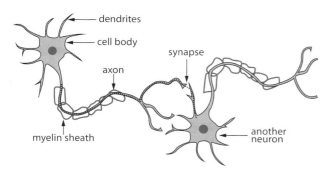

- dendrites
- cell body
- synapse
- axon
- myelin sheath
- another neuron

When we learn something new, an electrical signal travels down the brain cell's axon to the end of the dendrite and across the neural synapse to another brain cell.

Understanding how the brain works doesn't necessarily tell what works best in the classroom (that's more the role of cognitive psychology), but it does help to explain WHY repeated practice and effort make sense.

The brain is constantly changing and is in fact adaptive, or 'plastic'. The more often you do something, the stronger the pathway between neurons. For example, when learning multiplication, you strengthen the pathways associated with multiplying. There is a common saying among neuroscientists: 'Neurons that fire together wire together.' When teaching very young children about the brain, we explain that the neurons are talking to each other. If information is sent but not thought about again (e.g. you learn a highly scientific term but you never use it or hear it again), those pathways weaken. As the saying goes, 'Use it or lose it.'

LIKE A PATHWAY IN A PARK

In many ways, learning is like a dirt pathway in a park that is made by people using that route (sometimes called 'desire paths', as I learned from another teacher). The first time we learn something, it is as if we are putting footprints in the grass. It may even be hard to make your way, but the more you walk on the path the more visible that pathway becomes until eventually it is clear, wide and easy to traverse, like the signals firing in our brain. But the path in the park will become overgrown with grass if no one walks there for a while. Because we know that the brain is made up of connections, scientists tell educators that we should begin our lessons by retrieving what students already know about the topic at hand. Tapping into a student's prior knowledge is like having students think about particular pathways in the park that they've already traversed.

PATHWAY IN A PARK
Learning is a lot like forming a dirt pathway in the park. The more you walk on the path the more visible it becomes and the more quickly you can traverse it. This is a great analogy to neural pathways growing stronger each time we practise something.

It is during adolescence (starting around age 12) that human brains go through a period of heavy pruning, when the brain sheds connections it doesn't use to make processing more efficient. 'Use or lose it' is on overdrive! (Siegel, 2014) During this phase of brain development, the prefrontal cortex (PFC) also goes through dramatic development. Recall our discussion of the PFC, or thinking brain, in Relationships: Research on page 25. The PFC is the control tower, in charge of higher-order processing and executive functions such as reasoning, planning, self-regulation and abstract thinking. The more we practise thinking, using executive functioning skills, the easier it is to retrieve those habits when needed.

RECOMMENDED READING
For an in-depth look at the teenage brain, see Sarah-Jayne Blakemore's TED Talk, *The Mysterious Workings of The Teenage Brain* (2012), which explains other aspects of teen behaviour.

LEARNING AND TEACHING ABOUT THE BRAIN

'Teachers who are prepared with knowledge of the workings of the brain … can help all children build their brain potential – regardless of past performance,' writes Judy Willis in 'A Neurologist Makes the Case for Teaching Teachers About the Brain' (Willis, 2012). Barbara Oakley, author of several books and courses on how we learn, agrees that both students (and teachers) should 'know how their brains learn. It's a big motivator for [students] to know physically what is happening when they're learning' (Oakley, 2019). When students learn about the brain and how it works, they do better in school.

Neuroplasticity is the process by which our brains' neural synapses and pathways are altered as a result of life experiences. It means that our brains are constantly changing.

Two major reasons reasons to teach students about the brain: firstly, neuroplasticity – the fact that the brain is constantly changing – offers a positive message to students about their potential, especially for those who may have faced failure in the past; secondly, when children learn about the brain, they learn to associate repetition and effort (which is uncomfortable at times) with getting smarter or better rather than being 'dumb'. The authors of *Make it Stick* say it well:

> It comes down to the simple but no less profound truth that effortful learning changes the brain, building new connections and capability. The single fact – that our intellectual abilities are not fixed from birth but are, to a considerable degree, ours to shape – is a resounding answer to that nagging voice that too often asks us, 'Why bother?' We make the effort because the effort extends the boundaries of our

abilities. What we do shapes who we become and what were capable of doing. (Brown et al., 2014, p. 199)

LEARNING IS A PROCESS

Learning doesn't happen in an instant, but each instance counts.

Growing up, my mother liked to stow things away. In a box under my bed were my first attempts at writing (a story about my dad), old reports about Delaware (it's a state, in case you don't know), letters to friends (folded to hide from teachers), and an interview with my grandfather about what it was like growing up (he had an outhouse!). Later, I added things to the box, like an English essay about *Animal Farm*, short stories and a collection of news articles published in my university newspaper. Years later, as a teacher, I would bring these written artefacts to my English class, put them on a table, and ask my students to guess the identity of the writer. I loved showing young writers my journey. It was a visual depiction of the learning process – a lesson in practice and process. Students think that knowing just happens, yet everything we can do now is based on all of the incremental steps we have taken along the way in our learning process. There is a story to everything we have learned. Effective teachers help students think about learning as a journey – one that includes bumps and the desire to give up at times. Understanding the difference between learning and performing is an important distinction for both teacher and students in the pursuit of cultivating a learning mindset.

LEARNING vs PERFORMING

The best learners move between the learning and performance zone, according to co-founder and CEO of Mindset Works Eduardo Briceño, a speaker and facilitator on learning. In his TED Talk (titled *How to get better at things you care about*), he says that one of the reasons we may not improve much at a skill, despite hard work, is that we spend too much time in the performance zone, focusing on the final outcome, and not enough time on focused improvement. In other words, we prioritise right answers over understanding how to work out solutions. Spending time in the **learning zone** means you spend time in the process of learning, exploring concepts and deliberately improving your learning – for example, by practising having conversations in new language. Focusing on the process helps to get kids into a learning zone, which is where they should spend most of their time as they develop a learning mindset. The **performance zone** is about showing others what you know or have mastered, such as doing an oral report in a foreign language for the class. Performance usually signals the end of learning. When we focus only on the end point, we miss opportunities to reflect.

RECOMMENDED READING
(for students): *Learning How to Learn* by Barbara Oakley et al. (2018); *Your Fantastic Elastic Brain* by JoAnn Deak (2010). For very young children, check out ClassDojo for videos explaining the brain and the struggles of a character called Mojo.

 SPOTLIGHT

**LEARNING ZONE vs
PERFORMANCE ZONE**
In the learning zone, one focuses on the process of learning; while in the performance zone, one shows off what one knows.

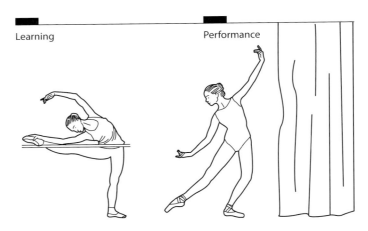

Learning   Performance

Despite this, many schools spend too much time preparing for or within the performance zone (e.g. exams). When that occurs, students cease to learn and instead focus on preparing/exhibiting what they know already. In the business and finance department of a secondary school in England, a group of teachers noticed that their students were in the performance zone way too much because of the nature of their course (which requires students to document each step for a grade). They made a decision to explain the two zones to their students and designate 'learning zone'-only time. Students were given the opportunity to genuinely try to get better at something without the pressure of performing and the teachers saw results: an increase in focus when learning (Sherrington, 2019a). Note that it's essential for students to feel comfortable in both zones, and each one has its advantages when we have a goal.

At a New York City girls' school, a group of 14- to 16-year-old girls were taught how to play darts as part of a study conducted by Barry Zimmerman and Anastasia Kitsantas (Zimmerman and Kitsantas, 1997). They were split into different teams. One team was directed to focus on **product** or outcome; they were told they should learn how to play darts by getting the best score. Another team focused on the **process** of learning; they were given lessons on technique – for example, how to throw the darts and position their bodies. There was also a third team where the **goal shifted from process to product**; once the students showed some proficiency, they were told to hit the target, thus changing their goal from practising skills (the process of learning) to demonstrating skills (the performance). The fourth team was the control group and were just told to 'do your best'.

The result? The girls in the shifting-goal group significantly outperformed the other groups. Another key factor was that half of the girls, who were asked to self-record their progress throughout, scored even higher, concluding that the metacognitive practice of recording your process benefits learning. These girls also displayed the strongest self-efficacy beliefs, the highest dart skill, the most positive self-reactions and the greatest intrinsic interest in the game.

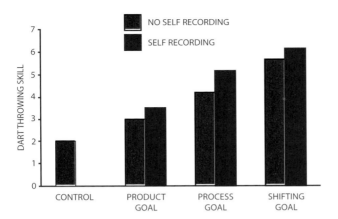

DART STUDY
Students in the shifting-goal group who self-recorded their progress outperformed the other groups. Researchers also found that the self-recording shifting goal group developed the highest levels of self-efficacy. (Zimmerman and Kitsantas, 1997)

'The takeaway from the dart experience is a straightforward one, one supported by a great number of studies,' writes Ulrich Boser in his book *Learn Better* (2017), 'because learning turns out to be a process, and method, a system of understanding. It is an activity that requires focus, planning and reflection, and when people know how to learn, they acquire mastery in much more effective ways.' In fact, Boser argues that learning methods that focused more on process (being in the learning zone) than performance significantly shifted outcomes in 'just about every field' (p. xv). Aiming for your target is important, yet the focus on improvement and the process of learning aids you most in hitting the bull's eye.

THE POWER OF PRACTICE and PERSEVERANCE

Although not the average student, Wolfgang Amadeus Mozart's success, I'm afraid, can not be put down to him being solely a gifted genius. While at only seven years of age he was astonishing audiences of symphony- goers, Mozart's expertise was more a result of 'deliberate practice' than innate talent. The same is true of a number of athletes, artists, writers and scientists, their stories covered in Anders Ericsson and Robert Pool's book *Peak: How All of Us Can Achieve Extraordinary Things* (2016), based on more than 30 years of research into the psychological nature of expertise and human performance. Ericsson, an expert on experts, coined the term **deliberate practice**, which is practice that is purposeful and systematic. This is distinct from naive practice; for example, a child repeating a task such as practising the same guitar chords. On the other hand, if they want to get better at music, according to Ericsson and Pool, this child shouldn't just practise repeatedly in his room; they should work towards a specific goal and get help from someone who is more expert and who can pinpoint what exactly they need to do to improve.

In the school setting we prefer the term **purposeful practice**, because it can apply to a number of types of learning, from cooking to swimming to writing an essay. Purposeful practice has a few essential components. According to Ericsson, these include (1) a challenging goal, (2) concentrated focus, (3) focused feedback, and (4) getting outside of your comfort zone (Ericsson and Pool, 2016, p. 15–18). Goals and feedback (covered

SPOTLIGHT

extensively in the coming pages of this section) are often at least talked about with students. **Concentrated focus** refers to paying attention to what you are trying to get better at and not falling back into just doing something automatically. This necessitates reflection – the ongoing process of monitoring our progress – and effective effort. When you engage in purposeful practice, you switch gears when needed, ask for help and feedback and use resources. In Peak, the authors remind us, 'Generally the solution is not to try harder but rather try differently. The best way to get past any barrier is to come at it from a different direction, which is one reason why it is useful to work with a teacher or coach.' Dweck concurs: 'Students need to know that if they're stuck, they don't need just effort. You don't want them redoubling their efforts with the same ineffective strategies. You want them to know when to ask for help and when to use resources that are available' (2016b, p. 19).

Getting outside of your comfort zone is incredibly difficult for students of all ages, especially teens who are constantly weighing up if the effort is worth it. To avoid plateauing, learners must push past what is comfortable. If we want to build our muscles at the gym, we can't keep lifting the same amount of weight. To get stronger, we need to add more weight to our dumbbells each visit. No pain, no gain. In fact, this metaphor is perfect for students when persuading them of the value of persevering through challenge and/or some discomfort. As we explained earlier in 'The Neuroscience of Learning', the brain also strengthens with increasing effort. This is a powerful reminder for students who might want to push themselves to practise more at drawing, redraft an essay or speak in front of the class. Educators can provide a safe environment for this to happen. 'This is a fundamental truth about any sort of practice: if you never push yourself beyond your comfort zone, you'll never improve' (Ericsson and Poole, 2016).

Purposeful practice is repeated practice that is well defined, thoughtful and feedback-driven.

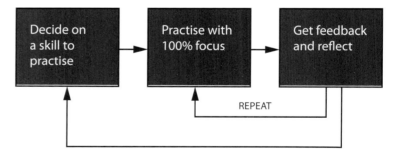

THE POWER OF SUCCESS

For some, success is seen as inevitable; for others, it may feel elusive or even unattainable. For all, it's an essential building block for a learning mindset that we must engineer for every student.

'Engineering small successes is how you get the mindset for more success. Make success the goal; make it seem possible,' writes Tom Sherrington in his blog (Sherrington, 2019b). So far, our focus has been on the process rather than the product of learning. Just to be clear: success is part of the process too. It's the endpoint, and it's paramount. In fact, one of the most effective influences on self-efficacy is 'mastery experiences', when students overcome obstacles. Bandura explains:

If people experience only easy successes, they come to expect quick results and are easily discouraged by failure. A resilient sense of efficacy requires experience in overcoming obstacles through perseverance and effort. Some setbacks and difficulties in human pursuits serve a useful purpose in teaching that success usually requires sustained effort. After people become convinced they have what it takes to succeed, they persevere in the face of adversity and quickly rebound from setbacks. By sticking it out through tough times, they emerge stronger from adversity. (Bandura, 1994)

Hence, these 'mastery experiences' help students to form a learning mindset, which in turn helps them to face challenges that arise in new learning experiences. In the 2019 Review of Research by Ofsted (the Office for Standards in Education), they conclude that 'there is a significant effect of attainment on self-belief'. In other words, 'the key to promoting positive self-belief is to ensure that pupils experience successful learning in school.' There are two more important caveats: (1) these successful moments need to be a result of effective learning habits like working hard and persevering – easy wins won't work here; and (2) Students need to reflect on these moments of success in order to identify what processes they will employ for future learning. Where do we start?

SCAFFOLD THE STRUGGLE

Years ago, I would have advised teachers to let students struggle through difficulty. Avoid, at all costs, giving the answers too quickly or asking loaded questions that have predictable responses. That said, mistakes, struggle and effort are important; but if there is too much of them, something isn't right. In *Practice Perfect*, Doug Lemov writes: 'If error is persistent and prevalent, ask yourself whether there needs to be so much of it. Why not redesign the process instead eliminating complexity or variables to make the task temporarily simpler, breaking down a chain of skills down to focus on just one, or slowing down so there's time to process the complexity and then speeding up later on' (Lemov et al., 2012). And then give students time to practise that success so that practice become permanent. Lemov refers to this as 'encoding success' (Lemov, 2010, p. 25).

Students need to experience success firsthand, and that can happen every day in many ways. In *How I Wish I'd Taught Maths*, Craig Barton writes, 'For them to truly believe they can be successful, students need to taste success for themselves, not just be told they can be successful' (Barton, 2018, p. 86). Barton makes the point that the road to success, and therefore motivation, is great teaching. In an interview with Tes (the *Times Educational Supplement* magazine), professor of psychology John Dunlosky, whose important research we put to use in Memory, suggests we manage our expectations: 'Sometimes – at least in education – people believe that simply motivating students, giving them the right mindset or grit is going to help them out, and it turns out I could develop a really motivated student who wants to achieve or thinks they can achieve, but yet if they don't have the right tools (the right strategies and the right background knowledge) they will still struggle' (Dunlosky, 2019). Therefore you give them the right strategies and opportunities to practise within the context of your content so they do well. 'Success is not generic,' writes Sherrington. 'It's very specific to each learning sequence' (2019b). And success happens is small increments as we slowly work through our goals. Using goal setting effectively within context scaffolds success.

CONNECT TO MEMORY
Mental effort contributes to cognitive load. Putting in the wrong effort that leads nowhere is not only pointless, it takes up precious working memory that could be used for other learning.

GOAL SETTING SETS THE STAGE FOR SUCCESS

Goal setting can seem tedious or even boring – we know. I can recall as a new teacher, year after year earnestly sitting down with my tutees (advisees) and writing goals on our school's official Goal Setting Day, filling in boxes that would be put somewhere central and seldom referred to again, often unfortunately forgotten completely – until the next Goal Setting Day months later. What I hadn't clocked yet was that my students needed nudges to keep on track, strategies to fight fatigue and guidance to break big goals into smaller chunks. It wasn't until years later, in my subject lessons, that I started to approach goal setting in a more systematic way (regular check-ins, a simple tracking system, etc.). These experiences, coupled with strong research on goal setting, excited me about the potential they have for supporting a learning mindset.

CLASSROOM
In Mindset: Classroom, find strategies and templates you can use with students to help them set and plan for goals and tools for keeping them on track.

We all reach goals through a 'one step at a time' process. Goals can be personal – like losing weight, learning to play the guitar or saving to buy a car – or they can be professional – relating to performance management, marking papers on time or learning a new skill. However, the real value in setting goals is not in the goal itself, but in the process that one goes through to reach that goal and the level of awareness of that process. This awareness of the process supports the development of a learning mindset and is an opportunity to reinforce metacognitive skills. The goal setting process starts with setting the right goal (more about this later) and then planning the steps (small and incremental). Lastly, monitoring and reflecting on the whole process impacts future thoughts, behaviours and actions.

SUCCESS: WHAT IT REALLY LOOKS LIKE

What people think it looks like.   What it really looks like.

Although most of the substantive research on goals comes from occupational settings, there has been a lot written about goals within the field of education. American psychologist Edwin Locke and his colleague Gary Latham have researched goal setting over more than four decades, looking at over 100 different tasks and 40,000 participants in at least eight countries. They know a thing or two about goals, and their conclusions are backed up by a dozen studies all pulling apart the role of goal setting in motivation, learning and performance (Latham and Locke, 1991). According to Latham and Locke, goals affect performance in four ways. Goals:

1. **Help with focus** by directing attention and effort towards activities that are relevant to reaching that goal – and away from irrelevant activities.

2. **Lead to greater effort overall**. In fact, challenging goals lead to greater effort than easy goals. They have an energising function.

3. **Encourage persistence** to stick with something.

4. **Affect which strategies we use**, pushing us to retrieve information or seek out new knowledge or skills.

PROMISING GOALS, NOT EMPTY PROMISES

 SPOTLIGHT

Setting goals is an obvious learning mindset tool – if done well. Students of all ages can have goals (learning to write your name, reading bigger books or building your own website). And there is nothing more exciting than seeing children reach their goal. Setting the right goal is important. Research shows that people who have more challenging (but realistically attainable) goals perform better than those who set less challenging goals for themselves. According to Locke and Latham's extensive research, in order for a learner to be motivated and increase productivity, goals need to have the following six characteristics: clarity, challenge, commitment, feedback, complexity and context. Strong goals have three other key elements that teachers should know:

- **Type of goal:** while both learning and performance goals are important, and performance goals can be motivating (students may work hard to get a good grade), students should be working more of the time in the learning zone and setting learning goals. These are those small, incremental goals that I neglected to monitor as a new teacher.

- **Method of monitoring goals:** students benefit from some type of monitoring. In fact, they crave it. Have you ever sat down and taught a GCSE (exam-level) student how to make a revision (study) calendar that they can actually use? It's like you've told them some ancient secret. After coaching one Year 11 (10th grade) student for almost a year, she recently told me the most important thing I did was help her fill in a calendar and ask her how it was going each week. A tool that may seem so obvious to an adult can be a mystery to a young person.

- **Incremental goals:** research overwhelmingly shows that students who set specific and proximal goals (smaller incremental goals leading to a main one) for themselves display superior achievement and perceptions of personal efficacy (Shapiro, 1984, cited in Zimmerman, 2002; Locke and Latham, 2002).

BUILDING BLOCKS: GOAL SUCCESS and METACOGNITION

Goal attainment is one of the building blocks of a learning mindset. According to Locke and Latham and consistent with Bandura, studies whereby participants have been taught metacognition and self-regulation skills, such as how to think through solutions and to overcome obstacles, showed that self-regulation training helped them reach their goal and improved overall self-efficacy. They gained a greater sense of control and influence over their behaviours. Thus, another building block is metacognition and it's our role, as educators, to give goal setting priority and make metacognition explicit to learners. Zimmerman's research led to his conclusion: 'Each self-regulatory process or belief, such as goal setting, strategies, and self-evaluation, can be learned from instruction and modelling by parents, teachers, coaches and peers' (Zimmerman, 2002).

RELATIONSHIPS | MEMORY | **MINDSET**

METACOGNITION: A CLOSER LOOK

Students who hone their metacognitive skills do better in school. Teachers play a crucial role in modelling and managing this skill on a daily basis.

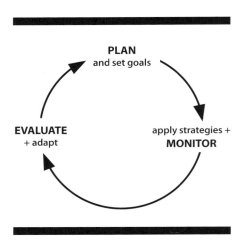

PLAN
and set goals

apply strategies +
MONITOR

EVALUATE
+ adapt

RECOMMENDED READING

These two free resources give practical advice all teachers will want to know: The Sutton Trust EEF Guidance Report *Metacognition and Self-regulated Learning* (Quigley et al., 2018) at www.bit.ly/2YZvdqE and 'Getting Started with Metacognition' from Cambridge Assessment International Education at www.bit.ly/2nv6Ump

Often thought of as 'thinking about thinking', **metacognition** is more accurately described as actively monitoring one's own learning. This is not a new concept. John Flavell (1976, cited in Fisher, 1998) introduced the term 'metacognition' as a result of his research in the 1970s; and since then, metacognition has been studied extensively to better understand its impact on learners. Dignath and Büttner's (2008) meta-analyses – based on real classroom contexts from 49 studies in primary schools and 35 in secondary schools – gave metacognition strategies high marks compared to other interventions (with an effect size of 0.69). The results of more recent studies and their significant impact on learning provide clear evidence that metacognition increases academic achievement, according to Daniel Muijs (now Deputy Director, Research and Evaluation at Ofsted) and his colleagues in a report on teacher effectiveness (Muijs et al., 2014). In *The Ingredients of Great Teaching*, Pedro De Bruyckere writes, 'There is a closer correlation between school success and metacognition than there is between school success and intelligence, something which led Muijs and his colleagues to conclude that metacognition can compensate for "cognitive limitations"' (De Bruyckere, 2018). The Sutton Trust's Education Endowment Foundation (EEF) has most recently brought metacognition and self-regulation to light by highlighting them in a recent guidance report on recommendations for implementing metacognitive strategies, drawing on a review of extensive evidence by Muijs and Christian Bokhove at the University of Southampton and their findings that these strategies account for an average of seven months of progression (Quigley et al., 2018).

THE BIG REVEAL

When I talk to adults about metacognition, I begin with a broken vacuum (a picture of it, that is) and ask, 'What would you do if your hoover was broken?' (Living in England, I've learned to call vacuums 'hoovers'). Someone always says they would kick it, but most people take a more measured approach. They might begin by opening it up to see if anything is caught in it, perhaps checking to see if it's plugged in or if a fuse is blown. (If not, a kick might be useful. I once fixed a printer that way.) These are basic troubleshooting strategies, each decision informing the next. After a while, they might evaluate whether it's time to buy a new hoover. This is a classic, everyday example of **metacognitive regulation**: planning, monitoring and evaluating our learning. This metacognitive regulation is informed by **metacognitive knowledge**, or what we know about: ourselves ('I can usually fix things that break'); the task ('I understand the basics of how a hoover operates'); and strategies ('When something breaks, I usually find a video online to help'). As adults, we are so used to this kind of thinking that we are hardly aware we are doing it, and even less aware that young people are still developing these important metacognitive skills. We have the gift of age (acquired metacognitive skills) and the **curse of knowledge** (being unaware of how much we know compared to what students may know). Our job as educators is to help students notice and articulate the strategies they use to solve problems, both successful and unsuccessful, and reflect on that process.

Successful learners use a learning mindset to tap into their metacognitive knowledge of self, task and strategies as they engage in any learning experience. Recall the case of Leah, from the beginning of this chapter. She was preparing a report on the American Civil Rights Movement. Leah might know she finds organising reports to be difficult, especially organising paragraphs (knowledge of self); she will know the task will require a chronological order (knowledge of the task); and she remembers halfway through that she can use a graphic organiser to help organise the information (knowledge of strategies for task). Leah will also use metacognitive regulation. This includes planning how to approach the task at hand ('What should I do first?'), monitoring the progress and the strategies being used ('Did I choose the best graphic organiser for this task?') and, lastly, evaluating the outcome and overall process ('How did I do?'). In a final reflection stage, Leah may consider how that experience relates to her understanding of the process of learning. Metacognitive knowledge and metacognitive regulation are linked and influence each other as the learner completes a task. 'Metacognitive thinkers change both their understandings and their strategies and they exhibit a sense of control over their learning. The clearest definitions of metacognition emphasize its nature as a process or cycle,' writes Barbara J. Millis (2016), educationalist and author of several books on learning. As Leah monitors her thinking, for example, she is making changes to her own learning behaviours and strategies – 'This is working. I'll use this method again.'

The **curse of knowledge** refers to being unaware of how much we know compared to what students may know. This applies to both metacognitive skills and knowledge we have stored in our long-term memory.

METACOGNITION IN ACTION
As students independently progress through a specific task (planning, monitoring and evaluation), they make decisions based on their knowledge of the task, strategies and self.

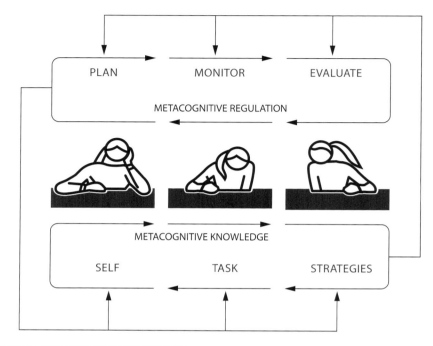

HOW TO IMPROVE METACOGNITION

The good news is that there is plenty of research indicating that we can teach metacognitive regulation to students through explicit instruction, lots of modelling and practice. Several large studies have taken on the task of researching the 'how' of teaching metacognition. Below is a list of recommendations based on Dignath and Büttner (2008), Hattie (2011), Hattie et al. (1996), the Sutton Trust EEF Guidance Report *Metacognition and Self-regulated Learning* (Quigley et al., 2018) and *Getting Started with Metacognition* from Cambridge Assessment International Education (no date).

Evidence-informed recommendations for improving metacognitive skills:

- MODELLING: Modelling metacognitive thinking to help learners develop their metacognitive and cognitive skills.
- EXPLICIT INSTRUCTION: Explaining what is meant by metacognition (or thinking about how we learn); explicitly teaching students metacognitive strategies; and embedding metacognitive instruction into content areas, rather than teaching as a separate 'study skill'.
- VERBALISATION: Verbalising metacognitive talk in the classroom; supporting students to strengthen their articulation skills in a safe environment.
- DIFFERENTIATION: Considering the appropriate level of challenge and need for guidance for the learner's developmental level (generally speaking, younger students need more scaffolding for this content).
- SELF TALK: Infusing self-talk strategies help learners reframe thinking to impact their attitude and regulate emotion to cope with difficulty.

MODELLING: MODELLING IS A MUST

SPOTLIGHT

The best teachers know what they know and show how they think through modelling. Modelling is the vehicle for sharing the teacher's learning process with students. When we model our thinking, we let learners inside our heads so that they can understand what expert thinking sounds like. One example offered by Ellis et al. (2013) using a Think Aloud is below:

> A teacher might say the following while modelling a strategy for solving a one-step algebra equation: 'The first step is to identify the unknown variable...there it is, x. Now I look to see if there is a coefficient greater than 1. Yes, the coefficient in this equation is 2. I can go to the next step.'

> Teachers can use an I Learned Statement to conclude Think Aloud modelling ... In keeping with the algebra example, a teacher might summarise her learning by saying or writing the following comment for students, 'I learned how to divide all of the expressions in an equation by the coefficient to reduce it to one.'

This live demonstration of our thinking, as we think aloud in front of the class, reveals deep understanding of the mysteries of the mind, including when one solves a maths problem, writes a sentence, reads difficult text, sets up an experiment, etc. Teachers should do this repeatedly, providing numerous examples of the thinking process, naming the steps and providing structures along the way. Naming the steps they take when solving a problem is important because novice learners will be using their working memories to sort through other information as they think; this allows them to focus on developing useful learning strategies, versus missing key information due to cognitive overload. (See Memory: Research for more on working memory and cognitive load.)

THE IMPORTANCE OF EXPLICIT INSTRUCTION

The promise of pedagogy is 'that students might do something more than attempt to solve problems and engage in learning; they might also reflect not only on **what** but on the **how** and **why** of what they have learned as a result of their experiences' (Ellis et al., 2013). Teachers should explicitly teach metacognitive regulation to children by telling students that good learners plan, monitor and evaluate as part of the process of learning. Below are some examples of questions teachers can use to encourage learners to ask themselves to illustrate that process.

BEFORE (Planning)	DURING (Monitoring)	AFTER (Evaluating)
'What do I know about this topic?''Have I done a task like this before?' 'What strategies worked last time? 'What will be my first step?'	'How am I doing?' 'What should I do next?' 'Should I try a different strategy?' If stuck: 'Where am I stuck?' 'What resources can I use?'	'How well did I do?' 'Did I get the results I expected?' 'Is there anything I still don't understand?' 'What could I do differently next time?'

CLASSROOM
Find simple strategies and procedures such as Model, Teach, Practise, Connect, to ensure that you are utilising the research on how to teach metacognition, starting on page 280.

 SPOTLIGHT

RECOMMENDED READING
At School 21, an all-through school in London (Pre-K to high school), teachers developed a programme in conjunction with Cambridge University that puts student talk centre stage. Watch students in action in this video from Edutopia (2016): *Oracy in the Classroom: Strategies for Effective Talk* www.bit.ly/2IWi8iV

Metacognitive strategies include questions, such as those in the table above as well as routines or strategies that we teach children in order to help them use metacognition as they learn (for example, Think Alouds). Regardless of the strategy, we've got to be 'meta' about metacognition as we model and explain how and why strategies work. The most significant gains in student achievement result from students being taught to use metacognitive strategies in explicit ways, rather than using them implicitly (Haidar and Al Naqabi, 2008, cited in Ellis et al., 2013; Kistner et al., 2010, cited in Ellis et al., 2013). This means not only modelling metacognition and strategies, but also explaining the benefits of each when introduced: 'I'm doing this because...'.

VERBALISING METACOGNITIVE THINKING

Classroom talk, when purposeful and repeated, cements metacognitive skills in students. An international study conducted in primary classrooms in five countries found that the most common examples of classroom talk – such as rote, recitation and instruction – do not promote metacognition (Alexander, 2005, cited in Scott, 2009). The types of classroom talk that do develop metacognition in students are classroom discussions where there is 'an exchange of ideas' and thoughts between students as well as dialogic teaching, meaning a back-and-forth sharing of ideas between the teacher and students, spurring students to have the aha moments that are so important to learning. There are simple classroom strategies that teachers can employ to effectively use classroom talk and help students to move from knowing about metacognition to internalising it through verbalising their thoughts (e.g. telling your partner about the steps you used to solve a problem or why you chose a certain strategy) (Mercer and Littleton, 2007, cited in Scott, 2009). The verbalisation of one's thoughts helps to solidify understanding, much like the self-explanation discussed in Memory, whereby students are asked to articulate how they were able to solve a problem. Having students express their thoughts aloud also benefits the teacher, who gains a greater understanding of the students' thinking and can respond supporting whole-class learning of the content as well as a reflection on the process of learning.

Class discussions whereby the talk is accountable to the learning community, to accurate knowledge and to rigorous thinking help foster communication skills, thus building students' confidence to express ideas, build on those of others and take academic risks so essential to learning. This is the type of talk that can be taught and practised (Wolf et al., 2006). At School 21, an all-through school in London (Pre-K to high school), for instance, teachers developed a programme in conjunction with Cambridge University that puts student talk centre stage. Their goal is to create opportunities for children to learn 'both to and through' talk. Firstly, students learn effective ground rules for discussion. Teachers demonstrate what effective talk looks and sounds like. Secondly, students are taught that there are different purposes to talking, different discussion roles and types of talk. Setting up protocols for how we actually talk helps to guard against falling into that trap of thinking that just because a classroom is abuzz with chatter that students are learning.

DIFFERENTIATION

Metacognition is not reserved for older students, a common misconception in educational settings (Dignath and Büttner, 2008). The authors of the EEF Guidance Report (Quigley et al., 2018) sum up the research well:

> Children as young as three have been able to engage in a wide range of metacognitive and self-regulatory behaviours, such as setting themselves goals and checking their understanding. They also show greater accuracy on tasks they have chosen to accept than on tasks they would have preferred to opt out of.

> There is clear evidence that the level of security and self-knowledge remains rather inaccurate until about eight years of age, with children being over-optimistic about their levels of knowledge. However, although older children typically exhibit a broader repertoire of metacognitive strategies, the evidence suggests that younger children do typically develop metacognitive knowledge, even at a very early age.

Of course, different approaches to teaching metacognitive and self-regulation skills will depend on the child's age and development. For example, primary school children will benefit from a much more direct one-on-one instruction rather than working in groups when using strategies. Furthermore, some students find it hard to complete a task and 'think about their thinking' at the same time, especially novice or younger learners. Metacognitive reflection is best employed after the task has been completed. I observed this in a Year 3 (2nd grade) classroom when a teacher asked the children to listen to her read a story (listening for understanding) but at the same time try to remember the questions they were asking themselves. Suffice it to say, neither comprehension nor metacognitive thinking took place for these novice learners. Metacognitive reflection is best employed after the task has been completed. For older students, metacognitive strategies (such as Think Alouds) work well during and after a task (although they tell me that it's weird to think about your thinking).

SELF-TALK

Trying to manage our thoughts is like catching smoke with a net. Thought patterns have been built up unconsciously over years. Ways of thinking and our attitudes to learning are malleable with conscious practice and repetition. Teachers can help students reframe negative self-talk – which can have a detrimental impact on their motivation, effort and learning – into positive self-talk. According to Tod et al. (2011), who conducted a systematic review of 47 studies, **positive self-talk** has beneficial effects on cognition (in particular, concentration and focus-related variables), cognitive anxiety and the technical execution of movement skills. Researchers like Martin Seligman – author and professor of psychology, best known for his work on positive psychology – have been advocating the use of consciously challenging any negative self-talk as a tool to counter learned helplessness, which many of our students face (Seligman, 2018).

When students are aware that they can change their attitudes about tasks or their beliefs about their capabilities, they are more likely to use self-talk as a tool. The first step is to become aware of our current self-talk ('What do I say to myself about my abilities? What do I say to others?'). The next step is to pause and recognise you have choice ('I just started to think I was stupid again. Not today!'). Then choose a more positive self-talk statement over a negative ('Actually, self, you're NOT stupid. You're just new to this.'). And continue to repeat that over and over again.

Self-talk can play a really important role in refocusing children. For example, instead of saying, 'I'll never be able to do this,' students could be redirected to stop and first ask themselves, 'What do I already know about this task?' and say to themselves something like, 'The first step in new learning is always the hardest. I can do this' or 'This is hard, but that's not a bad thing.' Ultimately, when students know that they can exercise a sense of control over their anxiety (and in fact realise that being a bit nervous about learning something new is normal), they develop the capacity to persevere, a higher level of self-efficacy and learning mindset for future experiences.

MAKING MISTAKES

Posters celebrating 'marvellous mistakes' may obscure the reality that students' fear of getting it wrong (especially in front of peers) is a foundational barrier to learning.

MAKING MISTAKES IN A PICTURE PERFECT WORLD

In 2006, Dove released a video called *Dove Evolution*, developed at Ogilvy & Mather, Toronto. It went viral. The video portrays a woman being 'made over'. The woman transforms into a supermodel before the viewers' eyes as make-up and digital wizardry soften her skin, thicken her lips and elongate her neck. With small tweaks, her hair flows, her eyes widen and her face is narrowed. This was a mind-blowing video to show teenaged students back in 2006 in my media studies class. Many felt duped by the media. This kind of digital manipulation is an example of how image is everything in our picture-perfect, social-media-driven society. In the age of social media, young people spend hours curating images of themselves as popular, attractive and having the time of their lives.

RECOMMENDED READING
To watch the eye-opening advert *Dove Evolution*, go to www.bit.ly/2khObcS

This pressure for perfection is compounded by our performance-driven, high-stakes education culture, where the difference (a few marks) between getting a C and getting a D in your GCSE (final exams) can impact what sixth form (11th and 12th grades) you go to, what university you get into and a plethora of other life experiences. The higher the stakes, the more discomfort students feel when making mistakes, especially if their peers see them struggle. The thing is that failure actually helps us learn, achieve academically and grow emotionally. Revealing our imperfect selves helps us practise courage and fosters growth. We want kids to value these fits and starts, but that takes a level of resilience and self-confidence that must be nurtured by us. Errors are opportunities to draw attention to the learning journey and understand that mistakes and struggle are an important part of that journey.

DIFFERENT EMOTIONAL RESPONSES TO MISTAKES

In a study across five different schools with 4th to 6th graders (Years 5–7), researchers measured different 'styles' of emotional responses to mistakes and identified distinct styles, in order of frequency (McCaslin et al., 2016):

- **'Distance and displace'**: when students withdraw and blame someone else
- **'Regret and repair'**: students engage in less self-blame, participate more actively in problem solving with their peers and earn greater respect from teachers (though they do experience some guilt)
- **'Inadequate and exposed'**: students blame themselves and feel embarrassed
- **'Proud and modest'**: students feel pride, with self-recognition tempered with humility

The study brings to light the fact that the emotional impact of making mistakes is highly influenced by the social aspect of making them in front of peers. For instance, the authors write: 'Inclusion of "regret and repair" students with those who characteristically display "inadequate and exposed" emotional adaptation, for example, might unintentionally reaffirm one's sense of control and the other's inadequacy' (McCaslin et al., 2016, p. 34).

The study also found that 'it is difficult for students with fewer resources (due to a high density of students in poverty or readiness to learn) to cope with negative emotions when making mistakes and to realize pride upon success'. Also, a student with a low sense of self worth will connect failure to their self-concept – 'This is who I am, it's no wonder I failed.' Children with a high level of self-worth, however, will treat failure more as being caused by lack of effort: 'I really should have revised (studied) harder for that.' The good news: the authors state that 'students' emotional responses are malleable and open to intervention'. We outline a number of strategies in Mindset: Classroom that are recommended to help students cope and subsequently learn when faced with mistakes, such as self-talk, modelling, whole-class discussion to normalise mistakes, and of course, teaching metacognitive strategies – all of which support a learning mindset.

GETTING IT WRONG – IN FRONT OF THE CLASS

One day when I visited a Year 10 (9th grade) music class, I caught the teacher Brad Schmaus directing each of his students to sing out of key. He went first. Children giggled. It's funny, especially considering that they knew Mr Schmaus can sing and he leads the choir – and is the lead singer in a professional band. 'Singing is amongst the things people are most self conscious about,' Brad later told me. 'It's simultaneously a technical, expressive, and very personal thing. At the same time, everyone can do it, so the focus must be on developing confidence and not fearing mistakes. I take lessons from jazz, and the mantra: "There are no mistakes in jazz."' Quotes by famous musicians line the walls – 'Do not fear mistakes, there are none' (Miles Davis) and 'It was when I noticed I was making mistakes that I realised I was on the right track' (Ornette Coleman) – but the real lesson was the embodiment of these messages as students sang out of key. 'We also make deliberately bad noises, laugh with each other and celebrate mistakes, praising those who "go for it" and are brave enough to do so,' Brad further explained. It's in moments like these that this teacher supports students to have a learning mindset about mistakes.

One study comparing how Japanese and American teachers treat mistakes in maths exemplifies different cultural approaches. It was initially inspired by the researcher

> The study brings to light the fact that the emotional impact of making mistakes is highly influenced by the social aspect of making them in front of peers.

SPOTLIGHT

Jim Stigler's observations in a Japanese classroom during a visit to observe teaching practice. In a radio interview, Stigler recounts how he watched as students openly struggled in front of their peers to solve problems. Stigler says:

> The teacher was trying to teach the class how to draw three-dimensional cubes on paper and one kid was just totally having trouble with it. His cube looked all cockeyed, so the teacher said to him, 'Why don't you go put yours on the board?' So right there I thought, 'That's interesting! He took the one who can't do it and told him to go and put it on the board.' (Stigler, 2013).

Surprisingly to Stigler, the child didn't shrink into his seat. Instead, he went to the board and struggled through the problem until he got the answer. The class applauded. The subsequent study, using video cameras to record maths lessons, revealed that in the Japanese classrooms, teachers tended to embrace mistakes by equating success with resilience and effort: 'You got the problem wrong; let's work on it together.' In contrast, the study found that in the majority of American classrooms surveyed, teachers tended to ignore errors made by students and praised students for correct answers.

PAY ATTENTION TO MISTAKES

When teachers put a spotlight on mistakes, students build resilience. When the student from the Japanese maths lesson finally got the answer, the class's reflection and praise were more about the process than the final answer (Stevenson and Stigler, 1994). A study of 123 seven-year-olds, using neural evidence (electrodes measuring responses), found that children who pay closer attention to mistakes are better able to bounce back from them and have the resilience to push through (Schroder et al., 2017). 'Paying attention to mistakes is a crucial mechanism of recovery' and leads to 'post-error accuracy'. In short, the study showed that when you look closely at what went wrong the first time, you are less likely to get it wrong again. To do this, we need to value mistakes and failure (Moser et al., 2011). This is echoed by what Lucy Crehan noticed in the most successful school environments. Crehan, the author of Cleverlands: *The Secrets Behind the Success of the World's Education Superpowers*, said in an interview with me: 'If children are constantly experiencing failure at something, but not experiencing the follow-up where we go back over it and we spend the time on it until you get it, then they'll just give up' (Crehan, 2018b). According to Crehan, we should reward the ones who worked the hardest to overcome this barrier rather than the attitude we see in some UK and US classrooms: 'Let's not talk about the fact that they didn't do very well, because it's a bit embarrassing that they are not very bright.'

Celebrating mistakes is not the answer. On the surface, and perhaps superficially, young people know the rhetoric about mistakes. In my conversations with students over the years about learning, it is rare to find one who will not agree – or at least know that they should agree – with the statement 'Everybody learns from mistakes.' Although teachers often refer to 'marvellous mistakes', rarely will you find a student who truly celebrates mistakes – and why should they? Nobody actually likes mistakes and nobody likes failure. (In fact, many students have told me the word 'failure' is too final, too emotive.) Yet intellectual struggles are essential to learning. To get the most out of mistakes, we need to examine them more closely and be a bit pickier about which are truly

Although teachers often refer to 'marvellous mistakes', rarely will you find a student who truly celebrates mistakes – and why should they?

marvellous and which are simply messy. We can remind our students that the goal isn't to make mistakes, but to learn from them by paying attention to how they happened and how we can fix them.

OUR ROLE MODELS ARE PEOPLE TOO

Scientists are like superheroes – or at least seem to have superhero brains. Students tend to have the perception that to be a scientist, you must be brilliant and solve problems without help from others. In fact, in a 2016 survey of students, most said that scientists are 'geniuses' (Lin-Siegler et al., 2016). Cognitive studies researcher Xiaodong Lin-Siegler and her colleagues at Columbia University's Teachers College found, however, that high school students' science grades improved after they learned about the personal and intellectual struggles of scientists including Einstein, Marie Curie and Michael Faraday. The stories (like the one about Einstein having to ask a friend for help with maths or the one about Marie Curie finding school difficult because people disapproved of women being educated (she had to move to France)) matter – and matter more than stories about the scientists' achievements. In fact, students who only learned about the scientists' achievements saw their grades decline (Lin-Siegler et al., 2016). Presumably, these students who read about the scientists' struggles internalised the learning mindset: success comes not from inherent genius, but from applied effort.

Perhaps not surprisingly, teaching students about the struggles of scientists was most beneficial for students who were low performing. It may also be, as postulated by the authors of the study, that if case studies had more 'sharing ethnic matches' with students (most students were Latino and black) there may have been even more academic impact. (Recall our discussion about expectations and stereotype threat in Relationships.) The benefits of the intervention were domain-specific, like most of the strategies we discuss; in other words, the intervention works when it is applied with the content or context in which you are using it. The children's general beliefs about intelligence and effort did not change, but these stories positively affected their outcomes in science. Here would be an opportunity for the teacher to make an explicit connection between self-efficacy within a domain and our macro understanding of the role of mistakes and struggle as part of the learning process generally.

THE IMPORTANCE OF RELATABLE ROLE MODELS

Take a moment to think about role models in your life. Are these people famous celebrities? Or are they a favourite teacher, coach, a parent or successful friend? If we want students to strengthen self-efficacy and develop a learning mindset, the role models we introduce to students should be relatable and like them in some way. Too often, students are pointed to celebrities or people who do not share students' racial, religious, gender, ethnic or other identities. 'Seeing people similar to oneself succeed by sustained effort raises observers' beliefs that they too possess the capabilities to master comparable activities to succeed,' according to Bandura (1994). 'By the same token, observing others fail despite high effort lowers observers' judgments of their own efficacy and undermines their efforts.' For example, observing someone from a similar background try hard and succeed at school will raise self-efficacy, while seeing

SPOTLIGHT

RECOMMENDED READING
J.K. Rowling's Harvard University commencement speech, *The Fringe Benefits of Failure,* is an inspiring true story about how 'failure' made her who she is today: www.bit.ly/2kfwSsV

someone who resembles you try and fail (and not recover) may lower self-efficacy. Teachers can control the examples they provide to their students to expose them to their optimal role models.

Students can be their own role models. According to Ericsson, it's important to identify (or even help students discover) experiences in their own lives when they have been successful due to behaviours such as purposeful practice, effective effort and learning from mistakes. In fact, students often work really hard without realising it when engaged in activities they are passionate about (sports, video games, etc.). Teachers should help students make connections between the things they work hard at and learning in general, and develop a repertoire of experiences for talking about learning. Once students have a repertoire and a feel for what success is, says Ericsson, they can begin to translate that to other content. We remind them, 'Learning how to write is a lot like riding a bike: you need to keep at it.'

CLASSROOM
Make models matter: share struggle stories, spotlight on relatable heroes and support reflection of students' past success through struggle.

FEEDBACK

On the surface, the purpose of feedback is to direct a learner to improve. Done well and following some straightforward guidelines, it is so much more.

Teacher feedback is either (1) actionable and about the task, relating to the success criteria ('Please add more detail to your characters') or (2) about the learning process, as it relates to behaviour, actions and metacognitive skills ('I noticed you stuck with that until you got it.'). When teachers focus feedback on what struggling learners did correctly as well as on the steps necessary for improvement, they give learners a roadmap for success, which strengthens their self-efficacy and learning mindset (Schunk and Zimmerman, 1997). Feedback on the task and feedback on the learning process are both essential elements of the teacher-student academic relationship. Below, we offer the research and benefits of these forms of feedback.

FEEDBACK ON THE TASK

The goal of **task feedback** is to close the gap between where the student needs to be and where they are now. Throughout this chapter, there have been several references to the importance of feedback, such as it relates to purposeful practice, effective effort, mistakes and goal setting. 'Feedback is among the most powerful influences on achievement,' according to Hattie (2009), whose research gives feedback a high average effect size (level of impact) of .79, twice the average effect of all other schooling effects. This comes from 12 meta-analyses that have included specific information on feedback in classrooms. Feedback gets a gold star from the Educational Endowment Foundation's Toolkit, with a rating on average of eight months of progression. And yet, the most comprehensive review of research on the effects of feedback (Kluger and DeNisi, 1996) found that, while feedback did on average improve performance, in 38% of cases it lowered performance. 'In other words, in over one-third of cases, learners would have been better off without the feedback,' writes Dylan Wiliam about the study (Wiliam, 2017). What does this contradictory research show? That it's essential that we get feedback right. When we do, it has the potential to:

- increase effort.
- increase willingness to embrace challenge, set high goals.
- lead to successful learning.
- reinforce a learning mindset.
- support a climate of care.

Feedback plays an important role in our daily lives. For instance, take Nina's commute to different schools in New York City. On her smartphone, she types in where she is headed, which gives her directions based on her current location. Once that's done, her app offers options of how she might travel (subway, walking or by car) and how long each will take. Paul Black and Dylan Wiliam, experts in assessment for learning, suggest a similar process for most effective feedback: identifying where the learner is going; determining where the learner is right now; and then exploring how they might get there (Black and Wiliam, 2009).

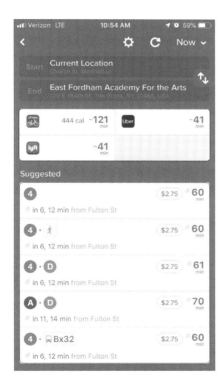

EFFECTIVE FEEDBACK
Just like when we use a smartphone app, feedback should be based on current location and the end destination.

WHERE IS THE LEARNER GOING?

Maps are useless if we don't know where we are going. It may seem an obvious point, but before we give feedback, it's important to create clear success criteria for your students and articulate student goals (see Goal Setting in this chapter for more details). Success criteria is a description, or list of features, that guide what success will look like on a particular task. It helps to distinguish between 'what I'm doing' ('I'm writing a ghost story') versus 'how I got there' ('I used spooky adjectives and ended with a cliffhanger'). Clear success criteria makes it easy to offer specific, relevant feedback about the task that is aligned with the end result students are working toward. It is also important for students as they work towards a goal.

In an interview about learning intentions and success criteria, John Hattie uses an analogy to explain how a lack of success criteria makes it hard to accomplish goals:

> If I said to you I was going to teach you what Australian rules football looks like, but I'm not going to tell you what the rules are and I'm not going to tell you how to score, but I want you to go out and play it, for many of you, you'd give up very quickly. Unfortunately, for a lot of kids in our schools, that's what learning looks like. 'All I have to do is wait and I'll be guided or I'll be told off.' (Hattie, 2015)

At Julian's Primary School in London, they start new writing units with an activity called What Makes Good, scrutinising a particular genre or type of writing, outlining the conventions and setting up the success criteria. The teacher then prioritises the criteria, based on their expertise, and the students and teacher work their way through, step by step. In my A level (11 and 12th grade) film studies classes, we would watch and unpack the conventions of documentary films before creating our own five-minute version. In the US, success criteria often take the form of rubrics, which simultaneously act as guidelines for learning expectations and an evaluation tool. See Mindset: Classrooms for an example of a single point rubric.

WHERE IS THE LEARNER RIGHT NOW?

As David Ausubel wrote back in 1968, 'The most important single factor influencing learning is what the learner already knows. Ascertain this and teach accordingly' (Ausubel, 1968). Teaching and feedback go hand in hand, at play in the classroom as we question, confer and observe. Assessment is the gateway to offering great feedback. Assessing what a student already knows at the beginning of new units of study helps teachers know exactly where students are relative to where the teachers want them to be. Formative assessment continues throughout the unit as teachers continually adapt to students' learning or lack of understanding. In fact, a more useful term for formative assessment is 'responsive teaching', as suggested in a tweet by Dylan Wiliam (2013), who has written extensively on the positive impact of formative assessment on learning.

RECOMMENDED READING
For a good and practical guide to feedback, we recommend *Visible Learning Feedback* (Hattie and Clarke, 2018) and *Responsive Teaching: Cognitive Science and Formative Assessment in Practice* (Fletcher-Wood, 2018).

HOW THEY'LL GET THERE: THE FOUNDATIONS FOR EFFECTIVE FEEDBACK

How many times have we spent hours writing detailed feedback that we think students are going to be so grateful for, only to watch it being stuffed carelessly into a backpack or – worse – finding it left behind on the desk after the bell rings? We daren't think that perhaps it also wasn't even read. For this reason, teachers need to design systems for giving feedback that includes specific timeframes and methods that facilitate student reflection and response. For feedback to be most effective, it needs to be formative, not final. If we don't have a plan for giving students an opportunity to act on feedback, then it gets lost – along with the opportunity to reflect on their learning process.

How frequently we give feedback and how immediately it should happen depends on how familiar the content is to the student, the student's prior knowledge and their self-efficacy. For new learning, feedback should be immediate and detailed, especially as students build knowledge and skills around a subject. When students gain more experience with a concept, delayed feedback can be more effective, as offering feedback too frequently means that students will not have time to struggle a bit on their own.

For novice learners, it is crucial to continually build up their understanding and sense of self-efficacy as they acquire knowledge. Build in small moments to highlight success using pointed, specific and limited feedback, such as 'You have stated several causes of the Great Fire of London. Now you can make it stronger by detailing what houses were made of at that time.' Keep in mind that if a teacher offers a large amount of feedback at once, this may overload students' working memories. (Think back to our working memory buckets and cognitive overload from Memory: Research.) Focused feedback takes up a lot of working memory capacity but is very important. To ensure they can hear and use the feedback, students need space and time for processing. Teachers must regularly check in using formative assessment. We discussed this balancing act in Research: Memory with the expertise reversal effect (see page 125). As with using too many worked examples for students who have a high level of expertise, too much feedback may provide an unnecessary crutch for more experienced learners.

AMOUNT AND FREQUENCY OF FEEDBACK
How we deliver feedback should be based on the amount of prior learning of the student. Typically, new learning requires more detailed and immediate feedback than when students have more acquired learning, or prior knowledge.

If we use success criteria to guide our feedback to students, as discussed above, this ensures that we keep feedback focused, regardless of how tempting it is to remind students of all the other things they might have done wrong. I have observed dozens of lessons where the learning intention was something like 'using more adventurous adjectives in writing', but teachers could not restrain themselves from also commenting on everything else that needed improvement. As a former English teacher, I am very guilty of having thought that the more things I could help fix, the better. I was wrong. Focus your feedback and park other comments for later.

PEER FEEDBACK

Graham Nuthall, an education researcher introduced in the Relationship chapter, spent a year of his life recording conversations of students by day and listening to the recordings at night. Among many insights, he discovered that about 80% of verbal feedback in the classroom was peer to peer. Most of the feedback was incorrect (Nuthall, 2007). Also, students who had the loudest voices or highest peer group status had more influence in these private conversations. Improving peer feedback has the potential to have a significant impact in the classroom if done well. Peer feedback is most effective when students have secured a foundation in the concepts they are giving feedback back on (Hattie and Clarke, 2018). Students also need to be trained in how to give feedback, with clear protocols (for example, use Kind, Useful and Specific Feedback) and an

'The only good feedback is that which is used,' advises Wiliam (2018). Students are more receptive to feedback when teachers communicate high expectations that the student can improve. Relationships matter too.

understanding of how to respond to success criteria. We pick up peer feedback in Classroom, with suggestions based on Ron Berger's models of excellence, and advice on how to implement in the classroom or whole school.

AUSTIN'S BUTTERFLY

SPOTLIGHT

Based on feedback from his peers, 1st grader (Year 2) student Austin makes several attempts to draw a butterfly. Austin's Butterfly is a story of the power of specific feedback, specific criteria and a learning mindset that helps him persevere to reach his goal, which is depicted in the fantastic online video from EL Education (www. bit.ly/2mupJFN). See page 304 in Mindset: Classroom for ideas on how to use this with your teaching.

NORMALISE ERROR

How teachers provide feedback on errors or mistakes is extremely important to student learning and their learning mindset. If we want to create spaces where children will openly make and calmly reflect on mistakes – in front of peers and their teacher – we must prioritise strategies for a climate of comfort, similar to what Doug Lemov calls a 'culture of error'. Lemov, author of *Teach Like a Champion* and educationalist, rigorously studies the habits of the most effective teachers (Lemov, 2010). Lemov says about mistakes, 'I won't tolerate anyone getting in the way of other people feeling comfortable enough to make them'. This statement should be said aloud if a mistake induces snickers. Robert Bjork, in an interview about best practice for memory, echoed these sentiments: 'You need to do a certain kind of socialization with your students if you want to optimise learning' or 'an attitude change' (Bjork, 2017). One way, Bjork suggests, is to say to students that raising your hand and giving a wrong answer to something is a contribution, because it's helping us think. Whole-group instruction (and feedback) is a perfect opportunity to normalise struggle and set norms about how to regulate for mistakes (self-talk) and treat each other. However, 'As much as we say mistakes are part of learning, you can't help but be disappointed,' admits Chris Hildrew (2019) – headteacher of a secondary school and author of *Becoming a Growth Mindset School* – when I ask him about the challenges of implementing growth mindset at his school. 'There is still an almost human-nature aversion to mistake-making.' It takes reflection and practice to change this human response, Hildrew adds. Yeager at al. (2019) found that mindset inventions were more impactful in schools where peer norms supported intellectual challenge. The researchers suggest, 'Perhaps students in unsupportive peer climates risked paying a social price for taking on intellectual challenges in front of peers who thought it undesirable to do so.'

COMPARISONS AND COMPETITION

The greatest motivational benefits come from focusing feedback on the quality of the child's work, not as a comparison to other children. 'Many teachers believe that competition for grades can increase performance, and to some extent they are right. Students who feel that the goals are within their grasp are likely to be motivated by competition to do even better' (Wiliam, 2012). The problem with this strategy, according to Dylan Wiliam, is that 'many students do not feel they're able to compete, and therefore give up – so competition produces gains for some students at the expense of others.

This might be acceptable in the adult world in competition for jobs and for other scarce resources, but it is unacceptable in primary and secondary education, where we want every student to achieve at high levels' (Wiliam, 2012). Feedback should be individualised; learning mindsets are about an individual's growth, not how they compare to others.

FEEDBACK ON THE LEARNING PROCESS

In a Year 6 (5th grade) classroom, students are working quietly on their own. I'm a guest, and the teacher has invited me to have one-on-one chats with the students. I lean down to ask one girl what she's working on. 'Maths,' (obviously, says her look). I smile and she explains that they are solving multi-step problems. I ask her, 'If I were to ask your teacher, "What does it take to learn in this classroom?", what would she say?' I ask this question often to children and get a mix of responses, including, 'Listen to what the teacher says' and 'Be good. Sit up in your seat.'

The girl I'm speaking to today says, 'Ms Booth is always saying you can improve. She likes hard work.'

At the risk of getting another look, I ask, 'What does that mean?'

The girl points to the wall. 'See there, that's our working wall.'

I leave her alone and check out the wall, which displays the first, second and third attempts at problem-solving, showcasing how students corrected themselves.

If someone had come to my classroom when I was a new teacher many years ago and asked the same question, I'm not sure what my students would have said. It's a good question that teachers should ask themselves. Our students should know what we value as important learning habits.

POINT OUT THE PROCESS...RATHER THAN PRAISE THE PERSON

 SPOTLIGHT

When students associate their success with positive learning habits, they are more likely to use these learning habits in future tasks. Consider the example on page 217 of five-year-old Mohammed who made small improvements as he persevered to learn to write. The teacher observed these increments and helped Mohammed to be aware of what he was doing – how each attempt helped him get better. This is particularly important when learning something new as students build confidence and self-efficacy. Knowing this teacher well, I think she likely added some encouragement (like 'Keep it up, I know you can do it') along the way or some metacognitive prompts ('What do you think you should do next, Mohammed?'). By pointing out the process, the teacher helps students become aware of how their positive behaviours and effective efforts add up.

FRUITLESS EFFORT

Valuing effective effort is an important component of a learning mindset; however, when teachers overly praise effort that doesn't get learners anywhere, their feedback is futile and even counterproductive.

RECOMMENDED READING

Mindset: Changing The Way You think To Fulfil Your Potential (Updated Edition) (2017) by Carol Dweck is a seminal, accessible book. Make sure to get the updated edition.

Effort praise has been written about extensively and most famously by Mueller and Dweck (1998). For example, the results in one study – with five hundred 5th graders (Year 6 students), reflecting a range of ethnic, racial and socioeconomic backgrounds and geographic areas – showed that children who received **effort praise** ('You must have worked hard at these problems') were more likely to engage in subsequent, more challenging tasks than students who received **intelligence praise** ('You must be smart at these problems'). Dweck concluded, 'When we praise children for the effort and hard work that leads to achievement, they want to keep engaging in the process. They are not diverted from the task of learning by a concern with how smart they might – or might not – look.' We praise students' innate talents or natural ability – 'You are so smart' or 'You are a natural' – with the best of intentions, but this type of praise may devalue learning habits such as hard work, interpreting struggle to mean that they aren't as smart or talented as they thought they were (Dweck, 2002; Kamins and Dweck, 1999; Mueller and Dweck, 1998).

When we, as educators, point out the process, we must first be authentic and specific in our feedback. Relate the comments to specific learning experience within that domain. Then, in line with our bigger point about learning mindset, find opportunities to connect these classroom moments to the desired learning habits of a learning mindset. Because students build self-efficacy through vicarious experiences (such as watching their peers succeed through, for example, hard work and using strategies), these types of acknowledgements also help students to be aware of the positive learning habits peers use, rather than thinking someone was successful due to sheer innate intelligence (Bandura, 1994).

THE RISKS OF PRAISING EFFORT

General or verbose praise about effort has little meaning, and kids can see right through it. Telling a class that 'everybody put in good effort' is not convincing, especially for older students, and certainly when they are aware that they didn't try their hardest. The risk of using effort-focused feedback is that it is likely to be too general and thus counterproductive for many reasons. If students put a lot of effort toward a task and still do not succeed, congratulating them on effort is like the consolation prize. Even if children are successful, if it took a lot of effort – maybe more than it took their peers

– emphasising the effort may be interpreted as the teacher pointing out, 'Well you got it, but it took you a lot of effort so really you aren't as smart as Johnny.' Lastly, effort is one component needed for learning, but it's not the endgame. Learning is the goal. Dweck writes about the problems with effort-praise with relation to growth mindset in *Education Week*:

> Certainly, effort is key for students' achievement, but it's not the only thing. Students need to try new strategies and seek input from others when they're stuck. They need this repertoire of approaches – not just sheer effort – to learn and improve ... The growth mindset was intended to help close achievement gaps, not hide them. It is about telling the truth about a student's current achievement and then, together, doing something about it, helping him or her become smarter. (Dweck, 2015)

SELF-EFFICACY SHAPES HOW WE INTERPRET FEEDBACK

The best way to ensure that all students get the most from our feedback is by being authentic and specific. General comments, such as those in the chart below, run the risk of being interpreted very differently depending on the self-efficacy level of the student. Have a look at the chart to see how two different children in your class might hear the same well-intentioned message completely differently. This interpretation then has an impact on their effort, perseverance and goal attainment.

ONE COMMENT, A VARIETY OF INTERPRETATIONS

WHAT THE TEACHER SAYS	LOW SELF-EFFICACY, LACK OF TRUST IN TEACHER/ FEELINGS OF ISOLATION	HIGH-SELF-EFFICACY, TRUST IN TEACHER/SENSE OF BELONGING
'You are so smart. You have so much potential'	'My teacher thinks I'm smart. If I try and fail, they'll discover that I'm not really smart. I'll play it safe'	'My teacher thinks I have potential. I'm going to trust them on this one'
'Good effort'	'The teacher's only praising my effort because there's nothing to praise about my work and they don't want me to feel bad'	'The teacher recognises that I'm working hard. I am working hard and it's important to do so'
'Everybody makes mistakes.'	'My teacher is trying to make me feel better'	'I made a mistake. So what? I'll keep going.'

The take-away: Research shows that feedback is most effective when authentic, specific, based on the task (not the person), and when not used as a comparison to peers. Additionally, feedback is one element in the big picture in cultivating a learning mindset. Bandura, who sees educators as 'efficacy builders', notes the multidimensional approach we need to take with our students: 'Successful efficacy builders do more than convey positive appraisals. In addition to raising people's beliefs in their capabilities, they structure situations for them in ways that bring success and avoid placing people in situations prematurely where they are likely to fail often. They measure success in terms of self-improvement rather than by triumphs over others' (Bandura, 1994).

'Self-belief does not necessarily ensure success, but self-disbelief assuredly spawns failure' (Bandura, 1997).

IS THERE ANY ROOM FOR COMPLIMENTS?

The movement to focus more on effort-praise versus intelligence-praise is sometimes misinterpreted to mean that we can't say nice things to students anymore. Praising a job well done or a goal achieved is needed and valuable. Note that the most effective praise is still focused on the process, including low-inference observation and details that help them know specifically why you are praising them. For example, 'The way you delivered that speech was excellent. You had a strong start by asking a question and made three clear arguments. Well done!'

TEACHER MINDSET

Teachers who believe in their own capabilities, and who work in schools that believe in them, benefit students the most.

A teacher who lacks confidence in their own practice is less likely to push students, try new strategies, or persevere when things don't work out as planned. This is a common problem for new teachers, who often try a succession of (usually classroom management) strategies only to quickly ditch them when they 'don't work' immediately. These teachers may even see early failures as a sign that they just weren't cut out for teaching. A more seasoned teacher might stick to a strategy longer, challenging students to practise a procedure until they've mastered it. According to Anita Woolfolk, an educational psychologist whose primary research focuses on teacher self-efficacy, 'teachers who set high goals, who persist, who try another strategy when one approach is found wanting – in other words, teachers who have a high sense of efficacy and act on it – are more likely to have students who learn' (Woolfolk, 2004).

The learning mindset for teachers is no different from that of students. Teachers, as learners, must be being willing to make mistakes, try new strategies and get out of their comfort zones. They should engage in metacognition, evaluating their behaviours and strategies and making changes to hone them. On a school-wide level, this mindset is referred to as 'collective efficacy', a belief in the school's ability to support their students to learn and thrive – 'We can do this.' According to Rachel Eells's 2011 meta-analysis of studies related to collective teacher efficacy and achievement in education, teacher beliefs are 'strongly and positively associated with student achievement across subject areas ... and in multiple locations' (Eells, 2011). Eells adds:

> Low efficacy beliefs are contagious, and can influence willingness to try. If teachers don't feel that their efforts will lead to success, they are, potentially, less likely to dedicate the energy needed in order to make a positive impact. However, confidence in collective ability can also be contagious. If break room chatter revolves around successes, overcoming obstacles, and opportunities to make a difference, the social norms of a faculty may be established such that new faculty members realize that optimism, dedication, and resilience characterize the school.

According to Donohoo et al. (2018), leadership plays a major role in influencing collective efficacy by 'setting expectations for formal, frequent, and productive teacher collaboration and by creating high levels of trust for this collaboration to take place ... and this can account for results in the classroom'. In order to collectively reflect on practice, staff need to support each other. In a training about teacher-student

The learning mindset for teachers is no different from that of students. Teachers, as learners, must be being willing to make mistakes, try new strategies and get out of their comfort zones.

relationships at one primary school, headteacher Emilie Haston stood up and reminded the staff, 'We have to trust each other if we want students to trust us.' Haston, who encourages teachers to regularly reflect on teaching, later added, 'In order for staff to thrive they need to feel valued, trusted and supported by leaders.' This happens when leaders themselves model their enthusiasm and respect for the learning process as journey, and use observations as learning tools instead of punitive tactics.

There are mindsets which we urge educators to avoid. Unlike a learning mindset, which is beneficial to students, some new teachers enter the profession with an unfortunate 'saviour complex' – the desire to 'save' their under-resourced students whom they often see as unacculturated victims. This attitude negates some of the assets students already have, such as their resilience, and often results in low expectations by teachers. Additionally, Kathy Sun (no date) in a year-long study in 40 middle schools' maths classrooms found some teachers proclaim that they have 'growth mindset' yet carry on using strategies that are not aligned with growth mindset, such as grouping 'students together based on past achievement', and conveying high expectations for past high achievers and low expectations for past low-achieving students.

Despite the challenges, shifting a school's culture to one of a learning mindset is absolutely possible when leaders and educators take a learning mindset. But it does take time. As Chris Hildrew, the headteacher mentioned earlier, told me, Changing the culture of a school is 'like pushing a really big lever that slowly moves a massive object'. The bottom line is that we need to practise what we preach. Next stop in this chapter is to do just that. In Mindset: Classroom, we will suggest our best picks for cultivating a learning mindset in the classroom and school-wide.

MINDSET: CLASSROOM

Mindset:
in the **Classroom**

While 'You can do it!' posters can be eye-catching, it's intentional strategies embedded in authentic learning moments that foster a learning mindset.

The goal of Mindset: Classroom is to guide educators through concrete strategies to help students hone their learning mindset. As we mentioned in the Mindset: Research section, a **learning mindset** refers to a person's understanding of learning as a process (it takes time and effort, for example) and a belief that they have control over their own learning ('If this doesn't work, I'll try another way'). The roots of a person's mindset are complex, deeply grounded in individual experiences and thoughts and built up over time. In this section, we have picked a selection of strategies we use and have seen work in schools to shift students' mindsets. We start with a look at the habits of effective learners, including some brain basics; move to goal setting as a way to set up students for success; and then take a close look into metacognition and the value of mistakes. Throughout, we offer suggestions to use feedback and teacher talk. All of these elements work together to cultivate a learning mindset.

WHAT LEARNING LOOKS LIKE

We start this section with a broad approach, to establish a language of learning that is used throughout the section. Our objective is to aid you in helping students identify what it takes to learn, so that they can then apply this in their content areas.

DIRECT TEACH: BRING TO LIGHT WHAT EFFECTIVE LEARNERS DO

For older students, follow these steps:

1. **Prepare** by thinking of personal examples of things you have learned to do well, like speaking a foreign language, running long distances, knowing the times tables, etc. You could even bring in something you learned how to do over time and demonstrate how you learned it. My mother saved a lot of my writing from my school days, so I always share those examples with students.

2. **Share with students** your examples from number 1.

3. **Give one minute of think time** for students to write down their own learning examples: 'Give an example of something you have learned how to do or know a lot about.'

4. **Create groups** of three or four and ask students to write down ideas on chart paper. Alternatively, use a Think, Pair, Share.

5. **Elicit a few examples** from the class, but instruct students not to use names. (e.g. 'In our group, we had examples of...')

6. **Ask the whole class:** 'What did it take for you to become good at or know a lot about the things you wrote down? For example, to learn to ride a bike, I watched my big sister do it.' Students will likely say things such as trying hard, thinking about it, practising over and over again, getting help from others, sticking with it, having fun, being good at it. All responses are valid.

7. **Ask students to record** their responses on the chart paper, using a different coloured marker.

8. **Direct students to look at their brainstorm and ask them**, 'What does this list show us about learning (getting good at something)? What decisions did you make in the learning process?' Elicit answers and remind them (if they haven't already mentioned it) that for most of them, it took time, practice, and perseverance to improve at something.

9. **Introduce the effective learning choices chart** (on the next page): 'A lot of the strategies you listed align with what we call "effective learning practices". When we practise a learning mindset, we make decisions as we learn.'

10. **Debrief**. Two options:

    - **Self-evaluation:** explain the self-evaluation scale and that there are no wrong answers, because we respond differently in different situations. Put down what comes to mind.

    - **Spotlight:** ask students to pick one of the categories and give a specific example of what this looks like in school. When might they see themselves choosing these behaviours?

RECOMMENDED READING
Show the Khan Academy video
You Can Learn Anything at www.
bit.ly/2kogp5K or watch videos
of babies learning to walk to
illustrate how learning includes
making mistakes and (literally)
picking yourself up over and over.
A quick Google search will reveal
lots of videos of children learning
to walk.

EFFECTIVE LEARNING CHOICES CHART

3 = I do this a lot   2 = I do this sometimes   1 = I rarely do this   0 = I don't do this

WHEN FACED WITH	I CHOOSE TO	SELF-EVALUATION
Challenges	Embrace challenges; set high goals	
New learning	Put in effort and lots of practice; break down tasks	
Prolonged difficulty	Persist through difficulty; try new strategies; take a break	
Lack of understanding	Seek help; ask questions; start again	
Mistakes	Use mistakes to learn; figure out what went wrong and try to fix it	
Critical feedback	Listen and learn from feedback	

For **younger students**, ask this question: 'What is something you've learned how to do or are good at now, but at some point could not do?' as a whole-class discussion prompt. Be prepared with age-appropriate examples, such as learning to tie your shoes, putting on your jacket or writing letters. Chart all of their answers. Select one skill that many of them can do and ask these follow-up questions:

- How many times did you have to try it to do it well/right?
- Was it hard to learn/become good at it? What was hard about it?
- What kind of help did you get along the way? Who helped you?
- Did you make any mistakes? What did you do?

Teacher talk:

- 'All new learning takes time and effort.'
- 'We have control over the choices we make as we learn. Sometimes that might mean working harder; other times it means we need to try a different strategy or ask for help.'
- 'It's usually easier to have a learning mindset when we are doing things we enjoy, like getting better at a sport or playing a video game. Nevertheless, we can use what we learn about learning to help with getting better at anything.'

Optional extension: Ask students, 'What do you NOT know how to do YET, but would like to? How could you use these strategies you listed to help you?' or 'Please talk about an academic concept or skill you've mastered and which of these strategies you used to do that.'

TEACHER TIP
Make a note of the students'
learning experiences to reference
later. Students love to know you
remember things about them, in
particular their strengths. This is
a great opportunity to connect
the dots between building
relationships and mindsets.

CONNECT LEARNING MINDSET TO SPECIFIC CONTENT

For this activity, take the opportunity to explore with your students what a learning mindset looks like in your subject.

1. **Prepare** by planning what skills and habits you already think students will need (see graphic below).

2. **Ask:** 'What does it take to learn in (name a subject) ... or to be a scholar or specialist (mathematician, scientist, historian, writer) ... or what does it take to learn something new (new language, sport, skill ...)?'

3. **Students work in pairs** or small groups to identify what makes a strong learner in your subject.

4. **Debrief:** Work with students to identify key learning habits. Suggest specific words or phrases that are specific to your subject and use these when feeding back to students.

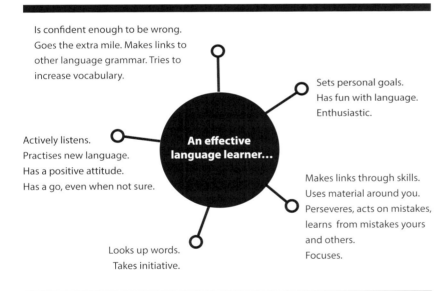

Is confident enough to be wrong. Goes the extra mile. Makes links to other language grammar. Tries to increase vocabulary.

Sets personal goals. Has fun with language. Enthusiastic.

Actively listens. Practises new language. Has a positive attitude. Has a go, even when not sure.

An effective language learner...

Makes links through skills. Uses material around you. Perseveres, acts on mistakes, learns from mistakes yours and others. Focuses.

Looks up words. Takes initiative.

SURVEY STUDENT ATTITUDES ABOUT LEARNING

Throughout this section, we'll introduce several surveys so you can learn more about your students' attitudes and help to build discussion. Often students choose the answer they think teachers want to hear, so encourage them to be honest and make surveys anonymous. Remind them that there are no wrong answers. We find this survey to be most helpful when given about a particular content area, since students' academic attitudes can vary from content area to content area.

TEACHER TIP
Create a digital survey, sending students the link to complete online. Google Forms creates a graphic display of results for you. It's great for quickly tallying results and presenting the information in a clear format for discussion. Kahoot! is another great one; it's gamified and has fun graphics.

1 = Strongly disagree 2 = Disagree 3 = Neither disagree nor agree 4 = Agree 5 = Strongly agree

Circle 1 (strongly disagree) to 5 (strongly agree)	
Everyone can change how clever/smart they are.	1 2 3 4 5
Setbacks make me want to give up.	1 2 3 4 5
It is possible for me to become even smarter by working hard.	1 2 3 4 5
Each person has a certain amount of intelligence and there's nothing you can do to change that.	1 2 3 4 5
I'd rather do an easy task than something challenging.	1 2 3 4 5
I like getting feedback from my teacher.	1 2 3 4 5

Comments:

For younger students: Create a handout that has several rows of frowning to smiley faces. Pass them out and explain to students what each face means (or elicit their meaning from students). Read one or several prompts aloud, such as 'I like to work hard', and ask students to circle or colour in the face that aligns with their level of agreement about each prompt.

SMILES TO FROWNS

 KEEP IT GOING

DIRECT TEACH: EXPLORE THE UPS AND DOWNS OF THE LEARNING JOURNEY

Using this image of a learning dip is a great (and visual) way of explaining to students that the learning journey includes moments when we are challenged and may feel stuck.

1. **Display** the Learning Journey (handouts or classroom display). You'll also need markers or sticky notes.

2. **Introduce** the concept of the Learning Journey. For example, 'The Learning Journey represents what it is like when we learn something new. The journey begins here (on the left) and ends here (the right side). Notice how the right-hand side is higher? This represents growth. The person has learned something! Based on the picture, what might happen to the learner along the way?'

3. **Relate** the Learning Journey to a character students have read about in a book, or talk about your own learning journey step by step, including places where you got stuck.

4. **Help** students find a concrete example in a whole-class discussion or a Think, Pair, Share: 'Think of times when you have been in the dip (in this lesson, this year, while studying…).' For younger students, give them some examples of things you observed in the classroom, such as learning how to write one's name, read or do number bonds.

5. **Record** student responses as they say them or talk through the visual.

6. **Debrief:** When did/do you get stuck? What does it feel like when you start to get stuck? How do you usually react when you're in the dip? What could you say to yourself in those moments?

Teacher talk:

- 'Learning is a journey, and that journey has ups and downs. Its a normal part of learning.'

- 'When you are in the dip, it might mean you need to work harder, try a new strategy or ask for help.'

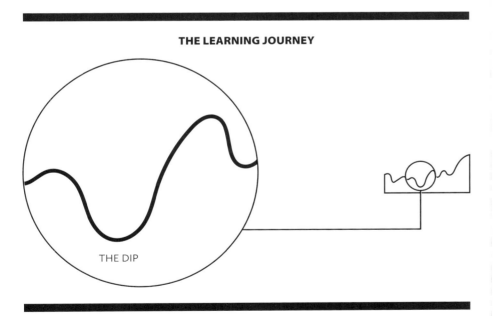

THE LEARNING JOURNEY

THE DIP

RECOMMENDED READING
This Learning Journey image is inspired by James Nottingham's Learning Pit, a model designed in 1999 (Nottingham, 2014). Others refer to the learning journey as the 'dip'. These include ClassDojo, who have a series of videos aimed at early elementary and primary school students.

TEACHER TIP
Display The Learning Journey in your classroom as a reminder of the ups and downs of learning. Use it as an interactive tool whereby students can reflect on where they are in the Learning Journey. Check out page 300 for an example from one school.

POINT OUT THE PROCESS

Explicit feedback on the learning process helps students to become more aware of when they are using effective learning habits. When students associate their success to positive learning habits, they are more likely to use these learning habits in future tasks.

Teacher Talk

In addition to Teacher Talk, suggest strategies students can use when they are in the dip. See Metacognitive Strategies, Make Meaning from Mistakes and Positive Self-Talk coming up soon in this section.

When students succeed as a *result of effective learning habits*, you can point it out: 'I noticed that...

> ...you figured out how to do that all by yourself by **trying different strategies**.'

> ...you really **listened** when (another student) made a suggestion. Listening to others helps you get new ideas.'

> ...you have clearly **thought about** that task by planning it out.'

> ...this was a hard assignment, but you **stuck with it**.'

> ...you kept trying **even after** you made a **mistake**.'

> ...you read the instructions **several times** until you understood them. That is what good learners do.'

> ...you chose a really challenging task. That's the best way to learn.'

or ask them to explain: 'Tell/show me...

> ...**how** you solved that problem/built that/created that.'

> ...about the **strategies** you used to figure out that problem.'

> ...where you had to **think hard** about what you were going to do next.'

> ...where you felt you were in the dip and you **kept trying**.'

> ...how you would **justify** that answer to prove you are right.'

🐧 KEEP IN MIND:

- Praising effort: There are many reasons why effort-praise can backfire. If it is too general, 'Good effort' sounds like the consolation prize and could send a message that we have low expectations of our students. If it is too verbose, it can also be interpreted as: 'Well, you got it, but it took a lot of effort so really you aren't as smart as Johnny, who did it easily.' Praising effort has little meaning if students put a lot of effort towards a task but do not succeed. Effort-praise should be used when pointing out the specific efforts that lead towards success or productive outcomes.

- Praise the job well done, rather than the person. Instead of 'You are a natural. Excellent speech!', you could say, 'The way you delivered that speech was excellent. You had a strong start by asking a question and made three clear arguments. Well done!'

ZERO IN ON THE LEARNING ZONE

In the classroom, students spend their academic time within two major zones. **The learning zone** means spending time in the process of learning like practising and getting feedback to be a better dancer. The **performance zone** is about showing others what you know or have mastered, such as in the actual dance recital. Both are useful. When we focus only on the end point (performance), however, we miss opportunities to reflect. Talk to students about the importance of being in the 'learning zone', which is where they should spend most of their time and where they will develop a learning mindset. See more on the 'zones' in Mindset: Research page 223. A great companion to the discussion of learning zones with older students is Eduardo Briceño's TED Talk, titled, *How to get better at things you care about*.

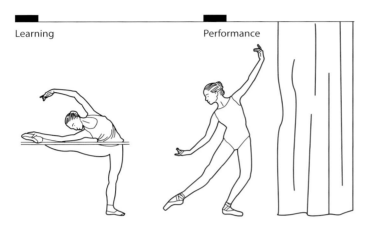

Learning   Performance

LEARNING AND PERFORMANCE ZONES
Talk to students about the importance of being in the 'learning zone', which is where they should spend most of their time and where they will develop a learning mindset.

BIG UP THE BRAIN

Although our brains are complex and mysterious machines, teaching a few small facts about how brains work can help students think about their learning process in a whole new way.

Children love to learn about the brain. Not only is it fascinating, but it gives students a clearer understanding of why learning takes repeated practice, increasing levels of challenge and lots of time. This is especially motivating for students who have associated their own struggle with a lack of intelligence. Teaching about the brain helps students understand why practising a learning mindset works.

 AT THE START

DIRECT TEACH: LEARNING STARTS SLOW, BUT PRACTICE MAKES PROGRESS

OPTIONAL OPENER: The following activity is a fun and quick way to introduce the brain and demonstrate that the hardest step in learning is often the start. Here we have linked this idea to how the brain learns.

1. **Start** with a simple activity that students need to practise a few times to get right. See figure on the next page for one suggestion. It helps students understand that new learning is challenging, but with practice and effort, the task is easier.

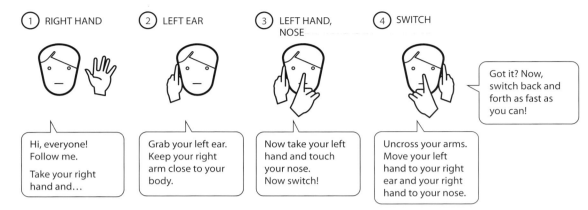

<table>
<tr>
<td>① RIGHT HAND</td>
<td>② LEFT EAR</td>
<td>③ LEFT HAND, NOSE</td>
<td>④ SWITCH</td>
</tr>
</table>

Got it? Now, switch back and forth as fast as you can!

Hi, everyone! Follow me.

Take your right hand and…

Grab your left ear. Keep your right arm close to your body.

Now take your left hand and touch your nose. Now switch!

Uncross your arms. Move your left hand to your right ear and your right hand to your nose.

EARS AND NOSE SWITCH

Slowly demonstrate the steps to students and then let them have a try. Give them several opportunities to practise. See how fast they can go.

RECOMMENDED READING

Do we only use 10 percent of our brain? Read 'Four neuromyths that are still prevalent in schools – debunked' (Busch, 2016).

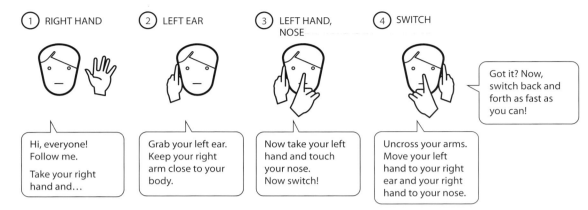

'Teachers who are prepared with knowledge of the workings of the brain … can help all children build their brain potential – regardless of past performance,' according to neurologist and educator Judy Willis (Willis, 2012)

2. **Debrief:** How difficult did you find the activity? Why? What did it take to get it right? What do you think would happen if we had another ten minutes to practise it?

Teacher Talk:

- 'This task might look easy at first, but it's tricky. You really have to concentrate and try it several times. Some people get it more quickly than others, but that's normal. It took me a while.'

- 'You can train your brain to move through challenges to get good at things that you might think you just can't do.'

- 'That feeling you had when you were struggling is what it feels like when your brain is getting a workout. Keep at it and it will get easier.'

DIRECT TEACH: COMPARE PATHWAYS IN THE BRAIN TO PATHWAYS IN A PARK

To help with student understanding of how the brain learns, it is useful to use the metaphor of a pathway in a park. This metaphor works with all ages. The first time we learn something, it is like putting footprints in the grass. It may even be hard to make your way at first, but the more frequently you do it, the more visible that pathway becomes until eventually it is easy to traverse. We form several pathways as we learn more things.

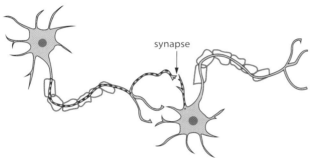

synapse

COMPARE PATHWAYS
Help students understand their
brain by comparing dirt pathways
in the park to the way their neural
pathways become stronger when
used more. That's how we learn.

RESEARCH
See Mindset: Research for a more
detailed description of what
happens when electrical signals
travel from one neuron to another.

DIRECT TEACH: A CLOSER LOOK AT HOW THE BRAIN LEARNS

Start by asking students what they already know about the brain. This will help you and
the students identify their prior knowledge and also help uncover some brain myths and
misconceptions that you can dispel.

Explain some brain basics that students should know:

For **older students**:

- Your brain has about 100 billion tiny cells called neurons that strengthen
  with effort and practice. The brain is constantly changing. This is called
  neuroplasticity.

- When you learn something new, your brain sends signals from neuron to neuron
  through neural pathways.

- The first time you learn something new is usually the hardest. The more you
  practise something you're learning, the thicker the neurons get, and the faster
  information can travel through the neural pathway, helping your learning.

- The brain has to be challenged to learn. You won't get bigger muscles if you always
  lift the same weights.

- With practice, the brain can learn new habits – ways of doing things and ways of thinking about things. You can retrain your brain!
- It takes time and effort, so persevere. Sometimes, it's uncomfortable to learn.

For **younger students**:

- The brain is like a muscle. It gets stronger with effort and practice.
- The first time you learn something new is usually the hardest.
- To strengthen your brain, you need to challenge it with more difficult tasks and practise a lot.

RECOMMENDED READING
Neuroplasticity by Sentis (www.bit.ly/2m0o3Dx) is an excellent video that reinforces the fact that we need to practise something in order to get better at it. It's great for discussing how we can form new habits and new ways of thinking with practice. For younger students, check out *Brain Jump with Ned the Neuron* (www.bit.ly/2klFFtb) or the book *Your Fantastic Elastic Brain* by JoAnn Deak.

🐧 KEEP IN MIND:

- The brain is like a muscle, but is not an actual muscle. It's much more complex. This is a simple metaphor for explaining that we learn from effort and practice.
- Brain training is a myth! You cannot work out your brain by doing maths in order to strengthen it in English. You only get better at the thing you practise.

KEEP IT GOING

BIG UP THE BRAIN: Reinforce the understanding of the brain's connection to learning, by 'bigging up' the brain when you talk to students.

WHEN YOU NOTICE...	YOU CAN SAY...
students are thinking hard	'I can see you are really giving your brain a workout.'
students start a new task	'Remember, the first time you start a new task is the hardest. Keep at it and it will get easier.'
students are practising something several times	'The neural pathways in our brains get stronger the more we practise something with purpose.'

GOALS: A ROADMAP FOR LEARNING
Creating goals sets students up for success, both now and into the future.

Goal setting is a powerful way to cultivate a learning mindset. Goals help focus attention, encourage more effort and teach metacognitive skills. Importantly, by explicitly teaching students about goals, we are spotlighting the learning journey and opportunities for small successes along the way. No matter how old your students are, we recommend setting up a system to help young people achieve their goals. Use the suggestions in this section to tailor a structure to suit your context.

 AT THE START

DIRECT TEACH: INTRODUCE GOALS

Below we describe a way to start talking about goals with your class to get the conversation started.

OPTIONAL OPENER: COUNTING TO 20

1. **Explain** to students that the class will play a game called 'Counting to 20' in which the goal is for the class, as a group, to count sequentially from 1 to 20. For younger students you may wish to count to 10 only. This game sounds simple, but there are a few guidelines:

   - There should be only one voice in the room at a time.
   - Hand-raising, gesturing or noise-making, other than stating a number, is not allowed.
   - The numbers must be stated sequentially.
   - When more than one person states the same number in a row or numbers are stated in the wrong order, the group will automatically start again at one and try again.

2. **Model** what not to do: point to a student to indicate they should talk next, raise your hand to talk or say a bunch of numbers in a row. Explain that the guidelines make the game challenging, but therefore the game is more fun.

3. **Frame the goal** by sharing that this is a challenging goal and usually it takes multiple attempts to reach it. When an error is made, students should just restart and work toward the goal of counting to 20 as a class again.

4. **Predict and strategise:** Ask students to predict how many times they think it will take them to reach the number 20. Elicit some things they want to keep in mind/do when working towards reaching their goal (e.g. make eye contact, be patient or focus).

5. **Start:** State you are starting and wait for someone to call out, 'one', and for others to follow with subsequent numbers. After a few attempts, have the group pause and ask them which strategies have been working, and what might be hindering the group from reaching the goal. Elicit any strategy suggestions. Remind students that this is a challenging goal and that the goal is likely to be reached sooner when the group is friendly and supportive of one another (see Relationships: Research about the importance of a 'relaxed-alert' brain state).

6. **Debrief:**

   - With **younger students**: 'In this activity, we set a goal (counting to 10 or 20). What is a goal? Why are goals important?'; 'What did we do when we didn't reach the goal on the first go?'; 'Did we have to do things differently?'
   - With **older students**: Elicit the value of having set a goal before starting the game by asking, 'How would we know if we were successful without having set a goal? Therefore, what purpose does a goal serve?'; 'How did it feel to have achieved the goal?'

RESEARCH
Goals affect performance in four ways. They help us focus, lead to greater effort, encourage resistance and push us to seek new strategies.
(Latham and Locke, 1991)

Teacher talk:

- 'In this game, like in all learning, having a challenging, yet doable goal is shown to keep people motivated. If the game was just to count with no end goal (e.g. the number 20), we might give up more easily and not be able to measure success.'

- 'Monitoring how we're doing in our journey to reach a goal helps us keep on track.'

- 'It is more satisfying to reach a goal when the goal is challenging. If we had counted to 20 on the first attempt, you might have found the game rather stupid. It's the difficulty that makes us motivated and excited to reach the end.'

KEEP IN MIND:

This game demonstrates that setting a more challenging goal can lead to more satisfaction when achieved. Having played this game with hundreds of students and adults, we've noticed that when a group has struggled to count to 20 the group breaks into spontaneous cheers and applause when they've finally done it. This doesn't happen when the goal is met after only one or two tries. When you see your students struggle and then celebrate, help make that link with them.

DEFINE GOALS:

1. **Explain** that a **goal** is something that you want to do or achieve that is reached through practice and effort. Offer a sports-related definition of a goal: in sports, a goal is when a player gets the ball into the target area (like a basket or between goal posts). Outside of the sports world, a goal is something that you hope to achieve, often requiring perseverance and effort. Share with students: 'Did you know that scientists study goals? Here are some of the things they learned:

   - When you set a goal that's more challenging (versus an easy goal), you are more likely to put in more effort and therefore reach your goal.

   - Making a public commitment to a goal increases the likelihood you will stick with it.

   - The brain learns better when you set challenging goals.'

2. **Think, Pair, Share:** 'With a partner, answer the following questions:

   - What are some of your goals outside of school (e.g. getting a high score on a video game, earning money, getting better at cooking or making new friends)? [If a student can't think of a personal goal, suggest a small one like cleaning their room, doing homework or getting to school on time.]

   - Why are these goals important to you? What do you hope to have or accomplish by them being met?'

3. **Debrief** with whole Group Share: A few students volunteer to share their goals and the importance of those goals to them. Remind them that goals work when we are motivated, and we work hard (practice and effort) to reach them.

Teacher Talk

'Setting a goal may seem like a simple task, but setting goals effectively is a science. I am going to help you at getting better at setting and reaching your goals.'

'We have different types of goals. For example, some are personal (relating to health, personality, friends, family) and some are educational, such as learning more about a topic, getting a certain grade or getting into the university of your choice. [**Older students** will also likely have career goals.] No matter what your goal, having a learning mindset will help you reach it.'

KEEP IN MIND

- Students may need a reminder of the difference between goals and wishes. A goal is something one wants to achieve that may require some effort, perseverance, strategies, and time. A goal ('I want to pass this class') is distinct from a wish, which is a desire for something that may not be in one's control ('I wish it would stop raining').

- There is a difference between performance and learning goals – a point that **older students** may find useful. You can explain that winning a game or performing in a dance recital is a performance goal (you are showing what you know how to do), and improving at dribbling the ball is a learning goal (a goal about the learning process). There are advantages to each kind of goal. For example:

  - Performance goals are motivating. They are something students can strive for in the long term. Examples include: earning a particular grade or winning a school talent competition.

  - Learning goals are essential because these goals actually help us improve our learning process and gain skills. They include goals like learning how to conduct an experiment to test a hypothesis or practising a dance move. In fact, in order to attain performance goals, a student will need to set and attain learning goals along the way.

TEACHER TIP
Create a class goal that is challenging yet achievable, such as learning everyone's first and last names by the end of the period or week, memorising a poem or writing down their homework in their planners each period.

CREATE A SYSTEM TO SUPPORT GOALS FROM START TO FINISH

Over the next few pages, we'll take you through the steps to plan, enact and reflect on student goals.

SUPPORT GOALS FROM START TO FINISH

SETTING THE GOAL	PLANNING	MONITORING AND FEEDBACK	FINAL GOAL REFLECTION
Stretch but difficult/smart goals	How I got there	Super quick check-ins	Questions about this goal
Goal timeframe	Steps for reaching the goal	Quick check-ins	Questions to reflect on learning mindset
Important questions for the teacher		In-depth check-ins	
		Survey says	

SETTING THE GOAL

STRETCH GOALS

Setting the right goal is crucial. Stretch goals are difficult yet doable goals. Recall what the research says about goal-setting and its relationship to difficulty. People tend to put more effort into more challenging goals; however, if the goal is too challenging or if there is not enough scaffolding or support, a student will likely not reach the goal. Help students find the right balance by setting stretch goals that are difficult yet doable.

THE LEARNING ZONE
Use this diagram to show students that learning happens just outside of the comfort zone, and it's smart to set stretch goals that push us into that learning zone. If something is so difficult that it creates anxiety, we enter the panic zone where thinking shuts down and learning is almost impossible.

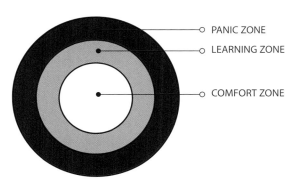

- PANIC ZONE
- LEARNING ZONE
- COMFORT ZONE

Goal setting and monitoring are metacognitive skills. There are plenty of opportunities for students to practise the metacognitive strategies coming up after this goals section.

For all ages, we recommend adopting the language of **SMART goals** as a way to talk about setting goals. Helping students think through essential elements of an effective goal, as they set and monitor it, sparks metacognition and commitment to the goal. Writing goals using the SMART goal definition is a tried and tested approach. There are plenty of resources available online to aid you more (with slight deviations on what each letter stands for), but all you really need are the essentials.

1. Start with a general goal, such as 'I would like to be more confident when I speak in class.' Then break it down. Think about what this might look like in practice. Visualise yourself having reached the goal.

2. Explain what a SMART GOAL is:

   A SMART goal is:

   Specific: the goal is clear and somewhat detailed.

   Measurable: we can measure our progress and success: how many, how much and/or how often? If it can't be measured, it can't be managed!

   Action-oriented: we can take steps toward reaching our goal.

   Reasonable: the goal is in our control, not just down to luck, and success is possible.

   Time-bound: we've set a timeframe for our goal.

   Goals should also:

   - Be stated in the positive: 'I will learn.../I will be able to...'
   - Require new learning along the way.
   - Recognise potential barriers and solutions.

3. Give examples of goals that are not so SMART and those that are SMART:

Not so SMART compared to . . .	SMART
I would like to be more confident.	I will participate more in my history lessons.
I will get better at homework.	I will turn in my homework on time for the next two weeks.
I would like to not get in trouble at school for being late.	I will get to school on time every day for the rest of the term.
I want to be a famous footballer player.	I will compete in a football match.
I want to do well on my GCSEs (exams).	I will get a B or above in biology.
I will get better at maths.	I will know my time tables (or number bonds) by the end of the year.

For **younger students**: Set a class goal, discussing and making decisions about each element of the SMART goal. Teachers can talk with students about individual goals, writing them down in templates such as this one below:

SMART GOAL FORM

> **My SMART Goal**
>
> I will _Learn my times tables up to 10_
>
> By _25 May_. I will reach my goal by _quizzing myself every day or asking my sister to quiz me for 20 minutes._
>
> Name: _Tom_ Date: _1 May_

GOAL TIMEFRAMES

Below are examples of goals and goal timeframes. Make the point that not all goals need to be long-term goals. Take this opportunity to share your own goals or to create a fun goal for the class.

- **Short-term goals:** These are the goals you set for yourself over a very short period of time, such a lesson, day or evening.
  - 'By the end of this period, I will have planned this essay.'
  - 'Today, I am going to focus. When my mind wanders, I will say to myself, "Re-focus."'
- **Intermediate goals:** These goals are still specific, but may take longer and require more self-regulation to change habits.
  - 'Over the next two weeks, I will organise my revision (studying) by using a calendar and tick off what I do each night.'
  - 'This week, I will practise always re-reading what I write.'

- **Long-term goals:** These are goals that require a longer period of time, have several sub-goals and require considerable monitoring and feedback. These include: learning a difficult skill, passing final exams, getting into university or finding a job.
    - 'This term (semester) I am going to learn to have a short conversation in Spanish.'
    - 'I will know my time tables (or number bonds) by the end of the year.'

KEEP IN MIND

- It is essential that teachers help students choose attainable goals so that students can experience small successes along the way. Recall the research on self-efficacy. People with high levels of self-efficacy have experiences of success as a result of effort and opportunities to reflect on what led to success.

- Often students already have experience with setting goals but haven't really thought about them deeply. Keep it positive at the start, but it may be helpful to acknowledge that we all have a lot of unmet goals. Discuss some of the obstacles and difficulties of goals. Remind students that goals are not easy because we may face challenges or lose the motivation to work on the goal – and that some goals take time to achieve.

- As teachers, we already set goals through learning objectives for students on a daily basis. This is a connection you could make with your students.

PLANNING

The expression 'Failing to plan is planning to fail' speaks to the importance of students putting together a well-thought-through plan. This requires forethought and a grasp of what will be needed in order to reach the goal. The following strategies support students to create a plan.

PLAN

REALITY

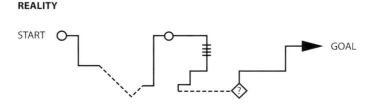

RECOMMENDED READING

When discussing life and career goals with students, we recommend *What Do You Really Want? How to Set a Goal and Go For It!* by Beverly Bachel and *The 7 Habits of Highly Effective Teens* by Sean Covey

For very young students, we recommend 'The Power of Yet' from Sesame Street – www.bit.ly/2kIwe7z

PLAN vs REALITY

It's important for students to understand that there is not always a direct route to reaching a goal, which is why it's so important to plot out a goal journey, keeping in mind that there will be twists and turns along the way, some of which can be predicted. (Inspired by image from www.bit.ly/2oLvxfx)

HOW I GOT THERE – A STRATEGY TO VISUALISE SUCCESS

'How I Got There' is a classroom activity that helps **older students** to be forward thinking about their goals. An added bonus is that students are explicitly practising metacognitive skills. This is one of our favourite tools.

1. Explain that one great way to reach your goal is to imagine what it took to reach your goal.

2. Give students a sheet of paper titled, 'How I (name the achieved goal).' For example, 'How I Got an A in the Class'; 'How I learned to be a better public speaker'; 'How I wrote an outstanding essay'; etc. Have them put a future date on the paper if there is a set date, like an exam, or have students fill in an end date that makes sense for the goal.

3. Ask students to look into the future and predict what they will have had to do to reach the goal. If you think your students may need more guidance, model this strategy using your own example.

   - What steps did you take? Be very specific.
   - What learning strategies did you use?
   - What obstacles did you face? What did you do to overcome them?
   - When was it the hardest? What did you do for help or motivation?

4. Whole-group discussion: Use teacher talk to help students think more precisely about the process of reaching a goal.

5. Create a goal planner handout: Use the chart below to customise a handout for your students to help them keep track of their next steps and deadlines.

Goal:		
Steps	**Deadline**	**Done?**

TEACHER TALK

Use the Learning Choices Chart on page 254, to help students reflect on decisions they will need to make when faced with obstacles, mistakes, difficulty, etc.

Encourage students to be specific. In my experience, they start with vague comments like, 'I worked really hard.' Be prepared to get them to think more deeply. For example:

If a student says…	Ask…
'I worked hard.'	'What did this look like?'
'I put a lot of effort into it.'	'How did you know your efforts were working?'
'I got help.'	'Where? Who? What did you do first?'

The Planning Fallacy is a phenomenon in which people are overly optimistic and underestimate the time needed to complete a future task (Kahneman and Tversky, 1979). Does this ring a bell?

MODEL AND TEACH STUDENTS THE STEPS FOR REACHING THEIR GOALS

Use the following chart for a more in-depth discussion. Explain that goals should be broken down into shorter increments so that they are manageable and more easily measurable. This practice builds confidence and teaches self-regulation. Use the chart below to talk through and model the steps for immediate and long-term goals by modelling the thinking process, using the example (or your own goal). For short-term goals, use three steps: Set a stretch goal, monitor and reflect.

RECOMMENDED READING
For GCSE, A level and high school students, *The GCSE Mindset Student Workbook* by Steve Oakes and Martin Griffin is a straight-talking guide for all students as they plan their studying and preparation for exams.

STEPS	EXAMPLE
1. Set a goal: Is it a stretch goal? Is it specific, measurable, action oriented, realistic, and does it have a timeline?	I will run a half marathon in the next six months
2. Break it down: What steps will I need to take?	1. Make sure I have the kit/equipment (proper running shoes, a timer). 2. Schedule training runs. 3. Start running.
3. Prepare for goal blockers: What obstacles may get in the way? What strategies can I put into place? Use If… then statements.	I might lose interest or get bored, injure myself or have to prioritise other things with my time. If I get bored, then I'll run with my friend. If I'm finding it hard to fit in running with my schedule, then I'll wake up earlier.
4. Make a commitment: Who will I tell? How will I stay motivated?	I'll tell my family that I'm going to run a half marathon.
5. Get feedback and monitor your progress: Who can support me to reach my goal? Who can inspire me to be resilient in pursuing my goal?	I have a phone app that records my miles and time. I'll talk to my PE teacher to get feedback on how best to work out for running. My mum can inspire me. She's a runner.
6. Reward yourself along the way for small successes: What small rewards (that aren't counter to the goal) would I have?	After I've reached a certain number of miles, I'll call a friend to hang out.

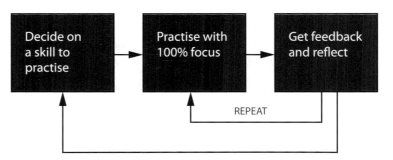

REACHING A GOAL TAKES PURPOSEFUL PRACTICE

Explain: Practice is a key part of reaching any goal. Explain to students that there is a special type of practice called 'purposeful practice' specifically needed to get better at something. Give examples from your content area, such as practising your letters or learning a new language.

Embed purposeful practice in the classroom:

- Identify one skill or process that you want your students to practise. This could even be a class routine, as discussed earlier in Relationships.

- Allow opportunities for students to practise this skill within the lesson. This means designating time for concentrated practice and focused feedback.

- Make each practice feel slightly different than the previous, so children are getting outside of their comfort zones – and be explicit about this design. Show students the comfort zone concentric circles on page 266.

- Build in early experiences of success.

MONITORING AND FEEDBACK
CHECK IN WITH STUDENTS ON A REGULAR BASIS

Self-monitoring and feedback are crucial in achieving goals. Regular check-ins show students that you have high expectations and that you want to support them. This part of the process is crucial for developing a learning mindset, and it is the perfect opportunity to 'point out the process' as students reach and reflect on small successes. Below are some ideas for checking in.

SUPER QUICK CHECK-INS

- Fist to 5: Use this quick strategy to monitor how students feel about their progress. Explain that you will make a statement and students will raise fingers to indicate their answer. Use prompts such as, 'Fist to 5: How much effort are you putting into your goal? Raise 5 fingers to indicate a lot, 1 to indicate only a little, etc.' or 'Fist to 5: I am on track with my goal. 5 being I am exactly where I should be.' (This also works with Temperature Check. See page 106 in Relationships: Leadership.)

- Weather report. Using the weather-related words only, ask students to rate how they are feeling about their goals. A Google search will give you several variations of the below.

WEATHER REPORT

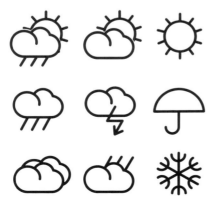

CONNECT TO MEMORY

Purposeful practice is in line with Memory strategies such as spaced retrieval practice, which requires repeatedly returning to previously learned skills, gradually removing clues or structures that might make recall easier. The effort put into recalling information helps fortify memories.

RECOMMENDED READING

We've said it before and we'll say it again: *Neuroplasticity* by Sentis is a great video (www.bit. ly/2m0o3Dx). Use it to explain how habits form in the brain.

QUICK CHECK-INS

- Exit Tickets or Entry Tickets with short-answer questions such as, 'What's one step you've taken toward reaching your goal?'

- One- to two-minute individual check-ins about goals during class time, or even in the hallway, can help keep students on track. Make a checklist of students with space for their goals and comments so that you can easily refer back later to ensure you check in with everyone.

- Goal Display: Display the goals in the classroom so that the goals are public, students can support each other, and you have an easy reference for check-ins. There is plenty of inspiration to be found online with an image search of 'goal display'. Obviously, ask students' permission first – students may want to keep them private. To keep track of this, we recommend a tracking sheet like the one used created for Classroom Connection Check-ins on page 74.

GOAL DISPLAY
Use sticky notes to display student goals, inspired by *Praising the Process: See it in Action* video by www.teachingchannel.org and www.mindsetkit.org

Gael	Keisha	Sam	Abdel
My goal is to use more adjectives.	I will check my spelling each time.	I am going to show, not tell.	I will use short & long sentences.
Bao	**Emily**	**Yessenia**	**Oscar**
	I will start sentences in different ways.	I will use more adventurous adjectives.	My goal is to show, not tell in my openings.
Jamal	**William**	**July**	**Ravi**

IN-DEPTH CHECK-INS

Use more in-depth check-ins to keep the momentum for long-term goals and for problem-solving any issues that may arise. Of course, these are also perfect opportunities to give feedback on process (see page 258 for 'I noticed that...' suggestions) and to celebrate achievements along the way. Example of in-depth check-ins include peer feedback (students pair up and interview each other about their goals), journal reflections, whole-class discussion and student conferences (individual or small group).

Use the following questions for the quick check-ins and in-depth check-ins:

- 'What is something you have done recently towards reaching your goal?'
- 'What are the biggest challenges you're facing in reaching your goal?'
- 'What are your next steps?'
- 'Is there anything you need help with? Please explain.'
- 'What can you do now to get back on track?'
- 'What kind of feedback would help you to reach your goal? Be specific.'
- 'What adjustments (if any) have you made to your plan? Be specific.'
- 'What have you learned about yourself over the past few days/weeks/months when working on your goal?'
- 'What achievements are you most proud of reaching on your way to meeting your goal?'

SURVEY SAYS: USE SELF-ASSESSMENTS TO REVEAL STUDENTS' HABITS

For **older students:** This survey can be used before, during or after long-term goal-setting. It also helps students reflect on how well they self-regulate their independent learning.

Scale from 1 to 4: How well did you do the following?

1 = Pretty dismal/no effort/gave up   4 = Excellent/really happy with my progress and effort

RATING	GOAL STRATEGIES	OPTIONAL FOLLOW-UP QUESTIONS
	I set **goals**.	Give an example.
	I monitor my performance (kept track of what I am learning/remembering).	What strategies do you use? (questioning, checklists, lists, quizzes, teacher feedback, etc.)
	I create an appropriate physical **space** for revision.	Where is it? What resources do you have there?
	I avoid **distractions** (notifications, online, family).	What are the hardest distractions to avoid?
	I give myself breaks.	What do you do?
	I use of my study **plan** and **calendar**, ticking things off.	What do you include on your calendar? Where is it?
	I manage **stress**.	What did you do to manage stressful times?
	From the above, which is the most challenging?	

FINAL GOAL REFLECTION

Reflection helps us become aware of strategies that worked, recognise obstacles (which can help us plan better next time) and develop a sense of accomplishment and pride for persevering. Reflections can take the form of whole group discussions, Talk Tasks (see page 282), written reflection, peer interviews, etc. We encourage you to model your own reflection with your students so that they become more aware of the ways that you set goals in your teaching practice. Goal Reflection questions include:

- How does it feel now that I have accomplished my goal?
- If I did not accomplish my goal, what are some of the reasons (was there a problem with the goal, one of my strategies, my motivation, etc.)?
- Did I get the results I expected or wanted?
- What have I learned from this experience? What would I do again or do differently?

 KEEP IN MIND

For **older students**, teachers need to be conscious that students will likely be asked to set goals for each one of their subjects. This is why it is important for schools to 1) think big-picture and support students in how to manage several different goals at once; and 2) develop school-wide systems and protocols for goal attainment to reduce student cognitive load (See Memory: Research) and stress. Ultimately, each department should be utilising the same approach.

 KEEP IT GOING

Goal-setting should be a regular practice throughout the year with key milestones and opportunities for success planned along the way as students develop a learning mindset. Use the chart on the next page to organise your thinking and outline any system you'll put in place before students set their goals.

RESEARCH
The pain of procrastination is worse than the actual task: 'Mathphobes, for example, appear to avoid math because even just thinking about it seems to hurt. The pain centers of their brains light up when they contemplate working on math. But there's something important to note. It was the anticipation that was painful. When the mathphobes actually did math, the pain disappeared' (Oakley, 2014).

See **Memory: Classroom** for ideas on how to create revision/study calendars with students.

GET READY, SET, GO: IMPORTANT QUESTIONS FOR THE TEACHER

AREA OF SUPPORT	QUESTIONS FOR TEACHER	RATIONALE
Setting the goal	Should this goal be co-created? teacher-created? Student-created (self-created)? Should I require they set one personal or social goal and one educational or career goal?	Self-created goals can lead to higher level of self-regulation. Appropriate and challenging teacher-generated goals lead to high level of self-efficacy and can demonstrate high levels of expectation from the teacher.
Type of goal	Are the goals performance or learning goals?	A combination of performance (outcome based) and learning goals (competencies and skills) have the highest overall impact. Wanting to get good grades works best as a goal when it is combined with the goal of wanting to understand the material. (Mayer, 2019)
Monitoring	When will I build in time for explicitly reflecting on goal progress and current strategies? Against which benchmarks will I monitor student progress?	Students benefit from practising metacognition when working on goals. Self-reflection has been shown to increase feelings of self-belief, which then leads to a positive impact on outcomes.
Feedback	How will I give feedback for short, intermediate and long-term goals? How will I facilitate effective peer feedback?	Feedback must be about the criteria, timely and based on expertise. Have a simple system for check-ins so you can sustain the process.
Strategies and resources	What strategies and knowledge will my students need to have in order to reach these goals? Do they have access to these? Is it clear where to find resources and get extra support?	Understanding of spaced practice and other memory strategies may be helpful for the student (See Memory: Application). Likewise, make sure students have essential knowledge needed to accomplish the goal and know how to access resources.

METACOGNITION: THINKING ABOUT LEARNING

Supporting students to get better at metacognitive strategies takes time and forward planning, but once a system is in place, metacognition becomes habit.

Metacognition is actively monitoring one's own learning and includes metacognitive knowledge and metacognitive regulation. Metacognitive knowledge refers to knowledge of oneself, the task and related strategies for completing the task. Metacognitive regulation refers to planning how to approach the task at hand, monitoring the progress and the strategies being used as well as evaluating the outcome and overall process. It's a cycle that we all undertake during a learning task. Each time we practise metacognition when engaging in a task, there is also an opportunity to reflect on the larger picture, relating the specific learning experience to the learning process in general, which fosters a learning mindset.

Metacognition, actively thinking of one's learning, is an ongoing process that includes metacognitive knowledge and metacognitive regulation. Teachers can help students reflect on the learner's decisions and relate the experience to the learning process in general. (See figure on next page.)

METACOGNITION IN ACTION

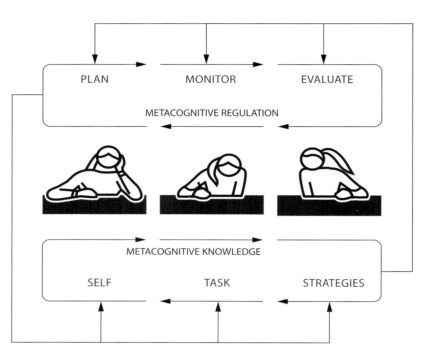

TEACHER WATCHES

REFLECTION

Reflect on learning as a process, and make connections.

 AT THE START:

DIRECT TEACH: INTRODUCE METACOGNITION

1. Explain metacognition or 'thinking about your thinking'

Teachers should explicitly teach metacognitive regulation to children. In other words, tell students that effective learners think about what they are doing as they work. Explain to students that learning metacognitive skills gives you more control of your learning! It's a bit like driving. You'll know when you need to put on the brakes, step on the gas or change direction. Again, it is crucial to explain WHY we use these metacognitive strategies as well as how to use them. Just like learning to drive, it takes practice, practice, practice.

Teacher Talk: 'As we become better learners, we develop the ability to think about our learning and how:

- We plan: Think first about the steps we will take to accomplish a task. We consider what we already know about ourselves, the task and the strategies that might work best. We set goals.

- We monitor: Keep thinking about how it's going and decide which strategy might be the best to use.

- We evaluate: Think back about how it went and evaluate your success and the process.'

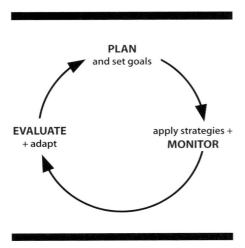

SIMPLE METACOGNITION CYCLE
This cycle illustrates how we are constantly planning, monitoring and evaluating. It's a good image to use when you introduce metacognition.

I use the word 'metacognition' with **older students** and 'thinking' or 'thinking about your thinking' for **younger students**. For younger students, you will need to explain the word 'thinking' first. One way of explaining thinking is to do the following activity:

Step 1: Show them three separate numbers (e.g. 1, 2, 3) or only two numbers, depending on your students' prior knowledge.

Step 2: Ask students to remember the numbers. Hide the numbers, and then ask them to recall the numbers.

> Although metacognition is more about 'thinking about your learning', we use the phrase 'thinking about your thinking' with younger students. It's more fun and easier to understand.

Step 3: Ask students to add a one to each number – in their heads. Explain that when they add a one in their heads, their brains are thinking: 'When we add numbers, we think in our heads. I see the number and put a one next to it and then see the answer. Some of you might count to yourselves inside your head. This is what thinking is.'

2. Give a concrete example.

Using the scenarios below (or your own), ask students to suggest things they might think about as they plan, monitor and evaluate the process. An example scenario might be: 'What would you be thinking if you are preparing to meet a friend?'

Teacher Talk

	SCENARIOS FOR TEACHER TALK
Planning	'If I have to meet a friend, I might think to myself, 'Hmm … What time do I need to leave to get there on time?"
Monitoring	'While I'm travelling, I could say to myself, *'Is this the best route? Am I going the right way?"*
Evaluation	'When I get there, I might reflect: *'It took me 15 minutes to meet my friend. Next time I'll try a different route to compare."*

Debrief

- Why is thinking about your thinking so important?
- Are there times when it is difficult to think? What can we do to help ourselves in those moments?

3. Explicitly teach students metacognitive questioning

Present questions students can ask themselves as they learn. For **younger students**, scaffold this by using only the questions in bold. When sharing this, ask students why each particular question might be important to ask oneself, so that students gain a deeper awareness of the importance of self-talk. Explain that these questions help us to be better learners.

BEFORE (Planning)	DURING (Monitoring)	AFTER (Evaluation)
'What do I know about this topic?' **'What will be my first step?'** 'Have I done a task like this before?' 'What strategies would work best?' 'Are there resources I will need for this?'	**'How am I doing?'** **'What should I do next?'** 'Should I try a different strategy?' 'What resources can I use?'	**'How did I do?'** **'What did I learn?'** 'Did I get the results I expected?' 'Is there anything I still don't understand?' 'What strategy was the most helpful for me?" 'What strategy was the most helpful for me?' 'What could I do differently next time?'

Adapt questioning to your context or subject. Also create sentence stems that apply to different situations and share these with students. Use these sentence stems to prompt student thinking. Differentiate for developmental ages. For example, in English, students can ask, 'How does this idea relate to my main point?'; or in science, 'What materials will I need for this experiment?' Teach these to your students.

4. Model metacognitive questioning in context

Task Example: What number is 49 less than 220?		
BEFORE (Planning)	**DURING (Monitoring)**	**AFTER (Evaluation)**
What do I know about this problem? This looks familiar. This looks like other word problems I've seen. I know that 'less than' means I subtract. 49 is really close to 50.	**What should I do next?** OK, I'm going to put the bigger number on top and subtract 49. At first I thought, but then I … I know I'm on the right track because … I need help. I'll use the (resource) I'll keep going.	**How do I know I got it right?** I know I got it right because I double-checked it. Next time, I might be able to do this in my head because 49 is so close to 50. I will use the key words (like 'less') to remember what strategy to employ.

CONNECT TO MEMORY
See 'Tap into Prior Knowledge' in Memory: Classroom for plenty of ideas on how to find out what students already know. We've also included a series of questions to probe understanding and help to uncover misconceptions.

🐧 KEEP IN MIND

According to the research, teaching metacognition works best when educators:

- **Explain** the benefits of metacognition ('Good learners think about their learning, because it helps them make good decisions and learn from mistakes').
- **Are explicit** about strategies to use ('It's important to plan, monitor and evaluate as we solve problems'; 'We can use planning tools to help us').
- **Model** ('First I will...').
- **Relate** to context and/or subject ('The first thing I'll do is look at the periodic table. I will...').
- **Incorporate verbalisation of thinking**, including Talk Tasks prompts and protocols ('Let's Think, Pair, Share...').
- **Practise, practise, practise** ('Remember when we... – let's use that strategy again here').

Teaching metacognitive skills will benefit all school-aged children; that said, children's ability to utilise these skills will vary significantly depending on their developmental stage. Children are around the age of 12 when they can begin to fully take advantage of metacognition (Peteranetz, 2016). See our discussion about age in Mindset: Research on page 235.

🐧 KEEP IT GOING

In order for metacognitive thinking to stick, it must be practised consistently, repeatedly applied to real learning contexts. As teachers progressively model and practise metacognition with their students, they begin to internalise these strategies and use them independently in everyday problem-solving, as well as in the way they express 'how' they learn.

Over the next several pages, there will be a number of metacognitive strategies. We start with metacognitive questioning and sentences, then introduce some specific Talk Tasks and reflection tools.

MODEL, TEACH, PRACTISE AND CONNECT

Model, Teach, Practise and Connect is a step-by-step guide for teachers to use to ensure that they are incorporating the key aspect of teaching metacognitive skills.

Before you begin, we suggest you:

- Identify a learning objective and task you often ask students to do. Consider what students could be thinking that would help them to better self-regulate and meet the objective.
- Use the metacognitive questioning grid above and plan what you are going to say when you model your thinking. This planning reduces teacher cognitive load experienced while teaching.

TEACHER TIP
A visualiser teaching aid is an excellent tool for modelling thinking in real time. The visualiser can easily project a draft piece of work, task to be completed or a mistake made, which the teacher can use as a live model for planning, monitoring or evaluation.

MODEL	TEACH	PRACTISE	CONNECT
Say aloud your thinking as you display the steps of the task.	Go back over the steps, reminding students what to do and what to notice about their thinking.	Students follow the steps the teacher modelled.	Teacher asks students to talk about the decisions they made during the task.

METACOGNITIVE TALK TASKS

Talk Tasks provide structure to help learners know what to do, how to do it and words to use, allowing them to focus on what really matters – metacognition. The emphasis is on the thinking process and helping students to plan, monitor and evaluate their learning. These tasks require that each student get a talk partner.

TALK TASK GUIDELINES

Students of all ages benefit when certain guidelines or protocols are established for talking in pairs or small groups. Train students how to do the Talk Tasks by introducing Talk Task guidelines.

TALK TASK GUIDELINES	
For younger students	**For older students**
Turn: Turn and face your partner. **Look:** Look at your partner or, if there is a written task, look at the task. **Focus:** repeat the talk task **Listen or speak** 　Listeners: show you are listening by nodding and avoiding any distractions. 　Speaker: give your opinion and then pause for other person to comment, or ask your partner a question. **Turn back and wait:** When you are finished, you can turn back and wait. If others are still talking, use the time to think about one point you would like to share with the class.	**Tune in:** orient your body to your partner, communicate that you are ready to listen. **Focus on task:** decide who will go first – or, one student repeats the question. **Everyone speaks:** make sure that each person speaks. (If someone has not spoken in a while, stop and listen. Ask a question.) **Actively listen:** when someone is speaking, show interest by nodding and making eye contact at points during the discussion. **Be prepared to share.**

 KEEP IN MIND

- For **younger students**, when introducing the Talk Task guidelines, keep it simple. Break the process into steps and model what each step looks like. Use a simple task to practise the guidelines in the beginning; otherwise, you may overload students with too much to think about. Although eye contact with a partner shows you are listening and is often a sign of respect, explain that it's OK to look away as well. Many people look up when thinking or will look at the work as they talk about it.

TALK TASKS

Think, Pair, Share: Teacher poses a question. Students first think on their own, then pair with one other person and share their thinking. Optional: share with the whole class after talking as a pair.

TEACHER TIP
When using Talk Tasks, be intentional about pairing students. Before you start, ensure every one has a partner. Having to pick a partner (or not being picked) can create anxiety for some students.

THINK   PAIR   SHARE

RECOMMENDED READING
For more examples of Talk Tasks, see *Visible Thinking* (www.bit.ly/2m5ujda), part of Harvard University's Project Zero, which has created a wide range of short 'thinking routines' for teachers. This is a great free resource, useful for all ages.

Think, Pair, Share, Square: Teacher poses a question. Students first think on their own and then pair with one other person and share their thinking. The pair 'squares up' with another pair and all four share their ideas.

Think, Pair, Listen: Teacher poses a question. Students first think on their own and then pair with one other person and decide who will go first. They listen to their partner (without speaking) and then switch.

Think, Write, Pair, Share: Teacher poses a question. Students first think on their own, then the students write their thoughts (this could also be in the form of notes). Then they pair with one other person and share their thinking.

See, Think, Wonder: Teacher shows a picture, video, diagram or some stimulus and poses a question. Students first look at the stimulus and think on their own about what it is and what it makes them wonder about (what questions they have). Students share their thoughts with a partner.

PAIRED THINK ALOUD

1. **Prepare** by coming up with a task that is difficult for students to do – something that will take some deep thinking. Put the task on strips of paper, so that each pair has one strip.

2. **Model:** (10 mins)

   - Explain that you (the teacher) will **think aloud** how to solve a task or figure something out.

   - (Note: Model a problem that you don't intend to give the students.)

   - Ask students to write down what you say – not your actions.

   - Model your thinking aloud. For example: 'Now where did I put my keys? I always do this. OK, I remember that I walked in the door first, then I...'

   - When done, ask students to recall the exact things you said, not a summary. For example, 'Now where are my keys?' – not, 'You were looking for your keys.'

- **Student paired task:**
- Separate into pairs and give each pair the task sheet, *turned down*. Remind students not to turn it over until you say go.
- **Explain the task:** 'I am going to give each pair a problem to solve. When I say "go", one of you will turn it over and think aloud as you solve the problem.'
- **Explain the roles:**

The Speaker:

- Say aloud what you are thinking. This might include:
    - Thoughts about the task as you try to complete it
    - Questions that come to mind
    - Steps you use to work it out
    - Decisions you make along the way

Make sure you are thinking ALOUD (verbalising your thoughts), not thinking in your head. If you don't know what to say next, you can say 'I'm not sure what to say, I'm stuck, let's see, um...' until you figure out what to say.

The Listener:

- Listen to the speaker and write down their thoughts.
- Allow the speaker to work through the problem at their own pace. (Do not interrupt or help. If you can't write it all down, do your best.) If they stop talking, ask, 'What are you thinking?'

PAIRED THINK ALOUD WALKTHROUGH

Turn over task

Student thinks aloud (thoughts, questions, steps)

Listener listens (takes some notes, encourages if needed)

Debrief the content

Switch roles with new task

Debrief content

Debrief the process

RECOMMENDED READING
Paired Think Alouds are based on Thinking Aloud Paired Problem Solving (TAPPS), one of our favourite strategies by Wimbley and Lochhead (www.bit.ly/2mspVpb)

TEACHER TIP
Display phrases that students
come up with. They can be posted
or aligned with the Learning
Journey diagram.

- **Start:** Say 'go' and give students a time limit, depending on task.
- **Debrief:** What did the speaker *think aloud*? On the board, list responses. Ask students to categorise their responses into 'helpful' and 'less helpful or not so helpful' in solving a problem. Students' answers will likely include strategies for solving the problem ('I used the graph to get information'), metacognitive talk ('Now is that right?') or more personal self-talk ('I'm rubbish as these types of problems'). Record all of the responses and help students to differentiate which are helpful and which are not. Teacher and students then come up with self-talk phrases to use when they're stuck. (See page 298 for more examples of positive self-talk.) Examples might include:
  - What is this asking me? Do I need to read it again?
  - What do I already know?
  - Learning something new can be hard at first. Keep going.
  - My brain's pathways strengthen with practice.
  - If I make a mistake, I can learn from it.
  - This is a hard problem that will challenge me. I like a challenge.

3. **Repeat and debrief again:**
- Allow the other partner to be the speaker and hand out a new task. Remind them of the roles.
- Debrief the second round: repeat the debrief process and note any new positive self-talk that might be inspired from the last debrief.

4. **Debrief the talk task:**
   Make it explicit that this Think Aloud strategy helps us to learn better. For **older students**, reiterate the word 'metacognition'. Elicit what they learned and remind them that research backs positive self-talk.

Younger students may benefit from using sentence stems:

BEFORE (Planning)	DURING (Monitoring)	AFTER (Evaluation)
This question is asking me to … I already know … First, I will … I notice … I wonder …	At first, I thought … but now I think . . I can tell I am on the right track, because … I am stuck because …	I can prove I got this right by … I got stuck on … so I … I can get better at this by … What I liked about my process was… what I might change is…

 KEEP IN MIND

- Once you have introduced any of these protocols and practised them several times, students will not need as much guidance.
- The teacher should group students. Having to pick your partner (or not being picked) can create anxiety for some students. Before you start, ensure everyone has a partner.
- Switch it up. Provide students with opportunities to work with different people.

ACCOUNTABLE TALK FOR THE CLASSROOM

Classroom talk that's accountable to the learning community, to accurate knowledge, and to rigorous thinking helps foster communication skills, thus building confidence and, ultimately, supports a learning mindset. It is the type of talk that can be taught and practised.

For **younger students**: you can introduce accountable talk in stages, starting with 'agree/disagree' and moving on to 'starting off', then 'ask for clarification' and 'summarise'. Give students many opportunities to practise these roles before moving on. For **older students**, you may want to customise the accountable talk stems for your subject. For example, in English ('The author has shown this through...'); in history ('This source shows...'); or in art ('The artist's technique reveals...').

Talk hand signals are non-verbal indicators that students can use to communicate their opinions and thoughts.

| I AGREE | I DISAGREE | I HAVE AN ANSWER | I'M THINKING | I'D LIKE TO BUILD ON THAT |

SENTENCE STEMS for ACCOUNTABLE TALK

Agree/disagree	Build on it	Challenge it
I agree/disagree with ..., because I agree with .., but I disagree with ... I understand your point, but I think ... I agree/disagree, because we already learned that ...	I would like to add ... To expand on what ... said, I would add ... This reminds me of ... (refer to previous learning/content)	That may be true now, but what about when ... ? OK, but don't you think that ... ? Have you considered ... ? I have a different point of view. I think ...

Starting off:	Ask for clarification:	Summarise:	Probe more:
I think/I believe ... In my opinion ... because ... Let's start by/with ... Based on ... it seems that ... I noticed that ..	Would you explain that again? What do you mean by ... ? Can you give me an example of ...? Is that the same as ...?	So what you are saying is that ... In other words, you think ... Am I right in thinking that ... ? I heard a lot of people saying that .. In summary ...	Why do you think that? Can you back that up with some evidence? If that is true, then why ... ?

CONNECT TO RELATIONSHIPS
Incorporating the use of accountable talk into the classroom norms can help students contribute to a positive classroom culture of respect. (For more about establishing classroom norms, see Relationships: Classroom)

 KEEP IN MIND:

- Encourage students to use each other's names when using accountable talk, not just pronouns ('I agree with what Naomi said' as opposed to 'I agree with what she said').
- Encourage students to refer to previously learned material and to use specific and technical vocabulary.

MORE METACOGNITIVE STRATEGIES

Because metacognitive skills are such an important aspect of learning mindset, you'll also find related strategies throughout Mindset: Classroom, especially when we discuss goals and mistakes. Likewise, there are several reflective tools in Relationships: Classroom and Memory: Classroom that connect the dots. We've collected a few more good ones for you on the following pages. Select ones that are the most appropriate for your students' ages and the content you teach. Practise these strategies regularly with students so that they become habit. Keep in mind that introducing too many new strategies at a time can be overwhelming for students, so it's best to introduce these slowly throughout the year.

VISUAL MAPS (for planning)

Visual maps are a great way to get students to organise their thinking. We cover visual maps in Memory: Classrooms. Students can design their maps (such as mind maps or concept maps) or use graphic organiser templates, such as compare/contrast diagrams or T charts. Additionally, students can then explain their visual map to their partner or use it to aid themselves as both a reflective tool and memory strategy. For **younger students**, provide the map to help them plan. For **older students**, give them opportunities to practise designing their own maps based on how they think information should be organised.

CHECKLISTS (for planning and monitoring)

RESEARCH
After explicitly teaching and modelling metacognitive strategies, the research strongly suggests that these thinking skills are best learned when students apply them to a domain-specific learning experience (Dignath and Büttner, 2008).

Simple checklists aid students in following steps and monitoring their progress as they go. Checklists can include steps and questions to ask along the way about one's thinking or strategies. Examples include a checklist of what goes into writing a scary story (e.g. a suspenseful opening, imagery, etc.) or the steps to solve an equation. The teacher could either model how they came up with the list or the teacher and student together could generate a checklist. The actual creation of the list could additionally be a final reflection tool – and then the list can be used during the next attempt at the same type of task.

REFLECTION LOGS (for monitoring and evaluation)

A student log of thoughts about learning can be used for any stage of the process to mark strategies, reflections, progress toward one's goals and/or learning. These should be ungraded, but monitored by teachers for feedback on how students are using metacognitive thinking. Questions may include:

a. How would you summarise the main ideas of this lesson in three sentences or fewer?

b. What was the main idea of the whole lesson? How did it relate to what you already know?

c. How can you connect today's learning with your own personal experiences?

d. What was something you did today that you could have done better? What about a task or idea that you don't understand or don't agree with?

e. What was the most important thing you learned today? Why was it important? How was it the same as or different from what you already knew?

NOTE TAKING for older students (for monitoring)

Interactive notetaking, which is outlined in more detail in Memory: Classroom (page 174), encourages the learner to be more aware of the information they are writing down, rather than mindlessly copying notes. To enhance metacognition, take a brief break in the lesson and ask students to turn to a partner and explain their notes (elaboration). This is also a great opportunity to incorporate summarisation of the lesson. Summarising is a complex skill that takes a lot of modelling.

CONNECT TO MEMORY
Check out Memory: Classroom for tips on how to teach interactive note taking.

EXIT TICKETS (for monitoring and evaluation)

Exit Tickets, completed in the last few minutes of class, contain questions relating to the learning process. Use them to guide reflection:

- When students encountered a challenge
- When students chose a different strategy to solve a problem; and
- When students learned something new about the task or themselves

EXAM WRAPPERS (evaluation)

Exam Wrappers are customised questionnaires to give students after they have completed an exam, essay or longer project. They are a great tool for recording students' thoughts about how well they prepared for a task, how they felt about the task itself and/or what they learned. Exam Wrappers (see figure on next page) are also useful for setting new goals and ensuring students engage in the feedback once they have turned in a marked piece of work. They don't have to be about an exam, but they work best when they relate to a specific task that may have required significant prep work.

EXAM WRAPPER

When did you start preparing for this exam? Choose one option

	Since the start of the year
	About two weeks before the exam
	About one week before the exam
	The night before the exam
	I didn't prepare

How did you prepare for the exam?
Write the number that corresponds with how much you used the following strategies

1 - not at all; 2 - sometimes; 3 - a lot	
	Reread through my notes or book
	Highlighted my notes or text
	Re-wrote my notes or took notes from the book
	Created mind maps
	Used pictures/draw pictures
	Used flashcards and/or quizzed myself
	Answered past exam questions
	Looked at online resources
	Used mnemonics (using the clues to remember the rest)
	Other

What type of questions were the most challenging? What was challenging about them?

Name three things you will do differently to prepare for your next exam

1.

2.

3.

In what ways can I help you prepare for your next exam?

LETTERS TO ANOTHER OR FUTURE SELF (evaluation and reflection on the learning process in general)

Students write letters to you or a peer about their previous learning. Alternatively, they can write to their future selves. In this case, the letters can be sealed and either sent home to be opened later or given to them at the start of the next school year. Here are some prompts that may generate interesting responses:

- When I first looked at this assignment (topic or exam), I thought to myself...
- If I were to do this again/when I do this again, one thing I will definitely do differently/the same is...
- One piece of advice I would give a younger student is...
- One thing I learned or that happened that I don't think the teacher noticed is... (This can potentially be a fun one. One year a student confessed to popping my beach ball.)

PROCESS PORTFOLIO (evaluation and reflection on the learning process in general)

These process portfolios can be created in many different ways, from very detailed over a long period of time, to more condensed portfolios that cover a short unit of work. Essentially, the student collects 'artefacts' that demonstrate their growth over time. For example, artefacts could focus on their progression as a writer, their skills development in PE, or learning to draw or play a musical instrument. The collected artefacts are used to tell a story about how the learner progressed. There are annotated or narrated (this can take the form of sticky notes, an accompanying report, photos, videos or a recorded voice narration, for example), reflecting on their growth, the strategies they used and, of course, the metacognitive thinking they practised. These portfolios are great for displays and for showing incoming students the learning journey.

RECOMMENDED READING
To learn more about larger-scale process portfolios, see this inspiring article (www.bit.ly/2m3FrYo) from EL Education about Passage Presentations with Portfolios.

LONG-TERM METACOGNITIVE REFLECTION

The end of a unit, term or school year is a great time for students to take stock of their metacognitive skills through reflection. The sample questions below could be explored in a variety of formats (discussion, turn and talk, etc.):

- What are some examples of how you...? (Use the chart to guide responses)
- How was your learning process the same as/different from other learning experiences?
- How has your learning improved this year?
- How has your teacher helped you to learn? How could your teacher help more?
- What was the easiest/hardest assignment? What challenges did you face and what did you do?
- What mistakes or errors did you make? How did you resolve them?

🐧 KEEP IN MIND:

Model and scaffold strategies: metacognitive strategies should be modelled (e.g. the teacher models their thinking step by step) and then scaffolded (e.g. the students mimics the teacher) to prepare students practise on their own.

MAKE MEANING FROM MISTAKES

Take down those 'Mistakes are Great' posters and find authentic moments to make meaning from students' temporary setbacks.

Creating a climate of comfort – where students genuinely feel like they can learn without the fear of repercussions (from peers or teachers) from making a mistake – takes real effort. In Relationships: Classroom, we suggest a number of strategies for establishing classroom norms that support academic risk-taking. We address the important role of the teacher in setting the tone by being bold enough to call out snickers or looks and being wise enough to deal with sloppy mistakes (misspelling a word the student already knows) and stretch mistakes (forgetting lines during an oral presentation) in different ways. In this section, we offer some intentional strategies for supporting this climate of comfort and the promotion of a learning mindset, which values mistakes.

 AT THE START

SURVEY SAYS: USE ANONYMOUS SURVEYS TO FIND OUT STUDENT ATTITUDES ABOUT MISTAKES

Survey students about how they feel about making mistakes. This is a great strategy because it shows students that while we all learn from mistakes, it's normal to feel uncomfortable making them. Below are two sample surveys to get students thinking about their attitudes towards mistakes and to help teachers reframe those attitudes to be more aligned with a learning mindset. This survey can be followed up by one-to-one check-ins, Think, Pair, Shares and/or small group discussions.

1 = Strongly disagree   2 = Disagree   3 = Neither disagree nor agree   4 = Agree   5 = Strongly agree

Circle 1 (Strongly disagree) to 5 (Strongly agree)	
Making mistakes is one of the best ways to learn.	1 2 3 4 5
If I know I might make a mistake or fail, I would rather not try.	1 2 3 4 5
I give up easily when I don't understand what is happening in class.	1 2 3 4 5
I feel comfortable talking to an adult at the school when I don't understand something.	1 2 3 4 5
I worry about other students making fun of me if I make a mistake.	1 2 3 4 5

Comments:

Debrief:

- What is something you've learned from a mistake you made?
- Why do you think some people fear making a mistake?
- What can we say to our peers when they make a mistake or get the wrong answer?

USE SUBJECT SPECIFIC SURVEYS

Students' academic anxieties are often centred around a particular subject. When students are in a heightened state of anxiety, their brains do not process information as easily and learning can be compromised. Students may show signs of anxiety as early as Key Stage 1 (K–1st grade) and anxiety often increases with age, especially in subjects like maths and for high-profile tasks, such as public speaking. Eliciting students' anxiety levels and discussing the role of mistakes can support them to reach that relaxed-alert state we mentioned in Relationships: Research. Below is an example of a survey about public speaking:

PUBLIC SPEAKING EXAMPLE

Circle 1 (Strongly disagree) to 5 (Strongly agree)	
A person is either good at public speaking or not, and you can't really change it.	1 2 3 4 5
The best public speakers do not have to prepare much before speaking.	1 2 3 4 5
Public speaking is a natural talent. You're born with the ability or you aren't.	1 2 3 4 5
I worry about making mistakes in front of my peers.	1 2 3 4 5

Comments:

KEEP IN MIND:

When telling students they can learn from mistakes, explain why:

- Mistakes are an important part of learning because they help you to solve problems.
- Making a mistake often means that you challenged yourself or attempted something outside of your comfort zone, which is important when learning something new.
- Mistakes help you to better understand the correct meaning of something.
- Understanding your mistakes helps you develop stronger habits of learning.

SHARE STORIES ABOUT THE VALUE of MISTAKES and TAKING ON CHALLENGES

For **younger students**, use the children's books below to highlight how these young people have made meaning from mistakes:

- *The Girl Who Never Made Mistakes* by Mark Pett and Gary Rubinstein (mistakes and challenges)
- *Beautiful Oops!* by Barney Saltzberg (mistakes)
- *The Most Magnificent Thing* by Ashley Spires (determination)
- *What Do You Do with an Idea?* by Kobi Yamada, illustrated by Mae Besom (confidence)
- *Ish* by Peter H. Reynolds (confidence and not having to be perfect)

MAKE ROLE MODELS RELATABLE

All learners struggle; it's an important part of learning. Use the stories of famous people, local heroes, family and friends and your own examples to model and normalise this challenging part of the learning process. Research role models in your subject area and find out more about their personal struggles. Be sure to include a variety of representations and relatable role models. For more on this, see Mindset: Research and Relationships: Classroom.

RESEARCH
In a recent study by Lin-Siegler et al., (2016), researchers found that reading about scientist's struggles had a positive impact on student motivation and performance in science. Reach more about his study in Mindset: Research on page 239.

LOOKING BACK: LETTERS TO YOUNGER PEERS

For this activity, older students write letters to younger students about their struggles in school and how they overcame them. These letters don't have to be about struggles; they could also be some general advice about hard work and perseverance. (See page 290 for similar letter-writing tasks.) This strategy is particularly helpful for students in transition years – entering a new school or phase, such as primary to secondary school, or Years 3 and 7 (or 6th and 9th grade in the US). We recommend starting with a class discussion and setting some ground rules (after all, you don't want older students to give younger students inappropriate advice, like how to sneak out of class).

- What is one thing you found difficult at the start, but you find easy now? What did you have to do to get better? (Keep at it, don't be afraid to ask for help.)
- What was it like coming to a new school? What advice would you have for a new student (e.g. making friends, studying, navigating the lunchroom)?
- 'Everybody has the ability to get smarter.' Explain why this statement is true.

For **younger students**: Create a letter template that the class can complete collectively. Consider using prompts such as:

- Year 2 (1st grade) is fun because…
- On my first day I felt…Now I feel…
- It's important that you…
- Remember to…
- One way to make friends in ___ year/grade is to…
- One thing I wish I knew at the beginning of the year is…

Alternative: Have older students visit younger students' classrooms as guests or 'experts' to talk about overcoming struggle. Of course, make sure that they are prepared in advance by thinking and writing about their own struggles and what strategies they used to overcome them.

RESEARCH
In one large-scale study, researchers found that students who reflected on ways to strengthen their brains and also wrote letters to younger students about their struggles were more motivated to take more rigorous learning experiences and persist with difficulty (Yeager et al., 2019).

KEEP IT GOING:

SPOT CHECKS

Spot Checks are short starters or Do Nows that purposely have errors in them; students are tasked with spotting the errors. These should be based on common mistakes you've seen in student work or errors you know students commonly make, such as confusing homophones (the difference between their, there and they're). Students usually enjoy Spot Checks. To utilise Spaced Practice (See Memory: Classroom), you can use content from your previous unit of study. Ensure that you eventually provide the answers and include a few examples that aren't mistakes.

STUDENT CHECKS

SELF-CHECK

Set a protocol in your class for students to self-correct before handing work over to a peer or teacher. This should become a classroom habit. It is best if you provide a rubric or checklist of 'common errors'. This could also take the form of a checklist of things to look for.

BRAIN, BOOK, BUDDY, BOSS

Ensure there are resources available to help students if they are finding the work difficult. Display 'Brain, Book, Buddy, Boss' (or Brain, Board, Buddy, Boss) as a reminder for students to be resourceful by thinking of the answer first, then checking a book, turning to a peer, then asking the teacher.

GUIDED PEER CHECKS

Peer checks can also help to build a supportive learning environment and de-stigmatise mistakes, but students need to be trained in how to give effective, supportive feedback and need specific guidelines. Without proper structures in place, peer checks can be a source of anxiety and embarrassment. (See Peer Feedback at the end of this chapter, on page 304.)

PREDICT YOUR MISTAKES

Ask students to predict the types of mistakes they might make when given an upcoming assignment or task. Students will likely mention 'sloppy' mistakes. Brainstorm what strategies they could put into place to avoid these sloppy mistakes or resources they could use to avoid mistakes during more challenging work.

CALLING ON STUDENTS

WITHHOLD THE ANSWER (by Doug Lemov)

We recommend checking out the protocols for calling on students that we've outlined in other chapters of the book. See high expectation questions on page 68 and Cold Call Recall on page 170.

Ask the class a challenging question, take several responses, but withhold the answer. By withholding the answer, you create suspense and therefore keep the attention of the students. As you discuss the question more, students can weigh up different responses and formulate an opinion of their own. Doug Lemov also suggests using multiple-choice questions for challenging content; well-designed multiple-choice questions have answers that are nearly right or reflect common misconceptions or mistakes.

MY MUDDIEST POINT

In this quick writing activity, students write down their 'muddiest point', meaning where they might have got stuck or found the content confusing. Prompts include:

- What do you know the least about?
- What was the hardest part of this task/problem for you?
- What would you like repeated or expanded on?

Although it is just a question, calling this activity the 'muddiest point' adds a fun element and a shared language that quickly connotes what the teacher is asking. These can be used mid-lesson or collected for the teacher to review (Angelo and Cross, 1993, cited in Tanner, 2012).

KEEPING TRACK OF MISTAKES

MISTAKE LOGS

Mistake Logs help highlight how much we learn from mistakes, as well as the different types of mistakes we make. They help teachers to notice mistake patterns and identify the potential need to re-teach something. Students can keep their own logs or you can keep a class log, with either you or the students jotting down when stretch mistakes happen. Make a point of only logging the stretch mistakes or the most common mistakes (e.g. 'Everybody keeps using the _____ incorrectly'). These logs are also great resources for Spot Checks (see above).

Date	What was the mistake?	What's the correction?	What did I/we learn?

RECOMMENDED READING
'Mistakes are not all created equal' (www.bit.ly/2kwlb14) is a great article to share with students. Author Eduardo Briceño explains that not all mistakes are the same. Sloppy mistakes can be quickly self corrected, while stretch mistakes happen when we are doing something challenging.

CORRECTING MISTAKES

Although it's tempting to correct every mistake or make improvement suggestions on all aspects of student work, the research is overwhelmingly clear that this has little impact – and we all know how time consuming it is for teachers! Use very specific success criteria or a rubric that makes clear what it is you are correcting (and not correcting) for each learning objective. (For more on this topic, see guidelines for giving effective feedback on page 301.)

STUDENTS IN CHARGE

Students review their past work, success criteria (for the current task), comparatively exemplary work, or the mark scheme or rubric to help them think about what they'd like to improve during the task. Students tell the teacher (with the help of a simple prompt sheet), 'I would like help with_____.' Then the teacher must restrain themselves and offer feedback only on what students asked for. Getting students to take ownership of their learning and to have an opinion on how they'd like support is empowering and builds metacognitive knowledge.

UNGRADED CORRECTIONS

Avoid putting a grade or level on work when it is passed back. Use a highlighter to mark mistakes or areas that need improvement and have students self-correct – with appropriate scaffolding.

RECOMMENDED READING
Another great activity for normalising mistakes is called My Favorite No from the Teaching Channel – www.bit.ly/2ozngLh

NORMALISING MISTAKES AND DIFFICULTY

How a teacher responds when a student makes a mistake or struggles with learning sets the standard for the whole class. No snickers, no stares allowed. Effective teachers demonstrate that mistakes are normal and beneficial to the learning process.

Teacher Talk

The following starters – 'Did you know that… ' and 'Ask yourself … ' – are useful prompts for the teacher to use to support students when they are faced with mistakes, struggle and/or disappointment:

'Did you know …	**'Ask yourself:**
I try things many times before I get it? Try **having another go**.	What do I **already know**? What part do I want help with?
it is good to ask for help when you need it; that is how we **learn from others**. We call that using a strategy.	**Where** am I stuck? What **tools** can I use to help me now?
that feeling of **struggle** is what it feels like to learn?	What **steps** did I already use to get to this point?
all successful people have made **mistakes** along the way?	How can I **learn** from that **mistake**? What part should I **try again**, differently?
one of the hardest parts of learning is the beginning – **starting something new**? It's normal.	What am I being asked to do?
Or explain: 'Here is what I was thinking when I solved it: _____.' (Think the entire thought process aloud. Then give a new question, issue, problem.)	*Or say to yourself: 'The **brain** learns better when it has to work hard and really **think**.'*

 KEEP IN MIND

- Be sensitive to students' emotional responses to failure. Fear of failure can be directly linked to self-worth or the belief that one is not valuable as a person. It might also be caused by negative responses to and consequences of mistakes within one's own family or other learning communities.

- If a child does make a seemingly careless or a silly mistake, it could be due to cognitive overload. (Check out the Memory chapter for more on cognitive load and working memory.)

POSITIVE SELF-TALK

Self-talk – that little voice inside our heads – can encourage or discourage us, impacting how much effort we put into a task, how long we stick with it, and how we interpret mistakes we might make along the way.

 AT THE START:

Self-talk is a metacognitive act that refers to a way of talking or thinking to ourselves about ourselves. This can be related to a situation or task. In the journey to support students' development of a learning mindset, teachers can model and teach ways to engage in positive self-talk, allowing them to think more positively about the task and their capacities. Below are some steps for introducing positive self-talk.

HANDLING SETBACKS WITH SELF-TALK

1. **Explain self-talk**. 'Self talk is what we say or think to ourselves about ourselves. We use it all the time! The way we talk to ourselves influences how we feel about a task, situation or our own abilities. Our self-talk can be negative or positive. Negative self-talk can impede learning, while positive self-talk is helpful because it can help us to persist when learning becomes difficult or we experience a setback, like making a mistake or struggling to figure out what to do.'

2. **Model** with an example:

   - Negative: 'I don't understand any of this! I give up. I'm just not clever!'
   - Positive: 'Let's break this down. I can get this.'

3. **Elicit** from students examples of self-talk they already use when faced with difficulty.

4. **Hand out** the chart below. Ask students to circle which of the positive self-talk statements 'fits' ('I can imagine saying this to myself') and which ones seem like a stretch ('I wouldn't say that'). Ask them to add additional (realistic) examples of positive self-talk they might use.

5. **Whole-class discussion**: Elicit some responses from the students. Discuss which positive self-talk examples seem most realistic to them and which additional statements they added.

6. **Debrief:** Remind students of how positive self-talk can really shift their thinking and learning process. Ask them to write down two examples of positive self-talk that they will practise saying the next time they are faced with a setback or difficulty. Have students keep these examples of self-talk somewhere that is easy to get to so that they can refer to them when they need them.

> The way we talk to ourselves influences how we feel about a task, situation or our own abilities.

NEGATIVE SELF-TALK (SHUTS DOWN LEARNING)	POSITIVE SELF-TALK (HELPS YOU TO CONTINUE TO LEARN AND CHALLENGE YOURSELF)
'This is too hard.'	'This may take some time and effort. The first time learning something is the hardest.'
'I can't do this any better.'	'I can always improve, so I'll keep on trying.'
'I got it wrong. I'm no good at this.'	'Mistakes help me learn better. Where did I go wrong?'
'They are so clever. I'll never be that clever.'	'Everybody can learn. I can figure out how they did it.'
'It's good enough.'	'Is it really my best work?'
'I tried and failed. I don't want to try again.'	'Most successful people have had failures along the way.'
'My teacher is always criticising me.'	'Feedback helps me learn.'

TEACHER TIP
When talking privately to students as they work or at the start of their task, ask, 'What can you say to yourself right now to stay motivated?' Then write their (positive) self-talk on a sticky note and stick it to their desk as a reminder. Encourage students to use this strategy themselves at home when they need a little motivation or to shift their mindset.

USE SCENARIOS TO PRACTISE SELF-TALK

1. **Explain the task.** 'Each pair or trio will get a scenario of negative self-talk. These are real examples collected from other students. Your task is to advise a peer on what self-talk they could use in this scenario. Write 3 examples in your book.'

2. **Model one example:**

   Scenario: 'I am really horrible at writing. I never know what to write.'

   Peer advice: 'In the past, I found writing hard, but I know I can get better at this if I practise more.'

   For exam-level students:

   Scenario: 'I want to do well on my GCSEs, but I'm so lazy. I'll never do it.'

   Peer Advice: 'I got this. It will take effort, but once I get a routine, it will be easier.'

3. **Assign each pair or trio one of the** scenarios on the next page or make your own.

4. **Then start the task.**

5. **Whole-class discussion:** Elicit a few responses from pairs. Ensure the peer advice self-talk suggestions are positive and realistic. Use the Teacher Guide: Sample Responses for Self-Talk Scenarios, on the next page, to offer additional examples, if needed.

6. **Debrief**
   - Explain that negative self-talk is normal and can be changed to positive self-talk.
   - If you practise saying something to yourself, it can become a habit – a new way of thinking. It helps us develop a learning mindset.
   - Positive self-talk can help you in stressful situations, because it helps you see new perspectives and solutions to problems.
   - Before you start a task, ask yourself: 'How do I feel about this task?'; 'What could I say to myself right now to help? What can I say to myself if I get stuck?'

For self-talk to be effective, it should be positive and realistic. It is not helpful to say to yourself, 'I can do it. I'll keep trying' when in fact you need help or you should use a different strategy.

SCENARIOS	PEER ADVICE EXAMPLES
Taking an academic risk 1. 'I'm really good at science, but my homework was really hard. I chose not to do it so no one would know that I didn't understand it.'	'Not understanding something is part of learning.' 'It's when I show what I don't know that a teacher (and friends) can help me get better.' 'I'll start with what I can do and work from there.'
Getting outside of your comfort zone 2. 'I am just bad at doing presentations in front of the class. And today when I was asked to present my work, I didn't do it.'	'Presentations take practice, practice, practice. Even if I stand up and don't do as well as I would've liked this time, I know that it will get easier with practice. That's how the brain works.' 'I'll ask a friend who is very comfortable doing public speaking to give me advice and practise with me.' 'Most people are nervous when they present. It's normal.'
Putting in effort 3. 'I didn't understand, so I raised my hand right away for help and waited for the teacher to give me the answer. That was easier than trying to figure it out.'	'Usually, when someone gives you the answer or helps you before you've really struggled to figure it out, you won't remember the information as well.' 'That uncomfortable feeling of trying to figure it out is your brain working. I'll reread the question before asking for help.'
Facing criticism 4. 'I tried really hard to write an essay. I thought it was pretty good, but my teacher only criticised it.'	'What positive things can I learn from this? My teacher has high expectations for me and wants me to do well. Their job is to push me to improve. This is a positive thing.' 'Feedback is not about me, it's about the work.' 'Sometimes teachers forget to comment on what they liked and just focus on what could be improved. I'll ask my teacher to point out some of my strengths.'
Attitude toward failure/ comparing self to others 5. 'I know I'll never get picked for the team, so why bother even trying? I'll never be as good as everyone else.'	'Trying to do something that is scary means I can take risks, which is a really important skill.' 'Everybody can get better from whatever point they are at – I should compare myself to myself, not to others.'

 KEEP IT GOING

STUDENT-CREATED SELF-TALK POSTERS

1. **Ask** students to select a positive self-talk statement from the chart on page 298.
2. **Create** posters with students, completing a prompt template such as:
   When I think, '_____', I can say to myself, '_____'
3. **Hang** posters on the wall. As an option, invite students to place a sticker on the poster each time they've used this positive self-talk prompt.
4. **Reflect** with students after a week or so to see how or if they've referred to the posters.
5. **Consider** other ways to show posters if these have become part of the 'wallpaper'. Taping a different poster to the classroom door each month or integrating the prompt into a Do Now or Exit Ticket can keep this alive.

THE LEARNING JOURNEY

Create a Learning Journey on the wall (see page 257) and ask students what they can say to themselves if they are 'stuck in the dip'. Post examples of positive self-talk on the dip graphic. Use the Learning Journey to discuss where students might be in their learning. One secondary school teacher I know created her own version for display. (See a reproduction of this below.) It is now printed in all of the student planners and used by all subject teachers to facilitate discussion about the ups and downs of learning.

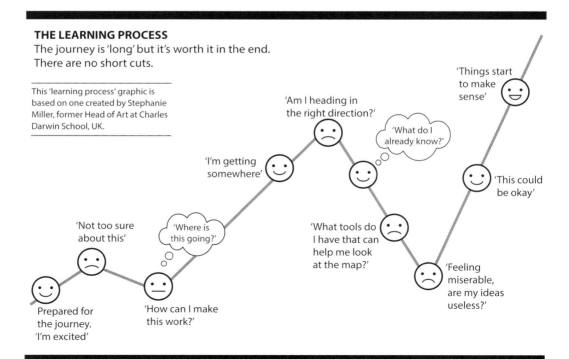

THE LEARNING PROCESS
The journey is 'long' but it's worth it in the end. There are no short cuts.

This 'learning process' graphic is based on one created by Stephanie Miller, former Head of Art at Charles Darwin School, UK.

'Things start to make sense'

'Am I heading in the right direction?'

'What do I already know?'

'I'm getting somewhere'

'This could be okay'

'Not too sure about this'

'Where is this going?'

'What tools do I have that can help me look at the map?'

'Feeling miserable, are my ideas useless?'

'Prepared for the journey. 'I'm excited'

'How can I make this work?'

FEEDBACK

Not all feedback is the same, yet there are some rules feedback should follow to promote student learning, increase effort and bolster more positive self-belief.

As we discussed in Mindset: Research, teacher feedback can be either (1) actionable and about the task, relating to the success criteria ('Please add more detail to your characters') or (2) about the learning process, as it relates to behaviour, actions and metacognitive skills ('I noticed you were stuck with that until you got it.'). For the next few pages, we'll look at feedback on the task. For more about feedback on the learning process, see Point Out the Process starting on page 257 and Normalise Mistakes and Struggle on page 296.

CONNECT TO MEMORY
For plenty of suggestions to find what a student already knows, see 'Prior Knowledge: Find Out What Students Already Know' on page 161 in Memory: Classroom.

GUIDELINES FOR GIVING FEEDBACK

Preparing for Feedback: Teacher Checklist

__ **Success criteria:** Are you clear about what success looks like? How will you know the learner has learned what you intended them to learn?

__ **Formative assessment:** Are you clear about what the learner already knows relative to the success criteria?

__ **Student response to your feedback:** Have you factored in when the learner will have time to review and reflect on the feedback?

Timing and frequency: when and how often? Give frequent and immediate feedback as a general rule

Do...

Build in strategies for students to respond to feedback.

Return student work in a timely manner.

Give immediate, verbal feedback to relevant questions and to any misconceptions.

Delay feedback for more expert learners.

Give more expert learners less frequent feedback, so that they can work independently through problems.

Don't...

Go over the work without providing opportunity to respond to the feedback.

Return an assignment or assessment two or more weeks after it's been completed.

Dismiss misconceptions, thereby implying they are accurate.

Give so much feedback that learners depend on it and do not think for themselves.

Quantity: how much?

Do...

Select about two or three points to make per assignment.

Include strengths as well as weaknesses in equal measure.

Be cautious not to overload novice learners with too much feedback.

Don't...

Return assessments with every single small mechanical error corrected (eg. punctuation, spelling, etc.); focus on the key skills you are evaluating.

Write long, wordy feedback.

Lots of comments on poor quality papers and almost nothing on good quality assignments.

Focus: on what? Specific aspects of the success criteria

Do...	Don't...
Give feedback based on success criteria that students understand (e.g. student-friendly rubrics).	Make criticisms without offering any insights and how to improve.
Compare student work to their previous work.	Display class lists that compare students to each other.
Avoid personal comments.	Make personal comments, like 'This shows laziness'.

Process of learning: learning choices that lead to success

Do...	Don't...
Be specific and authentic.	Comment solely on intelligence and/or natural ability.
Point out when students have displayed the choices on the Learning Choice Chart on page 254.	Overpraise effort.
Relate effort, practice and challenge to how the brain learns.	Compare students.

 KEEP IT GOING

STRATEGIES TO FINE-TUNE FEEDBACK

Because feedback is so central to learning and a learning mindset, there are numerous feedback strategies we recommend throughout the book. For **assessment for learning**, you'll find a lot of ideas in Memory: Classroom, where we discuss ideas for tapping into prior knowledge and questioning on page 161. We have also included numerous reflection tools on the metacognition pages in this section. Below are some strategies specifically for feedback.

QUICK CHECK-IN DURING THE LESSON

Use traffic lights to quickly assess understanding. Make the frown red; the neutral face amber and the smiley face green. Give each student a set and possibly laminate them for continued use.

TRAFFIC LIGHT COLOURS

RED	AMBER	GREEN
'I don't understand this yet.'	'I think I understand but could not explain it to someone else.'	'I understand this well and could explain it to a friend.'

RUBRICS

A rubric is a guide that helps the teacher and student clearly communicate about the different levels of the **success criteria**. They are most effective when provided alongside the assignment so that students know how they're being evaluated and, therefore, what goals to set for themselves. It is also a great tool for **student responses to your feedback**. Under each of the rubrics is space for students to review and reflect on the feedback in some form. They are similar to an exam board mark scheme, but rubrics are more specific to the task and, if shared with students, written in accessible student-friendly language. Rubrics can be time-consuming, which is why we love the single-point rubric. It's interactive, spells out the success criteria and takes up less time. Below is an example of one:

SINGLE-POINT RUBRIC

Success Criteria	Student Comments	Areas that need improvement	Areas that shined

Teacher comments:

RECOMMENDED READING
cultofpedagogy.com has a number of excellent blog posts about rubrics. One really useful one for helping you construct your own format and criteria is Rubric Repair: 5 Changes that Get Results by Mark Wise (www.bit.ly/2mqOiDq).

A FEW MORE GOOD IDEAS for STUDENT RESPONSE TO FEEDBACK

- Make corrections. (Be specific about which corrections should be worked on and how many opportunities there will be in the future to work on them.)
- Explain the feedback to a partner. Having to explain one's feedback helps them to better understand it.
- Reword the feedback – put it in your own words.
- Identify a similar task so they can implement the feedback.

KEEP IN MIND:

- A students' ability to absorb and respond to feedback will be determined partly by their level of self-efficacy for the task at hand. Students with high self-efficacy will tend to receive feedback more positively than students with low self-efficacy. Remind students why you are giving feedback – because you have high expectations and you want to help them get better. (See Relationships: Classrooms for tips on establishing high expectations.)
- Feedback followed by a caveat indicates that you really were looking for something else. 'Excellent job getting your maths homework in on time. Now if you could do that in English too, that would be great' emphasises a deficiency and is less effective.

RECOMMENDED READING
Visible Learning: Feedback by John Hattie and Shirley Clarke (2018) and *How to Give Effective Feedback to Your Students*, 2nd edition by Susan M. Brookhart (2017).

PEER FEEDBACK

Peer feedback is powerful when learners are trained in how to give and get feedback.

INTRODUCE PEER FEEDBACK THROUGH AUSTIN'S BUTTERFLY

Teaching students to give more effective peer feedback is essential for both primary and secondary students and should be introduced using simple, explicit protocols that are repeatedly practised. At Julian's Primary School in London, peer feedback protocols are reintroduced each year by adapting the following steps to different content, and the same protocols are practised across the curriculum from English and art to science and PE. In secondary schools, different departments can adapt the same protocols so that effective peer feedback becomes the norm.

Set up: You'll need to watch the fantastic video about Austin's Butterfly (www.bit. ly/2mupJFN), which shares a student's multiple attempts at drawing a butterfly (including the final, far more detailed version). Consider showing images of Austin's attempts (see page 244 or search images online) and a photograph of a tiger swallowtail butterfly, which Austin draws. Teachers can draw their own butterfly to get feedback from students. Have your example butterfly ready – and don't make it too good if you happen to be an artist!

1. **Optional. Prepare** by drawing your own butterfly or a first attempt, as some tasks relate to a learning task.

2. **Introduce peer feedback**
   - **Explain peer feedback** 'Today, we are going to think a lot about how to improve our work with the help of others. I know everyone can do this task, no matter how good at art you are already.' Ask students what the word 'feedback' means. 'What makes feedback effective or helpful?' (Optional: Discuss why simply using the words 'good' and 'I like it' don't help someone get better.)
     - **Prediction:** 'In the video, a six-year-old student is asked to draw a butterfly. How many times do you think he'll keep trying until he is satisfied?' Show students the photo of the real butterfly.
     - **Watch** the video. Ask students how many versions Austin drew. 'What do these young students in the video notice and say? Why was the feedback helpful?' For example, the students used specific language like: 'The wings need to be more pointy and more triangular' compared to vague feedback such as 'Try to make the wings look better.'
     - **Explain:** Feedback should be:
       - **Kind** (but honest)
       - **Helpful** (offer suggestions for improvement)
       - **Specific** (precise and detailed)

3. **Model your own thinking of how you would draw the butterfly**. Show your first attempts at drawing. Model self-talk as you make a second attempt. ('I noticed the butterfly has pointed wings so I...') Ask for **feedback** from students and write down their suggestions.

4. **Evaluate as a class** the feedback they have given you. Use different colours to help them differentiate. Was it kind (but honest)? Helpful (suggestions for improvement)? Specific (precise)? **Pull out phrases** they used that were effective or that could be improved.

 **KEEP IT GOING**

Have students practise giving and getting feedback on a piece of work, using Kind, Helpful and Specific feedback. Peer feedback is best when students have (1) a clear understanding of the success criteria; (2) a foundation in the content they are feeding back on; and (3) opportunities to improve each time. This will set them up to give and receive feedback more effectively. Otherwise, they may reinforce misconceptions or waste time with general statements.

Optional: Introduce Peer Feedback Prompts (below) to use. In pairs:

- Do peer feedback one at a time, with the speaker reading their own work out loud to a partner. Feedback could be about written text or a maths problem, for example.
- The listener fills in the prompt sheet that contains sentence starters (see below).
- The listener then reads the prompt sheet to their partners. Discuss.
- Switch roles and repeat.
- Students use feedback to improve their work.
- Students share their final work with the class and name the specific changes they made as a result of feedback.

WHAT'S GOOD?
"I like the way you_____, because_____"
"I can see you really improved with _____ or thought a lot about." (Explain more below.)
"Well done. This shows _____" (Point to something successful and explain why below.)

HOW CAN I HELP?
A suggestion: "You can make this even better by_____" (Be specific)
Or question: Have you considered_____?
What would you like help with? (Then write the response.)

RECOMMENDED READING
Watch *An Artist's Journey at Dunraven School* (www.bit.ly/2m9xocc), which shows how we implemented Austin's Butterfly at the primary school where I taught. The following year, we involved Year 8 (7th grade) and they taught five-year-olds using some sentence starters.

TEACHER TIP
Student prompt sheets help to scaffold the language learners can use to give and receive feedback.

MINDSET: LEADERSHIP

Mindset: Leadership
and professional learning

 For a learning mindset to become the norm, not a nag, leadership must walk the talk.

This Mindset: Leadership section focuses on ways school leaders can help teachers practise a learning mindset while supporting their students to hone their own attitude toward learning. Educators are learners too and great teachers never stop reflecting on their practice. As we state in Mindset: Research, a teacher's adoption of a learning mindset helps educators improve their practice and understand that learning to teach is a process that requires practice, perseverance and metacognition. Teachers must also model and use classroom strategies that are aligned with a learning mindset in order to genuinely communicate that they value its worth.

As with the Leadership sections in Relationships and Memory, this section includes **Professional Learning: At the Start** for ideas on how to introduce concepts and research to your staff and **Professional Learning: Keep it Going**, which outlines suggestions for maintaining and developing educators' implementation throughout the year. Together these two parts provide multiple experiences for leaders to model to teachers, practise and share, creating a positive learning environment that supports the teachers' learning mindsets.

Professional Learning: At the Start

BAGGAGE CLAIM: THE LEARNING JOURNEY

FACILITATOR TIP
To ensure that good ideas are put into practice, build in time for staff to reflect and plan their next steps during the professional learning session. Otherwise, good intentions can get pushed to the bottom of the list during a busy school day.

This activity is a great starter to get everyone thinking about learning. It's also a great way to build relationships, because participants are connecting through commonalities and learning new things about their colleagues. You'll likely find out some fun and fascinating information about colleagues.

1. **Prepare** by printing out the Baggage Claim template so that each person has one suitcase (print and cut). Think of some examples of things you are good at or know a lot about.

2. **Ask** staff to write down three things they are good at or know a lot about on their suitcase. Share your own examples.

3. **Explain** Baggage Claim:

   a. 'You will circulate around the room and find a partner. One of you will introduce yourself by saying your name and reading what is on your baggage claim. Then the other person shares.'

   b. 'Next, exchange cards with your partner and find a new partner. This time you need to introduce the person whose baggage claim you just received: "I've got Emma's suitcase (point out Emma). She's good at…".' Explain that they will repeat the process for one to two more rounds.

4. **Start:** 'Let's go. I will tell you when to stop.' Circulate around the room. Ensure that everyone is finding partners quickly.

5. **Stop and ask** the whole group: 'What are some things your colleagues are good at or know a lot about? What are some common themes, skills or topics you heard?'

6. **Pair and discuss:** 'Share with your partner what you need to do to become good at or know a lot about that thing.' Prompt participants to consider actions and thoughts. They are likely to share responses that relate to practice, making mistakes, hard work, help from someone and sheer enjoyment.

7. **Whole-group discussion:** 'Let's share with the group some strategies, actions and thoughts that made you or your colleague good or know a lot about your topic or skill'; 'What patterns do you notice? What might this teach us about learning?'

8. **Introduce learning mindset:** Display the Effective Learning Choices Chart below: 'A lot of the strategies you listed are similar to what we call effective learning habits or choices.' Present the chart. If time allows, ask staff to annotate the chart by writing comments next to descriptors about how these choices might be useful for their students, which they think students do well/need to improve and where they have seen evidence of these behaviours in action.

WHEN FACED WITH:	I CHOOSE TO:
Challenges	Embrace challenges; set high goals
New learning	Put in effort and lots of practice; break down tasks
Prolonged difficulty	Persist through difficulty; try new strategies; take a break
Lack of understanding	Seek help; ask questions; start again
Mistakes	Use mistakes to learn; figure out what went wrong and try to fix it
Critical feedback	Listen and learn from feedback

9. **Debrief:** Use the facilitator talking points in the Jigsaw Method Content Guide on the next page.

RESEARCH INTO MINDSETS AND METACOGNITION

THE JIGSAW METHOD

Since the Jigsaw Method has such a high effect rating (Hattie, 2011), we recommend you use it when turnkeying research to your staff. This is a great way to model the strategy so that educators feel more comfortable using with their students. Please refer to Relationships: Leadership, page 96 for instructions on how to facilitate it. Use the Jigsaw Method Content Guide to adapt the Jigsaw Method to the teaching of strategies and concepts relating to learning mindset.

JIGSAW METHOD CONTENT GUIDE

TOPIC: MINDSET	
EXPERT GROUP TOPICS	**FACILITATOR TALKING POINTS**
Choose approximately five from the list: • Learning vs performing • The power of practice and perseverance (purposeful practice) • Promising goals, not empty promises • Modelling is a must • Verbalising metacognitive thinking • Getting it wrong – in front of the class • Our role models are people too and relatable role models • Normalise error • Point out the process … rather than praise the person. (See Point out the Process below for a closer look.)	• A learning mindset means having an understanding that learning is a process (it takes time and effort, for example) and a belief that we have control over our own learning ('If this doesn't work, I'll try another way'). • In the classroom, when one practises a learning mindset, they recognise that getting better at something necessitates perseverance, practice, effort and metacognition skills.
GUIDING QUESTIONS FOR JIGSAW GROUP QUESTIONS	• As educators, we play a pivotal role in cultivating our students' learning mindsets. It's up to us to educate students about the process of learning in general, teach them strategies that put them in the driver's seat of their own learning experiences and ensure opportunities for reflection.
• For your subject or student age group, which of the topics are the most relevant and why? • How would you define a learning mindset? • What ideas have you heard that relate to what you already do or know? • In what ways will this research inform your teaching? What actions will you take?	• We, as educators, are learners too. Classroom management and effective teaching improve when we learn from our mistakes, reflect and keep going. I support you in that process.

SPOTLIGHT

FACILITATOR TIP
Don't forget to look for the spotlight icon to find our suggestions for expert group topics.

Alternative for Jigsaw Method: Spotlight on metacognition

Use the diagram of metacognition on page 232 to define the term. Then give each Expert Group one of the five ways for How to Improve Metacognition (modelling, explicit instruction, verbalisation, differentiation, self-talk). Pose the Jigsaw Guiding Question: How could we improve metacognition skills in our subject? Use the list on page 232 to summarise how to improve metacognition.

CLASSROOM APPLICATIONS THAT CULTIVATE A LEARNING MINDSET

There is not only one strategy or type of strategy that fosters a learning mindset. What is crucial is that teachers help learners make the connection between the specific learning experience and the broader understanding of learning. We suggest this Adopt, Adapt or Add activity to arm teachers with concrete strategies that help learners make that connection.

ADOPT, ADAPT OR ADD

In Adopt, Adapt or Add (AAA), staff are asked to engage with classroom strategies and decide whether they would like to either **Adopt** a strategy *as is* for their classrooms,

Adapt it to better fit their classroom context or **Add** a different, related strategy they could share with the group. For consistency and practice, we use the same strategy for the Leadership sections in Relationships, and Memory. See Relationships: Leadership on page 100 for detailed steps on how to facilitate this. There are three different variations for delivering Adopt, Adapt and Add. Choose the one that works best for you!

For Mindset, we have not labelled strategies AAA strategies throughout, because we suggest taking a focus on a particular topic (e.g. metacognition). Begin with an explanation of what is meant by metacognition by referring to Direct Teach: Introduce Metacognition on page 277 in Mindset: Classroom. Give each group one of the following (which start on page 280):

- Model, Teach, Practise, Connect
- Talk Task guidelines
- Talk Tasks
- Paired Think Aloud
- Accountable talk for the classroom
- Visual maps, checklists, reflection logs and/or Exit Tickets
- Letters to another or future self, Process Portfolio and Long-term reflection
- For **older students**, note taking on page 174 and Exam Wrappers on page 288

POINT OUT THE PROCESS

The scenarios below are examples of when a student has been successful as a result of practising a learning mindset. Ask staff to use one of these scenarios or make up one of their own and then practise how they would respond. Follow the guidelines for Pointing out the Process on page, starting their feedback with 'I noticed that...:

- ...your student put on a coat independently instead of getting an adult to help or dropping it on the floor after the first try like they did last time.'
- ...your student wanted to have a go at a multi-layered maths problem that was more challenging than one with a clear set of questions to answer.'
- ...your student worked for a long time on a writing assignment that was really difficult and took several attempts to get it right.'
- ...your student completed a group project, participating and even occasionally leading the group despite the fact that they told you they "couldn't work in a group".'
- ...before your student started their history essay, you saw them creating a plan for what to do.'
- ...your student wasn't sure about some facts, so they used resources to double-check.'

STUDENT SUCCESSES SCENARIOS	PROCESS FEEDBACK PROMPTS
Write down examples of when students have practised a learning mindset which has contributed to success	Write down process feedback you can offer students in this scenario 'I noticed that…'

 Keep in mind:

For leaders, we highly recommend reading the section on Feedback in Mindset: Research on page 244 and addressing:

- Normalising error
- Comparisons and competition
- Point out the process rather than praise the person
- The risks of praising effort

In my experience, just the word 'yet' has been a powerful game changer for teachers and students across the US and UK. First featured in Dweck's now famous TED Talk *The Power of Believing You Can Improve* (www.bit.ly/2l2JBPY), such a concise, powerful word can remind us that learning is a journey. This small word turns 'I can't' into 'I can't yet', which gives us the motivation to keep going, and a reminder that everyone can get smarter and become more skilled.

PROFESSIONAL LEARNING: KEEP IT GOING

SHARE PROGRESS AND NEW IDEAS WHILE BUILDING A LEARNING MINDSET

DEVELOPING EDUCATORS' OWN LEARNING MINDSETS

Leaders can set the stage for staff to become mindful of their own progress as they hone their mindset. These simple strategies can help.

- Survey staff to help them reflect on their attitudes toward learning. They are more likely to be honest if allowed to keep their answers to themselves and then reflect on the extent to which they align with a learning mindset.

Circle 1 (strongly disagree) to 5 (strongly agree)	
I welcome opportunities to learn new research about teaching.	1 2 3 4 5
I feel comfortable being observed by colleagues or by leadership.	1 2 3 4 5
It is important to me that I have the opportunity to learn at work.	1 2 3 4 5
I seek feedback from my students about my teaching.	1 2 3 4 5
When a lesson goes badly, I bounce back quickly and reflect on it.	1 2 3 4 5

Comments:

> How teachers feel about their ability to teach actually impacts their ability to teach. When leadership creates collaborative and reflective work environments, teachers get better and kids benefit.

- Use the learning journey on page 257 for staff to reflect on their own progress. Model your own journey to demonstrate a level of comfort with struggle, mistakes and challenges.

- Use the language of Pointing out the Process as described in Mindset: Classroom on page 257 when feeding back to staff privately and during whole-staff sharing moments, such as those we have outlined below. This works particularly well with Teacher Features.

TEACHER FEATURES

Teacher Features are 10- to 15-minute presentations by staff who share a classroom strategy they have implemented. They can be done during morning briefings, the start of staff meetings or any other time when the whole staff convenes.

Guiding questions for staff:

- What strategy did I implement?
- Why did I do it? 'I wanted students to...'
- How did I evaluate it? 'I noticed that...'; 'Student surveys showed...'
- What did I learn? 'I learned that I should...'; 'Next time, I would change...'

Remember that this is an opportunity for staff to share what they have learned. Encourage staff to share challenges, misconceptions and mistakes as well as successes. Acknowledge that these strategies take practice and explain that you encourage their continued professional risk taking and perseverance, even when the strategies don't go as planned at the beginning.

'KEEP IT GOING' STRATEGIES

Use the Keep it Going strategies (see Mindset: Classroom) to periodically reinforce learning mindsets and build on previous professional learning. Provide handouts for staff or templates so that the resources are easy to use and/or adapt. Follow this up by asking teachers if you can visit their classroom while they do the activity.

PRACTICE PARTNERS

Colleagues working on the same strategies (or different ones) pair up to prepare for implementation, and then visit each other's rooms to see the strategy in action. Post visits, the teacher pairs debrief about what they noticed: what worked, what might need to be adapted, the impact on students, etc. If possible, Practice Partners can share their findings with their department, year/grade-level colleagues, or the entire staff.

MAKE YOUR OWN #OBSERVEME MOVEMENT (or join the online one)

#ObserveMe is a movement created by Robert Kaplinsky, a maths teacher from California, which encourages teachers to post signs on their door, inviting others in to observe and give feedback. Not only does this strategy promote growth through feedback, it creates risk-free observation whereby teachers don't feel the pressure to get it right. You can find lots of examples by going to Kaplinsky's website at www.bit.ly/2l2CFlR or just searching online for #ObserveMe.

- Post a sign like the one below to let people know they are welcome in your classroom.
- List what you want feedback on.
- Consider including an observation tool, like a quick and easy feedback form or Exit Ticket. Some teachers have created online questionnaires (Google Forms are simple to use) and created a QR code so observers just need to snap a pic to go the form.
- You may ask the observer to offer feedback on the actions of the entire class (teacher and students) as this sign below does.

Optional: Take a picture of it and tweet it out using the hashtag #ObserveMe.

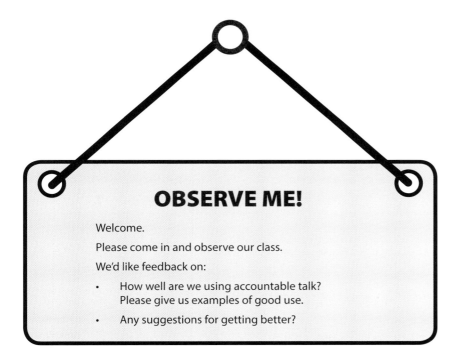

OBSERVE ME
This sign was created by the whole class, which is a great way to involve students in the process. Also, teachers can post when they are trying out something new, so colleagues help them learn what worked by being an extra set of eyes in the room.

TEACHER MINDSET SELF-ASSESSMENT

Use this self-assessment to identify what you already do and look for ways to embed ideas that promote a learning mindset into the environment and into your teaching. This is a guideline. You can add criteria that would be useful for your subject or for the age of your students. Use the following scale and write the number in the middle column. Add evidence.

1 = Never 2 = Rarely 3 = Sometimes 4 = Usually 5 = A lot of the time

Environment: The physical environment and surrounding areas		
Self-Assessment	1 to 5	Evidence:

Displays reflect:

Vocabulary that relates to the learning process

Student work that reflects the stages or the process of learning, not just final product (including photos)

Resources available in the room are clearly marked to help students if they need support with difficult work or if they want a challenge.

Quotes or profiles of successful people who achieved after setbacks or failures (check for representation of all students and genders)

Other:

The feedback and modelling

I use **think time** and make it explicit to the students.

When feeding back to students, I **point out the process**.

My feedback is **specific** and **authentic**.

I **model** an attitude and language that values mistakes and risk taking (getting out of my comfort zone).

I make **references to metacognitive skills; I model how I plan, monitor and evaluate** as I problem solve.

I **frequently refer to resources** in the room available to students, so that I'm modelling how helpful they are for independent use.

Other:

Curriculum and teaching strategies

Learning objectives are framed as challenging and I set **high expectations** for all from the start of the lesson.

My teaching strategies emphasise the **process** as well as progress and final product.

I teach how to use metacognitive strategies and why they are important.

I use strategies that introduce opportunities to work through **mistakes and failure**.

I embed **goal setting** into my teaching and support students to break down larger goals.

Other:

RECOMMENDED READING
10 Mindframes for Visible Learning: Teaching for Success by John Hattie and Klaus Zierer. Use the mindframes as a self-evaluation tool for teachers to reflect on their practice. Two mindframes I particularly like: 'I engage as much in dialogue as monologue' and 'I explicitly inform students what successful impact looks like from the outset'.

RECOMMENDED READING

Recommended Readings and Resources

BOOKS

Learning: general

Ambrose, S. A., Bridges, M. W., DiPietro, M., Lovett, M. C. and Norman, M. K. (2010) *How learning works: 7 research-based principles for smart teaching*. San Francisco, CA: Jossey-Bass.

De Bruyckere, P. (2018) *The ingredients for great teaching*. London: SAGE Publications.

Hattie, J. and Yates, G. C. R. (2014) *Visible learning and the science of how we learn*. Abingdon: Routledge.

Hendrick, C. and Macpherson, R. (2017) *What does this look like in the classroom? Bridging the gap between research and practice*. Woodbridge: John Catt Educational.

Nuthall, G. (2007) *The hidden lives of learners*. Wellington: NZCER Press.

Sherrington, T. (2017) The learning rainforest: great teaching in real classrooms. Woodbridge: John Catt Educational.

Learning: relationships

Benson, T. A., Fiarman, S. E. (2019) *Unconscious bias in schools: a developmental approach to exploring race and racism*. Cambridge, MA: Harvard Education Press.

Buck, A. (2018) *Leadership matters 3.0: how leaders at all levels can create great schools*. Woodbridge: John Catt Educational.

Dix, P. (2017) *When the adults change, everything changes*. Carmarthen: Independent Thinking Press.

Hammond, Z. L. (2014) *Culturally responsive teaching and the brain*. Thousand Oaks, CA: Corwin.

Pinkett, M. and Roberts, M. (2019) *Boys don't try? Rethinking masculinity in schools*. Abingdon: Routledge.

Learning: memory and cognitive science

Bailey, F. and Pransky, K. (2014) *Memory at work in the classroom: strategies to help underachieving students*. Alexandria, VA: Association for Supervision and Curriculum Development.

Brown, P. C., Roediger, H. L., McDaniel, M. A. (2014) *Make it stick: the science of successful learning*. Cambridge, MA: Belknap Press.

Carey, B. (2014) *How we learn: the surprising truth about when, where, and why it happens*. New York, NY: Random House.

Oakley, B., Sejnowski, T. and McConville, A. (2018) *Learning how to learn: how to succeed in school without spending all your time studying; a guide for kids and teens*. New York, NY: TarcherPerigee. (Great resource for teachers and students)

Weinstein, Y. and Sumeracki, M. (2018) *Understanding how we learn: a visual guide*. Abingdon: Routledge.

Willingham, D. T. (2010) *Why don't students like school?* San Francisco, CA: Jossey-Bass.

Vocabulary and reading

Beck, I. L., McKeown, M. G. and Kucan, L. (2013) *Bringing words to life: robust vocabulary instruction*. 2nd edn. New York, NY: Guilford Press.

Quigley, A. (2018) *Closing the vocabulary gap*. Abingdon: Routledge.

Wexler, N. (2019) *The knowledge gap: the hidden cause of America's broken education system – and how to fix it*. New York, NY: Random House.

Willingham, D. T. (2017) *The reading mind: a cognitive approach to understanding how the mind reads*. San Francisco, CA: Jossey-Bass.

Growth mindset and character

Dweck, C. (2017) *Mindset: changing the way you think to fulfil your potential*. Updated edn. New York, NY: Ballantine Books.

Gershon, M. (2016) *How to develop growth mindsets in the classroom: the complete guide*. Scotts Valley, CA: CreateSpace Independent Publishing Platform.

Hildrew, C. (2018) *Becoming a growth mindset school: the power of mindset to transform teaching, leadership and learning*. Abingdon: Routledge.

Tough, P. (2013) *How children succeed: grit, curiosity and the hidden power of character*. London: Random House.

Metacognition

Nilson, L. B. (2013) *Creating self-regulated learners: strategies to strengthen students' self-awareness and learning skills*. Sterling, VA: Stylus Publishing.

Feedback and formative assessment

Brookhart, S. M. (2017) *How to give effective feedback to your students*. 2nd edn. Alexandria, VA: Association for Supervision and Curriculum Development.

Fletcher-Wood, H. (2018) *Responsive teaching*. Abingdon: Routledge.

Hattie, J. and Clarke, S. (2018) *Visible learning feedback*. Abingdon: Routledge.

Wiliam, D. and Leahy, S. (2015) *Embedding formative assessment: practical techniques for K–12 classrooms*. West Palm Beach, FL: Learning Sciences International.

Teacher and learning strategies

Caviglioli, O. (2019) *Dual coding with teachers*. Woodbridge: John Catt Educational.

Frazier, N. and Mehle, D. (2013) *Activators: classroom strategies for engaging middle and high school students*. Cambridge, MA: Educators for Social Responsibility.

Lemov, D. (2010) *Teach like a champion*. San Francisco, CA: Jossey-Bass.

Lemov, D. (2014) *Teach like a champion 2.0: 62 techniques that put students on the path to college*. 2nd edn. San Francisco, CA: Jossey-Bass.

Mayer, R. E. (2009) *Multimedia learning*. 2nd edn. New York, NY: Cambridge University Press.

ARTICLES

Learning - general

Coe, R., Aloisi, C., Higgins, S. and Major, L. E. (2014) *What makes great teaching? Review of the underpinning research*. London: Sutton Trust.

Deans for Impact (2015) *The science of learning*. Austin, TX: Deans for Impact. Available at: www.bit.ly/2OEdhiV

Rosenshine, B. (2012) 'Principles of instruction: research-based strategies that all teachers should know', *American Educator* 36 (1) pp. 12–19, 39. Available at: www.bit.ly/2Kw17qg

Relationships

Australian Society of Evidence Based Teaching (no date) 'What everyone needs to know about high-performance, teacher student relationships', *EvidenceBasedTeaching.org.au* [Website]. Available at: www.bit.ly/2Y1qmri

Francis, B., Taylor, B., Hodgen, J., Tereshchenko, A. and Archer, L. (2018) *Dos and don'ts of attainment grouping*. London: UCL Institute of Education. Available at: www.bit.ly/33dhxtF

Korbey, H. (2017) 'The power of being seen', *Edutopia* [Website]. Available at: http://edut.to/2Gi3j1J

Rakestraw, M. (2017) '9 resources for teaching about unconscious bias', *Humane Connection* [Blog], 13 October. Available at: www.bit.ly/30UKCZe

Rimm-Kaufman, S. and Sandilos, L. (2011) 'Improving students' relationships with teachers to provide essential supports for learning', *American Psychological Association* [Website]. Available at: www.bit.ly/2JlCzz3

Working memory

Gathercole, S. E. and Alloway, T. P. (2007) *Understanding working memory: a classroom guide*. London: Harcourt Assessment. Available at: www.bit.ly/2SAfNqb

Sealy, C. (2017) 'Memory – not memories: teaching for long term learning', *Primary Timery* [Blog], 16 September. Available at: www.bit.ly/2IHSZIT

Cognitive load

Centre for Education Statistics and Evaluation (2017) *Cognitive load theory: research that teachers really need to understand*. Sydney: NSW Department of Education.

Centre for Education Statistics and Evaluation (2017) *Cognitive load theory in practice: examples for the classroom*. Sydney: NSW Department of Education.

Learning strategies

Dunlosky, J. (2013a) 'Strengthening the student toolbox: study strategies to boost learning', *American Educator* 37 (3) pp. 12–21. Available at: www.bit.ly/2YpLDeC

Weinstein, Y., Madan, C. R. and Sumeracki, M. A. (2018) 'Teaching the science of learning', *Cognitive Research: Principles and Implications* 3 (2).

Willingham, D. T. (2008) 'What will improve a student's memory?', *American Educator* 32 (4) pp. 17–25, 44.

Willingham, D. T. (2009) 'Why don't students like school?', *American Educator* 33 (1) pp. 4–9, 12–13.

Mindset

Dweck, C. and Yeager, D. S. (2019) 'Mindsets: a view from two eras', *Perspectives on Psychological Science* 14 (3) pp. 481–496.

Dweck, C., Walton, G. M. and Cohen, G. L. (2014) Academic tenacity: mindsets and skills that promote long-term learning. Seattle, WA: Bill & Melinda Gates Foundation. Available at: www.stanford.io/2SdpLOh

Hennessey, J. (2016) *Opportunity or setback?* Parents' views on failure influences children's mindsets about intelligence. Mindset Scholars Network. Available at: www.bit.ly/2M2JD5c

Yeager, D., Walton, G. and Cohen, G. L. (2013) 'Addressing achievement gaps with psychological interventions', *Kappan* 94 (5) pp. 62–65.

The brain

Cozolino, L. (2013) 'Nine things educators need to know about the brain', *Greater Good Magazine* [Online], 19 March. Available at: www.bit.ly/2MuXZdm

Willis, J. (2009) *What you should know about your brain*. Alexandria, VA: Association for Supervision and Curriculum Development. Available at: www.bit.ly/2G3kB2b

Metacognition

Cambridge Assessment International Education (no date) 'Getting started with metacognition', *cambridge-community.org.uk* [Website]. Available at: www.bit.ly/2nv6Ump

Quigley, A., Muijs, D. and Stringer, E. (2018) *Metacognition and self-regulated learning*. Education Endowment Foundation. Available at: www.bit.ly/2YZvdqE

Scott, C. (2009) 'Talking to learn: dialogue in the classroom', *The Digest* 2. Available at: www.bit.ly/2nd5soF

OTHER WEBSITES AND BLOGS

Cult of Pedagogy – www.cultofpedagogy.com

Daniel Willingham – Science and Education – www.bit.ly/310wQo7

Doug Lemov – www.teachlikeachampion.com/blog

Edutopia – www.edutopia.org

Efrat Furst – www.bit.ly/2AZ6590

The Education Endowment Foundation's Teaching and Learning Toolkit – www.bit.ly/2JwoJZH

EL Education – www.eleducation.org

Go Cognitive: Educational Tools For Cognitive Neuroscience – www.gocognitive.net

Greater Good Magazine – www.greatergood.berkeley.edu

Improving Teaching – www.improvingteaching.co.uk

Kate Jones – www.lovetoteach87.com

The Learning Scientists – www.learningscientists.org

Learning and the Brain blog – www.learningandthebrain.com/blog

Mindset Scholars Network – www.mindsetscholarsnetwork.org

Mr Barton Maths – www.mrbartonmaths.com

Oliver Cavigilioli – www.olicav.com

Ollie Lovell – www.ollielovell.com

The Teaching Channel – www.teachingchannel.org

Teaching Tolerance – www.tolerance.org

Tom Sherrington – www.teacherhead.com

UCLA Bjork Learning and Forgetting Lab – www.bit.ly/2Zb31kk

REFERENCES

References

Adesope, O. O., Trevisan, D. A. and Sundararajan, N. (2017) 'Rethinking the use of tests: a meta-analysis of practice testing', *Review of Educational Research* 87 (3) pp. 659–701.

Aitkenhead, D. (2018) 'Best teacher in the world Andria Zafirakou: "Build trust with your kids – then everything else can happen"', *The Guardian*, 23 March. Available at: www.bit.ly/30rV2zU (Accessed 22 October 2018).

Ambrose, S. (2014) *How learning works: 7 research-based principles for smart teaching with Dr Susan Ambrose* [Video]. Available at: www.bit.ly/2XSiYj0 (Accessed 8 November 2018).

American Psychological Association (2006) 'Multitasking: switching costs', *APA.org* [Website]. Available at: www.bit.ly/2lNiUPN (Accessed 14 November 2018).

Archer, L., Francis, B., Miller, S., Taylor, B., Tereshchenko, A., Mazenod, A., Pepper, D. and Travers, M. (2018) 'The symbolic violence of setting: a Bourdieusian analysis of mixed methods data on secondary students' views about setting', *British Educational Research Journal* 44 (1) pp. 119–140.

Atkinson, R. C. and Shiffrin, R. M. (1968) 'Human memory: a proposed system and its control processes' in Spence, K. W. and Spence, J. T. (eds) *The psychology of learning and motivation* (Vol 2). New York, NY: Academic Press, pp. 89–195.

Atkinson, R. C. and Shiffrin, R. M. (1971) 'The control of short-term memory', *Scientific American* 225 (2) pp. 82–90.

Australian Society of Evidence Based Teaching (no date) 'What everyone needs to know about high-performance, teacher student relationships', *EvidenceBasedTeaching.org.au* [Website]. Available at: www.bit.ly/2Y1qmri (Accessed 28 October 2018).

Ausubel, D. P. (1968) *Educational psychology: a cognitive view*. New York, NY: Holt, Rinehart and Winston.

Awh, E. (no date) 'Working memory and attention', *Go Cognitive* [Website]. Available at: www.bit.ly/2ZnL6Xf (Accessed 8 November 2018).

Baddeley, A. D. and Hitch, G. (1974) 'Working memory' in Bower, G. H. (ed.) *The psychology of learning and motivation: advances in research and theory* (Vol 8). New York, NY: Academic Press, pp. 47–89.

Bahrick, H. P. (1979) 'Maintenance of knowledge: questions about memory we forgot to ask', *Journal of Experimental Psychology: General* 108 (3) pp. 296–308.

Bailey, F. and Pransky, K. (2014) *Memory at work in the classroom: strategies to help underachieving students*. Alexandria, VA: Association for Supervision and Curriculum Development.

Bandura, A. C. (1994) 'Self-efficacy' in Ramachaudran, V. S. (ed.) *Encyclopedia of human behaviour* (Vol 4). New York, NY: Academic Press, pp. 71–81.

Barnado's (2018) 'New survey shows half of all schoolchildren feel sad or anxious every week', *Barnados.org.uk* [Website]. Available at: www.bit.ly/2Ll631h (Accessed 20 October 2018).

Barton, C. (2018) *How I wish I'd taught maths: lessons learned from research, conversations with experts,* and 12 years of mistakes. Woodbridge: John Catt Educational.

BBC (2010) *Take a walk in your mind – Brainsmart* [Video]. Available at: www.bit.ly/2lY69Bl (Accessed 20 November 2018).

Beck, I. L., McKeown, M. G. and Kucan, L. (2013) *Bringing words to life: robust vocabulary instruction.* 2nd edn. New York, NY: Guilford Press.

Berry, D. C. (1983) 'Metacognitive experience and transfer of logical reasoning', *The Quarterly Journal of Experimental Psychology: Section* A 35 (1) pp. 39–49.

Bethell, C. D., Carle, A., Hudziak, J., Gombojav, N., Powers, K., Wade, R. and Braveman, P. (2017) 'Methods to assess adverse childhood experiences of children and families: toward approaches to promote child well-being in policy and practice', *Academic Pediatrics* 17 (7S) pp. S51–S69.

Bian, L., Leslie, S. and Cimpian, A. (2017) 'Gender stereotypes about intellectual ability emerge early and influence children's interests', *Science* 355 (6323) pp. 389–391.

Bjork Learning and Forgetting Lab (no date) 'Applying cognitive psychology to enhance educational practice', *UCLA Bjork Learning and Forgetting Lab* [Website]. Available at: www.bit.ly/2Zb31kk (Accessed 10 November 2018).

Bjork, R. (2017) 'Robert and Elizabeth Bjork – memory, forgetting, testing, desirable difficulties', *Mr Barton Maths Podcast.* Craig Barton, 29 June. Available at: www.bit.ly/2Y3088U (Accessed 10 November 2018).

Bjork, R. (2018) *SOLER Symposium* [Lecture at Columbia University SOLER Symposium]. ColumbiaLearn, 11 October. Available at: www.bit.ly/32NVJ8r (Accessed 10 November 2018).

Bjork, R. A. and Bjork, E. L. (1992) 'A new theory of disuse and an old theory of stimulus fluctuation' in Healy, A., Kosslyn, S. and Shiffrin, R. (eds) *From learning processes to cognitive processes: essays in honor of William K. Estes* (Vol 2). Hillsdale, NJ: Erlbaum, pp. 35–67.

Bjork, E. L. and Bjork, R. A. (2011) 'Making things hard on yourself, but in a good way: creating desirable difficulties to enhance learning' in Gernsbacher, M. A., Pew, R. W., Hough, L. M. and Pomerantz, J. R. (eds) *Psychology and the real world: essays illustrating fundamental contributions to society.* New York, NY: Worth Publishers, pp. 55–64.

Black, P. J. and Wiliam, D. (2009) 'Developing the theory of formative assessment', *Educational Assessment, Evaluation and Accountability* 21 (1) pp. 5–31.

Blakemore, S. (2012) *The mysterious workings of the adolescent brain* [Video]. TED. Available at: www.bit.ly/2nuSpPv (Accessed 20 November 2018).

Boser, U. (2017) *Learn better: mastering the skills for success in life, business, and school, or, how to become an expert in just about anything.* Emmaus, PA: Rodale.

Brafman, O. and Brafman, R. (2011) *Click: the power of instant connections.* London: Virgin Books.

Brookhart, S. M. (2017) *How to give effective feedback to your students.* 2nd edn. Alexandria, VA: Association for Supervision and Curriculum Development.

Brophy, J. E. (1998) *Motivating students to learn.* Boston, MA: McGraw-Hill Education.

Brown, P. C., Roediger, H. L., McDaniel, M. A. (2014) *Make it stick: the science of successful learning.* Cambridge, MA: Belknap Press.

Bryk, A. S. and Schneider, B. (2002) *Trust in schools: a core resource for improvement.* New York, NY: Russell Sage Foundation.

Bryk, A. S. and Schneider, B. (2003) 'Trust in schools: a core resource for school reform', *Educational Leadership* 60 (6) pp. 40–44.

Buck, A. (2016) *Leadership matters: how leaders at all levels create great schools*. Woodbridge: John Catt Educational.

Busch, B. (2016) 'Four neuromyths that are still prevalent in schools – debunked', *The Guardian* [Online], 24 February. Available at: www.bit.ly/2mY5rVU (Accessed 5 December 2018).

Butler, A. (2010) 'Repeated testing produces superior transfer of learning relative to repeated studying', *Journal of Experimental Psychology: Learning, Memory, and Cognition* 36 (5) pp. 1118–1133.

Cambridge Assessment International Education (no date) 'Getting started with metacognition', *cambridge-community.org.uk* [Website]. Available at: www.bit.ly/2nv6Ump (Accessed 20 November 2018).

Campbell, T. (2015) 'Stereotyped at seven? Biases in teacher judgement of pupils' ability and attainment', *Journal of Social Policy* 44 (3) pp. 517–547.

Caviglioli, O. (2019) *Dual coding with teachers*. Woodbridge: John Catt Educational.

Centers for Disease Control and Prevention (2018) 'School connectedness', *CDC.gov* [Website]. Available at: www.bit.ly/2XCi3hF (Accessed 22 October 2018).

Centre for Education Statistics and Evaluation (2017a) *Cognitive load theory: research that teachers really need to understand*. Sydney: NSW Department of Education.

Centre for Education Statistics and Evaluation (2017b) *Cognitive load theory in practice: examples for the classroom*. Sydney: NSW Department of Education.

Cera, R., Mancini, M. and Antonietti, A. (2013) 'Relationships between metacognition, self-efficacy and self-regulation in learning', *Educational, Cultural and Psychological Studies* 7 (1) pp. 115–141.

Chandler, P. and Sweller, J. (1991) 'Cognitive load theory and the format of instruction', *Cognition and Instruction* 8 (4) pp. 293–332.

Chandler, P. and Sweller, J. (1992) 'The split-attention effect as a factor in the design of instruction', *British Journal of Educational Psychology* 62 (2) pp. 233–246.

Claro, S., Paunesku, D. and Dweck, C. S. (2016) 'Growth mindset tempers the effects of poverty on academic achievement', *Proceedings of the National Academy of Sciences of the United States of America* 113 (31) pp. 8664–8668.

Coe, R. (2015) *What makes great teaching?* [PowerPoint presentation at IB World Regional Conference]. 31 October. Available at: www.bit.ly/2MgsPrZ (Accessed 10 November 2018).

Coe, R., Aloisi, C., Higgins, S. and Major, L. E. (2014) *What makes great teaching? Review of the underpinning research*. London: Sutton Trust.

Cohen, G. L., Garcia, J., Apfel, N. and Master, A. (2006) 'Reducing the racial achievement gap: a social-psychological intervention', *Science* 313 (5791) pp. 1307–1310.

Collins, J. (2018) '45% of teens say they're stressed "all the time", turn to online resources and apps for help says poll on stress and mental health', *Globe Newswire* [Website]. Available at: www.bit.ly/2LdMgla (Accessed 20 October 2018).

Cook, C. R., Grady, E. A., Long, A. C., Renshaw, T. Codding, R. S., Fiat, A. and Larson, M. (2017) 'Evaluating the impact of increasing general education teachers' ratio of positive-to-negative interactions on students' classroom behavior', *Journal of Positive Behavior Interventions* 19 (2) pp. 67–77.

Cowan, N. (2010) 'The magical mystery four: how is working memory capacity limited, and why?', *Current Directions in Psychological Science* 19 (1) pp. 51–57.

Cozolino, L. (2013) *The social neuroscience of education*. New York, NY: W. W. Norton & Company.

Craik, F. I. M. and Tulving, E. (1975) 'Depth of processing and the retention of words in episodic memory', *Journal of Experimental Psychology: General* 104 (3) pp. 268–294.

Crehan, L. (2017) *Cleverlands: the secrets behind the success of the world's education superpowers*. London: Random House.

Crehan, L. (2018a) Telephone interview with Tricia Taylor, 12 October.

Crehan, L. (2018b) Telephone interview with Tricia Taylor, 13 July.

De Bruyckere, P. (2018) *The ingredients for great teaching*. London: SAGE Publications.

Deak, J. (2010) *Your fantastic elastic brain*. Naperville, IL: Little Pickle Press.

Delpit, L. D. (1988) 'The silenced dialogue: power and pedagogy in education other people's children', *Harvard Educational Review* 58 (3) pp. 280–298.

Department for Education (2018) *Pupil exclusions*. London: The Stationery Office. Available at: www.bit.ly/2JFzLvA (Accessed 26 October 2018).

Didau, D. and Rose, N. (2016) *What every teacher needs to know about psychology*. Woodbridge: John Catt Educational.

Dignath, C. and Büttner, G. (2008) 'Components of fostering self-regulated learning among students: a meta-analysis on intervention studies at primary and secondary school level', *Metacognition and Learning* 3 (3) pp. 231–264.

Donohoo, J., Hattie, J. and Eells, R. (2018) 'The power of collective efficacy', *Educational Leadership* 75 (6) pp. 40–44.

Dunlosky, J. (2013a) 'Strengthening the student toolbox: study strategies to boost learning', *American Educator* 37 (3) pp. 12–21. Available at: www.bit.ly/2YpLDeC (Accessed 10 November 2018).

Dunlosky, J. (2013b) *Improving student success: some principles from cognitive science* [Video]. Faculty of Science – McMaster University, 10 December. Available at: www.bit.ly/2YmZPFj (Accessed 12 March 2019).

Dunlosky, J. (2019) 'Podagogy – season 5, episode 5 – effective revision with professor John Dunlosky', *Tes – the education podcast*. Tes, 13 February. Available at: www.bit.ly/32S3pqo (Accessed 12 March 2019).

Dunlosky, J., Rawson, K. A., Marsh, E. J., Nathan, M. J. and Willingham, D. T. (2013) 'Improving students' learning with effective learning techniques: promising directions from cognitive and educational psychology', *Psychological Science in the Public Interest* 14 (1) pp. 4–58.

Dweck, C. (2002) 'Messages that motivate: how praise molds students' beliefs, motivation, and performance (in surprising ways)' in Aronson, J. (ed.) *Improving academic achievement*. New York, NY: Academic Press.

Dweck, C. (2015) 'Carol Dweck revisits the "growth mindset"', Education Week 35 (5) pp. 20, 24. Available at: www.bit.ly/2nswDM8 (Accessed 25 November 2018).

Dweck, C. (2016a) *Mindset: the new psychology of success*. New York, NY: Ballantine Books.

Dweck, C. (2016b) 'How praise became a consolation prize'. Interview by Christine Gross-Loh, *The Atlantic* [Online], 16 December. Available at: www.bit.ly/2Ilqi4t (Accessed 26 November 2018).

Dweck, C. and Yeager, D. S. (2019) 'Mindsets: a view from two eras', *Perspectives on Psychological Science* 14 (3) pp. 481–496.

Dweck, C., Walton, G. M. and Cohen, G. L. (2014) *Academic tenacity*. Seattle, WA: Bill & Melinda Gates Foundation. Available at: www.stanford.io/2SdpLOh (Accessed 20 October 2018).

The Economist (2018) 'England has become one of the world's biggest education laboratories', 31 March.

Education Endowment Foundation (2011) 'Teaching and learning toolkit', *Education Endowment Foundation* [Website]. Available at: www.bit.ly/2JwoJZH (Accessed 20 October 2018).

Edutopia (2016) *Oracy in the classroom: strategies for effective talk* [Video]. Available at: www.bit.ly/2IWi8iV (Accessed 28 November 2018).

EdX (2018) *The science of learning: what every teacher should know* [Course]. 10 January.

Eells, R. J. (2011) 'Meta-analysis of the relationship between collective teacher efficacy and student achievement', *Dissertations* 133. Loyola University Chicago eCommons. Available at: www.bit.ly/2lltKMr (Accessed 2 December 2018).

Ellis, A. K., Denton, D. W. and Bond, J. B. (2013) 'An analysis of research on metacognitive teaching strategies', *Procedia – Social and Behavioral Sciences* 116 (2014) pp. 4015–4024. Available at: www.bit.ly/2lO3Kd3 (Accessed 4 December 2018).

Ellison, K. (2015) 'Being honest about the Pygmalion effect', *Discover* [Magazine], October 29. Available at: www.bit.ly/2lyeex5 (Accessed 15 November 2018).

Encyclopædia Britannica (no date) 'Physiology' [Online]. Available at: www.bit.ly/2xELmp4 (Accessed 20 October 2018).

Eppler, M. J. (2006) 'A comparison between concept maps, mind maps, conceptual diagrams, and visual metaphors as complementary tools for knowledge construction and sharing', *Information Visualization* 5 (3) pp. 202–210.

Ericsson, K. A. (2006) 'The influence of experience and deliberate practice on the development of superior expert performance' in Ericsson, K. A., Charness, N., Feltovich, P. J. and Hoffman, R. R. (eds) *The Cambridge handbook of expertise and expert performance*. New York, NY: Cambridge University Press, pp. 683–703.

Ericsson, A. and Pool, R. (2016) *Peak: how all of us can achieve extraordinary things*. New York, NY: Vintage.

Felton, R. (2016) 'Black students in US nearly four times as likely to be suspended as white students', *The Guardian* [Online], 8 June. Available at: www.bit.ly/2GaDsbH (Accessed 24 October 2018).

Feor, J. (2012) *Feats of memory anyone can do* [Video]. TED. Available at: www.bit.ly/2lUVibT (Accessed 17 November 2018).

Fernandes, M. A., Wammes, J. D. and Meade, M. E. (2018) 'The surprisingly powerful influence of drawing on memory', *Current Directions in Psychological Science* 27 (5) pp. 302–308.

Fisher, R. (1998) 'Thinking about thinking: developing metacognition in children', *Early Child Development and Care* 141 (1) pp. 1–15.

Fletcher-Wood, H. (2018) *Responsive teaching*. Abingdon: Routledge.

Foster, R. (2016) '5-a-day starter', *The Learning Profession* [Blog], 26 May. Available at: www.bit.ly/2mPwimA (Accessed 15 November 2018).

Francis, B. and Hodgen, J. (2018) *The best practice in grouping students project: our findings* [Lecture at researchED National Conference]. 8 September.

Frazier, N. and Mehle, D. (2013) *Activators: classroom strategies for engaging middle and high school students*. Cambridge, MA: Educators for Social Responsibility.

Gallo, C. (2014) *Talk like TED: the 9 public speaking secrets of the world's top minds*. New York, NY: St Martin's Press.

Gathercole, S. E. and Alloway, T. P. (2007) *Understanding working memory: a classroom guide*. London: Harcourt Assessment. Available at: www.bit.ly/2SAfNqb (Accessed 6 November 2018).

Gilliam, W. S., Maupin, A. N., Reyes, C. R., Accavitti, M. and Shic, F. (2016) *Do early educators' implicit biases regarding sex and race relate to behavior expectations and recommendations of preschool expulsions and suspensions?* New Haven, CT: Yale Child Study Center.

Goldenberg, C. (1992) 'The limits of expectations: a case for case knowledge about teacher expectancy effects', *American Educational Research Journal* 29 (3) pp. 517–544.

Gonzales, J. (2018) 'Note-taking: a research roundup', *Cult of Pedagogy* [Blog], 9 September. Available at: www.bit.ly/32dlIE3 (Accessed 13 November 2018).

Good, T. L. and Brophy, J. E. (2000) *Looking in classrooms*. New York, NY: Longman.

Hammond, Z. L. (2014) *Culturally responsive teaching and the brain*. Thousand Oaks, CA: Corwin.

Haque, Z. and Elliott, S. (2015) *Barriers: visible and invisible barriers: the impact of racism on BME teachers*. National Union of Teachers and the Runnymede Trust. Available at: www.bit.ly/2xGDF1Q (Accessed 30 October 2018).

Hattie, J. (2009) *Visible learning: a synthesis of over 800 meta-analyses relating to achievement*. Abingdon: Routledge.

Hattie, J. (2011) *Visible learning for teachers*. Abingdon: Routledge.

Hattie, J. (2015) *John Hattie learning intentions and success criteria* [Video]. Lori Loehr, 26 February. Available at: www.bit.ly/2MlHsJO (Accessed 5 December).

Hattie, J. and Clarke, S. (2018) *Visible learning feedback*. Abingdon: Routledge.

Hattie, J. and Yates, G. C. R. (2014) *Visible learning and the science of how we learn*. Abingdon: Routledge.

Hattie, J., Biggs, J. and Purdie, N. (1996) 'Effects of learning skills interventions on student learning: a meta-analysis', *Review of Educational Research* 66 (2) pp. 99–136.

Haynes, T. (2018) 'Dopamine, smartphones & you: a battle for your time', *Science in the News* [Blog]. Harvard University Graduate School of Arts and Sciences, 1 May. Available at: www.bit.ly/32O3M59 (Accessed 12 November 2018).

Hildrew, C. (2019) Telephone interview with Tricia Taylor, 9 May.

Hughes, J. N. (2011) 'Longitudinal effects of teacher and student perceptions of teacher-student relationship qualities on academic adjustment', *Elementary School Journal* 112 (1) pp. 38–60.

Jensen, F. E. and Nutt, A. E. (2016) *The teenage brain: a neuroscientist's survival guide to raising adolescents and young adults*. New York, NY: Harper.

Jussim, L. and Harber, K. D. (2005) 'Teacher expectations and self-fulfilling prophecies: knowns and unknowns, resolved and unresolved controversies', *Personality and Social Psychology Review* 9 (2) pp. 131–155.

Kahneman, D. (2012) *Thinking, fast and slow*. London: Penguin.

Kahneman, D. and Tversky, A. (1979) 'Prospect theory: an analysis of decision under risk', *Econometrica* 47 (2) pp. 263–292. Available at: www.bit.ly/2oE8aEm (Accessed 20 November 2018).

Kalyuga, S., Ayres, P., Chandler, P. and Sweller, J. (2003) 'The expertise reversal effect', *Educational Psychologist* 38 (1) pp. 23–31.

Kamins, M. and Dweck, C. (1999) 'Person versus process praise and criticism: implications for contingent self-worth and coping', *Development Psychology* 35 (3) pp. 835–847. Available at: www.bit.ly/2mkGnrx (Accessed 8 December 2018).

Kang, S. H. K. (2016) 'Spaced repetition promotes efficient and effective learning: policy implications for instruction', *Policy Insights from the Behavioral and Brain Sciences* 3 (1) pp. 12–19.

Karpicke, J. D. and Roediger, H. L. (2008) 'The critical importance of retrieval for learning', *Science* 319 (5865) pp. 966–968.

Karpicke, J. D., Blunt, J. R., Smith, M. A. and Karpicke, S. S. (2014) 'Retrieval-based learning: the need for guided retrieval in elementary school children', *Journal of Applied Research in Memory and Cognition* 3 (3) pp. 198–206.

Karpicke, J. D., Blunt, J. R. and Smith, M. A. (2016) 'Retrieval-based learning: positive effects of retrieval practice in elementary school children', *Frontiers in Psychology* 7, Article 350. Available at: www.bit.ly/2Y864O5 (Accessed 12 November 2018).

The Key (2017) *State of education survey report 2017*. Available at: www.bit.ly/2S0LGry (Accessed 25 October 2018).

Kirschner, P. A. and Neller, M. (2017) 'Double-barrelled learning for young & old', *3-star Learning Experiences* [Blog], 30 May. Available at: www.bit.ly/2njT0mS (Accessed 12 November 2018).

Kluger, A. N. and DeNisi, A. (1996) 'The effects of feedback interventions on performance: a historical review, a meta-analysis, and a preliminary feedback intervention theory', *Psychological Bulletin* 119 (2) pp. 254–284.

Koedinger, K. (no date) *Leveraging examples in e-learning* [Presentation]. Available at: www.bit.ly/2UjPeql (Accessed 11 November 2018).

Kohli, R. and Solórzano, D. G. (2012) 'Teachers, please learn our names!: racial microaggressions and the K–12 classroom', *Race Ethnicity and Education* 15 (4) pp. 441–462.

Korbey, H. (2017) 'The power of being seen', *Edutopia* [Website]. Available at: http://edut.to/2Gi3j1J (Accessed 27 October 2018).

Kornell, N. and Finn, B. (2016) 'Self-regulated learning: an overview of theory and data' in Dunlosky, J. and Tauber, S. K. (eds) *The Oxford handbook of metamemory*. Oxford: Oxford University Press, pp. 325–340.

Kuepper-Tetzel, C. (2018) 'A note on note-taking', *The Learning Scientists* [Blog]. The Learning Scientists, 29 March. Available at: www.bit.ly/34bTcWj (Accessed 13 November 2018).

Latham, G. P. and Locke, E. A. (1991) 'Self-regulation through goal setting', *Organizational Behavior and Human Decision Processes* 50 (2) pp. 212–247. Available at: www.bit.ly/2nO3FqF (Accessed 10 December 2018).

Leana, C. R. (2011) 'The missing link in school reform', *Stanford Social Innovation Review* [Website]. Available at: www.bit.ly/2JJgc5A (Accessed 25 October 2018).

The Learning Scientists (2018) 'Episode 10 – concrete examples', *Learning Scientists* [Podcast]. Available at: www.bit.ly/326chqZ (Accessed 10 November 2018).

Lemov, D. (2010) *Teach like a champion*. San Francisco, CA: Jossey-Bass.

Lemov, D. (2014) *Teach like a champion 2.0: 62 techniques that put students on the path to college*. 2nd edn. San Francisco, CA: Jossey-Bass.

Lemov, D. (2017) 'How knowledge powers reading', *Educational Leadership* 74 (5) pp. 10–16. Available at: www.bit.ly/2LZBChz (Accessed 8 November 2018).

Lemov, D., Woolway, E. and Yezzi, K. (2012) *42 rules for getting better at getting better*. Hoboken, NJ: John Wiley & Sons.

Lin-Siegler, X., Ahn, J. N., Chen, J., Fang, F. A. and Luna-Lucero, M. (2016) 'Even Einstein struggled: effects of learning about great scientists' struggles on high school students' motivation to learn science', *Journal of Educational Psychology* 108 (3) pp. 314–328. Available at: www.bit.ly/2m148EI (Accessed 8 December 2018).

Locke, E. A. and Latham, G. P. (2002) 'Building a practically useful theory of goal setting and task motivation: a 35-year odyssey', *American Psychologist* 57 (9) pp. 705–717.

McCaslin, M. M., Vriesema, C. C. and Burggraf, S. (2016) 'Making mistakes: emotional adaptation and classroom learning', *Teachers College Record* 118 (2) pp. 1–46.

McCloud, C. (2015) *Have you filled a bucket today? A guide to daily happiness for kids*. Brighton, MI: Bucket Fillers.

McDaniel, M. A. and Donnelly, C. M. (1996) 'Learning with analogy and elaborative interrogation', *Journal of Educational Psychology* 88 (3) pp. 508–519.

McDaniel, M. A., Agarwal, P. K., Huelser, B. J., McDermott, K. B. and Roediger, H. (2011) 'The effects of quiz frequency and placement', *Journal of Educational Psychology* 103 (2) pp. 399–414.

Master, A. and Walton, G. M. (2013) 'Minimal groups increase young children's motivation and learning on group-relevant tasks', *Child Development* 84 (2) pp. 737–751.

Mayer, R. E. (2009) *Multimedia learning*. 2nd edn. New York, NY: Cambridge University Press.

Mayer, R. E. (2018) *How to be a successful student*. New York, NY: Routledge.

Mayer, R. E. (2019) 'Why keeping it simple is the key to multimedia learning'. Interview by Chris Parr, *Tes.com* [Website]. Available at: www. bit.ly/2lLfehs (Accessed 16 November 2018).

Mayfield, K. H. and Chase, P. N. (2002) 'The effects of cumulative practice on mathematics problem solving', *Journal of Applied Behavior Analysis* 35 (2) pp. 105–123.

Medina, J. (2008) *Brain rules: 12 principles for surviving and thriving at work, home, and school*. Seattle, WA: Pear Press.

Meyer, D. E. and Kieras, D. E. (1997a) 'A computational theory of executive cognitive processes and multiple-task performance – part 1: basic mechanisms', *Psychological Review* 104 (1) pp. 3–65.

Meyer, D. E. and Kieras, D. E. (1997b) 'A computational theory of executive cognitive processes and multiple-task performance – part 2: accounts of psychological refractory-period phenomena', *Psychological Review* 104 (4) pp. 749–791.

Miller, G. A. (1956) 'The magical number seven, plus or minus two: some limits on our capacity for processing information', *Psychological Review* 63 (2) pp. 81–97.

Millis, B. J. (2016) *Using metacognition to promote learning*, IDEA Paper #63. Available at: www.bit.ly/2lIKAoS (Accessed 8 December 2018).

Moser, J. S., Schroder, H. S., Heeter, C., Moran, T. P. and Lee, Y. (2011) 'Mind your errors', *Psychological Science* 22 (12) pp. 1484–1489.

Mueller, C. M. and Dweck, C. (1998) 'Praise for intelligence can undermine children's motivation and performance', *Journal of Personality and Social Psychology* 75 (1) pp. 33–52.

Muijs, D. (2019) 'Developing the education inspection framework: how we used cognitive load theory', *Education Inspection* [Blog]. Ofsted, 13 February. Available at: www.bit.ly/2M1Dwyp (Accessed 21 February 2019).

Muijs, D., Kyriakides, L., van der Werf, G., Creemers, B., Timperley, H. and Earl, L. (2014) 'State of the art – teacher effectiveness and professional learning', *School Effectiveness and School Improvement* 25 (2) pp. 231–256.

Myatt, M. (2019) Interview with Tricia Taylor, 17 January.

The National Child Traumatic Stress Network (no date) 'Child trauma – effects', *NCTSN.org* [Website]. Available at: www.bit.ly/2XEgDD3 (Accessed 25 October 2018).

Nottingham, J. (2014) *The learning pit*. Alnwick: Challenging Learning. Available at: http://bit.ly/2n7dMqb (Accessed 25 November 2018).

Nuthall, G. (2007) *The hidden lives of learners*. Wellington: NZCER Press.

Nuthall, G. and Alton-Lee, A. G. (1997) *Student learning in the classroom: understanding learning and teaching project 3*. Wellington: Ministry of Education.

Oakley, B. (2014) 'Procrastination', *You require more minerals* [Blog], 19 August. Available at: www.bit.ly/2moEnyI (Accessed 10 December 2018).

Oakley, B. (2019) Email exchange with Tricia Taylor, 5 March.

Oakley, B. and Sejnowski, T. (no date) *Learning how to learn: powerful mental tools to help you master tough subjects* [Online course]. Coursera. Available at: www.bit.ly/2L0zmWG (Accessed 11 November 2018).

Oakley, B., Sejnowski, T. and McConville, A. (2018) *Learning how to learn: how to succeed in school without spending all your time studying; a guide for kids and teens*. New York, NY: TarcherPerigee.

Oberfoell, A. and Correia, A. (2016) 'Understanding the role of the modality principle in multimedia learning environments', *Journal of Computer Assisted Learning* 32 (6) pp. 607–617.

OECD (2018) 'Teaching hours', *OECD iLibrary* [Website]. Available at: www.bit.ly/2NX8quv (Accessed 20 October 2018).

Ofsted (2019) *Education inspection framework: overview of research*. Department for Education. London: The Stationery Office.

Okolosie, L. (2017) 'Racism in schools isn't just part of the grim past – it's hiding in plain sight', *The Guardian* [Online], 7 July. Available at: www.bit.ly/2LJNoN7 (Accessed 20 October 2018).

Paivio, A. (1971) *Imagery and verbal processes*. New York, NY: Holt, Rinehart & Winston.

Parr, C. (2018) 'Do your relationships with students really matter?', *Tes.com* [Website]. Available at: www.bit.ly/2LPeEJW (Accessed 30 October 2018).

Pennington, C. R., Heim, D., Levy, A. R. and Larkin, D. T. (2016) 'Twenty years of stereotype threat research: a review of psychological mediators', *PLOS One* 11 (1) Available at: www.bit.ly/2JxFkgX (Accessed 1 November 2018).

Peteranetz, M. S. (2016) 'Fostering metacognition in K–12 classrooms: recommendations for practice', *The Nebraska Educator: A Student-Led Journal* 31 (1) pp. 64–86.

Quigley, A. (2018) *Closing the vocabulary gap*. Abingdon: Routledge.

Quigley, A., Muijs, D. and Stringer, E. (2018) *Metacognition and self-regulated learning*. Education Endowment Foundation. Available at: www.bit.ly/2YZvdqE (Accessed 30 November 2018).

Rawson, K. A., Dunlosky, J. and Sciartelli, S. M. (2013) 'The power of successive relearning: improving performance on course exams and long-term retention', *Educational Psychology Review* 25 (4) pp. 523–548.

Recht, D. R. and Leslie, L. (1988) 'Effect of prior knowledge on good and poor readers' memory of text', *Journal of Educational Psychology* 80 (1) pp. 16–20.

Rimm-Kaufman, S. and Sandilos, L. (2011) 'Improving students' relationships with teachers to provide essential supports for learning', *American Psychological Association* [Website]. Available at: www.bit.ly/2JlCzz3 (Accessed 20 October 2018).

Roediger, H. L. and Pyc, M. A. (2012) 'Inexpensive techniques to improve education: applying cognitive psychology to enhance educational practice', *Journal of Applied Research in Memory and Cognition* 1 (4) pp. 242–248.

Roehlkepartain, E. C., Pekel, K., Syvertsen, A. K., Sethi, J., Sullivan, T. K. and Scales, P. C. (2017) *Relationships first: creating connections that help young people thrive*. Minneapolis, MN: Search Institute.

Rohrer, D. and Taylor, K. (2007) 'The shuffling of mathematics problems improves learning', *Instructional Science* 35 (6) pp. 481–498.

Rose, N. (2018) 'The role of forgetting as we learn', *Ambition.org.uk* [Website]. Ambition Institute. Available at: www.bit.ly/2LDMKS2 (Accessed 10 November 2018).

Rosenshine, B. (2012) 'Principles of instruction: research-based strategies that all teachers should know', *American Educator* 36 (1) pp. 12–19, 39. Available at: www.bit.ly/2Kw17qg (Accessed 8 November 2018).

Rosenthal, R. and Babad, E. Y. (1985) 'Pygmalion in the gymnasium', *Educational Leadership* 43 (1) pp. 36–39.

Rosenthal, R. and Jacobson, L. (1968) 'Pygmalion in the classroom', *The Urban Review* 3 (1) pp. 16–20.

Routson, J. (2009) 'Heidi Roizen: networking is more than collecting lots of names', *Stanford Graduate School of Business* [Website]. Available at: www.stanford.io/2LPk8EL (Accessed 30 October 2018).

Rubinstein, J. S., Meyer, D. E. and Evans, J. E. (2001) 'Executive control of cognitive processes in task switching', *Journal of Experimental Psychology: Human Perception and Performance* 27 (4) pp. 763–797.

Schacter, D. L. (2015) 'Memory: an adaptive constructive process', in Nikulin, D. (ed.) *Memory: a history*. New York, NY: Oxford University Press, pp. 291–297.

Schmuck, R. A. and Schmuck, P. (1992) *Group processes in the classroom*. Boston, MA: McGraw-Hill Education.

Schroder, H. S., Fisher, M. E., Lin, Y., Lo, S. L., Danovitch, J. H. and Moser, J. S. (2017) *Developmental Cognitive Neuroscience* 24 (1) pp. 42–50.

Schunk, D. and Zimmerman, B. J. (1997) 'Social origin of self-regulatory competence', *Educational Psychologist* 32 (4) pp. 195–208.

Schwartz, D. L., Tsang, J. M. and Blair, K. P. (2016a) *The ABCs of how we learn: 26 scientifically proven approaches, how they work, and when to use them*. New York, NY: W. W. Norton & Company.

Schwartz, D. L., Cheng, K. M., Salehi, S. and Wieman, C. (2016b) 'The half empty question for socio-cognitive interventions', *Journal of Educational Psychology* 108 (3) pp. 397–404.

Scott, C. (2009) 'Talking to learn: dialogue in the classroom', *The Digest* 2. Available at: www.bit.ly/2nd5soF (Accessed 8 December 2018).

Seligman, M. (2018) *Learned optimism: how to change your mind and life*. London: Nicholas Brealey.

Senzaki, S., Hackathorn, J., Appleby, D. C. and Gurung, R. A. R. (2017) 'Reinventing flashcards to increase student learning', *Psychology Learning & Teaching* 16 (3) pp. 353–368.

Sheehy-Skeffington, J. and Rea, J. (2017) 'How poverty affects people's decision-making processes', *JRF.org.uk* [Website]. Joseph Rowntree Foundation. Available at: www.bit.ly/2XH7C15 (Accessed 25 October 2018).

Sherrington, T. (2019a) Telephone interview with Tricia Taylor, 14 June.

Sherrington, T. (2019b) 'Engineering success: a positive alternative to generic mindset messaging', *Teacherhead* [Blog], 1 June. Available at: www.bit.ly/2mfmiD2 (Accessed 30 November 2018).

Siegel (2014) 'Pruning, myelination, and the remodeling adolescent brain', *Psychology Today* [Blog], 4 February. Available at: www.bit.ly/2nQm4Tv (Accessed 29 November 2018).

Siegel, D. J. (2010) *Mindsight: the new science of personal transformation*. New York, NY: Bantam Books.

Singletary, S. L., Ruggs, E. N. and Hebl, M. R. (2009) 'Stereotype threat: causes, effects, and remedies' in Bogue, B. and Cady, E. (eds) *Applying research to practice (ARP) resources* [Online]. Available at: www.bit.ly/2XICRJe (Accessed 1 November 2018).

Smith, M. and Evans, J. J. (2018) 'Storytelling as transdisciplinarity: an experiment in first-year composition and communication' in Hokanson, B., Clinton, G. and Kaminski, K. (eds) *Educational technology and narrative: story and instructional design*. New York, NY: Springer, pp. 103–112.

Smith, M. and Weinstein, Y. (2016a) 'Learn how to study using…dual coding', *The Learning Scientists* [Blog]. The Learning Scientists, 1 September. Available at: www.bit.ly/2nmV1Pb (Accessed 17 November 2018).

Smith, M. and Weinstein, Y. (2016b) 'Learn how to study using…elaboration', *The Learning Scientists* [Blog]. The Learning Scientists, 7 July. Available at: www.bit.ly/2mRACBE (Accessed 17 November 2018).

Sorden, S. D. (2013) 'The cognitive theory of multimedia learning' in Irby, B. J., Brown, G. Lara-Alecio, R. and Jackson, S. (eds) *The handbook of educational theories*. Charlotte, NC: Information Age Publishing, pp. 155–167.

Spencer, S. J., Steele, C. M. and Quinn, D. M. (1999) 'Stereotype threat and women's math performance', *Journal of Experimental Social Psychology* 35 (1) pp. 4–28.

Steele, C. M. and Aronson, J. (1995) 'Stereotype threat and the intellectual test performance of African Americans', *Journal of Personality and Social Psychology* 69 (5) pp. 797–811.

Stephens, G. J., Silbert, L. J. and Hasson, U. (2010) 'Speaker-listener neural coupling underlies successful communication', *PNAS* 107 (32) pp. 14425–14430.

REFERENCES

Stevenson, H. W. and Stigler, J. W. (1994) *The learning gap: why our schools are failing and what we can learn from Japanese and Chinese education*. New York, NY: Simon and Schuster.

Stigler, J. (2013) 'Why Eastern and Western cultures tackle learning differently'. Interview by Alix Spiegel, *Morning Edition*, New Hampshire Public Radio, 2 September. Available at: www.bit.ly/2nPQ69W (Accessed 22 November 2018).

Stonewall (2017) School report 2017. London: Stonewall. Available at: www.bit.ly/2LOE62d (Accessed 1 November 2018).

Sun, K. L. (no date) *There's no limit: mathematics teaching for a growth mindset; a summary of dissertation work by Kathy Liu Sun*. Stanford, CA: PERTS, Stanford University.

Swartz, R. J. and Parks, S. (1994) *Infusing the teaching of critical and creative thinking into content instruction: a lesson design handbook for elementary grades*. North Bend, OR: Critical Thinking Press and Software.

Sweller, J. (2012) *An interview with John Sweller* [Video]. Veritasium, 21 March. Available at: www.bit.ly/2M8eP3c (Accessed 10 November 2018).

Sweller, J., van Merrienboer, J. J. G. and Paas, F. G. W. C. (1998) 'Cognitive architecture and instructional design', *Educational Psychology Review* 10 (3) pp. 251–296.

Sweller, J., van Merrienboer, J. J. G. and Paas, F. G. W. C. (2019) 'Cognitive architecture and instructional design: 20 years later', *Educational Psychology Review* 31 (2) pp. 261–292.

Tanner, K. D. (2012) 'Promoting student metacognition', CBE – *Life Sciences Education* 11 (2) pp. 113–120.

Taylor, K. and Rohrer, D. (2010) 'The effects of interleaved practice', *Applied Cognitive Psychology* 24 (6) pp. 837–848.

Terada, Y. (2018) 'Dos and don'ts of classroom decorations', *Edutopia* [Website]. Available at: https://edut.to/2NDPP4x (Accessed 10 November 2018).

Thabit, W. (2005) *How East New York became a ghetto*. New York, NY: NYU Press.

Tod, D., Hardy, J. and Oliver, E. J. (2011) 'Effects of self-talk: a systematic review', *Journal of Sport and Exercise Psychology* 33 (5) pp. 666–687.

Tough, P. (2016) *Helping children succeed: what works and why*. New York, NY: Random House.

UCL Institute of Education (2018) 'IOE research raises concerns about setting', *UCL.ac.uk*. University College London. Available at: www.bit.ly/2SaxL2p (Accessed 30 October 2018).

The University of Chicago (2011) '5 Essentials School Reports provide "annual physical" on 600 Chicago schools', *UChicago Urban Education Institute* [Website]. Available at: www.bit.ly/2JVikaL (Accessed 26 October 2018).

The University of Chicago (2018) *The role of noncognitive factors in shaping school performance*. Chicago, IL: The University of Chicago. Available at: www.bit.ly/2nURbwW (Accessed 3 December).

Walton, G. M., Cohen, G. L., Cwir, D. and Spencer, S. J. (2012) 'Mere belonging: the power of social connections', *Journal of Personality and Social Psychology* 102 (3) pp. 513–532.

Weinstein, Y. and Sumeracki, M. (2018) *Understanding how we learn: a visual guide*. Abingdon: Routledge.

Weinstein, Y., Madan, C. R. and Sumeracki, M. A. (2018) 'Teaching the science of learning', *Cognitive Research: Principles and Implications* 3 (2).

Wiliam, D. (2012) 'Feedback: part of a system', *Educational Leadership* 70 (1) pp. 30–34.

Wiliam, D. (2013) [Tweet] 23 October. Available at: www.bit.ly/2n6auUa (Accessed 24 November 2018).

Wiliam, D. (2014) 'Is the feedback you're giving students helping or hindering?', *Dylan Wiliam Center* [Website]. Available at: www.bit.ly/2xekiNf (Accessed 20 October 2018).

Wiliam, D. (2017) 'Getting educational research right', *Medium* [Website], 28 November. Available at: www.bit.ly/2nSw5PV (Accessed 30 November 2018).

Wiliam, D. (2018) 'An interview with Dylan William'. Interview with Greg Ashman, *Filling the Pail* [Blog], 11 August. Available at: www.bit.ly/2n5pAt3 (Accessed 30 November 2018).

Williams, S. (2018) 'Children's books are adding to science's gender problem', *The Conversation* [Website]. Available at: www.bit.ly/2LmMR49 (Accessed 28 October 2018).

Willingham, D. T. (2004) 'Ask the cognitive scientist – the privileged status of story', *American Educator* 28 (2) pp. 43–45, 51–53. Available at: www.bit.ly/2NpBhpm (Accessed 10 November 2018).

Willingham, D. T. (2006) 'How knowledge helps', *American Educator* 30 (1) pp. 30–37. Available at: www.bit.ly/2KMhAGu (Accessed 10 November 2018).

Willingham, D. T. (2008) 'What will improve a student's memory?', *American Educator* 32 (4) pp. 17–25, 44.

Willingham, D. T. (2009) *'Why don't students like school?'*, American Educator 33 (1) pp. 4–9, 12–13.

Willingham, D. T. (2010) *Why don't students like school?* San Francisco, CA: Jossey-Bass.

Willis (2012) 'A neurologist makes the case for teaching teachers about the brain', *Edutopia* [Website]. Available at: https://edut.to/2mny1Qa (Accessed 5 December 2018).

Willis, J. (2009) *What you should know about your brain*. Alexandria, VA: Association for Supervision and Curriculum Development. Available at: www.bit.ly/2G3kB2b (Accessed 24 October 2018).

Willis, J. (2012) *'Want children to pay attention?* Make their brains curious' at Young Minds 2012 [Video]. Happy & Well, 23 August. Available at: www.bit.ly/2Zzprvc (Accessed 12 November 2018).

Willis, J. (2016) 'Using brain breaks to restore students' focus', *Edutopia* [Website]. Available at: https://edut.to/2nowauo (Accessed 27 October 2018).

Willis, J. (2017) 'The neuroscience of narrative and memory', *Edutopia* [Website]. Available at: https://edut.to/2lKKM7a (Accessed 12 November 2018).

Wittrock, M. C. (1989) 'Generative processes of comprehension', *Educational Psychologist* 24 (4) pp. 345–376.

Wolf, M. K., Crosson, A. C. and Resnick, L. B. (2006) *Accountable talk in reading comprehension instruction* [CSE Technical Report 670]. Los Angeles, CA: UCLA National Center for Research on Evaluation, Standards, and Student Testing. Available at: www.bit.ly/2n5jeK4 (Accessed 12 December 2018).

Wooldridge, C. (2016) 'The importance of sleep for memory and cognition', *The Learning Scientists* [Blog]. The Learning Scientists, 11 July. Available at: www.bit.ly/2YjLOny (Accessed 10 November 2018).

Woolfolk, A. (2004) 'An interview with Anita Woolfolk: the educational psychology of teacher efficacy'. Interview with Michael F. Shaughnessy, *Educational Psychology Review* 16 (2) pp. 153–176. Available at: www.bit.ly/2nQJCHM (Accessed 5 December 2018).

Yeager, D. S. and Walton, G. M. (2011) 'Social-psychological interventions in education: they're not magic', *Review of Educational Research* 81 (2) pp. 267–301.

Yeager, D. S., Walton, G. and Cohen, G. L. (2013) 'Addressing achievement gaps with psychological interventions', Kappan 94 (5) pp. 62–65.

Yeager, D. S., Garcia, J., Brzustoski, P., Hessert, W. T., Purdie-Vaughns, V., Apfel, N., Master, A. and Williams, M. E. (2014) 'Breaking the cycle of mistrust: wise interventions to provide critical feedback across the racial divide', *Journal of Experimental Psychology: General* 143 (2) pp. 804–824.

Yeager, D. S., Hanselman, P., Walton, G. M., Murray, J. S., Crosnoe, R., Muller, C., Tipton, E., Schneider, B., Hulleman, C. S., Hinojosa, C. P., Paunesku, D., Romero, C., Flint, K., Roberts, A., Trott, J., Iachan, R., Buontempo, J., Yang, S. M., Carvalho, C. M., Hahn, P. R., Gopalan, M., Mhatre, P., Ferguson, R., Duckworth, A. L. and Dweck, C. (2019) 'A national experiment reveals where a growth mindset improves achievement', *Nature* 573 (7774) pp. 364–369. Available at: www.bit.ly/2n66WkN (Accessed 21 September 2019).

Zafirakou, A. (2018) *Andria Zafirakou's winning speech from the Global Teacher Prize 2018* [Video]. Available at: www.bit.ly/2nosuZD (Accessed 15 November 2018).

Zimmerman, B. J. (2002) 'Becoming a self-regulated learner: an overview', *Theory Into Practice* 41 (2) pp. 64–70. Available at: www.bit.ly/2nR0bU4 (Accessed 14 November 2018).

Zimmerman, B. J. and Kitsantas, A. (1997) 'Developmental phases in self-regulation: shifting from process to outcome goals', *Journal of Educational Psychology* 89 (1) pp. 29–36. Available at: www.bit.ly/2n625A3 (Accessed 5 December 2018).

Zulkiply, N. and Burt, J. S. (2013) 'The exemplar interleaving effect in inductive learning: moderation by the difficulty of category discriminations', *Memory and Cognition* 41 (1) pp. 16–27.